# TRIUMPH AND TRAGEDY

## THE LIFE OF EDWARD WHYMPER

# TRIUMPH AND TRAGEDY

## THE LIFE OF EDWARD WHYMPER

*For Anne —*
*Mon bonne amie et conseillère*
*de francais - With warmest*
*wishes,*
*Bill*

EMIL HENRY

Matador
5 Weir Road
Kibworth Beauchamp
Leicester LE8 0LQ, UK
Tel: (+44) 116 279 2299
Fax: (+44) 116 279 2277
Email: books@troubador.co.uk
Web: www.troubador.co.uk/matador

ISBN 978 1848765 788

British Library Cataloguing in Publication Data.
A catalogue record for this book is available from the British Library.

Typeset in 11pt Garamond by Troubador Publishing Ltd, Leicester, UK
Printed and bound in the UK by TJ International Ltd, Padstow, Cornwall

**Matador** is an imprint of Troubador Publishing Ltd

MIX
Paper from
responsible sources
FSC® C013056

For Elizabeth, Sherrye, and Emil,
*mes bons enfants.*

# TABLE OF CONTENTS

# GLOSSARY

| | |
|---|---|
| *aiguille* | sharply pointed peak (Fr. "needle") |
| *alp* | high mountain meadow (Ger.) |
| *alpenstock* | long wooden staff with pointed iron tip at bottom; later models added a flat iron piece on upper end, pointed on one side, bladed on the other, as a hatchet |
| *arête* | narrow top of a rocky ridge (Fr.) |
| *arriero* | mule-driver (Sp.) |
| *bach* | mountain stream (Ger.) |
| *bâton* | long wooden staff (Fr.) |
| *bergschrund* | large crevasse separating a glacier's head from the snow attached to the mountain's rocky surface, typically the last crevasse before a summit (Ger.) |
| *buttress* | projecting portion of a mountain or hill |
| *chamois* | agile mountain goat-antelope of Europe and Asia (Fr.) |
| *chimney* | steep rock gully, narrower than a couloir |
| *col* | mountain pass; a gap in a mountain ridge (Fr.) |
| *cornice* | overhanging crest of hard snow, often at the edge of a cliff or narrow summit |

| | |
|---|---|
| *couloir* | wide, steep gully, often filled with snow or ice (Fr.) |
| *crampon* | metal plate with sharp spikes, for attachment to bottom of boot |
| *crevasse* | fissure, crack, notch, or ravine in a glacier or snowfield (Fr.) |
| *dent* | peak ("tooth" Fr.) |
| *diligence* | stagecoach (Fr.) |
| *glacier* | slow moving mass of ice formed by compacted snow; its head nearest the mountain, its snout the lowest point, its plateau the level surface |
| *glissade* | act of sliding down a snow-slope on the feet, leaning slightly backward and dragging an alpenstock or batôn behind for support and balance (Fr.) |
| *grat* | ridge (Ger.) |
| *hörn* | peak ("horn" Ger.) |
| *joch* | mountain pass or gap (Ger.) |
| *massif* | mountain range or mass (Fr.) |
| *moraine* | debris of rocks and stones left by a moving glacier; lateral moraines left along the sides, terminal moraines at the snout |
| *moulin* | narrow, nearly vertical shaft in a glacier, formed by water percolating through a crack (Fr.) |
| *névé* | hardened snow at the head of a glacier (Fr.) |

| | |
|---|---|
| *pitch* | the steepness of a slope; a section of difficult rock or ice between rock ledges |
| *scree* | slope of small, loose stones; rocky rubble |
| *sérac* | large ice pinnacle, often in fantastic form, created at cracks in glacial surface (Fr.) |
| *schrund* | crevasse (Ger.) |
| *tambo* | country inn (Sp.) |
| *theodolite* | rotating telescope mounted on a tripod, used for measuring horizontal and vertical angles of points distant from the surveyor's location |
| *traverse* | horizontal crossing |
| *vallon* | vale; small valley (Fr.) |

# PREFACE

Framed in the window of my fifth floor room in Zermatt's Aristella Hotel, the Matterhorn filled the southwestern quarter of the sky. It stood majestic in the moonlight, a stone-grey silhouette under the night's cloudless black canopy. I had just finished *Scrambles Amongst the Alps*, Edward Whymper's stirring narrative of his five summers of Alpine climbs culminating in his being the first to set foot on the Matterhorn's summit. In 1865, at age 25, he had climbed what was then considered the Alps' most formidable peak. News of the conquest spread far and wide, but Whymper's notoriety came at a dreadful price. Four out of the seven climbers in his party fell simultaneously to their deaths in an accident still remembered as perhaps the most shocking in the history of mountaineering. "Climb if you will," said Whymper at the end of his story, "but remember that courage and strength are nought without prudence, and that a momentary negligence may destroy the happiness of a lifetime. Do nothing in haste; look well to each step; and from the beginning think what may be the end.'[1]

I first read those words in August of 1984 while preparing for an ascent of the Matterhorn in Whymper's pioneering footsteps. It would be my first attempt to climb any mountain worthy of the name, but thousands had reached this famous summit before me and I was fortunate to have teamed up with Rickie Andenmatten, one of the great mountain's most experienced guides. In the preceding year, he told me, seventeen souls had died on its slopes. During the current summer it had claimed two more lives, from along the same track we were to follow. Wisely, he waited to make these disclosures until we came down from a successful ascent, adding that all of the fatalities had been among climbers without professional assistance.

My acquaintance with the "impossible mountain," as it was once known, began many years earlier. In October of 1963, I was on a weekend holiday in the picture-book town of Zermatt, deep in Switzerland's Pennine Alps near the Italian border. In a casual street conversation with a local resident I learned a wonderful secret, as intriguing as it was startling. The Matterhorn's summit, he said, was accessible to almost anyone in reasonably good physical condition. Resplendent in full view on that clear day, the imposing peak looked beyond the reach of an inexperienced climber, no matter how many hours of dedicated jogging and weight workouts might precede a novice's attempt. Disregarding my protestations, my adviser held firm, suggesting only that I retain a Zermatt guide. With that gem of information cached in my brain, I returned to Geneva and thence to my life as a lawyer in the United States. Twenty-one years later I took advantage of a rare three-week travel window and proved my informant correct.

Although first published in 1871, an abridged version of Whymper's *Scrambles* was still in print and available at Zermatt bookstores in French, German and English. Feeding my interest in Whymper's Alpine exploits were keen recollections of camping out as a youth – sleeping under the stars, cooking on a campfire's hot coals, and singing to the moon along with good companions in the splendid isolation of a low-tech, pollution-free environment. As I eagerly turned the pages of *Scrambles* it mattered not that my adventures had been in the woodlands of the southern United States. They were my Alps, and the author's words resonated with the stirring recollections of many pleasant moments.

The quality of Whymper's narrative – showing exceptional talent for a champion describing his own deeds – stimulated my curiosity about the man himself, the author whose mountain escapades came so vividly to life on the printed page and the artist whose evocative drawings made the reader a part of the adventure. Researching the life of the "boy conquistador" of the Alps, I was drawn happily into the Victorian society that produced such an eccentric, multi-faceted character.

Whymper was born in 1840, three years after Queen Victoria's succession to the British throne. He was a consummate Victorian, not from living most of his life during the Queen's reign but because his character almost perfectly reflected the customs, beliefs and sensibilities of that sixty-four year period. Viewed from the 21st century, the Victorian age seems an historical curiosity – distant, antiquated and stylized, as in Charles Dickens and Arthur Conan Doyle. Its perceived remoteness, however, is due less to the passage of time than to the quantum cultural changes of the intervening period. In the year of Whymper's birth, Londoners were jailing Chartist leaders for their advocacy of universal adult male suffrage. Slavery was firmly entrenched in the American south. During Whymper's adolescence, England was fighting Russia in the Crimean War, and he had just turned twenty when the firing on Fort Sumter signaled the start of the American Civil War. His contemporaries were Charlotte Brontë and Thomas Hardy, Thomas Edison and Mark Twain.

Whymper and Victoria outlived their life expectancies by a considerable margin. By the Queen's death in 1901, Victorian society was steadily adapting to the 20th century. The industrial revolution had brought enormous economic growth. With greater social awareness had come expanded voting rights, improved labor laws and more public financial support for the poor. At Whymper's death in 1911, the internal combustion engine, the telephone and even the radio broadcast station were old news. By then, burgeoning technology had also produced a nascent commercial aviation industry, air-conditioned factories and neon lighting. That time does not seem quite so far away.

By a continuing consensus, the twelve-year period of 1854 to 1865 is known as the Golden Age of Mountaineering – for the sheer number of its first ascents (fourteen above 4,000 meters and scores of lesser peaks), and because those early Alpinists went virtually unarmed into hostile and uncharted territory. They had no special clothing, no huts for shelter, no reliable maps and only a few rudimentary climbing tools. There were no freeze-dried foods. The luxury of hot soup came in tin cans lugged aloft by porters, along with a primus stove and fuel to heat it. In many respects, Golden Age climbers resembled the pioneers of aviation who followed railway tracks for lack of radio beacons, squinted in open cockpits against rain, sleet and snow, and landed in pastures when fuel ran out or weather closed in. And as those aviators received help from farm families after emergency landings, so Whymper and his colleagues, after their climbs, found food and shelter in the chalets and hay-lofts of Alpine natives.

The mid-nineteenth century Alps, like the frozen wastelands of the Arctic Circle, were a frontier, and British mountaineers a special breed of frontiersmen. Amateur sportsmen, they climbed mountains not for scientific discovery, increased foreign trade or personal wealth, but for the thrill of testing themselves in one of nature's most challenging arenas.

Mountaineering was an outlet for energetic Englishmen to whom physical fitness was next to godliness, who believed that a strong body and clear mind were part of one's preparation for service to Queen and country. And, of course, the mountains offered escape from the daily work routine of summertime London.

The Alps sheer cliffs, icy rocks and frozen snow slopes exposed climbers to deadly risk. Hidden crevasses lurked in every glacier. Unstable snow on an underlying sheet of ice was a persistent menace. During the day, falling rocks demanded constant alertness. At night, to protect against rock slides tending to fall in the darkest hours, climbers bivouacked in the lee of fixed boulders or promontories. A life-threatening situation greeted Whymper on almost every climb. On the Matterhorn in 1862, "he had the narrowest escape from sudden death that has ever fallen to the lot of any climber."[2]

News of death or serious injury among climbers and their guides came regularly by word of mouth throughout Whymper' six summers in the Alps. While the mountains welcomed eager adventurers from all walks of life, they were no place for dilettantes or weekend warriors. Those who came to conquer had to be strong in body and dedicated in spirit – and among them Whymper was unique. An almost perfect physical specimen, he was also the most determined and ambitious. He was a "hard man,...only a hard man could have achieved what he did."[3] He was also unconventional. He never viewed mountain climbing as anything but a pure sport, and was quite open about putting first ascents above all other considerations. Said one of a later generation's climbers, "Through the conventions of his contemporar[ies]... he crashed with a rude and well directed vehemence that remains as individual as it was in his own day."[4]

In contrast to the severity of their summits, the Alps offered Golden Age climbers mountain scenery of unsurpassed beauty. Approaches to their peaks and passes held mountain vistas, flower-carpeted meadows, fragrant pine forests and paths through orchards in green valleys beside clear rushing streams. Along the way, Alpinists found welcome if sometimes rustic and uncomfortable lodging at local inns and chalets. Points of departure for even the most difficult climbs were easily accessible; there were no hundred-kilometer treks to the base of the targeted mountain, no month-long periods of acclimatization at varying heights, and no prolonged exposure to below-zero temperatures in oxygen-depleted air. The Alps of today are much the same; unlike the Himalayas, they are not icy moonscapes for semi-professionals with space age equipment.

Victorian mountaineers often needed more than one day to make an ascent. On those occasions they and their guides scratched out camp sites on rock ledges or narrow ridges. They built campfires for cooking, warmth and light – centerpieces for easy banter and a few songs before turning in for the night. Leather wine-bags usually got as far as a campsite; a wine or champagne bottle might make it to the top. Though fashionable city-dwellers would have sniffed with displeasure, this young wine of the country became a complex Rothschild in the tin cup of a tired climber. It also increased the palatability of stale mutton, overripe cheese and rock-hard bread. Though the weather was fickle and sometimes harsh, bivouacking climbers grew accustomed to spectacular sunsets of red, yellow, pink and purple in the western sky as the topmost snows of eastern slopes glowed with a spectral blush in that same light. Some nights would bring the silhouette of a jagged peak against the glowing orange of a rising full moon; other evenings would form an overlay of bright stars in a clear black sky. Midnight among snow-clad peaks and frozen glaciers brought a deep chill, an awesome stillness regularly punctuated by the sharp staccato of falling rocks in the continuous grind of Alpine erosion. This juxtaposition of danger and picturesque beauty gives the Alps an eternally romantic appeal. Exotic Alpine images beckon even today as they did in Whymper's time: the Grand Saint Bernard Pass, the long plateau of the Mer de Glace, and the majestic summits of the Matterhorn, the Jungfrau, Mont Blanc, the Eiger, and the Monte Rosa. The Alps snow-covered peaks and lush valleys are still there for the modern amateur with spare time and modest means. When we meet Alpine climbers today, they are us. But the Alps were the Himalayas of the Golden Age pioneers, whose courage and determination showed us the way.

The appalling loss of four lives in a single accident on the first ascent of the Matterhorn created a maelstrom of public controversy with Whymper at its high-pressure center. It forced him to deal with grieving relatives and a horrified public, and despite his youth he did so, sensitively and forthrightly. He was open and honest with the facts as he saw them, but restrained in casting blame. His account of the accident earned him the respect of his peers and the gratitude of the families of his dead companions.

As the news of the Matterhorn incident spread, it reinvigorated a standing dispute among guardians of the Victorian ethic: was mountaineering, without scientific or other practical purpose, a reckless and therefore immoral endangerment to life? Or was it a true sport, like cricket and football, which improved stamina and built character? As late as 1882, seventeen years after Whymper's first ascent of the Matterhorn, Queen Victoria noted with alarm that three serious accidents had occurred that summer. She consulted with Prime Minister Gladstone about expressing her disapproval of these dangerous Alpine excursions, but the horse had left the barn. The development of mountaineering as a sport was well underway, spurred in no small measure by the popularity of Whymper's writings and lectures.

The Matterhorn disaster ended Whymper's unparalleled climbing career when he was only twenty-five. Soon after his years in the Alps he turned to exploration and scientific observation, first in Greenland and then in a major climbing safari to the high Andes of Ecuador. His last foray was into the Canadian Rockies. In all of these there was a strong element of adventure, with Greenland and the Andes contributing some additional "firsts" to Whymper's record. Following his practice of keeping a detailed daily journal while abroad, he returned from Ecuador with copious notes that became another best-selling book, *Travels Amongst The Great Andes of the Equator.* This title appealed to his earlier readers, and critics hailed it with as many or perhaps more plaudits than first greeted *Scrambles.* Whymper is "a many-sided traveller...an artist...a humorist of the driest brand, a raconteur hardly surpassed," said *The Times.* With another exciting tale of foreign lands and mountain adventure under his belt – spiced with local color and a bit of banana republic intrigue – he was again a popular figure on the lecture circuit.

After the publication of *Andes,* Whymper focused once more on his first love, the Alps, using his knowledge of them to write two popular guidebooks, *Chamonix and the Range of Mont Blanc,* and *The Valley of Zermatt and the Matterhorn.* He travelled these regions until the day he died, promoting and updating his books, assiduously collecting revenues from their sales. Income from book royalties and lectures in England and America gradually supplanted his engraver's earnings. But he never acquired the means – or the inclination, for that matter – to live a life of leisure. His intellectual curiosity and quick mind kept him informed and productive, ever unwilling to suffer fools quietly. Physically he stayed resilient and tough; at sixty-two he walked from Edinburgh to London, averaging over fifty miles a day. To the end he retained a combination of wanderlust, scientific curiosity and artistic talent, along with the will and the energy to pursue them all.

In my quest to understand Whymper I found him good company. I was his armchair companion among the Alps and the Andes, the rustic villages of western Europe, the high plateaus and tropical rain forests of Ecuador, and the frozen wastes of Greenland. He introduced me to engaging characters and customs, bringing to life an era more appealing on many levels than our own. His ironic wit and sardonic humor, though abrasive in his later years, had a Twain-like appeal for me. But he could also be exasperating. I empathized with some of the guides, civil servants, hotel managers and others who sought to serve him, and in so doing suffered his high-handed disdain. I wished that the complaints in his later journals had shown some emotional depth beyond anger. At the end I understood his desperate attempt to find intimacy with a wife and child, and regretted his inability to do so.

Until now, the only full biography of Whymper was written by Francis S. Smythe and published in 1940. An accomplished mountaineer himself, Smythe grudgingly praised the grit and determination that made Whymper's remarkable climbing record possible, but painted a poorly illumined picture of him as an arrogant, alienated loner. With the exception of a facile critic of recent date, the wheel came full circle as later writers were able to look with greater insight into Whymper's personality. "Smythe's lack of sympathy," said one, "amounted to a positive dislike [from someone] overfond of the clichés and half-truths with which a certain school likes to belabor the Victorian age and those who lived in it."[5]

The journey to an understanding of Whymper's heart and soul is as tortuous as his most difficult mountain passage. His diaries, journals, lectures, and the classic memoirs of his climbs and explorations – replete with personal opinions and observations – are the most fertile ground for the researcher's probing. The letters of his waning years furnish additional detail and provide color. Family members, critics and a few friends of these times have their say, highlighting some of the shadows. But even after the biographer's interpretative touches, the portrait remains a work in progress.

Whymper was unquestionably the most controversial character among the principal players during mountaineering's Golden Age and the later Victorian era. He was deeply and permanently affected by the intense trauma of the Matterhorn accident and the cruel complicity of fate. Some say that the episode embittered him; more accurately, the accident seems to have aggravated an inherent depressive condition. His brusque manner alienated many, and he became emotionally abusive as his marriage disintegrated. But he made friends among some who refused to be intimidated, and there were times when he showed kindness. He stayed, however, relentlessly self-contained. Sadness was also a part of his post-Matterhorn makeup, arising out of increasing loneliness and perhaps a realization that he was his own worst enemy.

Certain of those qualities generate distaste and dislike, but as parts of a complex whole they also induce empathy. Some of them, and the continuing emotional struggle they reflected, are to one degree or another our common lot. Whose life is without disappointment and failure, or feelings of real or imagined inadequacy? Who does not erect barriers, sometimes outwardly unpleasant, to hide vulnerability and protect against hurt? Whose equanimity can suppress all feelings of anger? These internal conflicts are grist for the biographer's mill.

Reflecting on his mountain climbing days, Whymper spoke of "joys too great to be described in words, and...griefs upon which I have not dared to dwell."[6] Over a lifetime, however, he revealed more than he intended.

# LIST OF ILLUSTRATIONS AND MAPS

Full-Page

In the Text

Maps

# PROLOGUE

## *Storm on the Mountain*

The Matterhorn sits astride the boundary between southern Switzerland and northern Italy. On the Swiss side, the mountain's north and east faces meet to form a towering monolith of almost 15,000 feet. Chiseled by eons of wind and weather, it stands apart from its neighbors in glorious isolation. Its massive presence dominates the nearby village of Zermatt. From there, looking southwest, the crown of the Matterhorn's summit appears to have been wrenched sideways in the throws of its pre-historic formation, creating an overhang on the eastern face and a near-vertical surface on the northern. It was this view from Zermatt that gave the Matterhorn of Whymper's day its reputation as the "unassailable summit," the "impossible mountain" from which any climber reckless enough to challenge it would never return.[1]

In Italy the southern flank of this three-sided pyramid is an incredibly rugged series of ridges, jagged cliffs, and buttresses topped by a narrow but flat summit whose approach is severe but lacks the extreme verticality of the Swiss sides. These features, intimidating in their own right, kept all but a handful of mid-nineteenth century climbers from attempting the mountain's summit from Italy. Those brave or perhaps foolish enough to go beyond the lower glaciers on the Italian face found themselves in a fantastic expanse – a wild jumble of huge boulders, abrupt and often ice-covered rock precipices, deep crevasses and ravines, narrow ledges, rocky ridges, and steep gullies of frozen snow and fallen debris. To make climbers' lives even more interesting, avalanches and rock slides were common on all sides of the Matterhorn during the summer months when unpredictable weather frequently brought gale-force winds and below freezing chill at the higher levels.

*Photograph of Edward Whymper, age 25*

\* \* \* \*

In the summer of 1863, twenty-three year old Edward Whymper cut a striking figure. His bright-eyed gaze was steady and penetrating, complementing the firm line of his jaw and the cleft chin. Slight hollows below raised cheekbones softened the regular features of his face, hinting at the artist within. His nose was rather long from bridge to tip and his ears a bit on the large side, though both were proportional to his head and the crowning mop of dark hair. In serious moments his mouth turned down slightly at the corners but offered a subtle smile in repose. He was above average height, and in the minority of clean shaven men among his bearded compatriots. His upper body showed great strength, in part from exercising with home-made weights, but he had the sloping shoulders and long muscles of a well-conditioned swimmer. His hands and fingers were large; his thighs and calves sinewy from strenuous year-round walking, and from hard mountain scrambling in his last three Alpine summers. Somewhat surprisingly for one with so powerful a frame, his movements were those of a lithe athlete. His erect carriage gave him the look of a poised and self-confident young man.

In August of that year, Whymper was in Breuil, a village at the head of the picturesque valley known as the Val Tournanche that led southward from the foot of the Matterhorn into the Val d'Osta region of Italy. He was there for one reason only: to make another attempt in his unwavering assault on the Matterhorn's virgin summit. On this occasion his spirits were high. After numerous scrambles on the mountain's southwest side during the preceding two summers, he knew its daunting terrain like his own face in the mirror. He had hired Jean-Antoine Carrel, the most respected of the Val Tournanche guides, to lead his party. Another guide and several porters would strengthen their group. Adding to Whymper's buoyant mood was the weather, which had been threatening but was now clearing up.

Carrel, a native of the valley, had grown up in the Matterhorn's shadow and explored its slopes while still a youth. He had twice been called into the army of the Savoy, fought in the ranks as a rifleman – a "bersagliere" – and had returned to his home in the town of

Valtournanche a battle-hardened veteran. He was the one guide whom the great mountain had never intimidated, and who was as determined as Whymper to reach its summit. Twice before they had attempted the Matterhorn together. They both knew the landmarks along the ascent route, as well as the names they or other climbers had given them: the "Great Staircase" at the head of the "Glacier du Lion," followed by the "Tête du Lion," the "Col du Lion," the "Chimney," the "Great Tower," the "Crête du Coq," the "Cravate," and the "Shoulder" that led to the final peak. These labels were not for campfire stories alone; they had practical use as reference points on a climb, much as the bearings of promontories and other landmarks keep sea-going vessels away from hidden reefs and shoals.

As the leading guide on the Italian side, Jean-Antoine insisted on choosing his assistants and was not shy about using nepotism and patronage in the process. On this occasion his cousin Caesar Carrel would be the second guide. He had chosen three local peasants, including Luc Meynet, "the hunchback of Breuil" and one of Whymper's favorites, as porters to carry the bulk of the equipment needed for the climb. If all went perfectly – which was never one's anticipation on the Matterhorn – a successful ascent would require at least two days. There were no huts or other shelters above the glaciers, and the possibility of bad weather forced parties to prepare for several nights in the open. The mountain's upper terrain was still relatively unknown; climbers might unexpectedly encounter wide crevasses not seen from the valley, and high cliffs that could not be scaled without extra equipment. Whymper and the guides would carry ice axes and bâtons or alpenstocks, rope for tying up, and a rucksack containing extra clothing and personal items. The porters would bring the heavy baggage, including a tent, ladder, blankets, provisions, utensils, brushwood for fires, and 450 feet of extra rope.

The six men left Breuil just before dawn on the tenth of August, 1863. Whymper's party was heavily burdened but his heart was light. "A still and cloudless morning seemed to promise a happy termination to our enterprise."[2] They followed the usual route, hiking first through meadows and then onto the slopes of the Glacier du Lion. There they met crevasses to be skirted or crossed on snow bridges at a slow crawl. Next came the rocks Whymper called the "Great Staircase" for their ease of ascent. These led to the base of a small rocky peak known as the Tête du Lion. Angling to their right around this formation, they started up the rocks along one side of the gully or couloir leading to the Col du Lion, a high pass between ten and eleven thousand feet that joined with the side of the great mountain itself.

Recent bad weather had covered the couloir's rocky slope with loose snow, under which lay a treacherous varnish of ice. Here, as in the shadows of most Alpine peaks, danger lurked. Carrel was in the lead – swinging his axe to carve a foothold or to gain a purchase on the slope – when the surface beneath his feet suddenly gave way. Streams of snow cascaded down the mountain, leaving "long, bare strips of glassy ice" in their wake.[3] Instantly, with cat-like agility, Jean-Antoine threw himself back onto the rock from which he had slipped and stopped his fall. Regaining his feet the imperturbable guide remarked simply, "it's time we were tied up," and went back to work as if nothing had happened.[4] Above this point, however, when passing over a difficult stretch, Carrel would tie an extra rope around a nearby rock, letting a length of it hang down for the next climber's use as a "guard rope" for additional security. This created a series of fixed ropes which all climbers below Carrel could hold onto as they went higher.

Such episodes and tactical adjustments were all in a day's work, and by "steady going" the party reached the Col du Lion before 9:00 a.m. Whymper noticed that the terrain had changed drastically since his ascent of the preceding summer. The Col's summit had shrunk from a "respectably broad," snow-covered surface to a narrow band of hard ice "sharper than the ridge of any church roof."[5] The area where he had camped a year earlier looked desolate; ledges then present were gone, and newly fallen stones littered the surface of the snow on the col's downward slopes. This was typical of the ever-changing features of the Alps, whose wind and weather could turn ridges to rubble in one season or block one summer's open route with an impassable crevasse the next.

After inching across the narrowed col the party went slowly upward for the next two hours, mindful of the need for extreme caution under these conditions. They climbed in groups of two or three, but all were tied together with a single rope. Jean-Antoine, in the lead, cut footholds where possible, and when no other support was available used Whymper's shoulder or the head of Whymper's embedded ice axe to hold his weight. As one man in a group advanced, the others remained stationary, digging their hobnailed boots into packed snow or the narrow lip of a newly cut step. For additional balance, a climber would plunge his ice axe – usually a store-bought, ordinary pick axe – into the snow, or clutch a rock crevice that happened to be within reach. When a man moved upward, the climber above him slowly reeled in rope, keeping the line taut. If there was a climber below, that member of the party slowly paid out rope as needed. Occasionally one or another would slip, but the taut rope would enable the higher climber to stop the slide after "scarcely a foot."[6] None needed to be reminded in this situation that failure to follow this first rule of mountaineering could be fatal.

As the party labored on, the sun shone brightly in a cloudless sky and the air was still. They had the rhythm now and were making steady progress. Their mood was exuberant, almost playful. They "shouted to raise the echoes from the Dent d'Herens," a neighboring peak.[7] They were confident of spending the night on the Matterhorn's high Shoulder, and were already imagining a triumphant march to the summit the following morning. In less than an hour they reached the Chimney, a narrow shaft formed by three sides of smooth rock. The usual procedure at that point was for the most agile climber – Carrel, in this instance – to squirm upward, unassisted, and then lower a rope for others' use if needed. As they completed this maneuver the atmosphere was still tranquil, the air dead calm, not a speck of cloud in sight.

They were now on the ridge above the Chimney that led to the foot of the "Great Tower." Suddenly, a rush of cold air descended upon them, an icy "shower-bath" from out of the blue. A fresh wind of enormous force came at them from all sides, "beating against the ridge and screaming amongst the crags." Patches of fog appeared, swirling about, "showing blue sky for a moment, blotting it out the next." The patches quickly grew bigger "until the whole heavens were filled with whirling, boiling clouds." A furious snow storm then engulfed them and in a few minutes blanketed the ridge on which they stood.

Their only choice at this point was to provide cover for themselves as quickly as possible. Bracing against a freezing gale they worked steadily for two hours to dig a hole in the snow and erect a tent, anchored with

*Matterhorn Crags at Midnight*

pegs or boulders to hold against the fierce wind that tore at the canvas.

> The clouds had blackened during that time, and we had hardly
> finished our task before a thunderstorm broke upon us with
> appalling fury. Forked lightning shot out at the turrets above, and
> at the crags below. It was so close we quailed at its darts. It seemed
> to scorch us – we were in the very focus of the storm. The
> thunder was simultaneous with the flashes; short and sharp...like
> the noise of a door...violently slammed, multiplied a thousand-
> fold....[8]

Throughout the storm the wind blew so furiously that Whymper
feared the tent might be blown away with the entire party inside. To
prevent that – after making sure their clothes were fastened tightly about
them – they all went outside, leaning into the wind to present a lower
profile, with knees bent and feet planted in the snow. In this manner
they endured long enough to build a wall of rocks and snow on the
windward side of the tent. After crawling cautiously back into their
makeshift shelter they shook the snow from their clothes and huddled
together until the storm abated and the sky cleared, about three-thirty
that afternoon.

As their tent would accommodate only five people at night, packed
like canned sardines, they sent one of the porters to the lower slopes for
the evening, leaving the hunchbacked Meynet and another man with
them. The weather kept changing throughout the afternoon; snow would
return, stop suddenly, and then begin again. In moments of blue sky
they saw the Monte Viso clearly, a hundred miles to the south in Italy. In
the west they watched the sun set behind the range of Mont Blanc. They
ate little. When darkness came on they settled "comfortably – even
luxuriously – in our blanket-bags," but lay awake in their tent more than
they slept.[9]

Throughout the night, rocks plunged down the Matterhorn's side –
some closer than others – crashing loudly as they fell. Lightning flashes,
though now farther away, lit the black sky at close intervals. The sounds
of rushing wind and distant thunder also continued intermittently in the
darkness. The storm and the falling rocks presented little immediate

danger but when darkness hides the origins of sounds, "even a sigh may be terrible in the stillness of the night."[10] Snug in their nest, they had survived a difficult day and were hopeful that tomorrow would bring their prize. Lying there, Whymper reflected that he had never seen "a more splendid spectacle than the…illumination of the Matterhorn's crags. I forgave the thunder," he said, "for the sake of the lightning."[11]

It was a short night. Anxious to get underway again, the men turned out at 3:30 the next morning. They were discouraged to find that snow was still falling. When it stopped about nine o'clock they packed up their canvas bags – not yet dry from the prior day's exposure – and set out for the summit, some eighteen hundred feet above them. For two hours they struggled upward, but by eleven o'clock had gained only three hundred feet and snow had once again begun to fall. They held a council: at this pace it might take five hours or more to reach a suitable campsite on the Shoulder, and continuing bad weather might pin them there for several days. Whymper, like most of his British climbing colleagues, was a true amateur with obligations to meet at home. It was now Tuesday, and he had a business appointment scheduled in London at the end of the week. After deliberation, the party reluctantly turned and retraced their steps down the mountain. Their descent was uneventful and they were in Breuil as twilight turned to dusk.

The other guests at the Breuil inn were skeptical of Whymper's description of the weather conditions his party had encountered. They were shocked to hear how he and his colleagues had been in a severe snow storm for twenty-six hours, fighting the elements for survival. The weather in Breuil had been beautiful during the two days Whymper and his party had been gone. Indeed, said Monsieur Favre, the innkeeper, "we have had no snow; it has been fine all the time you have been absent, and there has been only that [one] small cloud upon the mountain."[12]

So ended Whymper's 1863 climbing season. His failed attempt on the Matterhorn's southwestern side was a perfect example of the difficulties of climbing in mountaineering's Golden Age. The wonder is not about how so many Alpine expeditions of the time failed, but how so many, despite these difficulties, succeeded. What kept them going, particularly the British, was a love of adventure and a strong national tradition – indeed, a duty – to persevere in the face of setbacks and losses. Among this earnest group Whymper proved ultimately to be the most committed.

In five seasons of climbing he would scale many peaks – more than half of them as first ascents – but his focus would stay on the Matterhorn. Now, however, in the summer of 1863, Whymper dutifully returned to work in his father's engraving business, and to a more sedentary life in London. But he was already thinking of the challenges of the following summer, and how he could improve his chances of gaining the success he longed for. Only twenty-three years old, he was gaining in strength and experience. He would return.

# CHAPTER 1

## A Victorian Family

The Whymper family's earliest ancestors came to England from the Netherlands in the latter part of the seventeenth century, settling in Suffolk, East Anglia. They were fairly recent adherents to the Baptist faith, a denomination formed in Holland in 1609 by John Smyth, an exiled British dissenter. An accompaniment to their religious beliefs was the solid work ethic evident in the family's history from the time its name first appeared in Suffolk's records.

These early immigrants used "Whimper," the Dutch spelling of the family name. The oldest family member shown on the genealogical chart in Whymper's papers was his triple great-grandfather, "William Whimper of Trimley, Suffolk."[1] The first relative he knew more about was his grandfather, Nathaniel Whimper, born July 24th, 1787. Nathaniel wed Elizabeth Orris and established a home in Ipswich, the "county town" of Suffolk, located about 65 miles northeast of London. Reflecting his Dutch heritage, and perhaps a family tradition, he was a brewer. Edward's father, Josiah Wood Whimper – one of twelve children born to Nathaniel and Elizabeth – entered the world on April 24th, 1813. Josiah showed an artistic bent early on, particularly toward painting, with no interest in his father's brewing business. At age sixteen – determined to put his talents to work and showing more courage than caution – he left home to seek opportunity and recognition in London. He walked the entire distance, arriving in the big city with only the proverbial few shillings in his pocket.

Josiah found employment in London as an apprentice engraver and in his spare time began to paint watercolors and sell them in a neighborhood market. He soon met and married a slightly older woman who died childless in 1835. Two years thereafter, relying solely on his rather tenuous but gradually growing sources of income to support a family, Josiah persuaded Elizabeth Claridge, a young woman he met at the Baptist chapel they both attended, to be his bride. They married on August 12th, 1837; she was eighteen, he twenty-four. One writer, years later, labeled this union an "improvident marriage," presumably in light of Josiah's willingness to take on family responsibilities with few financial means to meet them.[2] But along with the self-confidence that had pushed him to London in the first place, Josiah showed good judgment in choosing Elizabeth. She became a supportive wife, nurturing mother, and a helpmate in her husband's business.

Once married, and wanting to reap the full fruits of his talents for his new family, Josiah began to think seriously about striking out on his own. He had come from Ipswich to London unemployed, inexperienced, and essentially penniless. By scrimping during their first year together he and Elizabeth increased the meager savings of his prior years, sufficient in his judgment to make the move. Again risking everything, he left his employer to form his own engraving company. Though he may have had promises of support from some publishers who had seen his work, Josiah's future now depended solely on his own artistic talents and business acumen. This was around the time of the birth of Frederick, his first child, in 1838.

Josiah's earnings as a sole proprietor were small at first but the business survived and grew, enabling him to remain self-employed for the rest of his long life. It was years later, probably when Edward joined the firm, that Josiah decided to anglicize the family's Dutch surname. "Whimper," the spelling Edward had used in elementary school, had an unfortunate connotation and a somewhat foreign ring. "Whymper" looked more like an English proper name, better for Josiah's company and for the family's social position. Adventurous on the larger issues, the elder Whymper was cautiously pragmatic on matters of everyday business.

Edward was born April 27th, 1840, in the fourth year of the Victorian era. Alexandrina Victoria, niece of Britain's King William IV, had succeeded to her uncle's throne at his death in 1837. She became William's successor because all of his ten children were illegitimate, a contributing factor, in the eyes of some, to the Victorian emphasis on marriage, family and sexual continence. At her coronation in 1838 she was barely nineteen years old. Two years later Victoria married her cousin on her mother's side, Prince Albert of Saxe-Coburg-Gotha. Albert was twenty-one, the same age as his new bride. Together they set a perfect example of abundant productivity, having nine children in the course of their twenty-one year union. They were as susceptible as their subjects, however, to the various diseases that periodically scourged the British Isles and continental Europe. Albert contracted typhoid fever and died in 1861 when only forty-two, leaving his devoted Queen bereft and heartbroken. Victoria herself, sound in body and strong in spirit, lived and ruled until her death in 1901 at the age of eighty-two. When Whymper died ten years later, he had lived sixty-one of his seventy-one years during Victoria's reign.

Whymper spent his early years in a family with barely enough income to stay fed, clothed and sheltered, whose children were in school instead of at work. In 1840, the year of his birth, the British economy was in depression. It soon recovered slightly but lapsed into a recession a few years later. Amid these business cycles Josiah's company faced the usual start-up problems of gaining reputation and revenue before its limited capital ran out. Every other year brought a new mouth to feed. The family and the business survived, but hard times were a constant companion. Whymper noted in his diary: "January 28, [1856]. Business bad – very. It did not pay its expenses last year.[3] "November 1, [1858]. Business is very, very bad, although we expect [it] shortly to be much better, but we have expected that so long and so often that I almost despair of ever seeing it so."[4] Habits acquired in these lean years would last a lifetime, as when travelling abroad in later days he would keep account of his expenses down to the last penny, and fret about overcharges, even for a bottle of beer.

Intermittent penury was only one of the early influences on Edward's character. He was born into a rigid class environment, accepted by English society collectively even as individuals fought to move upward within it. Wealth created by Britain's vibrant industrial growth in the mid-Victorian period swelled the ranks of the middle class, bringing to it increasing numbers of successful businessmen. But for tradesmen and artisans such as the Whympers, upward movement was a continuing struggle – initially to reach the lowest rung of London's middle class and then to stay there. Josiah and his family gained that level but hardly knew from one year to the next whether they could retain their tenuous perch.

Ironically, a particular mindset among the middle and lower classes – from which the Whymper family was not immune – helped to entrench power in the higher ranks. Pride of nationality and respect for British institutions were deeply rooted in the population as a whole, passions absorbed from birth as easily as the oxygen in the air they breathed. Prime Minister William Gladstone (1868-74) called this tendency "a sneaking kindness for a lord."[5] Some scholars placed its origin in the country's early history, when Britain had been "hammered into unity by a strong Crown."[6] Later, as ranking English families gradually acquired the Crown's decreasing power, "something of the mysterious ascendancy of the royal symbol" was transferred symbiotically to them.[7] The House of Lords retained its popular support well into the 20th century, long after the extension of voting rights to the general public. Thus amid the discontent, turmoil, and social change of the Victorian era, the class system endured.

The London of Whymper's adolescent years was an astounding mixture of contrasting styles and competing ideas. Darwin published his *Origin of Species* and John Stuart Mill his discourse *On Liberty*. Thomas Carlyle challenged them by advocating a benevolent aristocracy, and from church pulpits across the land came regular reaffirmation of the creation theory of the universe. The writings of George Eliot and Charles Dickens vied with penny comics and the melodrama of serialized weeklies. Prime ministers from the Whig, Conservative and Liberal parties played a constant game of musical chairs. Notorious couplings between unmarried men and women were not uncommon: "Eliot lived with G. H. Lewes for more than twenty years...as if his wife," and Mill openly courted a married woman for as many years. Carlyle and John Ruskin also flouted convention, but in a different style. They "managed to offend propriety in reverse," perversely honoring their respective marriages by "living in permanent celibacy with their wives."[8]

From this fermenting mixture came measurable social progress, as well as two abiding pillars of modern life: representative institutions and the family, neither of which was seriously challenged by Victorian society. History's hindsight allows us to rationalize the coexistence within Victorian society of a repressive moral code and openly licentious behavior. "[E]ven the scandals of the age – demonstrating the Victorians' capacity to *be* scandalized as much as [their] capacity *to* scandalize – testified to the intensity of [their] moral fervor, the measure of [their] earnestness. Even the *violations* of propriety reinforced the *sense* of propriety."[9] From that perspective, the era's contrasting viewpoints and pursuits appear more a pattern than a paradox.

In the early years of Whymper's life commoners had few civil liberties, many of which are now considered basic human rights. The intensely conformist tenor of the times naturally stimulated broad opposition. On the political agenda of mid-nineteenth century Britain there was always a "movement" seeking to abolish or lessen society's restrictions. Mounting one of the broader challenges to the established order of the day were the Chartists, through a so-called People's Charter drawn up in 1837 by members of the London Working Men's Association. In their petition the movement sought six specific political reforms: "universal adult male suffrage; the secret ballot; parliamentary constituencies of equal size; the abolition of property qualifications for Members of Parliament (who were then required to own land or have an independent income); salaries for [Members of Parliament] so that working men could serve [there]; and annual elections for parliament."[10] Those in power considered petitions of this kind to be the product of political radicalism, and the petitioners themselves rabble rousers. The term "radical" seemed generally to apply to any group seriously challenging embedded privilege. Chartism died by 1840 but its ideals stayed alive and ultimately became the law of the land.

Power resided in the upper classes – the nobility, peers of the realm, the landed gentry, and a few of the wealthiest merchants and industrialists. Although these classes fiercely resisted efforts to diminish their influence, the rise of the middle class was gradually eroding it. A far larger group felt downtrodden and hopelessly situated – the underpaid laborer, the overworked factory hand, the endangered miner, the sick whom no one cared for, the debtor facing prison, and the vast numbers who had no land and thus no vote. Advocates for these unfortunates fought doggedly for legislative measures to improve their lot, with gradual but steady success. For example, the Second Reform Act of 1867 extended voting rights to over one million "working men."[11] Three years later the Married Women's Property Act allowed women to inherit property without ownership passing immediately to their husbands. The Education Acts of 1870 and 1876 made sweeping reforms in elementary school governance.[12] In the same period the Factory Act mandated improved working conditions in larger industries, and the Public Health Act and the Sale of Food and Drugs Act brought the government actively into the field of health protection and promotion.[13]

More than any other factor tending to perpetuate conformity to the system was the influence of the churches. In England, the central pillar of the establishment was the Anglican Church. In the 1840s, seventy-three per cent of all graduates of Oxford and Cambridge were ordained as Anglican priests or deacons, many of whom were second or third sons not eligible or not named as inheritors of their wealthy fathers' lands.[14] Many of these received supplementary incomes from trusts or outright parental gifts. Well-educated and establishment-oriented, these clergymen were able to diminish the discontent within congregations that might otherwise have spawned serious critics of the status quo.

In 1844, only a tiny fraction of English marriages took place outside a church, and during most of the 19th century close to one hundred per cent of the funerals were religious in nature.[15] Church congregations' profound belief in the literal truth of the Bible, and in the moral imperatives of its stories as interpreted by the clergy, enhanced the power of the churches – Anglican, Catholic and Dissenting alike. Priests and pastors shepherded their flocks through this life, meanwhile teaching the rules of behavior for gaining entry into the next. This congruency of religious belief, in turn, promoted congruency of social thought.

Like secular critics of the establishment, religious dissenters formed their own church groups. Although Anglicans held most centers of power in the early Victorian years, an 1851 census found that almost half of the church-goers in England were not of that denomination. Probably the largest of the nonconformist groups were the Evangelical Methodists, whose first leader was John Wesley, a former Anglican. As Baptists, the Whymper family was part of the group known as Dissenters, which also included Quakers, Congregationalists, and Unitarians. These Dissenters epitomized Victorian religiosity: worship of a judgmental God, literal scriptural interpretation, and strict adherence to Biblical rules for observing the Sabbath. They emphasized the values of home and family headed by a strong father. They stressed a modest social life that resisted the lures of the flesh and the pitfalls of low society. Politically they were advocates of respect for the established government – whatever its current composition – and of severe punishment for those who broke the government's laws. The Anglicans were equally, if not more, politically conservative than the Dissenters, and shared their views on morality.

Religion thus played a major role in the development of the Victorians' harsh code of sexual conduct. As in the forces perpetuating the class system, there was great irony here, too. The effort to smother the sexual drives of its people came to be the Victorian era's most notorious characteristic, largely for the carnal excesses it tried to suppress but could not. Brothels and taverns in Victorian London were busy from sunset to dawn, their clientele often spilling riotously into streets near the Haymarket and the Strand, and in other back-alley neighborhoods. Prostitution flourished, becoming so widespread that efforts to quell it became a prime charitable activity. Its reformers included ordinary citizens along with people of prominence and power. Among the latter was Prime Minister Gladstone, who helped found "reclamation homes" and who actually walked "the streets at night looking for women to help."[16] Though he never mentioned such homes in his books, Charles Dickens chaired a group that ran a "reformatory home" for prostitutes.[17] In a particularly Victorian approach to this problem, the commercial promotion of prostitution was not made a crime. Pimps and other procurers operated surreptitiously, out of the public eye, so the Victorians simply pretended they did not exist. Only the women who openly practiced their vocation were subjected to public ostracism and potential penalties, beginning with the controversial Contagious Diseases of Act of 1864 which required the forcible examination of prostitutes for disease.

The most influential figure in all of this was the Queen herself. The public saw her as serious, God-fearing, industrious and straight-laced. With Victoria as their model, women were the custodians of morality – mothers who tried to keep their daughters chaste until marriage, and wives who joylessly submitted to their husband's carnal desires. The claim that some homemakers put frilly material on piano and table legs lest they appear too suggestive is probably false – an "old chestnut," as some would have it. It is probably true, however, that when Victorian wives sent out valentines depicting the figure of Cupid, he wore a skirt.[18]

Men also played a role in the attempt to repress the sexual urges of the populace. As head of the household, a father was expected to keep his son away from "women of the street," at least until the young man's imminent marriage called for his indoctrination to copulation at a carefully selected brothel. Clergymen preached against sins of the flesh; Members of Parliament made regular though largely unsuccessful attempts to enact sexually repressive laws. Both groups, at the time, were male monopolies. In 1857, Parliament passed the Obscene Publication Act, allowing authorities to seize and destroy literature that offended Victorian sensibilities about sexuality. Most Victorians still read Bowdler's 1818 *The Family Shakespeare in Ten Volumes,* which omitted words and phrases "which cannot be read with propriety in a family."[19] Male doctors examined the sensitive anatomical areas of female patients through multiple layers of the women's garments.

These same doctors believed that traces of semen in a male's urine signaled the presence of Spermatorrhea, a potentially harmful disorder thought to be caused by excessive masturbation. Doctors issued dire warnings against the practice and anxious parents sought ways to discourage their sons from engaging in it. The marketplace responded by developing various cages and other devices for fathers to fit onto their sons at night in order to prevent the act if not the temptation. The most elaborate of these involved a leather harness attached to wires that would ring a bell in the parents' bedroom in the event of "a filial erection."[20] Female self-stimulation was thought rare enough to be of little concern, or perhaps so far beyond the pale as to be unmentionable.

As a counterpoint to clandestine offerings of sexually-oriented activities, Victorian society provided ready access to abundant cultural diversions, especially in London. There were performances at Covent Garden Theatre, exhibitions of paintings and photographs at the Royal Academy and Pall Mall, and water shows at the Crystal Palace. For the more literary there were readings by Hardy, Eliot, the Brontës and

Dickens from their own works. Daily lectures were available on a myriad of subjects ranging from arctic exploration to cooking and table manners. Victorians revered Tennyson, Byron, Shelley and Keats. Wordsworth still spoke to poetry lovers as did contemporary American poets Longfellow and Whittier. Installments of new works by popular authors appeared in magazines just ahead of their books' publication. Readers devoured this material in both of its forms. There were magic lantern shows and re-enactments of famous events from exotic lands, including Albert Smith's acclaimed production of the first ascent of Mont Blanc. Popular music entertainment ranged from music hall choruses to Gilbert and Sullivan. Through every media, however, the Victorian ethic of taste and propriety exerted its leavening influence. Operas, for example, were well attended but sometimes censored by government watchdogs. In 1850, Verdi's *La Traviata* was approved for performance but the libretto – with its story of a scandalous liaison between an unmarried gentleman and a Parisian courtesan – could not be distributed in the theatre in English.[21]

In this milieu the Whymper family led a classic middle class life faithfully reflecting Victorian styles and attitudes. Following the birth of Edward, their second son, Josiah and Elizabeth produced nine more children, two girls and the rest boys. Josiah was an industrious father and conscientious family provider. Popular illustrated books created a strong demand for woodblock engravings, and Josiah's output became known for its high quality as the years went by. Among his clients were two of London's largest publishing houses, John Murray and William Longman. His reputation for excellence spread as far as Paris, which he visited occasionally to promote his talents. In time he also became a respected painter, primarily for his works in watercolor. He held classes for aspiring young artists, one of whom, Charles Keane, later became a noted artist for *Punch* magazine.[22]

Even with Josiah's and later Edward's reputation and business success, the Whympers remained lower middle class tradesmen in the eyes of British society. Engraving was a trade whose fortunes ebbed and flowed with business cycles and almost completely dried up in flagging economies. Additional pressure on the Whymper's family finances came from the need, for both business and social reasons, to maintain a standard of living higher than the lower classes which was not all that far beneath them.

Elizabeth, homemaker and nurturing mother, spent her time raising the children and trying to instill in them, by example, the Victorian values of thrift, character and duty. She also joined with Josiah in presenting to the world the appearance expected of a family in their social position. In doing so she fulfilled her role well. Nature had given all of the children strong bodies and good health which she sustained with attentive loving care. "Illness is not scarce in our house," wrote Whymper in his diary, but remarkably all eleven offspring lived to maturity.[23] Elizabeth found time for charitable work with families and schools in poor neighborhoods where once, with Edward's help, she endeavored "to get a blind boy into the school in St. George's Fields."[24] Her relationship with Edward was warm, and he worried about her health as she grew older and weaker.

By the late spring of 1859 Elizabeth's health was noticeably failing from some undisclosed and perhaps unknown illness. Her doctor advised the family to move away from London to the fresh air and open fields of the neighboring countryside. This would create some commuting problems for Josiah and Edward who had joined his father's company a few years before. But the doctor's advice prevailed and in June the family moved to a residence known as Town House in the village of Haslemere, about seventeen miles southeast of London.

Elizabeth was happy with her new home. The air was cleaner and she now had space for gardening and even a few farm animals. With the help of a hired hand or two, and of the children who were able, she reworked the old garden with new flowers and vegetables. She planted her favorite yellow-blooming jasmine vines near the house. She bought a piglet and delightedly watched its rollicking exploration of the premises. The move had energized her, and more time in the open air brought back some of her natural color. But there was one aspect of her condition a change of scene could not alter: that June, Elizabeth was four months pregnant. In November she gave birth to the family's eleventh child and second daughter, Annette. The pregnancy was probably one of the reasons her doctor had prescribed a change of scene, and a possible factor in her continuing decline. On December 9th, while talking to the new baby's nurse, she collapsed onto the kitchen floor and died instantly. After more than twenty-two years of marriage and eleven children she was only forty.

The suddenness of Elizabeth's death shocked her family. She had been the emotional center of their lives, their chief caretaker and comforter when things went wrong, their source of praise when things went well. Her absence left a void in their lives making her loss deeply felt. Nineteen at the time, Edward was probably the child who knew her best and was closest to her. Annette said many years later, after Edward's death, "The loss [of our mother] cut Edward to the heart. Such affection as he held, he never forgot [his] adored mother."[25] Annette was remembering, perhaps, a letter Edward had written her: "[Our] mother [once said] that she would live in the memory of some of her children more than others, and she was right."[26]

The family continued to live at Town House. After arranging for additional help with the children Josiah went back to work. Without Elizabeth's aid his responsibilities as father and family bread winner were greater than ever. He was forty-six at the time of her death, still healthy and vigorous. Seven years later he married again, this time to Emily Hepburn who at thirty-four was nineteen years his junior. Edward liked her and appreciated her affection for his father and the considerate attention she gave to the rest of the family. In later years she had her share of sickness, which offered Edward and her other step-children opportunities to show their concern. In 1886, when she was fifty-four, Whymper wrote to her, "The trifling attentions I am able to pay you are a very inadequate return for eighteen years of unvarying kindness. We should all desire to do more for you if we could, to testify to our respect and affection, and to express our sympathy with you during your severe trials."[27] Emily died later that same year of a lengthy and undisclosed illness.

Although the engraving company's earnings fluctuated with the economy, they were always the mainstay of the Whymper family's finances. Josiah's work ethic stayed strong throughout his long life. He gained recognition as one of London's leading engravers and remained in the business until photography made it obsolete toward the end of the century. He continued to paint watercolors which sold well in good times and later brought him membership in The Royal Society of Painters in Water Colours. Josiah hung tenaciously to life for seventeen years after Emily's passing and died in 1903 aged ninety. Edward was in Switzerland at the time and did not make it back to London in time for the funeral.

At work, Josiah had been a strict taskmaster. Edward chafed under orders that occasionally struck him as wrong-headed and arbitrary, convinced he could complete tasks "quicker and better" if left to his own discretion.[28] They shared a mutual respect, however, and Edward wrote regularly to his father – not perfunctory notes of duty but letters describing in detail his wanderings and adventures. At the end of his life Josiah could take pride in all of his children. Except for his last-born they led active lives in a variety of pursuits in both England and India. Annette, the youngest, never married. Perhaps because she grew up without a mother's loving care or affection, the family took a special interest in her – particularly Edward, her next-to-oldest brother. During her periodic bouts of ill-health he took the lead among several brothers to help pay her rent and other bills. Toward the end of her life, at the request of Frank Smythe, Whymper's 1940 biographer, she wrote thumbnail sketches of her sister Elizabeth and her nine brothers.

Frederick, the oldest, wrote professionally and authored several books. Alfred became an Anglican priest "much beloved and widely respected as the editor of [various] church papers." Charles developed into an artist of some renown, best known "as a painter of animals and birds." Henry went to India where "as a busy man of affairs" he was financially successful and widely known for his "relief works in time of famine." Henry also helped three of his younger brothers – Joe, Frank and Sam – obtain positions in India. Joe was Henry's business assistant; Sam became the manager of a brewery (like his grandfather) and was known as a "big game hunter and naturalist." Frank held several positions in the British colonial government of India, including Postmaster General of Bombay. Like Henry he was considered a great friend of the local people. William, who was younger than all except Sam and Annette, was "the one on whom all the family relied," the one who helped in family disputes and in times of illness or other distress.[29] Elizabeth, who also never married, spent her life as a social worker, becoming a Captain in the Salvation Army in her later years.

According to Annette, Edward was "the dominating personality" of the group and the only one to achieve international recognition.[30] That personality trait began to show quite early on in the foremost member of the large Whymper family.

CHAPTER 2

*Ambitious Dreams*

"How 'squisite," said Edward, age four, surveying the landscape around Shanklin where the Whymper family was spending its annual summer holiday. "How 'squisite."[1] This was his rather high-blown word for "beautiful" though he could not yet pronounce it properly. He was doubtless trying to repeat what he had heard others say. Flowery language was the custom among educated Victorians, most of whom used superlatives as often as not to describe a scene or to characterize their feelings. They were "shocked" and "furious" not merely surprised and angry. When out of sorts they felt "wretched" not simply bad. Perhaps verbal exaggeration was one way to let off steam in a society that demanded circumspect behavior. Edward adopted the speaking style of his elders at a very young age.

His formal education began the next year when he entered the first grade at Clarendon House School near the Whymper home in the Lambeth area of South London. During his nine years there, the only school he ever attended, he won a number of prizes both in specific courses and in overall conduct. He showed particular interest and aptitude in scientifically oriented subjects but also did well in French. One of his citations, dated December 9th, 1851, was a recognition of improvement and an encouragement to do better: To "E. Whymper for his improvement in Latin class 3 in the hope that it will serve as an incentive to future exertion."[2] Someone, probably his mother, had attached a daguerreotype picture of Whymper, aged 11, to the certificate. Accuracy, attention to detail and good organization were his strengths. Developed early they would last a lifetime.

Several notebooks in Whymper's handwriting from his last four years at Clarendon House survive today. Well-organized and neatly written they appear to be summaries of classroom lectures prepared from notes and submitted to the teacher for grading. All are science-related and cover a wide range of subjects: chemistry, physiology, steam engines (including a paper on Mr. Watt's invention), electrolytes, heat, pneumatic pumps, mechanics, magnetism, barometric pressure and Galvanism. A mark of 50 appears to be the top grade awarded for subject matter which could be raised by additional points for penmanship, illustrative diagrams and charts, and even "diligence." Whymper's lowest mark, on an unidentified topic, appears to have been a "25" prompting a note of chagrin: "Oh, what a great falling off was there, my countrymen." His highest marks, ranging from 50 to 60, were for papers on barometric pressure (with good drawings), Galvanism (including the story of Galvani watching his wife cut frog legs as she prepared a medicinal broth), and magnetism (with a description of a shipwreck at Beachy Head due to a faulty magnetic compass). Even then Whymper had a talent for storytelling.[3]

The young student turned fourteen in the spring of 1854. That summer Josiah decided that Edward would begin working in the family engraving business and not return to Clarendon School. Most likely the money for Edward's continuing education was in scarce supply. Business was bad and getting worse: next year the company's receipts were expected to be less than its expenses.[4] There were many mouths to feed now so it made sense for one of the children to earn his keep. With a good head on his shoulders Whymper was also the son who had most evidently inherited his father's artistic talent. The other side of this coin was that Edward did not want to end his studies and was decidedly unenthusiastic about working as an engraver. He had hoped to study law or civil engineering and had dreamed of arctic exploration and a life at sea. But he dutifully obeyed Josiah's decision. That was his nature and besides, he saw no good alternative.

For the next five years (1855-59), virtually the entire span of his adolescence, Edward kept a personal diary brimming with places and people in his life along with highly personal opinions on politics, religion and various less emotionally charged subjects. The youthful journal is a volatile mixture of substance and style. Some of its entries, on fires and railroad accidents for instance, show a classic boyish enthusiasm. He describes murders, robberies, hangings and suicides. Side-by-side with them are insightful observations on events and issues of the day ranging from the conduct of foreign wars to the need for fair criminal trials at home. Mature, informed judgments mingle with adolescent theories straight off the top of his head. He is empathetic one moment and hard-boiled the next. Many entries are quite mundane: he notes the weather as faithfully as a sailing captain keeping his ship's daily log. He acknowledges his own boredom almost as frequently, usually when he had to "chop wood" to make engraving blocks. He also complains of having to baby-sit a younger brother. As a whole, for its scope if not its depth, it is a remarkable record of early Victorian London as seen through male adolescent eyes. At one point in his diary he claims to write little about himself beyond his daily work. In fact almost every diary entry reveals something of the young author's character or personality.

Edward's years of apprenticeship with his father were difficult. Both were strong-willed and independent-minded. It would not have been unusual in these circumstances for a rift to have developed between them that would widen over the years. But throughout their contemporaneous long lives – Edward outlived Josiah by only eight years – their relationship would be one of mutual respect enriched by a degree of cordiality shown more in behavior than in words. Whymper's diary revealed something of how that relationship developed. He felt at times that he and his brothers were pawns in their father's grand plan, a blueprint he believed would fail. In one entry referring to himself as "Ted" his frustration was evident.

> In pursuance of his plan regarding us, my father sends my brother, Alfred, to Edinburgh next Friday to Clark's the printers. Thus Fred engraver, Ted draftsman, Alfred printer and so on. But shall we finally keep to this – I think, in fact I *know*, we shall not. Then what is the use in pursuing the plan and making us all those different trades? None whatever, if we could have got anything else that *we liked* and *should* keep to. In such a case, all the present time is being wasted.[5]

Whymper chafed at the lack of discretion allowed him on business decisions even when his father was out of town. "If I were left to do entirely as I thought proper, I [have] little doubt that I should get on with it both quicker and better."[6] But his warm feelings for his father predominated. "My father has...at last got one of the jobs settled which we have been looking...for. I sincerely rejoice, more for my father's sake than my own, as it is very dispiriting to a man with 10 children and no great fortune not to be able to obtain work...."[7] He was pleased when his father's paintings drew "exceedingly flattering" reviews in the press.[8] Perhaps the truest testament to the good will between them was the survival of their working relationship through so many lean and difficult years in Whymper's youth and after.

Some of his youthful diary's more striking entries concerned Britain's and its allies' war with Russia in the Crimea. Edward listened to his father and others talk about this and other issues of the day. He also read newspaper accounts of Crimean battles along with their editors' views of the war's impact on domestic politics. But the selection of subjects, the facts recited, and the reasoning applied to them clearly bore his personal stamp.

> Today the Ministers resigned in consequence of a motion by Mr Roebuck in the House of Commons to inquire into the conduct of the war, and the ministers, not wanting an inquiry, resigned. However, there will be one. The Queen sent for Lord Derby, but he refused to try and form a cabinet because Mr Gladstone and Lord Palmerston would not take office under him. The popular voice is for Lord Palmerston, but he has very little favor in the Queen's eyes.[9]

A month later he observed that "Yesterday in all probability the most important event took place that has happened in my lifetime...the death of the Emperor Nicholas 1st of Russia."[10] Whymper opined that Russian generals would be "uncertain" about what action to take in this temporary power vacuum thereby providing an opportune moment for British ministers "to press the siege of Sebastopol." He also hoped that the "milder" of the Emperor's two sons would become the new czar for "we shall be able to dictate much better terms to him."[11] At the time of these two opinionated but perceptive entries he had not yet reached his fifteenth birthday.

In June of 1855 Whymper grew angry at Russian soldiers who showed "their ignorance of the laws of humanity by firing...on a detachment of British sailors who were landing three prisoners under a flag of truce."[12] He did not fault the Russian soldiers for cruelty or consider the possibility that they failed to see the flag. Signaling his budding arrogance he simply branded the Czar's men as "ignorant" in contrast to the more enlightened views of himself and the British establishment. With brashness and shrewdness often clashing in a single observation he was sometimes wrong but never in doubt.

In early 1857 Edward deplored "bloodshed" noting that a potentially dangerous flare-up in Switzerland had been "at last happily settled...without having to resort to the stupid and cruel means of violence."[13] Later that year, however, came a steady flow of articles in the London press describing atrocities committed by sepoys, native Indian soldiers commanded by English army officers but rebellious in these cases. "General Havelock... when he took Cawnpore...found the great courtyard two inches deep in blood....[Sepoys] had stripped the women naked, beheaded them, torn the...flesh from their yet warm bodies, forced it into their children's mouths, [and] then thrown the bodies down a well [with] the living children on top of them."[14] Such descriptions hardened Whymper's heart. Agreeing with the British "General-In-Chief," he wrote a month later that the sepoys "must be given no quarter....[we must repay] what we owe...[them], the wretches."[15]

Political radicals who disturbed the peace at home also incurred Whymper's youthful displeasure. On Sundays in the summer of 1855 large crowds gathered in Hyde Park – "at least 150,000 people" on one occasion – to speak and protest against various perceived ills of the day. Violence would sometimes develop as it did on July 1st of that year when "the mob" broke windows in Belgrave Square. "As Mr Peel said in the House," reported Whymper, "they were mere *canaille* [rabble], and I quite agree with his suggestion that a few six-pounders fired into them would do a deal of good."[16] Edward and the Prime Minister were perhaps speaking metaphorically but their views, matching the temper and the language of the times, reflected the stern attitudes of the establishment against violators of law and order. They also reflected the intensity of the restless mob's anger.

When it came to individual cases Edward sometimes sided with the accused. He was upset in January 1856 when a court martial condemned a British naval officer to death for cowardice though the officer had not been in command of the action:

> The second master of H.M.S. Lynx, Mr Deheny by name, has been condemned to hang by the neck until dead, on charge of cowardice, in the action before Kinburn. He pleads nervousness. Now I do not think that such a crime should be made capital unless he is an officer in command...when it is obviously his duty to do such a thing, and he purposely or cowardly neglects doing so and by his conduct influences others....And as Mr Deheny had been some time previously ill, I do not think that the law, if that is the law, should be put in force in his case.[17]

Religion was as important to the young Whymper as law and order. A staunch Baptist he spent most Sunday mornings and evenings at Maze Pond House, a neighborhood Baptist chapel in which he had been baptized and had attended ever since. A variety of preachers passed through this church, many of whom drew Edward's scorn. "Mr Armstrong (an impudent, smeary-faced old ass) preached in the morning, and Mr Watts, an excited, affected young donkey, in the evening."[18] Three months later another preacher's text had a similar effect: it was "error...mixed with truth, being beautifully calculated to lead those astray whose opinions are not settled."[19] Further, he said, "I do not like dramatic preaching, I would rather hear a quiet sermon."[20] One may safely conclude from these entries that Whymper's views fell into the "settled" category. But though he believed strongly in the faith and in the teachings of the Bible he was not particularly sectarian in his outlook. Commenting on a preacher who had visited in the Whymper home he wrote:

> I like Mr Gosse exceedingly. Besides being a clever and learned man (and the conversation of such must always be pleasing to

me) he is an excellent Christian, brim full of his Bible, and very apt with his texts. He is a Plymouth Brother, which is the same as saying that he is no sect, and his opinions and views on religion coincide almost perfectly with my own."[21]

Along with most of his contemporaries Edward believed in a God that directly influenced the course of human affairs: one must work hard to be successful but God's help was an essential force in all human strivings. In February 1859 Whymper looked forward to a busy year "thanks be to our father in heaven from whom all blessings flow."[22] God was the ultimate judge of our guilt or innocence: "William Palmer was hung this morning....I am no[t] convinced he was guilty....If, however, he is innocent, he will not suffer in the next world for it, and if he is guilty...."[23] This sentence was left dangling like poor Mr. Palmer but Whymper's fatalistic attitude was evident, strengthened by his belief that "the soul is the peculiar property of the Lord."[24]

An ardent Sabbatarian in the Baptist tradition, Whymper noted that Sunday "was ordained and set apart by God himself for rest and is needed for religious purposes."[25] In this conviction Whymper was a product of his time. By a strong consensus virtually no one worked on the Sabbath. Even the British Museum, the National Gallery, and the Crystal Palace, places designed "to improve the national mind," were closed on the day God himself rested. But only one year after writing this entry Whymper confessed that he had "committed what I believe to be a sin" by taking an omnibus to Camden Road Chapel on a Sunday to hear his uncle preach there. He was ashamed of having helped "to keep [bus drivers] unnecessarily [at] work on the Sabbath Day, but hoped "not to be held accountable" for his lapse.[26] Using his diary as his confessor, he found absolution.

A business client once put Edward's sincerity on this issue to the acid test. A client named Macpherson, a Scotsman from Edinburgh, sent a wood block to the Whymper company for engraving.

He wanted it done quickly, in fact sooner than we could do it, [and we told him so]. [T]o our astonishment...[he replied], "As the block is for a religious publication, there would be no sin in working on the Sunday." No indeed, Mr Macpherson, not to please you or anyone else will that be done, [but]...we shall get it done as soon as possible. It is very strange that such an argument could be used [by] an educated person living in the 19th century. It would better suit the 12th or the 13th. [27]

Josiah Whymper and his son obviously saw eye to eye on this matter. Whymper's youthful fundamentalism, however, was not absolute. In May of 1856 the Prime Minister Lord Palmerston, "at the urgent petition of the Archbishop of Canterbury," ordered all bands to cease playing in London parks on Sundays. Whymper disagreed: "I do not consider that playing music (especially sacred which they did) is so criminal (in a religious light) as getting drunk or going excursions in the country on a Sunday."[28] Music, after all, was a restful pastime and thus in keeping with the purposes of the Sabbath. Less than a month later Whymper focused on another religious controversy. He noted with pleasure that "[t]he bill to remove the [civil] disabilities of Jews has just passed. It is a shame that it has met with such opposition as it has before now."[29] Since the Bible was usually interpreted to teach that the Jews killed the only son of God, the idea of admitting them into the mainstream of British life and politics was a difficult call for many Victorian Christians. But just two months into his sixteenth year Whymper seemed already to have learned that reason and experience were appropriate elements in the application of his faith.

On some issues of less emotional concern Whymper also expressed surprisingly mature opinions. In February 1856 aged fifteen, he noted that Parliament had recently created a new peer of the realm, a so-called "life-peer" whose title expired at death and could not, like classic peerages, be passed from father to eldest son indefinitely.

There has been a new peer created; but only for his life the peerage lasts. This is an innovation, but why should it not be? Some cry out that if that is done, the old families will become extinct. I should rather say, my lord may be a clever man and his son may be a stick....[I]f the father [be] a clever man, is it any reason...that the son should be rewarded for it? Not at all. But still I should not like to see the grandson of the Duke of Wellington starving. I think this shows that we are getting more enlightened, and if this goes on (which I have no doubt it will) there will be some chance for the poor deserving man getting to be a great man.[30]

Edward wrote these words too early in his life for them to be self-serving. Though he dreamed of fame he hardly saw himself as a potential candidate for lordship.

An ambitious teenager, Whymper found the job of apprentice engraver far more tedious than challenging. On at least one occasion – a visit to the Court of Queen's Bench – he "fancied himself" a lawyer even though the arguments of barristers appearing before the Court that day were "dull."[31] He also mused about becoming a civil engineer "where my head might be worked as well as my hands."[32] Many of his tasks were menial, particularly in the early years. Terse diary entries spoke loudly of his boredom: "Cut wood," "Went errands," "Drew diagrams, etc. Diagrams!"[33] This tedium occasionally triggered an explosion – as in September of 1857 – that splattered the pages of his diary with feelings of frustration: "Oh, sickening job....how I should rejoice to escape from this thralldom with scarcely any prospect of better times. The same everlasting filthy round day after day, one day not varying at all from the other."[34] But emotional outbursts of this intensity – or at least his recording of them – were limited. In a period of nearly five years only two of them, two days apart, appear in the diary.

Edward was now a young man and if his life sometimes seemed relatively sedate and boring it was not always so. Cricket was his favorite sport and pastime as a player, coach, and spectator. He regularly attended matches at the "Oval," a newly created cricket ground and viewing stand near his southeast London home still in use today in architecturally upgraded form. So often was he there that he once half-heartedly promised himself never to go again. "It is far too expensive for me at present. May God aid me in keeping" my vow.[35] Two months later his love of the game pushed him to participate in it at an even more time-consuming level. In August 1858 aged eighteen, he formed a new team, the North Lambert Cricket Club.[36] He was initially its coach and a year later played for the team as well.[37]

In an April 1859 diary entry Whymper noted his attendance at a meeting of the members of the Peckham Rye Albion Cricket Club at a local tavern. He referred to them as a "queer, beery lot" whose "bad habits" he wished to avoid.[38] This led some to conclude that his comment was aimed at all cricket players and showed him to be overly prudish and judgmental, not a regular bloke. Those critics might more reasonably have decided that the Albion Club had a disproportionately large share of hard drinkers and that he was faulting them alone. Indeed, Whymper went back to Peckham Rye two months later "intending to have an evening with the Albion Club."[39] A number of later diary entries also show his continuing association with his own teammates, quite content to be in their company.

Another of his favorite sports was horse racing. References to Derby Day – the weather, the size of the crowds, and the names of winning horses – occupy several diary entries. He also followed the Oxford-Cambridge boat races, and on one occasion noted the results of recent boxing matches.

Physical disasters were common at the time; raging fires regularly swept through London's wooden structures and deadly train wrecks occurred with alarming frequency. These events excited Whymper, often attracting him to see the destruction for himself. Individual calamities and executions also caught his attention. In just three months of 1856, February through April, his diary recorded "several" murders, two suicides by jumping (a woman from Westminster Bridge and a man from the "whispering gallery at St. Paul's"), an "abounding number of robberies," a boiler explosion in Whitechapel, and a "hanging at Newgate." Also in that period the Vauxhall Railway Station and the Covent Garden Theater burned to the ground.

> This morning I was woke up at quarter-past 5 by the bright light caused by the conflagration at Covent Garden Theater. I went at 7 o'clock to see it, and the inside was a mass of flames just like a furnace and they were as high as the roof had been....Eighty-five thousand pounds' worth of music and books, 100 complete suits of armour, are among the things destroyed, to which we must add one hundred thousand pounds at least for the superb building.[40]

This blazing fire animated Edward the youth even as Whymper the businessman took careful note of the financial cost. These facets of his personality showed themselves time and again in the future.

Whymper was an inveterate walker, often to a place for sketching, sometimes for pleasure and recreation, and on rare occasions to go tramping about with friends.

> In afternoon I walked down to Richmond and on to Twickenham to see my father sketching, and from there to Ham Common...where I had my tea, then walked direct up again, doing 25 miles between half-past 2 and half-past 9...[C]onsidering I am out of practice, and the roads bad, and I had new shoes on," that "was good for me. The longest distance I have walked yet in one day is 35 miles, and the longest distance without a halt is 27 miles."[41]

The following March Edward walked to St. Albans, stood 5 hours in the cathedral sketching the choir, and then walked back to his home in Lambeth, a round trip by his calculation of 21 miles. It was all in a day's work for an energetic seventeen year old.[42]

Whymper had a variety of other interests. He attended Albert Smith's hugely popular re-enactment of the ascent of Mont Blanc, which may have been his first exposure to Alpine adventure.[43] He enjoyed musical performances, most of all "the renowned Christy's Minstrels" whose talents received his unconditional accolades, tributes that came rarely from one so often difficult to please.[44] One entry, memorable for its youthful exuberance and lack of sophistication, notes the death of a minstrel favorite: "Today I heard that one of Christy's Minstrels has just died. It was Mr Peirce [sic], the inimitable singer and actor of the now world-wide song *Hoop de Dooden Doo*. I am very sorry for them and for myself."[45] Absent, however, was any expression of sorrow for Mr Peirce himself.

Newspapers and periodicals were the staples of Edward's wide-ranging intellectual appetite. He read Macaulay's History, 3rd Volume, but did not "like his style very much,"[46] Upon reading the diary of Thomas Moore he concluded without irony, "One cannot get a better idea of a man, than from his diary."[47] He read Dickens and other popular novelists, often by way of installments published in *Harpers* magazine. He also attended readings by these authors of their own works. *Tom Brown's Schooldays* was a favorite book, as was another written in the same style but not named in his diary.

> I cannot tell how it is but such books as these affect me more powerfully than any others. I feel convinced that a simple style, natural and unaffected, not too minute, but describing with power, will produce more effect and affect the mind more than the loftiest or grandest matter written in the most magnificent manner.[48]

He could not have known the portent these words carried when he wrote them, but his later writing style showed that he never forgot the lesson taught by these two books.

Whymper steadily developed his drawing skills as he gained experience in the engraver's art and this led naturally to a growing interest in the works of other artists. He regularly attended exhibitions of paintings at the Royal Academy and Pall Mall, and went to each of the Academy's annual exhibitions of the new art of photography, the first of which was held in January 1854. By mid-1857 the 17-year-old diarist considered himself an accomplished art critic. As such he continued to express opinions in his uninhibited style. In July of that year several of the artists on display at the Royal Academy evoked Whymper's royal displeasure: "especially the Academicians, oh! – Millais' insanities, Maclises' crudities and cut-out paper figures and some bad ones of Leslie, Redgrave I think, Ward, also Witherington, etc. I was horrified and disgusted."[49] That same day, as a cleansing antidote "to finish up the afternoon," he "went to the Oval and saw part of a grand cricket match between the Gentlemen and the Players of England." "The former will be beaten," he added confidently.[50] Perhaps Whymper was able to judge exhibitions at the Oval better than those at the Academy, but in any event he knew where to find relaxation and release.

The center of Edward's social life was his immediate family. The Whympers spent Christmases at home and took family holidays together in the summer. In London many of Edward's outings were with a family member or two – usually with his mother or sister Elizabeth who was just a year or two younger than he. Also part of the family picture were the internal stresses and strains that no large brood is without, including the proverbial crazy aunt in the basement.

> This evening there was another disturbance with that pest of ours, my father's sister, Mrs Bradlaugh. The cause of it need not be narrated here. Suffice it to say that I think this time we shall be rid of her. I lay the decline of our business principally to her coming to Canterbury Place [Whymper's home], for I believe that she has had more influence than any other single cause.[51]

Escape from crowded family quarters no doubt contributed to the fun and freedom of the family's summer holidays in Eastbourne, Shanklin, Ham and other nearby resort areas. Their time at Ham in August 1856 seemed special to Edward who wrote warmly and in a lightly self-mocking manner about it.

> I did but little good, my time being principally occupied with playing at cricket and trying to catch fish who laughed at my vain endeavors. I tried to sketch in color, but like my previous attempts it was a complete failure.[52]

His diary also records social evenings at home, dinner with a publisher who might order engravings for his next book or tea and supper with family friends: "Had Mr and Mrs W. Collingwood-Smith to tea and supper, he is amusing and she is as amusingly impudent as ever."[53] Mrs. Collingwood-Smith must have had extraordinary charm for Edward to tolerate her "impudence," much less to enjoy it as he did, apparently on several occasions.

His diary does not mention dinners or other visits at his house with companions his own age, and refers only to a few occasions outside his home in the company of friends. He managed, however, to attend parties in neighboring homes, several of which were sufficiently memorable to be recorded. The first was a "juvenile party" where the guests enjoyed "a good many games, some music, chemical experiments, etc."[54] Then came "*Good Friday!!* Bun day forever!!!," presumably at church.[55] He next noted three parties in the space of three weeks, beginning with "pleasant company and a very good supper" at Mr. Brown's house, where he "noticed especially a Miss Hivanry, a pretty and amiable little girl."[56] A party at Mr. Hepburn's followed – probably the home of his future mother-in-law – and then the wind-up of this social season, a party at Mr. Brown's from which Whymper returned home at midnight to receive a "scolding" for staying out so late.[57] A "soiree at Mr Beddome's" took place the next year and soon after a beautiful "spread at Mr Probart's with "music, singing and feeding."[58] Edward's last recorded party, noted when he was eighteen years old, was a "spread at Mr R Taylor's next door," where he danced – 24 dances – until midnight.[59]

Were these parties the only ones Edward attended in the roughly five-and-a-half years of his diary entries? Probably not; there are many gaps – a week here, two weeks there, and occasionally a blank month. The diary shows only that while he was a rather solitary youth he was not a social recluse. He admitted feeling "considerably awkward" at these events "not being used to female society."[60] Sometimes this shyness surfaced in ways he may not have recognized. His comment on the Princess Royal's marriage in January 1858 showed both his great interest in the affair and his sublimated feelings about emotional intimacy.

> To-day the Princess Royal was married and to-night there were and are a great number of illuminations up in the streets....It appears there was quite a scene in the central and most interesting part of the marriage ceremony yesterday. The Princess threw herself back into the arms of her mother who, it is said, was very much affected, hugged and kissed, etc., etc. Oh, humbug, bosh and foolery.[61]

The next month he commented in a similar vein about an Easter supper at the Blue Coat School attended by his mother, "at which they go through a considerable amount of mummery and bosh."[62]

He had few, if any, close male friends. Although Edward played cricket with boys in his age group and mingled with the younger men at neighborhood parties, his diary mentions only a couple of friends he once walked with, a few visits with former school chums, and a casual meeting with "an old schoolfellow, Chester Foulsham, who I was always partial to though I am not sure if the liking is reciprocal."[63] The wistfulness of the latter entry seemed to reflect a longing for the kind of easy companionship denied him by his shyness and budding self-absorption. This self-imposed solitude, and the boredom sometimes brought on by the repetitive tasks of the engraver's trade, no doubt heightened the intensity of his lonesome moments. But he was extraordinarily resilient and self-sufficient. Along with the usual stresses and strains of a large family he took comfort from family members, especially from his mother. His regular excursions outside the home, sometimes with family members, provided pleasure and intellectual stimulation. Boring and frustrating moments there were, but they did not dominate his outlook.

> Went to Maze Pond morning and evening. Dull. A regular muff preached. So many occurrences that were in last week, rarely happen together, viz. the trial and condemnation of Palmer, the Derby races, the illuminations and fireworks, and the altering rates of discount. Altogether it was a very exciting week."[64]

Surely any sixteen-year-old excited by changing bank interest rates – who also deems a dull Sunday sermon worthy of a diary notation – had a towering threshold against boredom.

Slightly more than three years after beginning his apprenticeship as an engraver Whymper wrote what he considered to be one of his most reflective moments. At age seventeen he dreamed of glory, tinged with second thoughts on where his true talents lay:

> Beyond my daily work, I seldom say anything about myself, but today I shall. I, when I first came to business (drawing on wood), did not like it at all and wished myself to go to sea. This wore off in course of time and I settled down to my fate (after a fashion) but very discontentedly. I had ideas floating in my head that I should one day turn out some great person, be the person of my

day, perhaps Prime Minister, or at least a millionaire. Who has not had them? They have not left me yet: time will show if they be true or false. But I can now settle down to whatever my lot in life is to be, much more contentedly than I thought I should then....[My drawing has been] "brought into notice...[and] there now seems a lead which I will follow as hard as I can and with God's help not only draw well but will draw better and better and, if possible, better than all.[65]

* * *

By the summer of 1860, Whymper had become a man of business and a skilled engraver and artist. Earning more now, he was beginning to feel greater independence from his father and more financially secure. He had developed superb physical strength and dexterity. His enormous stamina was matched by the power of a relentless will. He was thus perfectly suited for an assignment in the Alps that would soon come his way.

In a diary entry dated some three months before his eighteenth birthday Whymper expressed, perhaps without realizing it, the personal attributes that ranked highest in his credo. Paying tribute to General Havelock, a hero in the fighting against Sepoy mutineers, he wrote:

The brave Havelock is no more. Alas, at a time when the whole nation felt that he was a hero indeed, he was lying dead. Honor to the brave. He was one of 'nature's gentlemen,' truly religious, fearless and honorable.[66]

This brief tribute to the English general perfectly summarized the virtues Whymper valued most. Read as a whole his diary entries consistently showered admiration on God-fearing men of courage and honor, leaving no doubt they were models he hoped to emulate. His diary also gave hints of a feeling that the more successfully one developed these prime attributes, the less one might need or want to focus on other qualities in pursuit of personal fulfillment. He would not have put it that way but his mature years would reflect a continuing strain of this nature.

CHAPTER 3

*Beauty, Mystery and Adventure*

The Alps comprise an area of contrast and beauty, mystery and danger. Snow-covered peaks overlook deep fertile valleys. Distant summits at times seem close enough to touch. Paths lead through meadows and wild flowers into startling panoramas that change with the light and the season. Massive ranges evoke wonder and awe – at the unimaginable power of the forces that created them and the inexorable decay that began even at their birth. Although majestic and silent from afar, their treacherous heights are alive with ominous sounds of falling rocks and cracking ice. Every step there is cautious, every breath labored. In these moments the driving emotion is not fear but exhilaration; body and spirit are more alive, the awareness of life's frailty more intense. At the end of the day, whether in utter exhaustion or contented weariness, one's final thought is a profound gratitude for having been allowed the unique experience of Alpine adventure.

The Alps form a crescent that begins in an area above Nice in the south of France and extends eastward roughly seven hundred miles. From France they march upward through Switzerland and northern Italy and then spread across Austria and the southern edge of Germany to the Hungarian border. There, an offshoot reaches north toward Vienna and another goes southeast toward Croatia. Thousands of Alpine peaks rise above valleys and glaciers too numerous to count; 700 summits extend above 10,000 feet, 120 reach beyond 12,000, and 15 attain heights of over 14,000 feet.

The western Alps, from the Dauphiné range in France to the Simplon Pass in Switzerland, contain most of the higher mountains including the dramatic monolith of the Matterhorn at 14,780 feet and the snow-dome of Mont Blanc at 15,782 feet, the highest pinnacle in Europe. The Bernese Oberland, a beautiful area of Switzerland's Central Alps between Interlaken on the north and the Rotten-Rhone valley on the south, is home to several familiar giants including the Jungfrau, the Mönch and the Eiger. The massive chain of the Alps forces moisture from the clouds and northwest winds that blow steadily onto its northern slopes, producing year-round snow on the high peaks and drier warmer weather to the south. Three of the major rivers of the European continent begin in the Alps: the Rhine flowing up to the North Sea, the Rhone moving southward to the Mediterranean, and the Po running eastward to the Adriatic.

The latest chapter in the Alps' geological history was written only a few years ago. The idea of continental drift, originally put forth in 1910, was not confirmed until the 1960s when the theory of plate tectonics first explained movements of the earth's crust. Since then, geologists have mapped and acoustically measured rock formations hidden deep beneath the earth's surface. According to these measurements, the Alps evolved between ninety and twenty million years ago when the northern edge of the African continent smashed into the southern coast of Europe. Displacing the Mediterranean Sea that lay between these two land masses, the African plate ground upward over the sea's northern coast, digging deep valleys and thrusting skyward huge slabs of rock. The collision suture of the two continents, which is particularly noticeable near Zermatt, shows conclusively that the earthen material forming the Matterhorn and the peaks surrounding it was once part of Africa.

If we could look today at a series of time-lapse photographs taken during the Alps' multi-million year birthing period we would see a chaotic mixture of fiery avalanches, scalding steam geysers, and gigantic earthquakes that literally shook the planet. Out of that ancient turbulence, rising like a Phoenix from the ashes, came a unique section of the earth's surface. In the millennia after the mountains cooled, wind, snow and flowing glacial ice carved them into an infinite variety of formations. This erosion created the dreamlike figures of the Dolomite hills, the needle-sharp spires of the Mont Blanc Range, and all the fantastic forms in between.

The Alps lie at a relatively high latitude on the earth's surface. As a result, they have a snow-line of about 12,000 feet, which is low in comparison to mountains nearer the equator. They are also far enough south to have temperate weather on their lower slopes. This combination brings sporadic winter-like weather to the edge of upper mountain meadows in full summertime bloom. Howling winds and blinding snow regularly strike Alpine slopes with no warning in July and August. At the height of these storms tourists taking the sun at nearby resorts may see only a grey cloud placidly hugging a mountain's face, showing no sign of the turbulence within. Those summer storms usually depart as rapidly as they arrive.

From this mixture of climes comes a flourishing variety of animal and plant life. Mountain vegetation and water is sufficient year round for the support of chamois, ibex and marmot. Even among the higher Alpine peaks lichens smooth the pockmarked faces of rocks and cliffs; edelweiss and other small plants mimic the beauty of their larger cousins below. In the spring, rainbow-colored carpets of wild flowers adorn the high meadows where summer grasses and streams provide a seasonal home for cattle, goats and their shepherds. A myriad of snow-covered glaciers fill the high mountain valleys, glistening green and blue where deep crevasses expose their icy interiors. As they slowly wind lower on the southern side of the Alps, glaciers melt into streams and waterfalls that eventually form the lakes of Lugano, Como and others of world-renowned beauty. Even on the northern side, numerous Swiss lakes, including Geneva, Thuner and Brienzer, offer tranquil mountain vistas amid luxurious vegetation that blooms well into the autumn months. This combination of life and color contrasts vividly with the barren vistas and unbroken wintry landscapes of the Himalayan, Andean and other higher ranges.

British mountaineers of the mid-nineteenth century took readily to Alpine slopes. Prodigious walkers, they hiked from Mont Blanc and the Dauphiné Alps in France to the Matterhorn in Switzerland and on to the Monte Viso in Italy. From there they ventured into the Bernese Oberland of Switzerland, climbing peaks in each of these areas, all in roughly two months of summer. Tourists found their way to lower mountain reaches, the ladies in their long skirts and the gentlemen in their bowlers. Here they breathed pine-scented air amid views of snow-capped peaks in one direction and lush green valleys in the other.

As time went on investment capital followed, stimulating the growth of rail lines to the larger towns and coach roads into the heights. Inns sprang up to offer board and lodging for a variety of tastes and pocketbooks. *Murray's Handbook*, one of the early guidebooks for the area, lured tourists with linguistic flourishes typical of the times. "Their [lakes are] soft and smiling; blessed with a southern climate, their thickets are groves of orange, olive, myrtle and pomegranate; and their habitations villas and palaces." Of the roadways and railways, Murray waxed even more eloquent: they are "the most surprising monuments of human skill and enterprise, which surmount what would appear, at first sight, to be intended by nature to be insurmountable."[1] His flowery language aside, Murray's basic point was true: the Alps of his day were a wild and breathtakingly beautiful work of nature.

City dwellers' appreciation of mountain beauty was formed over many generations, and their recognition of mountaineering as a sport came even later. For thousands of years after modern man's appearance the Alps were considered a remote wasteland unworthy of civilized societies' interest or concern. In isolated circumstances, however, humans have been climbing mountains for almost all the years of recorded history. In 181 B.C.E. Philip of Macedonia scaled Mount Haemus in the Balkans, which some historians consider the first mountain to have been used as a strategic military lookout.[2] Taking military tactics a step further, on the Ligurian coast of Italy in 106 B.C.E, a Roman soldier climbed high above his bivouac in search of rock snails to supplement his diet. Emerging onto a high rocky promontory he found himself overlooking a Berber camp then under siege by his fellow legionnaires. He descended and later guided his comrades to the overlook from which they launched a successful assault against the enemy.[3] And so it went: in 1280, Peter III, King of Aragon, climbed Mount Canigou and reported the discovery of a dragon at the mountain's summit; in the fifteenth century Leonardo da Vinci climbed Mount Bo in the Pennine Alps;[4] and in 1786, spurred by an offer from H.B. de Saussure of two guineas to the first to attain Mont Blanc's summit, Jacques Balmat and Michel Paccard of Chamonix reached the top of the high mountain and claimed their prize.[5] Before that first ascent of Mont Blanc, "old school" Europeans clearly preferred the lowlands to the mountains.

The literature and architecture of that day perfectly mirrored this preference. Around 1715, one Bishop Berkeley, an Englishman "of fine taste and keen sensibility," wrote that structures of Greek design were flawless examples of "beauty, grace and ornament," reflecting man's higher nature.[6] In nature itself the counterparts of this Greek perfection were the rolling hills and cultivated fields of England and France. In contrast, Gothic architecture – its "fantastical [appearance]...not founded in nature or reason" – was an abomination.[7] Arbiters of contemporary taste cited "Westminster Abbey or Salisbury Cathedral as a specimen of simple ugliness."[8] Mountains, though a part of nature, were to them an ugly aberration, "great excrescences of the earth,...hideous rocks...which to outward appearances...have neither use nor comeliness."[9] Mont Blanc was known as "Mont Maudit," the "accursed mountain."[10] Said the noted French writer and diplomat Chateaubriand: "I cannot feel happy where I see weary men and their exhausting labour, which a harsh earth refuses to repay....I never discovered among...those celebrated [mountain] chalets... anything but dirty hovels full of cattle dung or the stink of cheese and fermented milk."[11]

Chateaubriand's words, written in 1805, were the dying gasps of the older view. A "new school" of writers had already popularized the view that the simple pastoral life of the mountains was morally superior to life in the city. Though founded in morality – a necessary base for anyone seeking converts to a new philosophy in mid-eighteenth century Europe – new school advocates were utterly fascinated with Alpine life and mountain travel. One remarkable contribution to this change was a single poem, *Die Alpen*, by Albrecht von Haller, a Swiss naturalist and philosopher. Published in 1728, it glorified the simple, luxury-free life of the Alpine peasant – where there "is no learning but plenty of common sense, where hard work [brings] security and comfort, and where the drink is pure water and the richest dishes are made of milk."[12] The appeal of this message generated thirty re-printings of Haller's poem, which devotees often recited from memory in European parlors and public houses. After Haller came Jean Jacques Rousseau, the most influential of the early romantics on the public's image of mountains, with *La Nouvelle Heloise* in 1759 and *Confessions* a few years later. "Rousseau [was]...the Columbus of the Alps, or [if you prefer], the Luther of the new creed of mountain worship....In the *Confessions*...there is an explicit avowal of his...love of torrents, rocks, pines, black woods, rough paths to climb and to descend, and precipices to cause a delicious terror...."[13]

By the middle of the nineteenth century, however, Rousseau's philosophy that vilified luxury and exalted life in the wild was no longer in vogue. British mountaineers in particular found reasons outside the strictly moral realm to escape to the Alps and embrace the challenges awaiting them there. Indeed, wrote Leslie Stephen, Rousseau's "eighteenth-century doctrine...has become...faded and old-fashioned for us", and his mode of expression "intolerably long-winded."[14] Today, of course, there is a certain discordance in Stephen's criticism of loquacity. His verbal excesses, as well as Whymper's, are now as dated as were the words of Haller and Rousseau to the Victorians. The florid expressions of Stephen and other Victorian authors have enduring appeal, however, because they spoke with the voice of first-hand experience. They deeply appreciated Alpine scenery but were not content merely to be observers. They were dedicated mountaineers. They devoted their minds and bodies – as well as their hearts – to Alpine climbing and then wrote, often eloquently, of their experiences. In so doing they gave the world a lasting appreciation of the rewarding adventure they found in this exotic land.

This, then, was the setting into which fortune would cast the twenty-year-old Whymper. In August of 1860 a London publisher sent him to the Alps to make drawings for an upcoming book. In just six short summers the young artist-engraver became the best known climber of the Golden Age of mountaineering and its most controversial figure. His exploits brought him exhilaration and melancholy in equal measure. His ascent and catastrophic descent of the Matterhorn provoked discussion and disagreement that became a permanent part of mountaineering lore. All that, however, lay in the unknown future as his train left London that summer for Brighton where, by steamer, he would head eastward into the Channel toward his destiny.

# CHAPTER 4

## *A Perfect Match*

In 1845 John Franklin and his expedition team of some 150 men set sail from England, bound for the Arctic Ocean in search of the legendary northwest passage to the Orient. Following John Ross's attempt of a decade earlier, Franklin was one of a steady stream of British explorers in the pre- and early Victorian periods who risked their lives in far northern waters for the advancement of science and commerce, and the growth of their nation's expanding empire. A successful mission would offer them a sense of national service and the promise of fame, fortune and high adventure. Franklin and Ross failed in their quests but both were knighted for their efforts. Franklin's recognition came posthumously, for though the British government mounted some thirty rescue missions in search of him and his men, they were never heard from again. In 1859 the last of these search parties found records kept by Franklin's expedition – along with skeletons and scattered relics – on King William Island.[1] This island is at the southern end of McClintock Channel, just north of the Arctic Circle, midway between Greenland and Alaska. The discoveries there showed that Franklin and his team had advanced farther west than any of the earlier British expeditions.

In London newspapers and periodicals stories of these harrowing Arctic adventures fired the imaginations of many readers, including young Edward Whymper. In 1857 he read "Dr. Kane's account" of the search for Franklin, paying particular attention to Kane's description of an unexplored part of Greenland.[2] This may have been the first of the various stories that would motivate Whymper to see Greenland for himself a decade later. In that same year he showed interest in the accounts of other British explorers, citing the popularity of *Livingstone's*

*Travels, Lord Dufferin's Yacht Voyage,* and other books on foreign adventure.[3] But he postponed serious thoughts of becoming an Arctic explorer himself when an unexpected assignment took him to an equally fascinating land, the Alps of western Europe.

William Longman, one of London's leading publishers, had seen Whymper's engravings and admired his work. In the summer of 1860 Longman asked him to make on-the-scene sketches of "great Alpine peaks" for a forthcoming book by an Englishman who planned to climb Mont Pelvoux in the Dauphiné region of France.[4] Now twenty, Whymper had never seen a mountain – not even the Scottish highlands or the peaks of northern Wales. But he was anxious to escape the tedious routine of the workshop and proud to have been selected for an important business project. He had read accounts of Alpine climbing and sat spellbound at Albert Smith's theatrical presentation of the conquest of Mont Blanc.[5] After five long years of apprenticeship to his father he saw the Longman project as an opportunity to be completely on his own in an arena promising the sort of adventure he had dreamt of. The offer came at just the right moment and Whymper eagerly accepted.

He left London on July 23rd, 1860. As his steamer ploughed through the choppy waters of the Thames estuary and into the English Channel, the grey bulk of Beachy Head cliffs came into view off the vessel's starboard bow. Looking at this coastline landmark he remembered the time he and his older brother Frederick, still schoolboys, had attempted to climb Beachy Head's chalk-like surface and found it deceptively treacherous. "With the impudence of ignorance," he later wrote, "we...nearly broke...our necks."[6] Though differing drastically in degree, that introductory scramble closely resembled the rather casual trial-and-error approach that Whymper and other Alpine pioneers would bring to the new sport of mountaineering. Those early climbers and their guides were largely self-taught, and most had similarly disquieting memories of near calamity in their early climbing careers. But he had no premonition of that now, or of how far the next few years would take him beyond this boyhood escapade.

Once in Europe a buoyant Whymper made what he labeled his "first...two ascents" up the stairs to an artist friend's seventh floor flat in Paris, and then a similar climb to the west parapet of Notre Dame

*Beachy Head*

Cathedral where, for half an hour, he stood beside a fiendish gargoyle overlooking the city.[7] After a short stay in the French capital he left for the Alps, travelling by rail to Geneva and then by coach through picturesque countryside to Montreux at the eastern end of Lake Geneva and on to Interlaken. Situated in central Switzerland amid green hills and lake vistas near the spectacular peaks of the Bernese Oberland, the quaint village of Interlaken sat on the narrow land bridge between Lake Thuner on the west and Lake Brienzer on the east. There Whymper hired a porter to carry his extra clothing, food, sketching materials, camping and cooking equipment, toiletries and other incidentals. The next day, dressed in the rough cotton or wool shirt and trousers he wore on walks at home, and with a knapsack of items he might need on the trail, he eagerly set forth.

Even by Victorian era standards when the competitive sport of "pedestrianism" was a favorite of many British youths, Whymper covered a remarkable amount of ground that summer. His body was near perfectly fashioned for the task – in sinewy strength, suppleness and deep energy reserves. In the forty-seven days of his first Alpine summer he walked over 600 miles through three countries on rugged, largely unmarked terrain: from Bern, Switzerland on the north to the Grimsel Pass on the east, Italy's Val d'Aosta and Valpelline regions on the south, France's Dauphiné Alps and the Mont Blanc Range on the southwest, and Grenoble farther west. For good measure he climbed several minor summits and passes along the way, acquiring "a passion for mountain scrambling" that would drive him ever more forcefully in the coming years.[8] Throughout that summer he wrote a daily journal and made drawings in a sketchbook kept always close at hand. These sketches captured the Alpine peaks and passes as Longman had ordered but they were only a part of his artist's bag. Almost daily he drew scenes of ordinary peasant life, finding human interest in local people and commonplace events that a less sensitive observer might have missed.

The route from Interlaken to Zermatt, Whymper's first long walk, went through some of Switzerland's most beautiful Alpine scenery. The young engraver from London was impressed, as if viewing the Mona Lisa for the first time: "[I] saw the sunlight lingering on the giants of the Oberland; heard the echoes from…cow-horns in the Lauterbrunnen valley and the avalanches rattling off the Jungfrau….[I] crossed the Gemmi into the Valais, resting for a time by the beautiful Oeschinen See."[9] From Visp on the Rhone River he proceeded up the St. Niklaus Valley to Zermatt where no panoramic views greeted him. Zermatt sat about 5,000 feet above sea level at the southern head of the valley, encircled by high hills whose abrupt rise began virtually at the town's borders. Shutting out views of the Monte Rosa, the Breithorn, the Dom and other nearby giants, those steep foothills seemed to concentrate the energy of the village toward its center like skyscrapers surrounding a park in the heart of a large modern city.

Amid the Pennine Alps, Zermatt acted as a magnet for serious climbers of the day. With them came talented guides from the surrounding Valais region, the Bernese Oberland and Chamonix. The climbers were predominantly Englishmen from a variety of professions and vocations, most of them interesting conversationalists and experienced travelers. The best of the Zermatt guides were impressive in their quiet strength and casual talk of mountain hazards routinely met. This environment immediately appealed to Whymper as he entered the

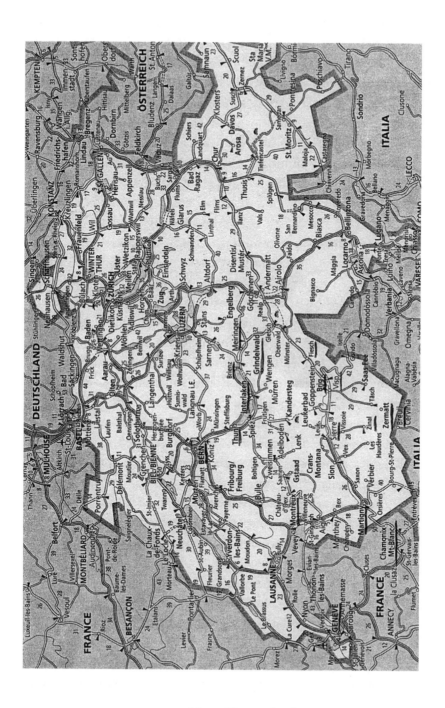

*Map of Switzerland*

Monte Rosa Hotel and was welcomed by its cheerful host and owner, Alexandre Seiler. The latter's genuine hospitality, along with his wife's adroit behind-the-scenes management, made the Monte Rosa the center of Zermatt's climbing activity and Seiler himself "the doyen of Swiss hotel-keepers."[10] Among the hotel's guests at the time of Whymper's arrival were three pioneers of those early days: Leslie Stephen, T. W. Hinchcliff, and Frank Walker. Whymper's excitement was almost palpable:

> The hotel is full of Alpine men, many of them very plucky fellows... Mr Walker... suggested we might knock up an expedition together; I shall be most happy....Mr. Hinchcliff offered to coach me on the Riffelberg, which offer was gratefully accepted.[11]

Just after dinner, Stephen, Hinchcliff and another came into the salon wet as water dogs, having just come from the Riffel for a walk. They did it in 35 minutes. Rather a contrast with my four hours of last night. I hear that Professor Tyndall is at the Eggishorn with Mr Hawkins, having just accomplished some wonderful

*Portrait of Alexandre Seiler*

climbs at Lauterbrunnen. Professor Hall of King's College is here today...so the table talk is continually interesting.[12]

Not completely overwhelmed by this experience, however, the young Whymper retained his resilient brashness. Along with the "plucky fellows" in the Monte Rosa Hotel were "the usual number of bores."[13]

Whymper took to the mountains like a bear to the woods. After a climb on the nearby Trift glacier he wrote:

The glacier is rather high up. I suspect the lowest part is at least 9,000 feet; we went a little way on it; I saw ice-tables for the first time – they were not good ones. We pitched stones down the crevasses and heard them leaping about, striking first one side and then the other, giving an impression of great depth.[14]

These "ice tables" were seracs – pinnacles of frozen snow that protruded from the surface of a glacier like stalagmites from a cave floor. Sometimes they curled over in wave-like crests, often growing to heights that made them dangerously unstable – or as Whymper put it, "not good." The next day on the Gorner glacier he had difficulty scrambling down three hundred feet on some steep rocks in part because "...my sketch-book rendered one hand always useless, and the rocks were nearly perpendicular."[15] Halfway down the rocky slope he came to a crevasse about seven feet across, too wide for a casual leap. After moving unsuccessfully along the ledge to find a narrower gap he decided that he had

...no alternative but to return and face the jump. Night was approaching, and the solemn stillness of the high Alps was broken only by the sound of rushing water or of falling rocks. If the jump should be successful – well.... [I]f not, [then] I fell in[to] that horrible chasm, to be frozen...or drowned in that gurgling, rushing water. Everything depended on that jump....So, finding my stick was useless, I threw it and my sketch-book to the ice, and first retreating as far as possible, ran forward with all my might, took the leap, barely reached the other side, and fell awkwardly on my

*A cure in difficulties*

knees. Almost at the same moment a shower of stones fell on the spot from which I had jumped.[16]

Whymper noted this incident in *Scrambles* but not in his journal. This raised the question whether it really happened and, if so, how much was fact and how much embellishment. Whymper was a stickler for accuracy throughout his life and quick to confront anyone claiming error in his writings or lectures. Here, as the only person present, he probably took some liberties. But his account of the episode – though over-dramatized – seems well within the bounds of literary license. In any case his description of the event would cause speculation among mountaineering's story-tellers and historians for years to come.

At that point, Whymper had been in the Alps only two weeks but the lure of the mountains already held him firmly in its grasp. He left Zermatt in high spirits on August 13th and went part-way down the valley to Stalden, still in thrall to his new surroundings.

The little inn at Stalden, in spite of its unpromising exterior, is as

*Diligence*

comfortable inside as any place I have been in....The day was perfect, and consequently I was able to sketch what I wanted; I was also very much amused by the people I passed on the road and...in consequence of succeeding in sketching, the exchequer is looking up, so I rejoiced.[17]

Being able to sketch the mountains around Stalden was financially favorable because his surroundings were often partially hidden by clouds. On a "perfect" day like this one the peaks and valleys become worthy subjects for his portfolio of drawings, many of which might be of value back in London. He had noted earlier that clouds above Zermatt's glaciers had frustrated his sketching efforts, which must have made him wonder if he could complete the Longman project before the onset of autumn's inclement weather.

Cloudy days that turned his attention to vignettes of everyday life were more valuable than Whymper realized. He later illustrated the *Scrambles* narrative partly with drawings of oddities and unexpected personal encounters not only to show his interest in them, but also to allow readers to share his lighthearted moments off the treacherous mountain slopes. These sketches gave his books much additional appeal. One from the Dauphiné Alps, for instance, showed a rotund French curé, exhausted and out-of-breath, being carted downhill like a sack of potatoes on the shoulders of a sturdy native. Along the path the peasant watched respectfully – hat doffed and eyes lowered – as the odd couple passed. The priest "was a helpless bundle and a ridiculous spectacle on the back of a lanky guide, while the peasant...stood by, with folded hands, [his] reverence for the Church almost overcome by [his] sense of the ludicrous."[18] Whymper's drawing perfectly captured the droll irony of that moment.

Leaving Stalden he descended to Visp and then walked up the Rhone valley to Fiesch, from which he climbed the Eggishorn, his first Alpine peak. On its summit he exuberantly carved his initials in a wooden cross already there and then painted them red – with a brush and coloring either purchased for the occasion or kept in his knapsack for just such an opportunity. Back in Fiesch he joined two tourists met along the way and went with them up the valley to Munster. There, on the following day, the trio hired a man to carry some of their baggage and to lead them to the top of the Grimsel Pass. On the ascent they encountered a savage hail storm whose fierce winds lashed at them like the knotted cords of a whip. Their feet got soaked as they struggled upward, splashing through two frigid streams in simple leather boots, and in due course reached their goal. This was Whymper's first climbing experience in bad weather, or with a native employed to lead the way. It was also the first time he had felt the addictive exhilaration of a successful ascent under trying circumstances.

That climb also highlighted Whymper's overwhelming self-assurance in an unfamiliar situation where looking and listening would have served him better than judging. Mistakenly assuming that his hired hand, a porter, was also a guide, Whymper wrongly faulted him for refusing to take the lead, and for overestimating the difficulty of the ascent to the high point of the pass. In his journal he mocked the man for carrying an umbrella much as any tourist might, and for taking shelter under a rock in the hailstorm where he "gasp[ed] and ma[de]... extraordinary India rubber-like faces" as a result of his discomfort. He went on to describe how, when the hospice on the far side of the pass came in sight, the native took the lead just "to make himself look smart and go into the place cocky."[19] Whymper might better have used those words to describe his own appearance and motivation as he "put...on a spurt [and] got in [the hospice] first, leaving the...dismal guide...in the rear with his umbrella turned inside out."[20] In *Scrambles,* a more mature Whymper wrote of this episode only that he "cross[ed] the Grimsel in a severe thunderstorm."[21]

From the Grimsel Pass Whymper went north through the Aare River valley and west across Lake Brienzer by steamer to Interlaken. This quaint, centuries-old town is situated on a narrow strip of land between Lake Brienzer on the east and Lake Thuner on the west. These long and narrow lakes are among the most serene and beautiful in Switzerland. Their deep blue waters, tinged with aquamarine near the shorelines, nestle among the wooded foothills of the snow-capped Oberland Alps on the south and more distant peaks on the north. Cottages dot the forest green borders of both lakes, clearly visible from steamers that regularly ply both bodies. Most often quiet and placid, their waters retain a pristine quality to this day.

Quite taken with the town's hospitable inns, luxuriant flower gardens, and walkways bathed in shimmering sunlight from the surrounding lakes, Whymper described Interlaken simply as the loveliest place on earth. Reflecting his own religious background, he expressed surprise at seeing Anglican worshipers here and in other Swiss towns using Roman Catholic churches "almost before the seats are cold from the previous congregations." This showed "some liberality of sentiment among...the R.C.s," quite a concession for a Maze Pond Baptist.[22] He wondered if an Anglican priest back home would do the same for the Catholics in his parish, and what the clergyman's parishioners might say if he did. This was the first indication that exposure to foreign customs might be tempering some of the fixed views so confidently set forth in the diary of his younger days.

From Interlaken he moved on to Bern but stayed there only one day. On August 24th he headed southwest to Montreux via Neufchatel and Martigny and then almost due south to the Great St. Bernard Pass. Going through the pass eastward into Italy he reached the town of Bionaz where he hired a porter. The two of them then went to the town of Valtournanche and from there proceeded toward Breuil at the foot of the Matterhorn.

Before their arrival Whymper and his porter had a dispute over the latter's fee. Without warning, as Whymper ranged confidently ahead of his slower companion, the porter simply turned on his heel and headed back to Bionaz, taking his employer's clothes and drawing materials with him. When Whymper reached the Breuil inn alone and without luggage the innkeeper refused him a room, forcing him to share a "sort of hay-loft in the roof" with four or five guides who smoked and talked most of the night.[23] He finally fell asleep only to be awakened at 3:00 a.m. when the guides departed. He had wanted to be up at first light to begin sketching the Matterhorn but "overslept" until 5:00 o'clock and did not begin drawing until 6:00, working in bright sunlight with makeshift materials. He noted how different the mountain looked from Italy: massive, with rocky ridges and rugged cliffs quite unlike the soaring monolith seen from Zermatt. Departing late that morning he was back in Bionaz by evening, thus ending his first brief visit to the Matterhorn's Italian side. There he reconciled accounts with the porter that had abandoned him and recovered his belongings.

Three days later, in early September, Whymper arrived at Chamonix, an ancient town in the valley immediately adjacent to the massive Mont Blanc Range. A Mecca for tourists even in 1860, the streets were bustling on the day of Whymper's arrival. Coincidentally the Emperor Napoleon and his Queen had chosen that day to pay Chamonix a royal visit. "The place is mad, yes, perfectly insane!" was Whymper's reaction to the crowds that jammed the town's inns and overflowed into the streets as they swarmed to catch sight of the Emperor and his wife.[24] The young English tourist walked about for a while but soon grew bored and returned to his hotel for the evening.

The next day, succumbing to the royal couple's magnetic presence, he chased after them but never got them in his sights. Abandoning his quest, for the next two days he sketched the magnificent views offered by Mont Blanc's lower slopes, particularly the broad expanse of the Mer de Glace, one of the Alps' longest and most dramatic glaciers. Feeling poorly the next morning – his third day in Chamonix – he took his ease sketching the town's villagers and the new English chapel that was to be consecrated in a few days by the Bishop of Winchester. Glad to be out of his "stinking" hotel Whymper left town the same day still under the weather and walked fifteen miles to Sallanches where he spent the night.

"Desperately tired" on his arrival, he wondered if his lack of energy was because he had taken it easy for the last two or three days. If so, he wrote, "I can soon cure myself."[25] And so he did in the only way he knew how. Arising early the next morning he set himself a good pace, stopped for lunch in Bonneville and arrived in Geneva, thirty-nine miles and ten hours from that day's starting point.

After only one night in Geneva Whymper doubled back into Italy, first by train and then on foot. Arriving at the hamlet of Paesana near the Monte Viso, he enjoyed an unexpectedly pleasant interlude.

> The inn was full, and I was tired, and about to go to bed, when some village stragglers entered and began to sing. They sang to Garibaldi! The tenor, a ragged fellow, whose clothes were not worth a shilling, took the lead with wonderful expression and feeling. The others kept their places, and sang in admirable time. For hours, I sat enchanted; and, long after I retired, the sound of their melody could be heard, relieved at times by the treble of the girl who belonged to the inn.[26]

This serenade, the only reported musical moment of Whymper's summer, occurred on September 10th. His days were now numbered and he moved rapidly on, headed first for Mont Pelvoux in the Dauphiné range and then on to Paris and the train to the Channel coast. Along the way he spent the night in Abriés where the innkeeper, having seen on Whymper's passport the name and signature of the issuing officer, Lord John Russell, mistakenly concluded that his guest was a member of the British royalty. The innkeeper then treated him with great respect, but as a consequence overcharged him, Whymper thought, for a bottle of beer: "1 franc for what ought not to have been more than 60 centimes."[27]

The next day he walked to the town of Montdauphin where he arrived after dark. En route to La Bessée the following morning, Whymper found himself on an unusually smooth road that put him in excellent spirits:

> What a luxury is a good road; one can go along without the slightest exertion at a swinging pace; everything seems jolly; fatigue seems a thousand miles off and one is in a good humour

with oneself and all the world. I think as a rule bad roads and incivility will be found to go together...Moral, the best thing a Government can do for a country is to make good roads."[28]

At La Bessée Whymper finally sketched Mont Pelvoux, the peak Longman had directed him to include among his summer drawings. There he met five climbers who had just finished an unsuccessful attempt on that summit. Among them was Jean Reynaud, a Frenchman and "right good fellow" who would become Whymper's climbing companion the following summer. Also in the group were Michel Croz, the guide who would lead Whymper on his two most successful summer campaigns, and Professor T. G. Bonney who would stay in touch with Whymper and write his obituary in the Journal of the Alpine Club many years later. From La Bessée he walked to Briançon, arriving at the town's inn around 7:00 in the evening. He calculated he had walked 34 or 35 miles altogether that day.

From Briançon Whymper set out the next afternoon for Grenoble, some seventy miles away on a twisting rough road leading over the Col de Lauteret. Along the way foul weather and miserable accommodations strengthened his view that bad travelling conditions and incivility – including his own – went hand in hand. He tramped through dirty villages in a driving cold rain, arriving at the Col's summit about 6:15. Bad weather and fatigue forced him to seek brief shelter in a "wretched little hospice...filled with workmen who were employed on the road, and with noxious vapours proceeding from them....Outside, it was disagreeable but grand; inside, it was disagreeable and mean."[29] He acknowledged, however, that in that foul place he received a "very civil reception" and got "wine and... hot water for tea for sixpence."[30] A good bargain always put Whymper in a mellower mood.

Continuing through a heavy rain along an unfamiliar road he reached the inn at La Grave about 10:00 p.m. sopping wet. The next morning, bound for Grenoble, he departed without breakfast, later than he had planned and angry with the innkeeper for failing to wake him. Around noon a diligence moving about six miles an hour came up behind him. After several days of unusually arduous walking, the temptation of a ride for the rest of the way was too great to resist. He flagged down the stagecoach and boarded it. His arrival in Grenoble that evening brought to an abrupt end his extraordinary walking tour of the Alps. The next morning he took the train to Paris, arriving there after "an uncomfortable and tedious journey of 18 ½ hours." At six o'clock in the evening of the next day he began the final leg of his trip, by train to the French coast and thence to London via the Brighton route."[31]

\* \* \* \*

Whymper's introduction to the Alps had gone well. His youthful excitement shone brightly from the early pages of his journal. He soon found, however, that the only constant in the Alps was change itself. Tramping from place to place he had encountered nasty weather, vermin infested accommodations, barely edible food and incompetent porters holding themselves out as guides to novice climbers who did not know the difference. Though he disliked cold rain when the going was easy he relished fighting against snow, sleet, wind and ice on the upper slopes. But he had been testy with people who contributed to his discomfort, and overly critical of service that did not meet his standards. These flashes of arrogance and irritability would become more pronounced in later Alpine summers as he grew more confident of his own abilities and less willing to accept the foibles of those around him.

The summer of 1860 drew a bright line between Whymper's past and future. Before then he imagined the Alps as "pretty," like artificial renderings on posters and post cards designed to attract tourists. Among the mountains, however, he discovered the harsh realities of Alpine life. Despite his appreciation of their rugged natural beauty he found them more a battlefield than a playground. But they offered the opportunities he yearned for: an outlet for his restless energy and superb physique, and a means to enter the society of the class of men he so admired. With innate self-confidence now fortified by experience he soon realized that he could hold his own among the established climbers of the day. By summer's end, as he sat on the train to London, he was already mentally mapping out the following season's strategy. He would focus on virgin peaks, notching his belt with first ascents until he conquered the most prized summit of them all: the Matterhorn. He could hardly wait for the contest to begin.

# CHAPTER 5

## *The Golden Age Begins*

Mountain climbing equipment in the mid-nineteenth century was primitive. The bâton, man's earliest peak-scaling aid, was still in use for balance and support. Originally this was a roughly hewn, undressed wooden stick about four feet long often made from a tree branch. Gradually replacing the bâton was the alpenstock – a finished somewhat longer wooden staff with a pointed iron-shod tip at the bottom – which could also be used for glissading and for probing glacial snows to locate hidden crevasses. Some alpenstocks were designed to give extra help by means of an iron "head" affixed horizontally at the top, one edge flat-bladed for hewing ice, the other narrowed into a point for wedging into crevices too narrow or too high to be grasped. An alpenstock also functioned as an extended arm to steady another climber or to pull a companion out of deep snow or the upper part of a crevasse. Though these cumbersome poles were a hindrance on rocks and icy slopes, serious climbers considered them essential.

Alpine ice-axes resembled commercial pickaxes – occasionally modified slightly by the climber himself – with a blade to cut steps and handholds, and a point to penetrate ice and snow-encrusted slopes as a means of hauling oneself upwards. In difficult places a climber's pickaxe plunged into the surface of an icy cliff could become a foothold for his companion. Sharply spiked crampons, strapped on one's boots to give traction on steep snow-slopes, were sometimes used but not universally favored. Climbers' clothes were as ordinary as their equipment, adaptations of shoes and garments made for other purposes. Their boots were hobnailed field boots; jackets, trousers and hats (sometimes with an added veil) were those used for other outdoor sports or worn simply to stay warm on cold winter days at home.

Ropes had gradually come into common use but roping techniques were not fully developed. Some guides, after tying the rope around a client's waist, would simply knot a loop at the other end and put an arm through it. Other early guides scorned the use of ropes altogether, even when crossing a field of hidden crevasses, trusting – not always successfully – in their ability to detect a cleft by the different color of the snow covering it from that on the surrounding glacier.

These were the prevailing conditions during the years between 1854 and 1865, the period known today as the Golden Age of Mountaineering. In that epoch a new breed of amateurs, most notably the British, scrambled up one Alpine peak after another acquiring the requisite skills as they went. Their climbs had no scientific, scholarly, or other utilitarian purpose. Seeking only the thrill of victory they made first ascents of some 140 summits over 12,000 feet.[1] Whymper's first visit to the Alps was in the middle of this period. The men he met at that time – Leslie Stephen, John Tyndall, T. W. Hinchcliff, Frank Walker – were already seasoned climbers. Whymper caught their enthusiasm and in two or three seasons became the most dedicated peak-bagger of them all. His ascent of the Matterhorn in 1865 climaxed the series of British successes and brought the Golden Age to an unforgettable end.

* * * *

This twelve year period had a less sensational but equally clear-cut beginning. On the 16th of September 1854, a twenty-eight year old London barrister named Alfred Wills, accompanied by four guides, climbed the 12,142 foot Wetterhorn. Though the Wetterhorn was not a virgin summit, Wills's ascent was significant among British climbers because it was a formidable Oberland peak and he the first Englishman to surmount it. That he had made the climb purely for the exciting challenge it offered added to the aura of his achievement. It is said that Wills, as if to emphasize his insouciant attitude, wore cricketing flannels and elastic-sided boots on the ascent.[2]

Back home in England Wills wrote a stirring account of his Alpine climbs that appeared in 1856 as a memoir under the title *Wanderings Among the High Alps*.[3] By a common consensus this book's wide popular

*Portrait of Alfred Wills*

acceptance gave birth to the sport of mountaineering, climbing for the purpose of pleasure alone. Wills was not the first to scale a mountain simply because – as 20th century British climber George Mallory famously observed – it was there. At the time of *Wanderings* publication, tourists were already laboring to the top of Mont Blanc each summer. In earlier years bold Alpinists had scaled a handful of other peaks, including two in the Bernese Oberland: the snow-covered Jungfrau in 1811 and, more surprisingly, the far more difficult Finsteraarhorn the following year.[4] But Wills was the first to write so vividly of his experience – with colorful detail to hold readers enthralled and a sincerity of style to foster empathy and respect. Like *Scrambles* fifteen years later, Wills's *Wanderings* became the talk of the mountaineering community and helped attract a growing number of men to its ranks along with a few daring women. A classic amateur who later became a judge, Wills gained renown in 1895 for presiding at Oscar Wilde's sensational trial for criminal indecency. He would also provide counsel and support to Whymper on the latter's return to London following the trauma of the Matterhorn descent.

*Wanderings* painted vivid pictures of mountain adventure: climbs beginning under bright stars in a black, pre-dawn sky; steep slopes overhung by towering cornices of frozen snow; fantastically formed ice pinnacles and looming seracs; ominous grey-green cracks marking the openings of glacial crevasses that turned dark blue as they went deeper; mountain air redolent of fir and pine; and the changing shapes and colors of peaks under the different lighting of sunrise, sunset, and misty cloud cover. The Wetterhorn ascent was the capstone of Wills's Alpine career and he wrote of it with the same youthful enthusiasm that had spurred him to climb it:

[Approaching the mountain's summit], the icy slope became steeper at every step [until] the angle of inclination was between 60 and 70 degrees!...An overhanging cornice of ice and frozen snow...curled over toward us like the crest of a wave, breaking at irregular intervals...into pendants and inverted pinnacles of ice, many of which hung down to the full length of a tall man's height. They cast a ragged shadow on the wall of ice behind, which was hard and glassy, not flecked with a spot of snow, and blue as the "brave o'erhanging" of the cloudless firmament. They seemed the battlements of an enchanted fortress, framed to defy the curiosity of man, and to...scorn his audacious efforts...

Suddenly, a startling cry of surprise and triumph rang through the air. [Hacked away by the blows of the lead guide's axe], a great block of ice bounded from the top of the parapet...and a thrill of astonishment and delight ran through our frames....That wave above us, frozen, as it seemed, in the act of falling over,...was the very peak itself!...I stepped [through the gap and] across...the ridge of the Wetterhorn! The instant before, I had been face to face with a blank wall of ice. One step, and the eye took in a boundless expanse of crag and glacier, peak and precipice, mountain and valley, lake and plain. The whole world seemed to lie at my feet.[5]

Descriptions of this sort took Victorian readers to a fantastic new world of science-fiction proportions. Wills showed them a thrilling new form of physical activity with the added benefits of foreign travel and exposure to a natural wonderland of awesome beauty. The heart of its appeal, however, was to its readers' deeper sentiments: duty, God and country. The sport of mountaineering fitted snugly into Victorian notions of physical fitness as a duty to country and empire. It helped to develop strong moral fiber. It was a way to serve God through clean living – a form of muscular Christianity – away from the temptations of European fleshpots. And it had all the requirements of a true sport: bodily strength and coordination, stamina and fortitude in the face of danger. Wills also showed his readers there was more to the Alps than the challenge of ice, snow and precipitous slopes. *Wanderings* promised the sheer fun of comrades-in-arms adventure in an ever-changing environment, the ultimate escape from the tedium of middle class life during the London summer. In time, mountaineering gained a cachet in England on a par with traditional sports like riding to foxhounds at home and stalking big game abroad.

On the Wetterhorn climb Wills stayed at the Grindelwald inn for a day or so prior to his departure. Unlike most climbers of the day he had brought his wife and brother-in-law with him. They bade him goodbye on a warm mid-September afternoon as his party headed for an evening bivouac on the mountainside, about a five hours' walk from the inn. With him were lead guides Auguste Balmat and Auguste Simond of Chamonix. The other two guides, Ulrich Lauener and Peter Bohren, both Oberlanders, would catch up with them later. From the inn the party's path led across a meadow and then a glacial stream in whose spray, higher up, a rainbow glistened and danced. At points along the path a profusion of mountain flowers and meadow grasses brightly dotted the landscape with varying shades of blue, red, yellow and green.

They reached their intended campsite in late afternoon, a hollow bordered by a glacial slope on one side and a rocky ridge on the other. Exploring the heights above the site before dinner Wills lingered for a view of the nearby peaks of the Lauterbrunnen valley bathed in purple by the setting sun. Returning to the bivouac he found a cold supper laid out, accompanied by coffee made with water from a stream rushing by the site and heated with firewood they had brought along. Their meal was "a mug of coffee without milk, a hunch of cold veal, and a log of sour bread, carved with one's pocket knife." Wills went so far as to call this a "cheerful...and hearty" repast, more a reflection of his lighthearted excitement than his taste in food. And happy he was, bivouacking under "bright stars [that] looked down on us with a merry twinkle...as if they too enjoyed the fun."[6]

Supper finished, cups rinsed in the stream, and the campfire stamped out, the party retired to a cave-like space under a large overhanging stone. Hunters had covered the sheltered area's floor with short mountain hay that made it look deceptively comfortable. In this long narrow enclosure lit by a single candle Wills and the four guides arranged their blankets after carefully inspecting them for fleas. Satisfied, they extinguished their only light and lay down in utter darkness. The Swiss guides struck up a hymn in German, their voices a soulful tenor and a rich bass, filling the natural chamber with melodious notes of praise to God. When they finished no one spoke, all settled down to sleep.[7]

An honest narrator, Wills was frank to acknowledge that this seemingly idyllic night quickly turned more sour than his supper bread. He dozed a while but soon became aware that his shoeless feet had become Lauener's pillow, and that Lauener kept his head there in his sleep even as Wills shifted about in futile attempts to dislodge him. The air in the campers' crowded space grew unbearably warm and smothering. When Wills's suppertime veal "seemed to rise up in judgment" against him he abandoned any hope of sleep and fled to the bare ground outside of the cave where he spent a short and miserable night. Astir long before dawn he stripped, and in the custom of many later English climbers "had a bathe" in the stream's icy waters, more refreshed by it than his restless evening. His party left the site in darkness guided by the dim light of a lantern until the dawn broke in a chilling grey sky.[8]

Simond, one of Wills's Chamoniard guides, was nicknamed "Sampson" for his great strength, allegedly such that he could pick up a grown man and hold him at arms length. Both he and Balmat were quite "business-like" in comparison with Lauener and Bohren, the rather carefree Swiss guides. The latter two, on the day before the party left Grindelwald, had pressed Wills for permission to take along a flag which they confidently expected to plant on the Wetterhorn's summit. Wills thought this would be tempting fate but he reluctantly agreed. Little did he expect to see, however, the monstrosity with which the Oberlanders cheerfully greeted Wills and the men of Chamonix when they arrived the next day. Strapped to Lauener's back was a 3' by 2' sheet of iron with two metal rings welded to one of the 2-foot sides, his "flag" which he proudly showed to Wills. Bohren carried a metal bar some 10 to 12 feet in length, the flagstaff that would fit through the rings and hold their victory flag aloft at the Wetterhorn summit.

Self-satisfied and excited on that first morning, the two of them shouted and yodeled notes of exuberant pleasure. To Wills's astonishment, faint answering shouts came from below: Bohren's proud family members were responding in kind with high-pitched *bon voyages* to their young kinsman. Wills could only look and listen in silent wonder; it was too late to rescind his agreement with these engagingly enthusiastic youths. The Chamoniard guides, their faces showing extreme displeasure, were less restrained than Wills. Balmat plainly told them the shouting should wait until they had returned safely to this spot from the summit. Simond called their 20 to 30 pounds of metal a *bêtise*, which Wills took to mean a "confounded piece of nonsense." But off the party went, with the turtle-backed Lauener and the strangely appended Bohren happily carrying their extra burdens.

About 10:00 a.m. on that first morning of their Wetterhorn ascent Wills and his party received a rather unsettling surprise. Looking down the mountain they spotted two men dressed in native clothes, apparently from the Grindelwald region. First thinking them chamois hunters, on closer scrutiny they saw that one of them was burdened as no hunter would be; strapped to his back was a freshly cut "young fir tree, branches, leaves, and all." The men were considerably lower, so Wills gave them little thought as his party stopped to take refreshment. Setting out again, however, they were shocked to see the newcomers "a good way ahead" of them. The Swiss guides were only mildly concerned but the Chamoniards were outraged. Balmat exclaimed indignantly that any climber in the Chamonix area who dogged the tracks of others in an attempt to beat them to the summit would be ostracized. He now threatened to go after these interlopers with "coups de poings" – his bare fists. Trying to resolve the matter Lauener and Bohren called out a challenge to these "pirates" who agreed, after a great shouting match, to wait for Wills's party to catch up with them.

It turned out that the man carrying the fir tree was Cristian Almer, perhaps influenced by the prophet Ezekiel who vowed to take "a shoot from the very top of a cedar…and plant it on a high and lofty mountain…"[9] Almer was then a young Oberlander who would guide Whymper a few years later (though not on the Matterhorn) and ultimately become one of Grindelwald's most respected guides. The other was Ulrich Kaufmann, Almer's brother-in-law. They said that they merely wanted to stay "even" with Wills and his guides, and to plant Almer's tree alongside Lauener's flag at the Wetterhorn summit. This satisfied Balmat, who now declared them "bons enfants" and sealed his new friendship for them by giving each a piece of chocolate cake.

Soon after this joinder of forces, the group of seven approached the Wetterhorn summit, unaware of how close they were to it. Before them they saw only the outline of a giant cornice of compacted snow looming above them like a breaking wave in the mist-filled air. In the lead, Lauener took out his axe and chopped away at the bottom of the snow-wall until he broke through. "I see blue sky!" he yelled excitedly, redoubling his effort to find out what lay ahead. Finally chopping an opening large enough to squeeze through he did so, grabbing Will's sleeve to pull him alongside. It was a breathtaking moment for the exuberant young climber; he and the guide suddenly realized they were astraddle atop the four-inch width of the Wetterhorn's white summit.

> I stepped across and had passed the ridge of the Wetterhorn!…The whole world seemed to lie at my feet. The next moment I was almost appalled by the awfulness of our situation. The side we had come up was steep, but it was a gentle slope compared with that which fell away from where I stood. A few yards of glittering ice at our feet and then nothing between us and the green slopes of Grindelwald nine thousand feet beneath.[10]

In contrast to the earlier comedic interplay between him and his flag-and-tree-burdened guides, Wills was serious in his description of the party's view from the mountaintop. It was 11:20 a.m.

> [T]he eye took in a boundless expanse of crag and glacier, peak

and precipice, mountain and valley, lake and plain. The whole world seemed to lie at my feet....[At] this wonderful prospect,...I experienced...profound and almost irrepressible emotion....Balmat told me repeatedly, afterwards, that it was the most awful and startling moment he had known in the course of his long mountain experience. We felt...in the more immediate presence of Him who had reared this tremendous pinnacle,...beneath the "majestical roof" of whose deep blue heaven we stood, poised, as it seemed, half-way between the earth and sky. [11]

Bohren, Almer, and Kaufmann also felt "irrepressible emotion" on the summit but had quite a different method of expression. Exuberant, they kept up a series of "discordant, unearthly yells" until silenced by Balmat. Never cry out on a summit, he warned, for the next moment may bring disaster. Only Lauener, one of the young Swiss guides, was uncharacteristically silent. Wills learned later that the guide's older brother, Johann, had died in a fall only a few months earlier after slipping over the edge of a far less dangerous precipice than the Wetterhorn peak. Lauener's pensive mood did not last long, however, and the party's unrestrained joy soon embraced him as well.

Still in the glow of success but aware that the day was fading, the group remained only twenty minutes on the summit. After descending about fifty yards someone remembered that they had forgotten to drink a toast to the newly conquered mountain. Wisely rejecting a first impulse to return to the top for that purpose they doffed their caps where they stood. After swallowing a draft of brandy and snow they cried out, "To the health of the Wetterhorn!" Farther down but still in high spirits they rested where they had left some provisions and reflected happily on their victory. Almer and Kaufmann had proved themselves to be truly "bons enfants" and all seven were now "the best friends possible." Here they drank again, this time more solemnly, "a rousing bumper of iced red wine to the health of the Wetterhorn." Then they gave a shout "as loud as human lungs could utter," to which Balmat raised no objection and may even have joined in. From there they began the last leg of the descent. After a rapid glissade and a tumble by Wills and Lauener without injury, they arrived at their prior night's campsite twenty hours after leaving it.

Here Wills broke out the bottle of champagne he had saved until victory was assured and they all had one final festive drink. This was the sportively adventurous young man who in later years would become a black-robed, bewigged member of the British judiciary with a history and temperament not likely shared by his peers on the bench.

Wills's Wetterhorn climb gained extraordinary attention in Grindelwald and Chamonix for an ascent of a mountain already scaled by others. It occurred before such climbs became commonplace and his guides were extremely popular in their respective home towns. Another reason was the relative lack of snow on the mountain that year, a condition rendering it considerably more difficult than in a season of normal snowfall.

Adding to the notoriety of Wills's climb was the striking clarity with which Lauener's flag and Almer's fir tree were visible from many points, far and wide. The recently developed telegraph enabled news of the climb to spread rapidly. The landlord of the Grindelwald inn, for example, lost no time in dispatching the news to Bern where the staff of the local observatory could clearly see both objects through its telescope. In a mule-drawn cart the day following his ascent Wills heard his driver, in an animated conversation with a companion, refer to him as the "Wetterhorn Herr." Balmat found himself "a man of note" in Chamonix, where he was summoned to the chief guide's office to repeat the story of the climb over and again to different groups that kept coming in to hear it. On his route home from Interlaken – along which he was a familiar figure – Balmat received the accolades of a returning war hero including a command performance in Martigny for villagers who wanted their questions answered before allowing him to move on. Like Whymper, Wills kept a strict accounting of all of his expenses, and also like Whymper – after some of the latter's climbs – found a large number of "disbelievers" in Grindelwald who doubted his claim and would not be troubled to go to a point where the evidence of his victory could be clearly seen.

Wills's unhurried climb of the Wetterhorn matched his easygoing approach to mountaineering and to the new sport he unwittingly inaugurated. In contrast, Whymper's Matterhorn ascent was a determined effort to win a fiercely competitive race. In 1854 Wills was one of a largely unnoticed handful of Alpine climbers; by 1865 Whymper was part of an established group of sportsmen, seeking to be their champion. Each ascent reflected the tenor of its time and the personality of its maker. Their two climbs made fitting bookends for the many compelling stories of mountaineering's Golden Age.

# CHAPTER 6

## The Wild Dauphiné

By 1860, when Whymper first visited the Alps, they had become readily accessible to foreign visitors. Switzerland was only two and a half days from London, first by steamer to France and then by railways which were spreading rapidly across the European continent. This was a mixed blessing to pedestrian purists, but tourists and climbers alike were delighted to spend more time in the mountains and less on the road. Modern transportation facilities had opened the Alpine gates and through them flowed a stream of British lawyers, clergymen, teachers and men of business, all eager to test their sporting skills in an exotic new land.

Whymper was one of that growing number. On his return to London after his first Alpine summer, his drawings drew high praise from publisher William Longman. They included high-peak profiles, deep valley vistas, life in the villages and on the roads, and sketches of climbers, guides, villagers and mountain animals. His simple style lent to the pictures an air of authenticity, conveying the impression of an artist intimately attuned to his subject. They gave the viewer a sense of being in the moment, like a poem whose words never grow old. Accurately portraying Whymper's experiences in the summer of 1860 they presaged the later drawings that so perfectly complemented his written words. With these sketches in hand Longman happily extended the young engraver's commission to the following summer. This assignment added to Whymper's reputation and his "exchequer," supplementing the funds he would need in order to follow his heart's new desire.

Probably due to the press of business, Whymper started for the Alps rather late in the summer of 1861. The end of July found him once again in Grenoble. While awaiting the Bourg d'Oisans diligence he learned that Reginald Macdonald, a London acquaintance, was in town and looking for him. Macdonald also intended to climb Mont Pelvoux and the two agreed to meet on August 3rd in La Bessée, a town near the mountain's base. With no time for an extended visit Whymper had to scramble aboard the departing coach, a "miserable vehicle" that took eight hours on a rough road to travel the thirty miles between Grenoble and Bourg d'Oisans.[1]

The dilapidated state of the coach and the poorly maintained road were typical of this least-travelled region of the western Alps. The Dauphiné had a wilder, harsher look, less majestic than the Bernese Oberland or the Pennine Alps of Switzerland. Its valleys were rockier and narrower; its rough trails led through bleak terrain offering few pleasant vistas to walking tourists. Its lack of travellers matched a scarcity of inns offering even modest accommodations. Peasant chalets willing to take overnight guests could be found, but they were for visitors with hardy constitutions who cared little for the basic amenities. The Dauphiné's assets were its many high peaks, fit objectives for the few pioneering climbers of 1861.

Jean Reynaud, a local road surveyor, was the "right good fellow" from La Bessée whom Whymper had met while breakfasting in a "cabaret" the preceding summer.[2] At that time, Reynaud and three Englishmen, with Michel Croz as their guide, had just made a failed attempt on Mont Pelvoux. In the intervening months Reynaud and Whymper had corresponded and arranged to meet at La Bessée in the summer of 1861 for another attempt on the Pelvoux, the mountain they believed to be the highest in the region. From Bourg d'Oisan Whymper walked first to Briançon where he spent the night, and then on to La Bessée the next day where Reynaud awaited him.

Inexperienced but overconfident, Whymper showed a surprisingly casual attitude in that first summer of serious climbing. He had arrived in the Daupiné without bâton or alpenstock, equipped only with a recently acquired green tree branch. Reynaud, saying he knew just how to fill that void, led Whymper to the local post office where the postmaster was said to have the finest bâtons in town. After banging on the door and "hulloing" loudly they finally roused its occupant. Whymper described the scene later in *Scrambles*:

[The postmaster was] endeavouring with very fair success to make himself intoxicated. He was just able to ejaculate: "France! 'tis the first nation in the world!"...The bâton was produced; it was a branch of a young oak about five feet long, gnarled and twisted in several directions. "Sir," said the postmaster as he presented it, "France! 'tis the first – the first nation in the world, by its," and [he stopped]. "Bâtons?" I suggested. "Yes, yes sir, by its bâtons, its – its," and here he could not get on at all. As I looked at this young limb I thought of my own, but Reynaud, who knew everything about everybody in the village, said there was not a better one, and we went off with it, leaving the official staggering in the road, muttering, "France! tis the first nation in the world."[3]

*Plus ça change, plus c'est la même chose!*

The next day, August 3rd, was the date set for Macdonald to join them but by noon their prospective companion was nowhere in sight. Hoping that he would catch up with them, Whymper and Reynaud set off for Mont Pelvoux accompanied only by Jean Giraud, a villager hired as a porter and nicknamed "petits clous," little nails, because he was the village shoemaker. Along the way, sensing the need for a guide more knowledgeable than the local cobbler, they hired a native known as "Old Sémiond" to lead them to the Pelvoux summit. Beyond the junction of two rushing mountain streams the new foursome entered a sprawling, rock-strewn valley forming the approach to the steep slopes of the Grand Pelvoux Massif – a barren wasteland of boulders, dirt, sand and natural debris with few trees and no trace of human or animal habitation. These mountains were "too steep for chamois, too inhospitable for the marmot, and too repulsive for the eagle. We did not see a single living thing in this sterile and savage valley during four days, except [a] few poor goats...driven there against their will."[4] After proceeding for some distance over and around rocks and boulders they reached the first mountain slopes and clambered upward for about thirty minutes. As the afternoon waned they halted beside a huge boulder – twenty feet high and fifty feet across – and after clearing away rocks and assorted refuse they gathered wood and made camp.

Despite their harsh surroundings Whymper was glad to be there. "The weather was perfect and our prospects for the morrow were good."[5] The party's wine-cask, which had survived a good bit of jostling, was tapped, and the three Frenchmen drank heartily of its contents. They sang snatches of French melodies, told stories, and recited bits of verse. The evening's frolics ended when one of them threw a handful of "red dust" into the campfire that sizzled, bubbled, and erupted into a bright flame that for a moment lit the surrounding crags.

Too reserved to participate Whymper sat like a schoolboy envying the older students at their games, wishing he could play but afraid of appearing awkward if he tried. He had sampled the wine but found it "execrable," so nothing had loosened his tongue or his inhibitions. The others tired "at last" and Whymper crawled into his blanket bag with high anticipation. The ground was rough and uneven, he dozed more than he slept, but he had no complaint. For the chance to scale the Dauphiné's highest peak at the next dawn he would have curled up with a porcupine.

Tomorrow came quickly. The party "roused at three and made a start at four-thirty."[6] "Little nails" Giraud had asked to be taken along. Although the shoemaker had been hired to go only as far as the first night's campsite Whymper agreed that he could join them. After mounting a series of chimneys, gullies, and several buttresses one after the other they sharply queried Old Sémiond. He assured them he knew the location of their elusive goal and that they were almost there. Proceeding farther they saw the old guide glancing about in apparent uncertainty. Again he reassured them but his employers would have none of it. Angrily frustrated – primarily by their own failure to find a competent guide – they did an about face and headed back toward their campsite of the preceding night.

Whymper's friend Macdonald joined their party the next day. They decided to allow Old Sémiond to come with them again but not as their leader. They also hired a young porter who turned out to have problems of his own: over the next two days, he drank Reynaud's wine, smoked the party's cigars, and secretly confiscated food for himself while the others lived on minimum rations. In the relatively unexplored Dauphiné region of 1861 this was what you got if you chose to come without guides from Switzerland or Chamonix. But the young novice was learning from experience, the best teacher. Enthusiasm alone was not enough; guides and porters should be hired in advance, and routes to the mountains – and to their summits, so far as possible – should be charted on a map having at least some semblance of accuracy.

By late afternoon of this third day on Pelvoux's slopes the party was once more on the mountainside well below its summit. The five men – Whymper, Macdonald and Reynaud, along with the old guide and a local porter – reached relatively level ground above the tree line where they stopped to make camp. Following the evening meal the three Frenchmen went soon to their blankets but Whymper and Macdonald – on their first night together – sat around the dying campfire drinking *café noir*. They talked at length, mainly about Macdonald's experiences trying to catch up with Whymper after missing him at La Bessée. By then their companions were asleep. The weather was excellent; the stars shone brightly in a cloudless sky.

When Whymper finally turned in, he found sleep elusive though apparently not from the coffee, which remained his after-dinner staple through many campfire nights to come. The Pelvoux was alive with the "dull boom" of boulders breaking off high above, roaring down the mountainside, sending sparks flying from crashes with other rocks in their paths. They presented no danger to the campers bivouacked in a promontory's lee, but their constant rumble was hardly soothing. The young Whymper was "too excited to sleep;" this was his first major climb, made even more thrilling by his belief that it would also be the first ascent of a virgin summit, about which he was mistaken. Unbeknown to them all a Frenchman had climbed the Pelvoux's highest peak in 1848. Such was the state of public record-keeping in the Dauphiné at that time.

The party was awake before dawn and on their way by 4:15. Roped together they soon met obstacles that often surrounded high Alpine summits. To continue upward they had to crawl across narrow snow bridges over deep crevasses and pick their way through high seracs that could kill if dislodged. They skirted or climbed buttresses blocking their upward path and scrambled up gullies filled with rotten rocks offering few if any handholds. They cut footholds in almost vertical ice falls. They ploughed through knee-deep snow, floundering when it became waist high in depressions and breaking free only with the help of a tug from their nearest companion. They labored thus for several hours and by noon were higher than all of the surrounding mountains except the Monte Viso far to the south.

Having yet to see the Pelvoux's summit they were beginning to think that the day might end before they caught sight of the hidden peak. Old Sémiond, though demoted from his leadership role of the day before, continued to bluster and bluff. After each resting point he would rise and say, "n'avez-pas peur, suivez-mois," ignoring the party's failure to pay him any attention whatsoever. Suddenly off to the left they caught sight of the snow-covered cone they knew instantly to be the mountain's pinnacle. Rejoicing they made a ninety degree turn and headed toward it. Old Sémiond – through doubt, fear, or exhaustion – elected to unrope and stay put. This was the brash Englishman's cue; he turned to the weathered guide and said, *"n'avez-pas peur, suivez-mois,"* gesturing to make sure his message was understood. The old-timer no doubt glared at his young employer but remained in place. The party scrambled up rocks and then traversed a short ridge of ice leading to the top. Macdonald cut a few steps for them and then they were on the final peak, nine and a half hours after breaking camp that morning. It was Whymper's first major ascent and he and Macdonald had become the first Englishmen to reach the Pelvoux summit.

Far and near, countless peaks burst into sight, without a cloud to hide them. The mighty Mont Blanc, full seventy miles away, first caught our eyes, and then, still farther off, the Monte Rosa group. [R]olling away to the east, one unknown range after another succeeded in unveiled splendour; fainter and fainter in tone, though still perfectly defined, till at last the eye was unable to distinguish sky from mountain....Southward, a blue mist seemed to indicate the existence of the distant Mediterranean, and to the west we looked over to the mountains of Auvergne. Such was the panorama; a view extending in nearly every direction for more than one hundred miles.[7]

After a celebratory half-hour at the summit the group reluctantly began its descent. The downward path offered almost as many challenges as the ascent. Macdonald slipped on the side of a glacier while making "a long stretch" to gain a handhold and "would have been in the bowels of a crevasse in a moment" had the rope not caught him.[8] The group then lost its bearings and wandered aimlessly for an hour. Acknowledging "the dreary fact" they would be unable to reach their prior night's bivouac before dark they cleared a small space on a narrow rock slope for the semblance of a campsite. They had eaten little that day and now had to make do with "six and a half cigars,...one-third of a pint of brandy, and half-a-pint of spirits of wine."[9] They mixed snow with the brandy and wine and then heated the mixture on a methanol spirit-lamp. Warmed by this "strong liquor" Whymper, Macdonald and Reynaud lay down on their bed of rocks and "pretended" to sleep.[10]

But they could not. Expecting to be back in camp for the night, they had brought along no extra clothing or blankets. They had nothing to use as ground cover and only Whymper's plaid to stretch over the three of them. The temperature sank almost to the freezing point and Reynaud suffered from a throbbing toothache. Whymper summed it up: "The longest night must end, and ours did at last."[11] Rising early they descended quickly to their original campsite, ending a rigorous but highly successful climb.

After spending the next night at La Bessée they went on to the inn at the neighboring village of La Ville for a few days of relaxation – consisting mainly of games of "bowls" played against locals who "invariably" beat them. They then split up and Whymper set out alone for the Italian border which he crossed during the day. Toward evening, somewhat beyond the village of La Chalp, he found a "lovely hole" which seemed to him a perfect campsite. It was near a stream, protected by "a rock to windward and some broken branches close at hand."[12] After a warm meal cooked on his spirit stove followed by a comforting pipe he wrapped himself in his blanket against the night's chill while the embers of the campfire still glowed, and was soon asleep.

...[B]ut not for long. I was troubled with dreams of the Inquisition; the tortures were being applied – priests were forcing

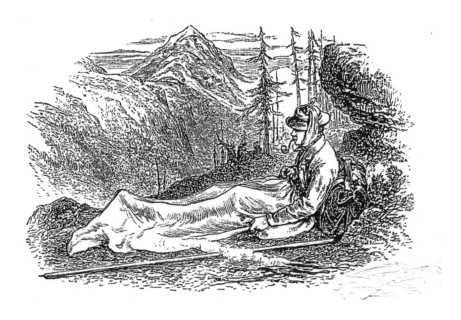

*The Blanket Bag*

fleas down my nostrils and into my eyes – and with red-hot pincers were taking out bits of flesh and then cutting off my ears and tickling the soles of my feet. This was too much; I yelled a great yell and awoke, to find myself covered with innumerable crawling bodies.[13]

It was not the Dauphiné's ubiquitous fleas but ants, whose home, he soon discovered, was uncomfortably close to his campfire. Moving to a neighboring spot he cleared another space and settled once more into his blanket bag. This time nature compensated him for the evening's earlier disturbance. "[A] brilliant meteor sailed across full sixty degrees of the cloudless sky, leaving a trail of light behind which lasted for several seconds. It was the herald of a splendid spectacle. Stars fell by the hundreds; and not dimmed by intervening vapours, they sparkled with greater brightness than Sirius...."[14]

At that moment of celestial fireworks Whymper must have thought how far removed from South Lambeth he was and how fortunate – indeed how blessed by the God of Maze Pond Chapel – to be in the natural wonderland of the Alps and to feel at home among them. Without a sense of their natural beauty he could hardly have written these passages. An open expression of his accompanying emotions, however, would have been uncharacteristic and perhaps even threatening – so much bosh and humbug to the intense young Londoner. However, descriptions of such events as the shower of stars above his snug bed – not uncommon in his writings – barely concealed his pleasure. His words in these instances struck an emotional chord with his readers and can hardly be dismissed as mere devices to attract a sentimental public.

Now on his way into northern Italy he was contemplating attempts on two of the Central Pennine Alps' tallest mountains: the Matterhorn and its neighbor 20 miles to the north, the Weisshorn, which he once called "the noblest [mountain] in Switzerland."[15] Both were virgin peaks. Although climbers considered the Matterhorn the most challenging of all the Alps, the Weisshorn also attracted Whymper because it had been "attacked numerous times by good mountaineers without success."[16] It never entered his mind that the Pelvoux was his only conquest to date and that he would be a complete novice on these difficult giants.

Surprisingly, Whymper had gone to the mountains that summer without arranging for guide services though he planned attempts on some of the Alps' most imposing summits. So far he had chosen guides on spur-of-the-moment recommendations by local villagers. The poor results of this process led him to believe that Alipne guides were unskilled opportunists, eager to take tourists' money but unable to provide quality service. In his view, they were unreliable leaders, mere "pointers [of] paths and large consumers of meat and drink."[17] He had not yet made it his business to learn the names of those he could rely upon. This attitude was consistent with Whymper's personality: he was young, strong, and overconfident. But the unforgiving mountains would soon teach him that expert guidance was a crucial component in the program of any climber as ambitious as he.

The need for guides would diminish as the passing years brought better equipment and improved techniques. In the Alps, guideless climbing would become the new frontier and eventually the norm for better climbers. But mountaineering in the Victorian era was attuned to the customs and attitudes of the day. The pace of life was slow; holidays were longer and more leisurely. Horse-drawn coaches were the Greyhound buses of the time and walking tours were the Alps' most popular outings. Victorian England also lauded the amateur athlete; the sporting professional was virtually unknown. Mountain climbers of the day fit perfectly into this relatively relaxed order. In spite of his ambitious plans for the summer of 1861, Whymper had spent most of June of that year travelling in France, perhaps devoting some time to contacting potential business clients in Paris but mostly visiting the popular sites of the continental tour.

In Italy, following his plan to attempt the Matterhorn and the Weisshorn, he headed for the Val Tournanche taking in the sights as he went along. Slopes near the village of St. Véran were abundant with chamois, the agile goat antelope prized for its meat and later on for the soft quality of its skin. In Ville Vieille he stayed at an inn "boasting the sign of the Elephant" which the villagers cited as evidence that Hannibal's Carthaginian army, marching toward Rome in the 3rd century BCE, had entered the Alps through the nearby gorge of the Guil. Whymper recalled the Elephant Inn for a different reason, one that spoke volumes about the lack of travel amenities in the back country of the Dauphiné and the dirt poor section of northern Italy adjacent to it. The Elephant Inn's bread "...being only a month old, was unusually soft....[and for] the first time [in] ten days [I could] eat some without first...chopping it into small pieces and soaking it in hot water."[18]

It was now late August. Passing through Briançon Whymper came finally to Châtillon at the entrance to the Val Tournanche about fifteen kilometers below Breuil. Here, as if magically transported from a monochrome Kansas into the technicolor land of Oz, he gazed upon a valley in full flower.

> The Val Tournanche is one of the most charming valleys in the Italian Alps. [I]t is a paradise to an artist...[with] groves of chestnuts,...bright trickling rills and...roaring torrents,...upland unsuspected valleys...and noble cliffs. The path rises steeply from Châtillon, but it is well shaded, and the heat of the summer sun is tempered by cool air and spray which comes off the ice cold streams.[19]

In Châtillon Whymper learned that Professor John Tyndall, an energetic Englishman with a reputation as one of the best climbers in the new fraternity of Alpinists, had recently scaled the majestic Weisshorn and was now at Breuil hoping to cap his latest success with a still greater one on the Matterhorn. This news triggered Whymper's competitive juices. Not yet at fever pitch, his interest in the Matterhorn took a significant leap.

In response to his inquiries about guides, several men of the Val Tournanche came forward to offer their services. They fit perfectly with his low opinion of the average guide's attitudes and talents. Their faces "expressed malice, pride, envy, hatred and roguery of every description" and he turned them all down.[20] He then met two climbers who recommended a guide whose service to them had just ended, whom they described as "exactly the man for the Matterhorn."[21] Their guide turned out to be an unimpressive person "of large proportions" but an Oberlander apparently not intimidated by the Matterhorn. So Whymper hired him for lack of a better choice and set out for Breuil at the mountain's southern base. Somewhere along the way he learned that the man had not been paid by the former employers who had recommended him so highly. Not wanting to lose the one guide that seemed willing and able to attempt the Matterhorn with him, Whymper simply assumed the obligation and went forward.

About half way up the path to Breuil lay the village of Valtournanche bearing the same name as its valley. Knowing he needed additional help on the Matterhorn, Whymper inquired in the town square about the availability of an additional guide. "With one voice" the villagers recommended Jean-Antoine Carrel, a native son of their valley.[22] Whymper sought out Carrel and found him "a well-made, resolute looking fellow with a certain defiant air which was rather taking."[23] Carrel was willing to join Whymper for a daily fee of twenty francs – about £0.80 at the time – which Whymper readily agreed to. Carrel – like any good bargainer whose initial offer has been too quickly accepted – tried to get more by insisting that his comrade also accompany them. As Carrel spoke, "an evil countenance came forth out of the darkness and proclaimed itself the comrade."[24] Put off by the second man's looks and cocky enough to think he could find another guide, Whymper declined any arrangement with Carrel. Though neither realized it at the time, their meeting was the beginning of a long-lasting relationship. They were to become fierce competitors for supremacy on the Matterhorn. Carrel would also be Whymper's principal Matterhorn guide on the Italian side and his lifelong climbing companion in the Alps and elsewhere. For now, however, they went their separate ways as Whymper continued up the valley.

On arriving at Breuil, Whymper went to the village inn and asked the questions uppermost in his mind: How had John Tyndall fared on the Matterhorn? Was he still there? He was relieved to learn that Tyndall had been in Breuil a day or so earlier but had departed without attempting a climb. No one seemed to know why; he and his guide had left without explanation. Whymper then inquired about guides. Several were there but all declined Whymper's offer except one. "A sturdy old fellow – Peter Taugwalder by name – said he would go," at a fee of "two hundred francs per day, whether we ascend or not."[25] He felt that Taugwalder's fee, astronomical at the time, was merely his way of avoiding a direct refusal.

From that day forward Whymper seemed convinced that even the guides who finally agreed to lead climbers on the Matterhorn "had no heart in the matter, and took the first opportunity to turn back."[26] The lone exception to this rule in Whymper's mind was Carrel although he later added J. J. Bennen, a Swiss guide from the Oberland region. As later events would show, Whymper was perhaps a bit generous in his estimation of Bennen's skills. He would also learn that the truth about Carrel was somewhat more complicated than he first thought. Carrel was dead set on being the first to scale the Matterhorn but he wanted to do it as the leader of an Italian party and was inclined to sound retreat if the going got tough when guiding an Englishman.

Unable to find acceptable help, Whymper decided that he and his Oberland guide would go it alone beginning the next day. From the inn at Breuil the Matterhorn loomed large in the northern sky and in Whymper's thoughts. This would be his first attempt and he had no illusions about the difficulties he would face. He also knew something of the mysterious aura that surrounded it.

[From the Italian side], the summit of the peak is nearly 15,000 feet above the sea, and rises abruptly by a series of cliffs [to] a clear 5,000 feet above the glaciers which surround its base...[I]ts invincible appearance...seemed to be a cordon drawn around it, up to which one might go, but no farther. Within that invisible line, djinns and effreets were supposed to exist – the Wandering Jew and the spirits of the damned. The superstitious natives in the surrounding valleys...spoke of a ruined city on its summit where...the spirits dwelt; and warned... against a rash approach lest the [furious] demons...hurl down vengeance [on unwary climbers].[27]

Whymper's plans called for a climb that would take at least two days. For their nights on the mountain he sought the loan of two blankets from the inn's proprietor Monsieur Favre. The innkeeper refused, noting that Whymper had brought a bottle of brandy with him from Valtournanche instead of waiting to purchase it at the inn. "No brandy, no blankets appeared to be his rule."[28] With meager provisions and no extra night-time cover he and his guide left in the late afternoon of August 29 and stopped for the first night at a cowshed in the high foothills about an hour above Breuil. "The cowherds, good fellows...hailed our company with delight, and did their best to make us comfortable....[But] as we sat with them round the great copper pot [enjoying their] simple food...they bade us with husky voices...to beware of the perils of the haunted cliffs."[29]

That night in the cowshed Whymper slept on and off as fleas buzzed in his ears and performed "a spirited fandango" on his cheek. As a result he awoke late the next morning; it was 7:00 a.m. when he and his guide started up the mountain. This was his first time on the Matterhorn and apparently the guide's as well, so they had to pick their route as they went along. They were aiming for the Col du Lion at something over 10,000 feet from which their next move would be plotted. A second night on the mountainside would obviously be required, and after exploring the lesser heights Whymper and his guide decided to spend their next night on the Col at its juncture with the Tête du Lion, partially sheltered by an overhanging ledge.

After selecting the location for their night's bivouac they returned to the cowshed, picked up their tent and provisions and climbed again to

*Portrait of Monsieur Favre*

the Col "heavily laden." Their chosen spot was narrow, barely wide enough to let them sleep side by side with a reasonable degree of safety. The tent Whymper brought with him that summer had looked fine in a London store but the mountain wind blew right through it, fluttering its flaps loudly and tearing loose its anchoring pegs. Judging the tent "thoroughly useless" Whymper and the guide dismantled it and wrapped themselves in its fabric in the hope of gaining a bit of protection against the icy chill of the oncoming night. At that point Whymper no doubt wished he had purchased an extra bottle of brandy from the hard-nosed innkeeper.

> On one side a sheer wall overhung the Tiefenmatten Glacier. On the other, steep, glassy slopes of hard snow descended to the Glacier du Lion furrowed by water and...falling stones. On the north there was the great peak of the Matterhorn, and on the south side the cliffs of the Tête du Lion. Throw a bottle down to the Tiefenmatten – no sound returns for more than twelve seconds....The silence was impressive. No living thing was near our solitary bivouac;....the stones had ceased to fall....It was bitterly cold. Water froze in a bottle under my head.[30]

They left the Col at daybreak glad to be moving again. The climbing was more serious now; each upward step had to be earned with effort. "But it was the most pleasant kind of climbing. The rocks were fast and unencumbered with debris; the cracks were good, although not numerous; and there was nothing to fear except from one's self."[31] They arrived with little effort at "the Chimney," a long and narrow vertical chute formed by smooth rock surfaces on three sides, its rear wall facing the climbers. The guide struggled to make it up this formation but could not. Whymper managed to do so but was unable to pull the heavy guide to the top. A confrontation ensued, similar to the one between Whymper and his inadequate guide at the Simplon Pass the preceding summer. The Oberlander untied himself and calmly announced he was going down. Whymper called him a coward and the guide responded in kind. Whymper then suggested that the guide return to Breuil and report that he had abandoned his "monsieur" on the mountain. This ploy was equally ineffective and the guide turned again to the descent. Whymper silently debated whether to continue upward by himself but decided against it. He had managed to scale the Chimney and could come down with little difficulty if another person stood at the bottom to help. Descending the steep rock shaft alone, however, "was quite another thing...as the lower edge hung in a provoking manner." Moreover, the Chimney was "a natural channel for falling stones."[32]

An internal bell also sounded, warning Whymper that an attempt to go higher on the Matterhorn alone would be foolhardy. So he ate humble pie and invited the guide to come back and help him get down the Chimney. The guide did so and together they returned to Breuil, arriving there around noon. Jean-Antoine Carrel and his uncle J. J. Carrel had been on the mountain that same day but had not crossed paths with Whymper. He learned later that they had not reached any great height and that the elder Carrel – for "convenience" – had temporarily taken off his shoes and tied them onto his waist. In so doing he had managed to lose one of them and thus come down the rest of the way with a piece of cord fastened round his naked foot. Undaunted, they had boldly glissaded down the Couloir du Lion, J. J. Carrel having tied up his shoeless foot in a pocket handkerchief."[33] Strong and tough indeed were these men of the Val Tournanche.

In describing his first attempt on the Matterhorn, Whymper expressed no disappointment at failing to hire the Carrels or fear they would ascend the Matterhorn before him. Most likely he and Carrel believed that before yielding its summit to anyone, this foreboding mountain would require further exploration at heights not yet reached. In the summer of 1861 he seemed content to be part of that undertaking, hoping good luck and a valiant effort and would bring him success. Now, however, his time to be abroad and away from the engraving business had expired and he left Breuil without a second attempt.

It is hard to say at what moment the Matterhorn became Whymper's obsession. He wrote in *Scrambles* that his do-or-die attitude developed as he left the Breuil inn "determined to return" in 1862, if possible, "to lay siege to the mountain until one or the other was vanquished."[34] His recent success on the Pelvoux had swelled his confidence more than it should have, making his defeat on the Matterhorn particularly galling. He knew that he faced competition from Professor Tyndall and perhaps others as yet unknown. Something also told Whymper not to underestimate Jean-Antoine Carrel, the Valtournanche native whose "defiant air" had so impressed him at their first meeting.

Soon after his return to London in the fall of 1861 the Alpine Club admitted Whymper to its select membership. At the Club, formed in 1857 as a place for climbers to share mountaineering information and experiences, he heard a good bit of additional Matterhorn lore. Stories of its invincibility and mysterious guardian forces created just the sort of challenge Whymper found irresistible. As he made plans for the following summer it had become clear in his eyes that the Matterhorn was the Alps' most valuable prize, and that he would mount an all-out effort to seize it.

# CHAPTER 7

## *The Monomaniac and the Bersagliere*

During the summers of 1860 and 1861, his first two climbing seasons, Whymper spent several nights in the open air at freezing temperatures. He had used a variety of different tents for shelter and been dissatisfied with all of them. Some were flimsy, some heavy and unwieldy. Others were drafty in moderate winds and unstable in storms. All took time to erect, a problem when a sudden weather change demanded immediate shelter. None came with waterproof ground cover.

Over the winter of 1861 Whymper designed a new tent and had it made to his specifications. The base area of his tent was a square, six feet per side. Its supporting front and rear frames were pairs of six-foot ash poles shod at the bottom with iron points, each pair joined in an "x" with a bolt through holes located near their top ends. A stout six-foot cord stretched between the frames at the bolt level established the top of the tent. The sloping two-sided roof was a six foot wide, continuous piece of rough calico that went over the top cord and down to the tent "floor" on either side. The square floor was made of mackintosh, a plaid of twill cloth rubberized to resist water and add strength. A calico triangle formed the rear wall; a slit along one edge of the front side created the entrance. The mackintosh floor material was about nine feet square, the extra length being sewn to the inner surfaces of the rear, the sides, and front flaps to hold all the pieces together and to block entry of cold wind at ground level. When the poles were spread apart sixty degrees and their tips pressed into the ground, the entrance side and the rear side of the erect tent each formed an equilateral triangle.

Reflecting Whymper's experience and the ingenuity of his design, the finished product was a major improvement over its predecessors. It met

*Whymper's Alpine Tent*

the practical demands of the Alps' harsh environment. It slept up to four – or five in a pinch – weighed only 22 pounds, and could be assembled by two people in three minutes, a welcome feature in extreme weather. As a new member of the Alpine Club he could now share anecdotes and information at meetings with Wills, Stephen, Tyndall and others he looked up to. It is easy to imagine him showing his new tent to these older hands and basking in their compliments.

Whymper left for the Alps again in early July of 1862. He and Reginald Macdonald, his Mont Pelvoux climbing companion of the previous summer, had agreed to meet in Zermatt. Whymper now realized the importance of arranging for guide services in advance. After trying without success to hire Melchior Anderegg or other "more notable" guides, he had employed two local men, Johann zum Taugwald and Johann Kronig. Neither Whymper, Macdonald, nor their two local guides seriously considered attempting the Matterhorn's Swiss side. Such was the strength of the common belief, as anyone who looked at the Matterhorn from Zermatt could plainly see, that while the Italian side was assuredly difficult, the steep slopes of the eastern and northern faces – and the northeastern ridge that separated them – were simply impossible.

Meeting in Zermatt as planned, Whymper and Macdonald set out on July 5th with their two guides across the Col Théodule, bound for Breuil. The weather was unsettled; there was rain in the valleys, snow on the mountain, and threatening black clouds overhead. The air around them as they walked was ominously still, punctuated with "mysterious, rushing sounds...like the swishing of a long whip."[1] What they were encountering was the common mountain phenomenon of static electricity which could make a climber's hair stand on end and his fingertips sizzle if moved fast enough through the air. Dr. Spence Watson, writing the following year about a similar experience on a nearby glacier, described how "the veil on [his] wide-awake stood upright in the air!"[2] Climbers sometimes hung loose veils from the front of their hats to protect against the glare of the snow in bright sunlight. "Wide-awake" was the name Victorian punsters gave to a soft felt hat with a low crown and wide brim – because its cloth material had no "nap." The members of Whymper's party, now without veils and under threatening skies, were not bothered with glare, but were apprehensive about becoming lightning rods. Maintaining a rapid pace, however, they soon arrived safely at the Breuil inn.

The party needed one further addition, a porter to carry supplies and equipment including Whymper's new tent. The innkeeper, Monsieur Favre, suggested Luc Meynet, a Breuil native, and directed them to Meynet's home. Whymper found it "a mean abode" full of cheese-making equipment and several "bright-eyed" children who said that "Uncle Luc" would be home soon. Not knowing quite what to expect,

...we waited at the door of the little chalet and watched for him. At last a speck was seen coming round the corner of a patch of pines [to the] south....[T]he children clapped their hands, dropped their toys, and ran eagerly forward to meet him. We saw an ungainly, wobbling figure stoop down and catch up the little ones, kiss them on each cheek, and put them in the empty panniers on each side of [his] mule, and then heard it come on caroling, as if this was not a world of woe....[A]nd yet the face of little Luc Meynet, the hunchback of Breuil, bore traces of trouble and sorrow, and there was more than a touch of sadness in his voice when he said that he must look after his brother's children.[3]

Whymper was attracted to this misshapen peasant from the moment they met. Meynet's unpleasant exterior reflected the burdens of a hard life but underneath, Whymper sensed, was a reliable worker with a positive outlook and congenial nature. After talking further Meynet decided that he could, after all, resolve his baby-sitting problems and come with them. Whymper was pleased and they agreed to meet early the next morning at the Breuil inn to begin the climb.

On Sunday, July 6th, rain in the foothills and snow on the mountain delayed their planned start. That night, however, the weather improved and the fivesome left early the next morning for the Matterhorn. As the only one who had climbed on the mountain before, Whymper led the way and promptly took them in the wrong direction to the top of the Tête du Lion. From there they overlooked the col below, the spot where they wanted to be. Descending, the guide Kronig slipped on a streak of ice and slid rapidly down, arms flailing and body twisting to retain his balance. With enormous effort he was able to stop his fall just before striking some rocks that would have propelled him up and over the high cliff to almost certain death. When Whymper got to him, Kronig's "face was corpse-like in hue" and he was "trembling violently."[4] When the guide recovered enough of his composure for them to continue they returned to the proper track and finally reached the Col du Lion in the late afternoon. Remembering the rocky perch of his night on the col the previous year, Whymper directed the party in the preparation of a platform made of debris from surrounding ledges smoothed over with dirt and mud.

Observing Luc Meynet during the porter's first day on the job, Whymper was pleased:

Meynet...proved invaluable as a tent-bearer....Although his legs were more picturesque than symmetrical, and although he seemed to be built on principle, with no two parts alike – his very deformities proved of service... [W]e quickly found he had spirit of no common order, and that few peasants [were] more agreeable companions, or better climbers, than little Luc Meynet, the hunchback of Breuil....He now showed himself not less serviceable as a scavenger, and humbly asked for gristly pieces of meat, rejected by others, or for suspicious eggs; and seemed to consider it a peculiar favour, if not a treat, to be permitted to drink the coffee grounds. With the greatest contentment, he took the worst place at the door to the tent, and did all the dirty work...put upon him by the guides, as gratefully as a dog who has been well beaten will receive a stroke.[5]

Whymper's praise was sincere, its condescending undertone the norm for an Englishman's view of a Swiss peasant. The young Londoner could relate easily to ordinary folk, whom he consistently brought into his travel narratives wherever he might be. Though he often found more to criticize than to praise, local villagers were a significant part of his Alpine experience. Other Golden Age climbers described close relationships with guides, hoteliers, and even a dog or two, but the bonding of such disparate personalities as Whymper and Meynet was unusual if not unique. And it would grow stronger as time went by.

During the night a sharp wind swept their bivouac on the Col de Lion and was blowing hard when they awoke at dawn. Whymper's new tent "behaved nobly" and with all five climbers cheek-by-jowl inside it they had little trouble from the cold.[6] The tent pegs held and the oversized mackintosh floor did its job. The morning was well along when the wind subsided enough to let them continue. They packed up and started out, hoping the weather would hold, but it was not to be. Hardly had they climbed a hundred feet when a windstorm of near hurricane force burst upon them, bringing swirling snow and flying debris: stones "as big as a man's fist [were] blown away, horizontally into space."[7] Caught in its grip they dared not stand, and so remained glued to the rocks unable to go forward or to return to the col. The temperature then

*My tent-bearer – the hunchback*

dropped swiftly. Finally, through brief lulls in the storm, they made it back to their tent site. At that point the two Oberland guides, thoroughly dispirited by the icy gale, announced that they had had enough. Meynet said that he had important cheese-making duties the next day; and there is no record of Whymper or Macdonald insisting or even suggesting that they keep trying. So they returned to Breuil, arriving at the inn at 2:30 p.m. "extremely chagrined at our complete defeat."[8]

This aborted second attempt on the Matterhorn forcefully reminded Whymper of the mountain's reputation for treating trespassers unkindly. Wanting to be sure that he and Macdonald would not reach Breuil and find themselves unable to hire competent professionals, he had engaged the reputed best of the willing and available Swiss guides. In hindsight the decision to try this mountain with guides who had never set foot on it seems almost reckless. But from Whymper's perspective at the time it was a natural step in the learning process. It would also give him a greater appreciation for Jean-Antoine Carrel's superior talents. And because it had been the guides' unwillingness to go forward – not any reluctance on his or Macdonald's part – he was determined to hire Carrel and try again, immediately.

In Whymper's absence while on the mountain Carrel had come up to

Breuil. Pride, curiosity and self-interest took him there whenever news reached Valtournanche that a party was attempting the Matterhorn. Before the day was over Whymper had approached Jean-Antoine and secured the guide's agreement to accompany the two Englishmen "on the first fine day."[9] Whymper thought himself fortunate, "for Carrel clearly considered the mountain a kind of preserve, and regarded our late attempt as an act of *poaching*."[10] To Whymper this was simply part of the "defiant air" Carrel had shown on their first meeting the year before. He did not resent it or think it would dampen the Italian's willingness to lead an Englishman to the top. He was wrong, but at the time only a clairvoyant could have seen that deeply into Jean-Antoine's heart.

\* \* \* \*

The area of the Val Tournanche had once been part of the former Savoie region of France. The Carrel family was well-known there and as with most Savoyards, French was their first language, Italian their second. Jean-Jacques, Carrel's uncle, was a noted chamois and marmot hunter who later joined his nephew as a porter and guide. Two cousins, Louis and Caesar, were porters who would occasionally accompany Carrel and Whymper on the Matterhorn. Other more distant relatives in the valley were G. Carrel, a church Canon, and Victor, another porter-guide. According to the records of Saint Antoine's church at Valtournanche, Carrel was baptized there on January 17th, 1829, but his exact age remained uncertain.[11] In his youth he was known for his strength and athleticism. He was bright, argumentative and reputedly had the wit to converse easily with the local priest, Amé Gorret, his friend and climbing companion.

Carrel was an ardent patriot, proud to be an Italian and galled by the oppressive rule of the Austrians who ruled the land at the time of his birth. At that time the Val Tournanche's region of Lombardy was part of the Kingdom of Sardinia, one of the stronger Italian mini-states under foreign dominion: in its case, Austria. When the self-appointed "King" of Sardinia decided to fight for independence as part of the Risorgimento, the 20 year old Carrel joined the Sardinian rebel army and became one of a group of expert riflemen known as *bersaglieri*. The war with Austria was intense but short, ending with a route of the Italian troops – Carrel among them – at the battle of Novara in 1849. He returned to Valtournanche saddened by the war's failure to bring independence but with his patriotism undiminished.

More mature and having seen battle and something of the larger world in the army, the veteran bersagliere carried himself even more confidently. He grew a moustache and an "imperial," a goatee-like beard popular at the time. His military bearing was softened, however, by the way he angled his hat and by the somewhat flippant look he cultivated. He also took to wearing a colorful feather in his hatband. Altogether he cut a dashing figure and was known among villagers as the "Cock of the Val Tournanche." By any name, he was an imposing young man.

Carrel grew up in the Matterhorn's shadow but had never climbed it or any other mountain. After returning home from the army and apprenticed for the requisite number of years, he became a stonemason and worked diligently at his new trade. For sport and extra earnings he hunted chamois and marmots on the mountains' lower slopes but saw no reason to climb higher. Life was hard enough without risking life and limb on the Matterhorn's rugged heights. What eventually spurred his determination to scale the great mountain remains unknown. It seems probable – as at least one author has speculated – that the catalyst for Carrel's interest was the church's Father Gorrett.[12] Like Carrel, Gorret was a son of the Val Tournanche and in that small community the two of them could easily have talked often. They were both young, athletic, intelligent, and proud to be Italians. As a member of the Catholic clergy Gorret had channels of information not readily available to the local citizenry. When news of the English climbers' onslaught into the Oberland Alps began to filter into Italy after the mid-1850s, Gorret and Carrel, both of whom had often explored the Matterhorn's lower slopes, would naturally have thought about claiming its summit for themselves and their country. There is no record that Carrel ever married.

In the summer of 1858 after several preliminary excursions, Carrel, Gorret and J. J. Carrel made their first attempt on the Matterhorn.[13] Each carried only a woodsman's axe and a graffito – a pole with a hook at one end for pulling marmots from their holes. One of their first obstacles was the massive ice-flow later named the Glacier du Lion. Still

*Portrait of Jean-Antoine Carrel*

a novice on that initial climb, Carrel abruptly sank into a hidden glacial crevasse. An ice outcropping luckily broke his fall not far below the surface and one of his companions used his graffio to pull Jean-Antoine to safety. On reaching the Col du Lion, Carrel got his first look at the green hills of his home valley and the broad vista of glaciers and peaks near the Matterhorn. Leaving the Col they climbed to a small peak at about 12,000 feet (later named the Tête du Lion) becoming the first persons to reach that point. By then it was late in the day so they turned and headed homeward.

It was the next summer before Carrel could make a second attempt on the Matterhorn. Sardinia had again gone to war with Austria, this time in an alliance with the French. Though brief, the war took an enormous toll of deaths and combat casualties. On June 24th, 1859, the two armies met at the battle of Solferino. After several hours of intense fighting the Austrians finally retreated, leaving behind over twenty thousand dead and wounded. This battle ended the war from which Lombardy emerged as a free state, ultimately to become part of a united Italy. Carrel, with a recent promotion to the rank of sergeant, had been in the thick of the fighting. He returned to Valtournanche a hardened war veteran, more sober in countenance, more independent in spirit, and more fiercely determined than ever to conquer the Matterhorn.

During Carrel's absence of almost a year, activity on and around the Matterhorn had increased. Vaughan Hawkins, an Englishman, had come to Breuil with a Swiss guide, J. J. Bennen, to survey the mountain for a possible future attempt. Others were talking about doing the same and attempts from the Italian side would begin in earnest the following year. After his second army stint Carrel made several further forays onto the Matterhorn with his Val Tournanche compatriots. In the year of his return they reached the bottom of a steep pitch they called the Chimney, at 12,650 feet the highest point anyone had yet reached on the mountain that was now Carrel's obsession. In the summer of 1860 Carrel's uncle, Jean-Jacques, was one of the guides leading a Matterhorn attempt by two Englishmen, Tyndall and Hawkins. Although that party ascended to almost 13,000 feet – the highest point reached by anyone before them – Carrel seemed unthreatened by their challenge and made no independent attempt on the Matterhorn that year. He believed that the mountain's last two thousand feet – steep, icy and separated from the final slopes by seemingly impassable crevasses – would continue to defy men with less skill, grit and knowledge of the mountain than he, and he had yet to meet his equal.

* * * *

On the morning of July 9th, 1862 Whymper set out from the Breuil inn on his second attempt of the Matterhorn that summer.[14] In his new party were Macdonald, with Carrel and his friend Pession as guides and Luc Meynet as their porter. At Carrel's suggestion they decided to encamp the first night considerably above the Col du Lion, near the foot of the Chimney. Arriving there without incident that afternoon they found a protected area under the Chimney's sharp rise. Led by Carrel they built a platform of earth and rocks, large enough to accommodate Whymper's tent and a space for their campfire. With the weather holding and the day not yet done, they decided to climb a bit higher to survey the first part of the next day's route. After an hour's scramble, at a height of about 13,000 feet, they reached the foot of the Great Tower, a large rock formation standing astride a ridge leading upward toward the summit. The task of finding a way around the Tower and onto the ridge would begin tomorrow. For now, they were content to return to their night-time bivouac.

At 5:00 a.m. the next morning they began the second leg of their ascent. Carrel, Macdonald and Whymper scrambled up the Chimney, followed by Pession. At the top, Pession said he felt quite ill and was unable to continue. The party waited for some time, hoping his condition would improve, but it did not, and Carrel flatly refused to go forward without his companion. Macdonald – "ever the coolest of the cool," and knowing that business in London would require his return upon their descent – suggested that he and Whymper proceed alone. Their "better judgment prevailed," however, and the party made their way back to Breuil.[15]

Whymper's second defeat in only four days left him deeply frustrated but with confidence in his own climbing ability as strong as ever:

Three times I had [attempted] this mountain and on each occasion failed....Up to the height of nearly 13,000 feet there were no extraordinary difficulties....Only 1,800 feet remained but they were as yet untrodden and might present the most formidable obstacles. No man could expect to climb them by himself. A...rock only seven feet high might at any time defeat him, if it were perpendicular. Such a place might be possible [for] two, or a bagatelle [for] three men. It was evident that a party should consist of three men at least. But where could the other two men be obtained? Only Carrel...exhibited any enthusiasm in the matter; and he...had absolutely refused to go unless the party consisted of at least four persons. Want of men made the difficulty, not the mountain.[16]

At that point Whymper was down but not out. The weather turned bad again at Breuil so he went over the Théodule Pass to Zermatt the next day on the chance he might find a guide there. But the problem persisted: he could not induce any of the town's "better" guides to come with him to the mountain they still feared. The snow and rain that had driven him to Zermatt continued intermittently, pinning him there for seven days. During that week, as casually noted in a one-line footnote in *Scrambles,* he ignored the weather and with a guide climbed the Monte Rosa – a snow mountain but nevertheless Switzerland's highest peak.[18] On July 17th, with the weather improving, he returned to Breuil hoping to sign up Carrel and Meynet for another attempt. But since he had given them no notice, the stonemason and the cheese-maker could not leave their work.

Whymper's rolled-up tent was still on the Matterhorn, on the platform constructed at the foot of the Chimney on their last attempt. Figuring he knew the way well enough he set out alone on July 18th to see if the tent was still there and in one piece. A solo climb, he noted, focused one's attention on details not always seen when accompanied by others. To assure coming down by the same route the single climber paid careful attention to landmarks and their "angles" along his ascent. Handholds got extra scrutiny to make sure they would not give way and footholds were tested a moment longer for there was no companion on the rope in the event of a miscalculation. On this climb he also observed, for the first time, tiny plants growing in nooks and crannies of the rocks above the tree line – "pioneers of vegetation, atoms of life in a world of desolation."[18]

In due course he reached the campsite's platform and found his tent rolled-up and safe under recent snowfall. Captivated by the striking view of the peaks surrounding his high perch he lost track of time until he noticed that birds on the neighboring cliffs "had begun to chirp their evening hymn."[19] He had come without provisions, intending to return to Breuil that evening. But the sky was calm and clear and when he unrolled the tent there was food enough for several days packed inside it. So he decided to stay and made the tent ready to receive a sole occupant. And yet he lingered outside, mesmerized by the view in the unaccustomed solitude of the moment. Spread around him in the still air were scores of majestic summits, near and far, including the Breithorn, the Monte Rosa, the Dent Blanche, the Dent d'Hérens, and, in the distance to the south, the isolated peak of the Monte Viso.

The sun was setting and its rosy rays, blending with the snowy blue, had thrown a pale, pure violet as far as the eye could see. [T]he valleys were drowned in purple gloom while the summits shown with unnatural brightness....As I sat in the door of the tent and watched the twilight change to darkness, the earth [became]...almost sublime....[T]he world seemed dead and I its sole inhabitant. By and by, the moon as it rose brought the hills again into sight and by a [thoughtful suppression] of detail rendered the view yet more magnificent. Something in the south hung like a great glow-worm in the air,...too large for a star and too steady for a meteor....[I]t...[took a long time for me to] realize the scarcely credible fact that it was the moonlight glittering on the great snow-slope on the north side [of the] Monte Viso, at a distance, as the crow flies, of 98 miles. Shivering, at last I entered the tent and made my coffee.[20]

At Whymper's bedtime there was nothing so soothing as the aroma and warmth of a hot cup of coffee, its caffeine no match for the sleep-inducing products of the day's arduous scrambles.

The next morning Whymper set his sights on the Great Tower – the spot where Pession's illness had forced a retreat nine days before – with the aim of exploring the route beyond the Tower as far as possible. He reached the first objective without difficulty. From the Col Théodule the Great Tower seemed only a slight bulge on an insignificant ridge in the Matterhorn's fractured southern side. Up close, however, it blocked the climber's view of everything above it. This was just one of the many surprises, not observable until close at hand, offered by the countless out-croppings, ridges, parapets and hidden crevasses on the Matterhorn's Italian side. The first step onto the ridge above the Tower was the most difficult: one had to spring up and then "haul oneself over [ridge's] sharp edge by sheer strength."[21] Climbing up the jagged center of the arête was impossible and to the left, steep precipices plunged almost vertically to the Tiefenmatten Glacier far below. The right-hand side of the ridge was narrowly passable, but its upward track was a series of enormous boulders and unstable rocky ledges. On that side and attempting to cross a narrow gully, he found himself spread-eagled on a rock "fixed as if crucified, pressing against the rock and feeling each rise and fall of my chest as I breathed.... Screwing my head round to look for [a] hold and not seeing any, [I] somehow jumped sideways...to the [gully's] other side."[22]

From there the rocks became loose and fragmented, "all was decay and ruin. The crest of the ridge was shattered and cleft, and the feet sank in the chips which had drifted down; while above, huge blocks, hacked and carved by the hand of time, nodded to the sky, looking like the gravestones of giants."[23] Some of them were so finely poised they looked as if a modest breeze or a light touch by a careless climber might topple them. Writing years later, Whymper said that he never again saw anything in the Alps "more striking than this desolate, ruined and shattered ridge at the back of the Great Tower."[24]

Surveying that barren scene Whymper found himself nearly as high as the 13,715 foot summit of the Dent d'Hérens, clearly visible in the western sky. He also saw that the cliffs ahead were so steep and broken that it would be foolish to attempt them alone. So he turned back, planning to return with Carrel as soon as possible and move beyond them to the summit.

On the descent he brought out for the first time two devices of his own conception and design. One was a grapnel-like claw that could be wedged into a rock crevice to secure a rope during an ascent or descent. The other was a metal ring attached to the end of a rope, through which the rope's other end could be threaded to make a loop. The loop could then be passed over a rock for support as a climber descended. A long piece of stout cord attached to the ring allowed the climber – after firm footing had been found – to pull on the ring, loosening the loop so the rope could be whipped off the rock and used again. Using these two devices on his solo climb, he "was able to ascend and descend rocks [that] would otherwise have been completely impassable."[25] Using both devices he made his way down to the campsite platform without incident, where he stopped to roll up the tent and stow it for future use.

Before continuing downward he decided to leave his "old navy boarding axe," the only one he had with him, on the platform with his tent. A climber normally carried his axe behind him, affixed to a rope commonly worn tight around his waist. On ascents, when he faced inward, the axe was well out of the way. On descents when he usually faced outward it could be a nuisance, as it had been that day as he came down from the high cliffs. Strapped to his back it had caught frequently on the rocks behind him, nearly upsetting him at several points. Now, free of it and ready for the last leg of the descent, he was well satisfied with the results of his solo scouting mission. Leaving the campsite area he "thought of [him]self as good as at Breuil."[26] Very soon, however, he would abruptly discover his mistaken judgment.

Moving downward he lowered himself through the Chimney, cutting his rope on reaching the bottom so as to leave the still-attached portion for his next ascent. He then descended steadily to the Col du Lion and a bit beyond, at which point the decision to leave his axe behind became a near-fatal mistake. Fifty yards above the safety of the Great Staircase's gentle angle he had to cross the upper edge of a steep snow-slope abutting the cliffs of the Tête du Lion. A corner of the cliff wall on his right side had to be turned in order to proceed. During the two days he had been alone on the mountain its warmth had melted the half-dozen or so steps he had cut in the frozen slope on the way up. Without his axe, his only recourse was to grasp with his right hand a rock in the corner of the cliff wall partially blocking his path, and with his long bâton in his left hand scratch out a step on the near side of the corner. Then, with his right foot in that step, he leaned around the corner and scratched another step on the rocky corner's far side. While making the precarious move to the second step he somehow slipped and fell headlong down the glassy slope.

> The [weight of the] knapsack brought my head down first, and I pitched into some rocks about a dozen feet below....[T]hey caught something and tumbled me over the edge, head over heels into the gully....[T]he bâton was dashed from my hands and I whirled downwards in a series of bounds, each longer than the last, now over ice, now into rocks, striking my head four or five times, each time with increased force. The last bound sent me spinning through the air in a leap of fifty or sixty feet, from one side of the gully to the other....I struck [some] rocks, luckily, with the whole of my left side. They caught my clothes for a moment, and I fell back on to the snow, [my] motion [momentarily] arrested. My head fortunately came the right side up, and a few frantic catches brought me to a halt in the neck of the gully...on the verge of the precipice. Bâton, hat and veil skimmed by and disappeared, and

the crash of the rocks which I had started, as they fell on the glacier, told how narrow had been [my] escape from utter destruction. As it was, I fell nearly 200 feet in seven or eight bounds. Ten more feet would have taken me in one gigantic leap of 800 feet onto the glacier below.[27]

Whymper stayed conscious but bleeding heavily from multiple cuts mostly about the head, some of which spurted blood with each heartbeat. Unable to stop the blood with pressure from his hands he kicked loose a clump of snow and stuck it on his head, diminishing the flow and enabling him to roll over and regain his feet. No sooner had he done that and limped to a place of safety, he fainted. Awaking later to a setting sun he started down the Great Staircase as darkness fell. "By a combination of luck and care" he made it down the remaining 4,000 feet of the descent, sneaking past the cowherds' hut and into the inn at Breuil hoping to reach his room unobserved.[28] But Favre the innkeeper saw him in the passageway and screamed with fright at the blood-spattered figure, waking the entire household. A score of people gathered around Whymper, unanimous in recommending that the wounds be treated with hot wine and salt. Ignoring his protestations they performed their home remedy and Whymper went to bed extremely uncomfortable but safe.

He arose the next day stiff and sore, grateful to be alive and no worse off. His injuries were severe. Several deep cuts on the head and temple and in his left palm had bled profusely. His arms and legs had multiple but less serious cuts and abrasions. The tips of both ears were gone and a sharp rock, in cutting away a section of his left boot and sock, had gouged a chunk out of his ankle. His entire body was bruised and he had no memory of the events of that day prior to his near fatal slip. His description of his climb to the impassable cliffs above the Tower, his use of the ring and claw as he came down, and his passage through the Chimney came later from notes made in the course of the descent.

The wine and salt did their work. His wounds healed rapidly, helped by the fitness of his young body and the ministrations of an English woman also staying at the inn whom he referred to without elaboration in his journal. Given the seriousness of his wounds, his recovery period was amazingly short. He fretted a bit under his bandages but managed to spend some quiet moments, many of them on the bank of a stream beside the inn. Near the bank was an iron spit, anchored at the stream's side, extending out over the flowing water. Fixed on the spit was an empty barrel and farther out a wooden paddle which the water turned rapidly as it rushed by. When the barrel was filled with clothes and soapy water it became the Alpine inn's washing machine. As he reclined and gazed at this home-made appliance – almost hypnotized by its motion – he recalled the moments of his near deadly fall.

> I was perfectly conscious of what was happening, and felt each blow, but, like a patient under chloroform, experienced no pain. Each blow was...more severe than [the one before], and I distinctly remember thinking, "Well, if the next is harder still, that will be the end!"...[A] multitude of [thoughts] rushed through my head, many of them trivialities or absurdities, which had been forgotten long before....[M]ore remarkable, this bounding through space did not feel disagreeable. But I think [I was about to lose] consciousness as well as sensation....[This makes me believe], improbable as it seems, that death from a fall by a great height is as painless an end as can be expected.[29]

In another reflective moment he vowed "that if an Englishman should fall sick in the Val Tournanche he should not feel so solitary as I did at that dreary time."[30] As fate would have it, events would call upon him to honor that vow at a critical moment in his climbing career two years later.

News of the accident brought Carrel to Breuil to see Whymper's condition for himself. With him was his cousin Caesar. Though the description of the fallen climber's wounds makes it difficult to see how he could mend so swiftly, Whymper engaged both of them, along with his favorite porter Luc Meynet, for what would be his fourth attempt on the Matterhorn that summer. Taking advantage of good weather they set out on the morning of July 23rd, only three full days after Whymper's fall. They reached the tent platform without incident, spent the night there and climbed to the Great Tower the next morning again with no

*I slipped and fell*

trouble. After negotiating the right side of the Tower ridge, as Whymper alone had done a few days earlier, they began scaling the loose rocks above and reached the point at which Whymper had turned back on his last attempt.

Suddenly, in a matter of minutes, the bright blue sky above them grew overcast. The temperature fell, mists formed out of nowhere, and in a few more minutes snow began to come down heavily. Reluctant to move about on this dangerous terrain they stayed put for several hours, unable to go forward and unwilling to retreat. But nothing changed and in time they retreated cautiously to the base of the Tower and there made another platform for their tent which Meynet still carried. With the snow continuing Carrel argued that the mountain would soon be glazed with ice and thus become inaccessible. Whymper countered that the rocks were still warm from the long period of sunshine before the storm and that the weather might abate shortly and allow them to continue. Carrel was insistent, however, that the mountain was unsafe so they headed back. Below the col they saw that the snow-cloud which had enveloped them was limited to the mountain's top 3,000 feet, leaving the lower slopes in brilliant sunshine. He had asked Carrel to spend one more night on the mountain and now felt cheated, checked again by an isolated storm and an obstinate guide. Back in Breuil he resembled an injured animal licking his recent wounds and nursing his deflated ambition.

Carrel may have been right. Whymper knew as well as anyone that the Matterhorn's weather was temperamental and unpredictable. But he was so aggressive in his pursuit that he hated to retreat when there shone even a small ray of hope of reaching the mountain's virgin summit. July was fading. He had failed on four attempts, frustrated each time by forces beyond his control. His mixed feelings about Carrel – begun at their first meeting and now at a high pitch – brought forth an unusually intense soliloquy.

Carrel [was a]...haughty chasseur... not an easy man to manage....He was equally conscious that he was indispensable to me, and took no pains to conceal his knowledge of the fact....[H]e was the only first-rate climber I could find who believed that the mountain was not inaccessible. With him I had hopes, but without him none; so he was allowed to do as he would.

His will on this [last] occasion was almost incomprehensible. He certainly could not be charged with cowardice, for a bolder man could hardly be found....There was no occasion to come down for want of food, for we had taken...enough to last for a week. [A]nd there was no danger...in stopping in the tent. It seemed to me that he was spinning out the ascent for his own purposes, and that although he wished very much to be the first man to the top, and did not object to be accompanied by anyone else who had the same wish, he had no intention of letting one succeed too soon – perhaps to give a greater appearance of éclat when the thing was accomplished. As he feared no rival, he may have supposed that the more difficulties he made the more valuable he would be estimated; though, to do him justice, he never showed any great hunger for money....[31]

This analysis did not change anything else Whymper wrote or said about Carrel. "Carrel was the finest rock climber I have ever seen. He was the only man who consistently refused to accept defeat, and who continued to believe, in spite of all discouragements, that the great mountain...could be ascended from the side of his native valley."[32]

Ever the aggressor, Whymper immediately made preparations for his fifth climb on the mountain that summer. Carrel had again agreed to be his guide. His plan was to take the tent from its platform at the Chimney and move it to a new campsite at the foot of the Tower. They would then mount the high ridge and affix ropes in some of the difficult places above the Tower, spend the night in the tent and attack the summit the next day. It was a good plan; Whymper's spirits again were high. But intractable fate, this time in the enigmatic personality of the Italian bersagliere, again intervened. The next morning "good little Meynet was ready and waiting" but Carrel was nowhere in sight.[33] According to Meynet, Jean-Antoine and Caesar had decided to go marmot hunting, just like that, without notice or explanation.

Whymper must have been boiling; without Carrel he felt he had no hope of reaching the summit. Determined, however, to spend the last of his summer days on the Matterhorn, he decided to climb with Meynet alone and get as far as he could. The two left together at the appointed time and soon stood on the Col du Lion. This was Meynet's first opportunity to see the lovely view from the col on a clear day. "The poor little deformed peasant gazed upon it silently and reverently for a time, and then, unconsciously, fell on one knee in an attitude of adoration, and clasped his hands, exclaiming in ecstasy, 'Oh, beautiful mountains!' His actions were as appropriate as his words were natural, and tears bore witness to the reality of his emotion."[34] Whymper was obviously moved by this sight but gave no sign of wishing he could occasionally be as open and demonstrative as his peasant companion.

On the col with Meynet his thoughts turned quickly again to the business at hand.

Moving easily upward they reached the first tent platform at about 12,550 feet in mid-afternoon. Since the two of them alone could not take the tent higher, Whymper decided to spend the night there. In good weather the next morning they were able to climb beyond the point Whymper had reached two days earlier with Carrel. Continuing they passed the spot at some 13,400 feet where Whymper had stopped on his solo climb. They struggled a few feet higher, but found the rocks difficult and treacherous, the ridge extremely unstable. It was clear to Whymper this time that prudence dictated a retreat: the way ahead was simply too difficult without at least one strong guide on his rope. Still, Whymper was not for a moment discouraged or deterred from his objective. As he thought things over on the descent, he decided to have a ladder made in Breuil that would be useful on some of the Matterhorn's steepest slopes above 13,000 feet. He also believed that when they arrived back in Breuil "Carrel would have had enough marmot-hunting and would deign to accompany us again."[35]

Whymper and Meynet were a unique twosome, perhaps the oddest pair ever to climb in the high Alps. Whymper was a middle-class, unsociable Englishman of uncommon strength, iron will and great ambition. Meynet was a misshapen, uneducated, Italian peasant whose spirit radiated cheerfulness, loyalty and humility. Whymper challenged the mountains for personal satisfaction; Meynet loved them for their own sake. They shared, however, a common courage and mutual respect. Whymper's trust gave the hunchback pride in himself; Meynet's unassuming ways and gentle nature gave Whymper opportunities for new insights into his own character. As they went toward Breuil that late July afternoon Whymper reflected on how well his porter had performed on the mountain's dangerous precipices earlier that day. "Meynet was always merriest on the difficult parts" where he kept saying 'We can only die once,' a thought which seemed to afford him infinite satisfaction."[36]

On his return to the inn Whymper learned to his dismay that Professor Tyndall had arrived in Breuil with two guides and was starting for the Matterhorn the next morning. Tyndall had prepared thoroughly for his second attempt on its imposing slopes. His guides were respected professionals Johann J. Bennen, Tyndall's favorite, and a Valaisan named Anton Walter. Porters would carry provisions enough for several days plus equipment that included a ladder for scaling difficult cliffs just as Whymper had planned for his next try. The most shocking news of all was that Tyndall had retained Carrel and his cousin Caesar for additional support. Uncustomarily flustered, Whymper now doubted he would have another chance.

Whether or not it suited Whymper, the decision by Tyndall and Carrel to join forces made perfect sense. Tyndall had no doubt learned of Carrel's reputation as the best guide on the Matterhorn's Italian side. Carrel knew the mountain better that Bennen or Walter. Hiring him would increase Tyndall's chance of success and undercut Whymper's ability to mount a simultaneous challenge. Without Carrel, Whymper might just as well twiddle his thumbs in Breuil. Carrel himself had much to gain and little to lose by joining Tyndall's party. If they succeeded, the bersagliere would be part of the first group to ascend the mountain, thereby bringing glory and pride to his fellow Italians. Given his reputation for knowing the Matterhorn better than anyone else, Carrel would get much credit for Tyndall's accomplishment. If Tyndall failed, Carrel would lose nothing because Bennen was the party's titular head. Whymper could only watch in anguish as the large party departed. "Everything seemed to favour [Tyndall], and they set out on a fine morning in high spirits, leaving me tormented with envy and all uncharitableness."[37]

Soon after the departure of Tyndall's entourage Whymper decided he had better get packing as he was due in London in a few days. But he could not tear himself away. He thought of some articles in his tent, still on the mountain, convinced himself that they were "necessaries," and set off to get them. He overtook "the Professor's army" as its members halted below the Col du Lion to have a meal, and continued on to his tent platform to await them. When they arrived he offered to leave the tent for their use and Tyndall accepted. Whymper then departed with his other items and returned to Breuil where he spent the night. The next morning, his knapsack packed, he again temporized. He and the inn's other guests saw what appeared to be a flag on a small peak about 800 feet below the summit that could have been left only by Tyndall's party. Whymper's heart sank. The pinnacle on which the flag now flew was the highest point anyone had yet reached. He had always felt, and Carrel had agreed, that the hardest part of the climb lay just before coming to that point and that "if it could be passed, success was certain."[38] Favre was "jubilant" at the prospect of the increased business a Matterhorn ascent would bring to his inn. Whymper joined him in a parting glass of wine – sweet as nectar to one, sour as vinegar to the other. Yet still he lingered, held captive in the tension of the moment.

\* \* \* \*

John Tyndall was one of the few early climbers with the courage to dare the Matterhorn. He was more experienced and twenty years older than his younger opponent. He was fresh from an impressive first ascent of the Weisshorn. With four guides, several porters and all the necessary equipment, he was now within reach of the mountaineering world's most prized summit. What Whymper would have given to have been with him! Instead, he languished at the Breuil inn, still scarred and bruised from his recent fall. But in this drama of man against mountain, the tortuous plot was just beginning to thicken.

# CHAPTER 8

## *The Professor and the Matterhorn*

In 1860 only two or three English climbers were eyeing the Matterhorn as a possible target. Professor John Tyndall was the boldest of these and would become Whymper's chief British competitor in the effort to reach the impossible mountain's summit. He would also be the source of a major dispute with his rival over why they did not join forces – when the opportunity presented itself in 1862 – and climb the mountain together.

Tyndall's first exposure to mountains was on a walking tour of the western Alps in 1849. Born in 1820, he was getting a relatively late start. As one of London's leading natural scientists he returned to the mountains in the next few summers to conduct experiments. During longer visits in 1854 and 1856, stirred by thoughts of Alpine conquest, he became a serious mountaineer. Wills, Hudson, Stephen and Whymper had all taken to the slopes in their early to mid-twenties. But by using his wiry strength and natural athletic ability to the fullest, Tyndall stayed in the front rank of British mountaineers. In 1860, drawn by the challenge of the "invincible" mountain, the 40-year old would be the first British climber to attempt the Matterhorn's summit from the Italian side.[1]

\* \* \* \*

Tyndall was born into a family of modest means in the small town of Leighlin Bridge, Ireland. In 1847, well-educated and with experience as a science teacher, the youthful professor joined the faculty of Queenwood College, a newly formed school near Stockbridge, England. After one year, too ambitious to continue teaching without an advanced degree,

*Portrait of John Tyndall*

Tyndall used all his savings to attend the University of Marburg in Germany. Graduating in 1850 with a Ph.D. degree in mathematics he returned to London and rose rapidly in the academic community.[2] In 1852 he was made a Fellow of the Royal Society, London's most prestigious group of scientists. By the mid-1850s he was a respected physicist known for developing original theories of heat transmission and magnetism. His study of suspended particles in liquids and gasses led him to become the first person to explain why the sky was blue. He wrote numerous articles and papers, lectured at London's Royal Institute, and for his work earned a medal from his colleagues in the Royal Society.

Had he lived a century later John Tyndall would have been called an egghead. In 1855, at thirty-five, he looked the part of an eccentric intellectual. His head was a large oval, often crowned with a Lincolnesque top hat. His long face was accentuated with a beard known as a "Newgate fringe." Not thick enough to be sideburns, this narrow band of whiskers came down both sides of his head to the back corners of his jawbones and then swept forward to meet under his chin. With his face and chin clean-shaven, the fringe magnified their length. He was thin and of medium height, with disproportionately large hands. Incongruously, he retained into his middle years the strength and muscular coordination of a good athlete.

Tyndall's behavioral quirks matched his appearance. Due to a low food intake, little sleep, and a dyspeptic constitution, he vibrated with nervous energy. He had an argumentative disposition, a ready sensitivity to criticism, and a volatile temper. He enjoyed intellectual infighting as in his notorious dispute with James Forbes, an implacable Scotsman, regarding who had first characterized glaciers as "plastic" and whose theory better explained glacial movement. Tyndall fought with enthusiasm. His lifelong friend Thomas A. Hirst described him as "a terribly rough and unconquerable antagonist....[H]e enjoys an intellectual fence for its own sake, and I am not sure that his...dexterity in inflicting sharp lashes is not a source of amusement to him."[3] In other words Tyndall was tough-minded and determined in his many endeavors.

Tyndall first attempted the Matterhorn in August of 1860. Then forty years old, with much of his youthful vitality still evident, he was eager to challenge the Alps' most threatening peak – or as he put it, lay "siege to the noblest fortress" of them all.[4] For this first attempt he teamed up with a fellow Alpine Club member, Vaughan Hawkins. Hawkins had examined the Matterhorn the previous summer with a Swiss guide people were beginning to talk about, Joseph J. Bennen. This survey had whetted Hawkins's appetite for an attempt on the Matterhorn as well as his appreciation of Bennen's skills. He passed along to Tyndall his enthusiasm for both man and mountain.

In Hawkins's eyes, the German-speaking Bennen was the perfect leader for the dangerous Matterhorn assault. Hawkins grouped him with the best Swiss guides of the day – Melchior Anderegg, Christian Almer, the Lauener brothers, and Peter Bohren – but put him first among them for his "combination of boldness and prudence," and his "peculiar power" to conceive and plan a mountain assault.[5] On the personal side, said Hawkins, Bennen was pious, cheerful, and a good storyteller without "a particle of mountain gloom."[6] Though these traits made him an ideal climbing companion in the eyes of his two English employers, later events would tell a somewhat different story.

This threesome arrived at Breuil on August 18th, 1860, a Saturday. There Tyndall looked for a local guide and porter to supplement his party, intending to start up the mountain the following Monday morning. On the recommendation of Monsieur Favre they met with Jean-Jacques Carrel,

Jean-Antoine's uncle, whom Hawkins described as a "shaggy, rough-breasted ...peasant," much older than he expected. [7] Whymper had brashly called the uncle an "evil countenance," and later on the mountain Bennen would say about the elder Carrel, "er weiss gar nichts," he knows nothing. [8] However, needing someone in their party with Matterhorn experience, they hired Jean-Jacques despite reservations about his climbing skills.

On Monday morning, August 20th, J. J. Carrel led Tyndall's party by lantern from the hotel into the pre-dawn darkness. By 5:00 a.m., as they began crossing the Glacier du Lion, Bennen was brought forward to take the lead. Without incident they arrived at the Chimney, its steep rock shaft coated that morning with black ice, "whose bottom leads out into space" and whose top is somewhere in the "upper regions." It looked impassable to Hawkins but Bennen "roll[ed] up it somehow, like a cat," followed by the wiry Tyndall who also mounted unassisted. Hawkins and J. J. Carrel needed help on the rope from the other two. The party then scrambled up another icy slope to a spot from which they could see "a line of towers and crags [rising] to a point just below the actual top." Looking for a route off the steep ridge, Bennen "peered wistfully about, exactly like a chamois," but found no alternative path. Struggling upward another two or three hundred feet they came to the Great Tower – a "mighty knob, huger and uglier than its fellows" – at which point Hawkins decided that he had had enough. Tyndall and Bennen, not ready to quit, left the others and continued upwards. Hawkins could hear them for a while, making "prodigious efforts, scrambling...among the huge blocks." [9]

Above the tower the going was difficult. They had to inch upward, one of them moving at a time only when the other was firmly anchored. All around them were huge masses of rock, wild looking "black eminences like tremendous castles in the air."[10] Standing before one of them Bennen paused and asked whether they should keep going. "Where you go I follow," replied Tyndall.[11] On reaching a ledge half-way up this ominous crag they paused to scan the heights in front of them. After a moment of silence Bennen said somberly, "Ich denke die Zeit ist zu kurz," I think the time is too short.[12] He feared that unless they retreated now, darkness would find them still high on the mountain, unprotected from the elements. With that, having climbed to 13,000 feet, they reluctantly turned downward, rejoined their party and returned to Breuil as darkness

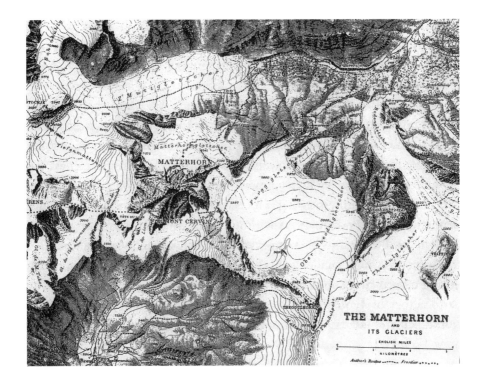

*The Matterhorn and its Glaciers*

fell. Though they stopped some 1,800 feet below the mountain's summit, they had gone higher on the Matterhorn than anyone before them.

This had been the first attempt on the Matterhorn's Italian side by English climbers. Though it had ended in failure, the experience had infused Tyndall with new confidence. Throughout the climb he had been the most aggressive and ebullient member of the party. "Splendid practice for us," he had said more than once, "splendid."[13] In addition to showing Tyndall's spirit, this first foray highlighted the relatively primitive state of early Alpine climbing. On what was perceived as the Alps' most difficult climb these English amateurs had hired only one professional guide, Bennen, who was as new to the mountain as they. J. J. Carrel knew the Matterhorn better but he relied more on strength than climbing skill. And without the valuable tool of a common language, good communication between these two men was lacking. These deficiencies seriously compromised their ability to perform a guide's basic responsibilities – to choose the best routes, avoid danger points, and strike a balance between the aggressive pursuit of a summit and the avoidance of foolhardy risks.

The guides of the day were for the most part still learning their trade. At one point on their ascent Bennen had accepted Tyndall's choice of an upward route over rocks, abandoning his own recommendation that the party go forward on an adjacent snow slope. This tentativeness on Bennen's part was hardly in keeping with his leadership role. In differences with their clients professional guides usually prevailed, but in this instance Bennen apparently acquiesced without a murmur. Also puzzling is why Tyndall and Hawkins – who viewed their guide with unqualified admiration – would challenge his initial decision. Such were the moments during climbs that could determine victory or defeat, life or death. The personalities of Tyndall and Bennen, and the interaction between them, would become increasingly important to the careers and achievements of them both.

\* \* \* \*

Tyndall came again to Switzerland on August 1st of the following year, 1861, just as the young Whymper was approaching the Dauphiné Alps to attempt his first major summit, Mont Pelvoux. Again the professor was with his "faithful and favourite guide, Johann Bennen."[14] Together they scaled the Weisshorn, a massive peak equal in height to the Matterhorn and, except for the "impossible mountain" itself, as arduous a climb as any the Alps had to offer. The ascent of this mountain's steep gullies, razor-edged ridges and sheer icy cliffs had taken nineteen and a half hours. That Tyndall was the first Englishman to reach the Weisshorn's formidable summit added exhilaration to his feat. In so doing the temperamental scholar proved to himself and his fellow Alpine Club members that he had the Victorian version of the right stuff. The Weisshorn conquest also heated his desire to add the Matterhorn to his list of first ascents, his next goal and the intended capstone of his Alpine career.

On August 20th, 1861, the day after his great Weisshorn victory,

Tyndall set out for Zermatt in the midst of a torrential rainstorm "arm-in-arm" with Bennen, both sheltered under a large umbrella.[15] No doubt this was the professor's way of showing that the Weisshorn's conquerors were ecstatic.

From Zermatt Tyndall sent Bennen ahead to Breuil on a mission to "reconnoiter" the Matterhorn. When Tyndall arrived in the Italian village around noon two days later he learned that his guide was on the great mountain, still scouting its terrain. As he awaited Bennen's return Tyndall's hopes were high. A year ago he had climbed to 13,000 feet on the Matterhorn's Italian side, a record that still stood. The Weisshorn experience had boosted his confidence and also strengthened his faith in Bennen's skill. Later that afternoon he caught sight of his guide coming down the hillside and strode rapidly out to meet him. As they came closer Tyndall searched Bennen's eyes for a hint of his thoughts but saw only a steady gaze that conveyed nothing. At length Bennen spoke:

> "Herr," [Bennen] said…in a tone of unusual emphasis, "I have examined the mountain carefully, and find it more difficult and dangerous than I had imagined. There is no place upon it where we could well pass the night. We might do so on yonder col upon the snow, but there we should be almost frozen to death, and totally unfit for the work of the next day. On the rocks, there is no ledge or cranny which could give us proper harbour; and starting from Breuil it is certainly impossible to reach the summit in a single day.'" [16]

Taken aback Tyndall urgently tried to salvage something from the wreckage of his plans. Could they at least attempt to reach the smaller peak near the mountain's summit? "Even that is difficult," Bennen replied, "but when you have reached it, what then? The peak has neither name nor fame."[17] This exchange left Tyndall painfully torn between two powerful and opposite forces: he desperately wanted the Matterhorn prize but the need to trust and respect his guide was also instilled deeply within him. He ground his boots into the grass in frustration and struggled with the decision which he knew was his to make. Had he overruled his guide, he felt certain, Bennen would have shrugged his shoulders and led the climb in dutiful service to his employer. Finally, he chose to honor his guide's judgment and postpone any further attempt on the Matterhorn to a later date.

That night Tyndall slept little and awoke the next morning feeling empty and disoriented, like a monk whose faith in God had suddenly been shaken. To his way of thinking, however, the only restorative tonic was further mountain exercise, so he and Bennen left Breuil and returned to Zermatt. They spent the few days left to them in the Alps that summer hunting chamois and climbing in the area around the Monte Rosa, and then headed home. The diversion of those days, followed by a productive year at home in London, revived Tyndall's spirits. As he made preparations to return to the Alps in 1862 his determination to claim the Matterhorn summit was stronger than ever.

* * * *

In the same year that Tyndall received Bennen's unexpected advice, Whymper had arrived at Breuil only nine days after the disappointed professor's departure. He and his inexperienced Swiss guide had then bivouacked on the snow-covered Col du Lion. Earlier that summer, with Macdonald, he had slept out on the side of Mont Pelvoux at 10,500 feet, almost the same elevation as the Col.[18] Though chilled to the bone on both occasions by strong winds and near freezing temperatures, Whymper had survived the exposure with no ill effects. Bennen, whose career had almost certainly included nights on a mountainside at that altitude, must have thought that the unusually heavy snowfall of 1861 would make a crucial difference – lowering evening temperatures on the col to the point where extra clothing and blankets would not provide adequate protection. Perhaps there was less snow on the heights when Whymper arrived or more, for that matter, but probably not enough difference to matter either way. Whymper's instincts were simply better than Bennen's and he had the self-confidence to follow them.

* * * *

Undeterred by the frustrations of that prior summer, Tyndall returned to Breuil with Bennen in 1862 intent on completing his unfinished business on the Matterhorn. Also in the party was Bennen's house-mate, a guide of extraordinary strength and stamina named Anton Walter. Tyndall seemed now to recognize that Bennen might welcome Anton's help and be "strengthen[ed], hand and heart, to have so tried a man beside him."[19] And this year Tyndall was all business. "There was nothing jubilant in our thoughts or conversation," he said, "the Matterhorn was our temple and we approached it with feelings not unworthy of so great a shrine."[20] He had planned an all-out effort to avoid surprise and to be prepared for anything the mountain might put in his path. The party was lavishly equipped with several new items: a stronger rope specially manufactured in London to withstand any strain it was likely to bear, a lightweight wooden ladder for assistance at crevasses and cliffs, and a number of long nails and a hammer. As a warm-up for the Matterhorn, Tyndall had spent three weeks climbing in the Bernese and Valaisian Alps. To further insure against failure he had hired two "porters" upon his arrival at Breuil: none other than Jean-Antoine Carrel and the bersagliere's younger cousin Caesar. This time Tyndall would attack the mountain with overwhelming force.

On the day Tyndall reached Breuil in 1862 Whymper was on the Matterhorn with Luc Meynet making his fifth attempt of the summer on the mountain's summit. By Whymper's calculation they reached an altitude of 13,460 feet before being forced to retreat, exceeding by some 400 feet the record set by Tyndall the preceding summer. On turning back he had planned to try again the very next day with the two Carrels as guides and Meynet as his porter. He was stunned to find this large and handsomely equipped party – "Tyndall's army," he called it – ready to attack the mountain in force on the same day *he* had planned to do so. Without the Carrels, his hopes were dashed. He had previously hired them, he felt certain, for the duration of his time that summer at Breuil. They had reneged on the first day of their engagement and gone marmot hunting. Now they had insulted him by joining his competition. He did not mention this to Tyndall, probably knowing it would have been futile to try to dissuade Carrel from his new commitment. It would also have cast him as a sore loser in Tyndall's eyes. Mustering his dignity and his better instincts, he offered the use of his tent to the professor's party.

While he might have been embarrassed not to do so – given Tyndall's seniority and his membership in the social tier to which the young climber aspired – it was nevertheless a sportsmanlike gesture. Tyndall felt that Whymper's offer was made "in the frankest spirit," and he accepted it gratefully as it would save his party one extra burden.[21]

So the question naturally arose whether Whymper would join Tyndall's party. Would the distinguished academic ask the bold youngster to accompany him, and if so would Whymper accept? This was indeed discussed, and both wrote later about it. Tyndall's explanation began with transparently exaggerated deference. "It certainly would have enhanced the pleasure of my excursion if Mr Whymper could have accompanied me. I admired his courage and devotion. He had manifestly set his heart upon the Matterhorn, and it was my earnest desire that he should not be disappointed." He then got down to the details:

> I consulted with Bennen who had heard many accounts – probably exaggerated ones – of Mr Whymper's rashness. He shook his head, but finally agreed that Mr Whymper should be invited 'provided he proved reasonable.' I thereupon asked Mr Whymper to join us. His reply was, 'If I go up the Matterhorn, I must lead the way.' Considering my own experience at the time as compared with his; considering, still more, the renown and power of my guide, I thought the response the reverse of reasonable, and so went on my way alone.[22]

Whymper's account of this exchange was quite different:

> An hour or so after he had accepted my offer (of the tent, etc.), he came to me and said (in a way which...seemed to imply that the answer might not be in the affirmative), "Mr Whymper, would you like to accompany us?" I replied warmly, "Certainly I should; it is the very thing I should like," or words to that effect. Dr. Tyndall then went on to say, "If you come with us, you must place yourself under Bennen's guidance; you must obey his instructions; you must follow his lead," and so forth. Now I was quite ready to place myself under Bennen; I would have done so

as a matter of course had I accompanied the party. But being called upon to declare that I would implicitly obey his instructions whether they were right or wrong, I could hardly avoid saying, "You will remember, Dr Tyndall, that I have been much higher than Bennen, and have been eleven days on the mountain, whil[e] he has been on it only for a single day. You will not expect me to follow him if he is evidently wrong?"...It was some time afterwards, half an hour or more, before Dr Tyndall came to me and said, "Well, after all, I think that you had better not accompany us."[23]

Both men had reputations to protect so each might have embellished the facts a little. Tyndall's account, however, has the opposite effect from the one intended. Its unctuous opening sentences send a warning, not a reassurance, of what he is about to say. His characterization of Whymper's demand to be the party's leader – without condition and above both Bennen and Carrel – rings hollow. Such a tactless proposal in these circumstances would have been uncharacteristic of any climber, even one so brash as Whymper. More likely Tyndall distorted Whymper's response to make it appear overreaching and easy for Tyndall to reject. Bennen was clearly the figure behind Tyndall's decision, and his proviso that Whymper must be "reasonable" – if indeed those were his words – must surely have been jarring to anyone with sensitivity to the situation. At that moment, Whymper had been on the Matterhorn more times than any other person, save perhaps Carrel, and had gone higher than anyone else. Moreover, Tyndall had acknowledged his gratitude for the loan of Whymper's tent and Whymper's generosity in making it. Tyndall's summary of their discussions seems embarrassingly inconsiderate and self-serving.

Whymper's account – though perhaps overstating Tyndall's demand for absolute subservience to Bennen – seems entirely characteristic of the man who wrote it: bold, self-confident and stubborn yet perfectly reasonable in the circumstances. It also fits with Tyndall's constant deference to Bennen's judgment and with the latter's paradoxical mixture of inspirational leadership offset by tentativeness in the clutch. Additionally, Whymper was desperate to be in the first group to scale the

Matterhorn and to have Carrel as his guide, so he would not have lightly dismissed Tyndall's offer. In any event, had Whymper joined Tyndall's party the history of the Matterhorn and Whymper's life itself might well have turned out quite differently.

At noon the next day, July 27th, Tyndall's party left the inn under Whymper's anxious gaze and headed up the mountain for the spot already chosen for the night's bivouac. They followed essentially the same route taken two years before and eventually reached the small area at the foot of the Great Tower where Whymper's tent awaited them. Well-situated in the Tower's shadow for protection against nighttime cannonades, this would also be their campsite. As darkness came on, fog rose toward them from the valley. By the time they retired its thick blanket enveloped them. Sharp peals rang intermittently from the heights followed by the roar of rocks tumbling down the adjacent couloir. It seemed to Tyndall as if the Matterhorn were disintegrating around them, which perhaps contributed to the party's being "astir" at 2:00 a.m. They got underway two hours later beneath a clear sky. Ironically their camp was well above the Col du Lion whose frigid terrain had intimidated Bennen the year before. Tyndall must still have been shaking his head over that piece of advice.

From the campsite they mounted the rocks of the mountain's southwest ridge. After some hard climbing they came to the base of "the conical summit seen from Breuil" which they could now see was not a peak.[24] It was only the edge of a foreshortened ridge running to the bottom of the Matterhorn's true summit. From there they could see the summit and felt it was truly within their grasp. "'In an hour,' cried Bennen, 'the people at Zermatt shall see our flag planted yonder.' Up we went in this spirit, [earlier failures] making our ascent a jubilee."[25] The entire party laughed excitedly at how close the final summit seemed. They scrambled to the top of the false summit and thereupon planted a flag which the people at Breuil saw through their telescopes and applauded in the mistaken belief it marked the success of Tyndall's mission.

As they started toward the true peak, the Matterhorn revealed its final surprise: the ridge leading to the precipice below the actual summit turned out to be "hacked and extremely acute," with "ghastly abysses on either side" along which they could move only slowly and cautiously.[26]

They were now close enough to the final cliff at the base of the summit to see the mountaintop clearly without a telescope. Almost instantly, in awed tones of deep disappointment, "three out of the four men muttered almost simultaneously, 'It is impossible.' "[27] Tyndall did not identify the speakers except to say that Bennen alone remained silent, so he must have meant Walter and the two Carrels although the image of Jean-Antoine doing so is unimaginable. More likely he too stood mute. The party nevertheless went forward to a point where they could see a "deep cleft" separating the ridge on which they stood from the final rock wall. As Tyndall described it:

> So savage a spot I had never seen, and I sat down upon it with the sickness of disappointed hope. The summit was within almost a stone's throw of us, and the thought of retreat was bitter in the extreme.[28]

Bennen pointed to a forward track he thought dangerous but not impossible and sought Tyndall's view on whether they should proceed. Sticking to his unshakeable belief that the professional guide should have the last word in a critical situation, Tyndall put the burden of decision on Bennen who reluctantly concluded that they should turn back. Tyndall felt Bennen had no choice. "[T]he other men had yielded utterly...[so] what could he do?"[29] Dejectedly they cut off a six-foot section of the ladder so laboriously brought to this point, leaving it to mark the high point of their progress. Returning to the steep cliff they had scaled that morning they anchored what remained of the ladder at the top, with their special rope attached. Upon descending farther to the base of the Great Tower, and as they were collecting their gear for the return, the mountain unleashed its final insult.

> A tempest of hail was...hurled against us, as if the Matterhorn, not content with shutting its door in our faces, meant to add to the process of kicking us downstairs. The ice pellets...hit us as bitterly as if they had been thrown in spite, and in the midst of this malicious cannonade we struck our tents and returned to Breuil."[30]

Tyndall's narrative of the 1862 climb in *Hours Of Exercise* ended abruptly at that point with no mention of his meeting with Whymper on the party's return to the Breuil inn. His description of the climb, published in the August 8th, 1863 issue of the *Saturday Review,* was also silent on their meeting. For Tyndall, the less said about this disheartening moment the better. This left Whymper, who had remained at the inn until the dejected party's return, to offer the last words on the subject:

> There was no spring in their steps – they, too, were defeated. The Carrels hid their heads, and the others said, as men will do when they have been beaten, that the mountain was horrible, impossible, and so forth. Professor Tyndall told me they had arrived within a stone's throw of the summit, and admonished me to have nothing more to do with the mountain. I...ran down to the village of Valtournanche, almost inclined to believe that the mountain was inaccessible....[I] le[ft] the tent, ropes, and other matters in the hands of Favre, to be placed at the disposal of any person who wished to ascend it, more, I am afraid, out of irony than for generosity. There may have been those who believed that the Matterhorn could be ascended, but, anyhow, their faith did not bring forth works. No one tried again in 1862.[31]

Tyndall's consolation prize for his last Matterhorn attempt was the assignment of his name to the "false peak" at almost 14,000 feet, now the highest point anyone had attained. It was there that his party had planted the flag which had led onlookers in Breuil to think that the true summit had been scaled. Since then the lower peak has been known as the "Pic Tyndall," a lasting tribute to the man who came so close.

\* \* \* \*

By the spring of 1863 – through Tyndall's description of his Matterhorn climb in the *Saturday Review* and possibly in correspondence with Carrel – Whymper had learned more about the circumstances of

Tyndall's retreat of the preceding summer. He was well aware of the ravine or notch, immediately below the mountain's true summit, which Tyndall described as blocking further progress. He and Carrel had often surveyed the upper part of the mountain with their telescopes. It lay at the northern end of the ridge – or "Shoulder" as the ridge was called – connecting the newly-named "Pic Tyndall" to the base of the mountain's final peak. Standing some 800 feet below the summit, Tyndall was not, as he thought at the time, a mere stone's throw away from victory.

Carrel and Whymper had frequently discussed the best route to use if they ever reached the Pic Tyndall and the shoulder behind it. Rather than proceeding along this ridge to the point where it overlooked the notch at the base of the Matterhorn's true peak, they decided that climbers should descend immediately, left or right, then proceed along the base of the ridge until reaching the bottom of the ravine. From there, they believed, climbers could move across the notch, scale its far side to a narrow ledge, and then climb to the mountain's true summit.

Carrel had told Whymper – probably when they met again in Breuil in the summer of 1863 – that Tyndall had been defeated simply because Walter, Tyndall's second guide, would not support Bennen, who was willing to go forward at the crucial moment of decision. At that moment, Carrel, refusing to be drawn into the debate about whether to continue or turn back, had given no hint to Tyndall of the plan he and Whymper had formulated for crossing the notch. He had been hired only as a porter and, more to the point, Carrel wanted to be the first on the Matterhorn summit. It stood to reason that had he been the Tyndall party's chief guide he might well have led them to the top. Indeed, events of the next three years showed it highly likely that Carrel *could* have done that. Whether he *would* have done so for an Englishman, who can say? What is known is that the ravine was eventually passed, by Carrel himself and one other, and the summit attained from the Italian side just as he and Whymper had predicted.

The events of the summer of 1862 gave considerable insight into the character of John Tyndall, scholar and mountaineer. His priorities and outlook were different from those of his younger countryman. Whymper's obsession was to climb, climb, climb. Professor Tyndall was not so possessed: he was more deferential to guides, more philosophical in nature, and less aggressive in his pursuit of Alpine peaks. Years later, Tyndall made a revealing statement, something Whymper would never have said: "Much as I enjoy the work [of climbing], I do not think that I could have filled my days and nights in the Alps with clambering alone. The climbing in many cases was the peg on which a thousand 'exercises' were hung."[32] Perhaps with that remark in mind Whymper said in *Scrambles* after describing Tyndall's defeat: "Tyndall...now disappear[s] from this history."[33]

# CHAPTER 9

## *Intermezzo*

The Alpine Club elected Whymper to its membership following his first Alpine climbing season in 1861. The Club had been organized only four years earlier, in September of 1857, at the home of William Mathews. At a dinner given for three relatives and a friend, Mathews had proposed the formation of a club for climbers who would "dine together once a year...and give each other what information they could" about their Alpine adventures.[1] All agreed and each contacted prospective members. Within three months twenty men had expressed interest in the idea. Eleven of those came to the Club's inaugural meeting held on December 22nd, 1857 at Ashley's Hotel in Covent Garden. A proposed rule to limit membership to those who had climbed a peak of 13,000 feet or more was promptly rejected. The founders well understood that a climber's performance was measured by the difficulty of an ascent and not necessarily by its height. The meeting also abandoned the idea of a yearly dinner in favor of monthly meetings to hear talks and lectures on mountain exploration and related subjects.

At a subsequent meeting the members decided to name the new organization simply the Alpine Club with no geographic or other identification. And why not? This was England, after all, whose countrymen were setting the pace in the Alps just as they had spread British influence to the far corners of the world. Their decision also had a recent precedent: when the first "world's fair" opened in London in 1851 – a huge exhibition of Britain's industrial and technological prowess – it was called simply the Great Exhibition.[3] Both the Alpine Club and The Great Exhibition were the first of their kind, and those who came later could distinguish themselves and their organizations however they might wish.

By the time Whymper joined its ranks the Club had grown to over 150 members who could now be admitted for "literary contributions or mountain exploits."[3] With this expansion it had gained wider recognition and a greater variety of occupations among its members but had not lost its spirit of convivial good fellowship. Ellis Hardman, a diarist and writer known as the "Victorian Pepys," captured this feeling in a vignette of after-dinner camaraderie at one Club gathering.

[There was] a jolly party round William Longman, the publisher...[with] Anthony Trollope sitting next to him. Longman is a glorious fellow, full of jokes and story, and beaming with good humour....Trollope is also a good fellow...with a large black beard...[Assuming the character of Silenus, a woodland deity sometimes depicted as a hearty drunkard] Trollope...made a funny speech, assuring the Club that he was most desirous of becoming a member [but that] both time and flesh were against him. He added that not very long since, in the city of Washington, a member of the U. S. Government [had]asked him if it were true that a club of Englishmen existed who held their meetings on the summits of the Alps. "In my anxiety," he said, "to support the credit of my country, I have transgressed the strict limits of veracity, but I told him what he heard was quite true." (Great cheers)[4]

By its sixth birthday in 1863 the Alpine Club had 281 members in a variety of occupations – from lawyers, academics and clergymen to merchants and civil servants.[5] This was welcome company for Whymper who found time to serve terms as a Vice-President and as a member of the Executive Committee a few years later.

In the winter of 1863 Whymper read a paper to the Alpine Club on the latest types of climbing and camping equipment, including those of his own creation. His basic theme was that well-equipped, well-rested and well-fed climbers were better able to avoid danger and climb higher. Rather dull going it might seem, but Whymper's promotion of new devices for greater safety and proficiency was a novel concept for Club members. Some resisted the use of man-made accessories as contrary to the tradition of true sportsmanship. To them mountaineering was the individual testing himself against the forces of nature, not competition among artifice-aided peak-baggers seeking to outdo each other. In their eyes Whymper's whirlwind pace and relentless pursuit of first ascents violated this precept. Moreover, they felt, it showed a boorish unconcern for the natural beauty of the Alps and their power to enrich the human soul.

Whymper's approach to this new sport had a modern look. Though he was the prototype of the self-taught amateur, his attitude was closer to the outlook of today's professional athlete. His fierce inclination was to be the best and he aggressively used every means legitimately available to him in the process. He was a forerunner, it might be said, of Coach Vince Lombardi's belief that "winning isn't everything, it's the only thing." Not surprisingly Whymper's stance came from a man barely able to claim middle class status and unaccustomed to the more privileged circumstances of many of his fellow Club members. Whatever these other Club members might think of his attitude they could not fault his credentials or his presentation. He spoke from experience with the conviction of one who had learned the lessons it taught.

Practicing what he preached he upgraded his own set of tools during that winter in London. Included were coils of rope, strong but light enough to be carried by a climber on steep terrain. His most prized device was a wooden ladder of his own design: two twelve foot segments joined end-to-end like those used by firemen which could be brought close together in the manner of parallel rulers. With these – along with his grapnel, iron rings and trusty tent – Whymper boarded a steamer bound for France on July 29th, 1863.

The first task of foreign tourists landing in France was to pass through customs. For Whymper it was an annual ordeal, a "purgatory of travellers where uncongenial spirits mingle together for a time, before they are separated into rich and poor."[6] His observations had the ring of first-hand knowledge:

> The douaniers look upon tourists as their natural enemies. See how eagerly they pounce upon the portmanteau! One of them has discovered something! He has never seen its like before, and

he holds it aloft in the face of its owner with inquisitorial insolence. "But what is this?" The explanation is only half-satisfactory, so he says, "But what is this," laying hold of a little box. "Powder." "But ...it is forbidden to carry...powder on the railway." "Bah!" says...an older hand, "pass the effects of Monsieur."...Our countryman – whose cheeks have begun to redden under the stares of his fellow-travelers – is allowed to depart with his half-worn toothbrush [and toothpowder] while the mighty douanier gives a mighty shrug at the strange habits [of the British]."[7]

This year Whymper found the French customs officials particularly curious about the nature and purpose of his equipment. "Numerous tools were of suspicious appearance," with the ladder and rope receiving special attention for being "highly suggestive of housebreaking." But he had little difficulty gaining their admittance after the "timely expenditure of a few francs."[8] At the next border crossing – with the formation of the European Community another century away – Whymper's difficulties increased. At the Italian town of Susa, the *doganieres* "were more obtuse and more honest" than their French counterparts, an unwelcome combination indeed. They refused to be bribed or to accept his

*But what is this? (Douanier)*

explanation of the true purpose of his unusual equipment. He was at a loss to know how to proceed until one of the agents, "cleverer than his fellows," rescued him without urging or additional incentive. The new officer suggested

> …that I was going to Turin to exhibit in the streets; that I mounted the ladder and balanced myself on the end of it, then lighted my pipe and put the point of my bâton in its bowl, and caused the bâton to gyrate about my head. The rope was to keep back the spectators…."Monsieur is [an] acrobat, then?" "Yes, certainly." "Pass the effects of Monsieur the acrobat!"[9]

Whymper arrived at the Breuil inn late in the evening of July 31st after all the other guests were asleep. This year he had made prior arrangements with Jean-Antoine to be his guide for the duration of his stay in Breuil, deciding to give "the bold cragsman another chance" after Carrel's desertion the preceding summer. Despite this characterization of his motive, Whymper was not being generous. Like a cricket team coach, he was using his star athlete despite the latter's off-duty misbehavior. Whymper wanted to win and at that moment had no one else to turn to.

Weather played the spoiler throughout Whymper's 1863 season as rain began to fall heavily the next morning. Later, during a break in the clouds, he and Carrel took the opportunity to ascend a nearby "degraded mountain", the Cimes Blanches, for its panoramic view. The day became overcast once more while they were on the summit, but being in no hurry they made friends with some mountain goats who had suddenly appeared, by offering them salt. As the two men began their descent the goats followed, hoping for more of the spicy treat. The downward route, rocky to begin with, was made treacherous by these four-footed companions. As a "number of stones [loosened by the goats] whizzed by" Whymper said to Carrel that they should rid themselves of what had become annoying pests. In agreement Carrel muttered "Diable, it is well to talk, but how will you do it?" Whymper's wits, always about him in the mountains, solved the problem. He poured some brandy into his cupped palm and offered it to the nearest goat, an "enterprising character" who had previously eaten the salt's paper container as well as its contents.

The animal:

> advanced fearlessly and licked up the brandy. I shall not easily
> forget its surprise. It stopped short, and coughed, and looked at
> me as much to say "Oh, you cheat!" and spat and ran away,
> stopping now and then to cough and spit again. We were not
> troubled any more by those goats.[10]

Free of their friends who had become hecklers, Whymper and Carrel
went back to Breuil.More snow fell on the heights that night, indefinitely
postponing their Matterhorn plans. The next day Whymper decided to
take advantage of the delay by making a tour of the mountain, surveying
the eastern and northern sides in particular to see if different views
might suggest other approaches to the summit. They went first to
Zermatt where Whymper took a room in the Monte Rosa Hotel.
Alexander Seiler, his favorite innkeeper, again impressed the young
Englishman with the hallmark personal attention afforded the Monte
Rosa's guests. On the morning of the 4th of August, knowing Whymper
wanted to get an early start, Seiler himself knocked on his guest's door
in the predawn darkness. Whymper acknowledged the call but
immediately rolled over for a few extra winks. Hearing no movement,
Seiler asked Whymper if he had a light in his room. When Whymper
grunted "No," Seiler "forced the lock off his own [hotel's] door" and
brought him one.[11] Monsieur Seiler indeed knew how to earn and keep
the loyalty of his regular guests.

Whymper and Carrel left the Monte Rosa at 4:00 a. m. accompanied
once more by Luc Meynet as their porter. They headed west, walking
upstream along the banks of the swiftly flowing Mattbach and through
the beautiful valley leading to the Z'Mutt Glacier. From the glacier the
"stupendous cliffs" of the Matterhorn's north face loomed starkly above
them. Whymper saw stones breaking away near the summit and falling
1500 feet without touching anything, with a momentum carrying
some of them over 1000 feet from the mountain's base. From afar the
north side of the mountain seemed quiescent but up close – as they
were – its unending erosion and awesome proportions made a visceral
impression:

...[S]it down by the side of the Z'mutt Glacier and you will hear...the incessant, piecemeal destruction...of the [north face's cliffs]....The descending masses thunder as loudly as heavy guns, and the echoes roll back from the Ebihorn opposite....You will hear but probably...not see [them], for...they will...be as pinpoints against the grand old face, so vast is its scale.[12]

The Matterhorn Glacier's surface was pock-marked by fallen boulders buried beneath its crusted snow. Hugging the mountain's northern base above the Z'Mutt Glacier, the higher glacier made its own contribution to the cacophony of the mountain's continuous erosion. Huge pieces of packed snow regularly peeled off its snout with a "wild uproar onto the slopes below." [13] Sparse pine trees at the base of the Z'Mutt Glacier, stripped of bark by weather and whitened by the cold, contributed to the portrait of barren wilderness at the foot of the Matterhorn's steepest side. Whymper's first stop on his tour of the great mountain confirmed in his mind the fearsome reputation of its northern face.

The following day, August 7th, the party headed for the Valtournanche. On the way they took a good look at the Grand Tournalin, farther west. Having heard that bad weather still surrounded the Matterhorn, Whymper decided to attempt the Tournalin, a minor Italian peak but one providing good views by reason of its height and relative isolation among its neighbors. Best of all it had never been climbed and the thought of another virgin summit was tempting. Early the next morning he and Carrel set out for their selected target, this time leaving a disappointed Meynet behind. "Pay me nothing, only let me go with you. I shall want but a little bread and cheese, and I won't eat much!"[14] But Meynet was too slow for the veteran climbers who were determined to return by nightfall.

They ascended without difficulty to a col about two thousand feet below the Tournalin's summit. There they were joined by a large group of chamois playing "like two-legged tourists" scattering rocks down the mountainside and taking no notice of the climbers' presence. Suddenly Carrel – finding the chamois a nuisance or perhaps wanting to see them perform – emitted a hair-raising whoop, the *bersagliere's* version of a Confederate rebel yell. At that the chamois dispersed wildly, plunging downward in "unfaltering and unerring bounds with... speed and grace that filled us...with admiration...."[15]

From the col they mounted a ridge appearing to lead to the summit. At its end, however, a fifteen foot cleft separated them from the mountain's highest point. The near side of the split was almost perpendicular so Carrel first lowered Whymper to the bottom with his rope. Whymper then jammed his axe into the earthen and rock wall, above his head, which Carrel used as a step to descend to his employer's shoulders and from there to the ravine's floor. The young climber marveled at his guide's agility: Carrel had moved "with a cleverness that was almost as far removed from my awkwardness as his own efforts were from those of the chamois."[16] A few upward steps from the bottom of the notch led them to the true summit. There, enjoying a magnificent view of the Monte Rosa, they built a "huge" cairn to celebrate the Grand Tournalin's first ascent.

Whymper had no complaints about his six-day tour of the Matterhorn. Back at the Breuil inn on Sunday, August 9th, he put the finishing touches on what was to be his grandest assault on the Matterhorn to date. His equipment was the finest available and he would be led by the great Carrel, the best of the Italian guides. Carrel's cousin and three porters would complete the party, which was fully provisioned for several days on the mountain. Everything within their control had been thought of and done. The only thing they could not control was the weather and that, of course, was what started out so beautifully but finally forced them to turn back. Defeated by "that small cloud upon the mountain," as Monsieur Favre reported it, Whymper was deeply disappointed but already thinking about his next attack:

> I arrived at Châtillon at midnight on the 11th, defeated and disconsolate....[B]ut, like a gambler who loses each throw only the more eager to have another try – to see if the luck would change – [I] returned to London, ready to devise fresh combinations and to form new plans.[17]

Whymper's failure in 1863 helped to perpetuate the myth of the Matterhorn's invincibility. In so doing it probably deterred others from making their own attempts on the Alps' most elusive summit. His competitors were now aware of his determination and skill; he had become the Ahab of the Alps and the Matterhorn his Moby Dick. Some must have silently thought that if the great mountain could defy Whymper's seven attempts, perhaps they should try lesser virgin peaks on which he had not yet set foot. His own plans, and the various schemes of the Matterhorn's other challengers, would play out in the not too distant future. Through various coincidences of time and place their efforts would eventually meld into a dramatic story whose climax and tragic aftermath would in retrospect seem inevitable.

CHAPTER 10

## "Strength and Skill Seldom Surpassed"

In the fall of 1863 and the following spring Whymper planned the most extensive climbing campaign of his career. His targets included several virgin peaks and passes with an all-out attack on the Matterhorn as the season's finale. Heading the list of other summits was the Pointe des Ecrins – the Dauphiné's highest peak – which he had first seen from Mont Pelvoux in 1861 and vowed silently to scale it. Now, three years later, he was ready. The experience gained from his Matterhorn attempts had led him to believe two things: that he would ultimately conquer that "impossible mountain," and that he and Jean-Antoine Carrel might be the only team capable of doing so. In any event he would acclimatize to the Alps this coming summer on other mountains in preparation for the grand assault. And those warm-up climbs, if successful, would add to his already outstanding record.

During the autumn and winter in London he hired Michel Croz as his guide for the 1864 season. Born in 1830 at Le Tour, a village near Chamonix in the Mont Blanc Range, Croz was probably the most respected of the Savoyard guides. Auguste Balmat of Chamonix – the great-nephew of Jacques Balmat who had guided Dr. Michel Paccard on the first ascent of Mont Blanc in 1786 – had been more widely known but had died in 1862. Croz knew the Pointe des Ecrins, having surveyed the mountain with British climber F. F. Tuckett in 1862. Later that same summer he had led an unsuccessful attempt on its summit by two other English climbers, William Mathews and the Rev. T. G. Bonney, who recommended Croz highly. The guide's skill and character were unparalleled, Mathews said, adding that Croz was happy "only...when upwards of ten thousand feet..."[1] Writing later in *Scrambles* Whymper echoed his friend:

Of all the guides with whom I traveled, Michel Croz was the man who was most after my own heart. He did not work like a blunt razor, and take to his toil unkindly. He did not need urging, or to be told a second time to do anything....Such men are not common, and when they are known they are valued. Michel was not widely known, but those who did know him came again and again.[2]

In talking with other Alpine Club members Whymper discovered that A. W. Moore and Horace Walker were planning a summer campaign in the Dauphiné. The Pointe des Ecrins was also in their sights and the three decided to join forces. Moore and Walker had retained Christian Almer as their guide, a respected 38 year-old Grindelwalder well known for having gate-crashed Alfred Wills's party on the Wetterhorn ten years earlier with a green fir tree strapped to his back. Years later, at age 70, Almer would cap a distinguished guiding career with a final ascent of the Wetterhorn accompanied by his wife in celebration of their golden wedding anniversary. He and Croz, now at the peak of their careers, were a matched pair. Each respected the other for his skill and diligence on the mountainside. "The temper of Almer was impossible to ruffle; he was ever obliging and enduring – a bold but safe man. That which he lacked in fire – in dash – was supplied by Croz who, in his turn, was kept in place by Almer."[3] Their one weakness as a unit was that Almer spoke only German and Croz only French, but they communicated effectively with gestures, looks and their common knowledge of the key words of their trade.

Supported by two able guides the team of Whymper, Moore and Walker made a powerful party. They planned carefully but climbed boldly, and each knew how to improvise in unanticipated situations. In the spring of 1864 they met to plot routes to the peaks and passes they would attempt. They decided to avoid sleeping in inns, as far as practicable, by bivouacking at the highest point reached each afternoon. This would enable them to see a good portion of the ground they planned to cover the next day, a valuable assist in the poorly charted area of the Dauphiné. Whymper liked the plan for an additional reason: he "detested" the region's filthy, flea-ridden inns and their "abominable"

*Portrait of Christian Almer*

food, noting at one point that he was not surprised to learn that a Dauphiné native was the inventor of insecticide powder.

Though young and healthy – and easily able to withstand physical stress – Whymper often fumed over inconveniences he attributed solely to the sloth and backwardness of Alpine peasants. The sociological roots of their lifestyles were of no interest to him whatsoever. This superior air – with its assumption that less developed cultures necessarily reflected ethnic or racial inferiority – was widespread among the more refined Alpine climbers. But with feelings of *noblesse oblige* and a practical sense of humor, Victorian mountaineers were often able to appreciate Alpine natives' generosity and strength of character even in the Alps' most primitive area, the Dauphiné.

At 23, A. W. Moore was a few months younger than Whymper. After studying at Harrow he had become a civil servant in the ranks of the East India Company in 1858. He first saw the Alps a year later. Less aggressive than his companions he was more a follower than a leader, but a welcome climbing partner for his sense of humor and calm courage under stress. Moore and Whymper had crossed paths at Zermatt in 1862, just before

Moore, Leslie Stephen and others made the first crossing of the Jungfraujoch. Horace Walker, the other member of the group, was a good friend of Moore's and three years older. He came from a well-to-do family in Liverpool where his father, Francis, was a successful merchant. Frank, as the father was known, had begun his mountaineering career as a youth in 1825 with a climb from Zermatt to the top of the Théodule Pass, an easy ascent but one considered challenging for tourists in those early days. Members of the Walker family – Frank, Horace and Lucy, Horace's older sister by two years – were in Zermatt in 1858 when Lucy decided to join the men in a climb to the Col Théodule, a nostalgic trip for Frank enhanced by the presence of both of his children. Lucy Walker would become a pioneer of women's climbing whose career would include, in 1871, the first ascent of the Matterhorn by a woman. Horace had scaled the Jungfrau at age 22, and would climb several major peaks with his friend Moore in the years to come. With Whymper in the forthcoming summer of 1864, Moore and Walker would engage in some of the most perilous ascents of their careers.

The five man party – Whymper, Moore, Walker, Croz and Almer – assembled on the morning of June 20th, 1864 in the village of St. Michel de Maurienne about 25 miles east of Grenoble in the central part of the Dauphiné. Their first objective was a group of three peaks known as the Aiguilles d'Arves which came into view as they went south over the Col de Valloire and into the d'Arves Valley. Their only reference to the area was Joanne's *Itinéraire du Dauphiné*, an elementary guidebook with an old map prepared by Sardinian engineers before the region became part of France. Devoid of other aids, their scrambles during the next three days would be a comedy of errors today but at the time were a classic example of the seat-of-the-pants method by which early climbers and guides surveyed and eventually climbed the great Alps, testing and training themselves as they went.

After spending their first night in the barn of a chalet – a no smoking area by most owners' rules – the party started up the valley at 3:55 the next morning. After several hours they topped a Col at about ten thousand feet from which they could study the two principal Aiguilles. Concluding that neither was accessible they continued surveying the area. At the head of a great snow-slope Walker, against the advice of both guides who thought it too steep, decided to glissade to the bottom, hundreds of feet below. He placed the iron tip of his alpenstock in the snow behind him and leaned back so as to lighten the weight on his boot soles. With his balance maintained and his speed controlled by the skillful use of his alpenstock – at least in theory – he began to slide swiftly down the gully. After maneuvering successfully for some distance Walker slammed into several projecting rocks that sent his feet flying from under him. Out of control he cartwheeled furiously down the slope finally crashing in a heap at the bottom. After a few moments of anxious silence his companions heard him calling to reassure them that he was in one piece and wryly charging them "not to keep him waiting down there."[4] From there they descended to the village of La Saussaz where they spent the night.

They left before dawn the next morning, June 22nd, "under a shower of good wishes from [the chalet's] hostesses" and headed for their next destination, La Grave.[5] At 9:15 after a five-hour relatively easy climb they stood atop the westernmost of two unnamed peaks they called the Aiguilles de la Saussaz, their first ascent of the summer. Looking southward from there the party had a panoramic view of the Dauphiné Alps including the col between the high peak of the Meije and the Râteau, a smaller mountain immediately to its west. This was a "brèche," or gap, known by the natives as the Brèche de la Meije, its crest as yet untrodden.

Deciding to put off an attempt of the Brèche until the next day they spent that night at La Grave's inn. It was "a rickety, tumble-down sort of place" doubling as a stable for the horses of couriers on the Grenoble-Briançon road, with stalls located immediately below the inn's dining area and bed chambers. Moore's reaction to this arrangement was that "there was nothing stable about [the inn] except the smell."[6] They nevertheless ate and slept there, wanting to spend at least one night out of a cattle shed's hay.

Starting out early the next day at 2:40 a.m. they got lucky: the ominous northern side of the Brèche turned out to be easy. They were on top of the col at daybreak in high spirits from the unexpected ease of the ascent. Some of the La Grave villagers who had been openly skeptical of the climbers' ability to reach the gap where none had gone before,

*Glissading*

watched the ascent in the rays of the rising sun. The young mountaineers were exultant: facing the villagers, they "screamed triumphantly as [the spectators] turned in to breakfast."[7]

About five o'clock that afternoon the party reached La Bérade on the other side of the Brèche. They had arranged to meet there with Alexandre Pic, a porter to whom they had entrusted their extra food and clothing, personal items, and tobacco. When darkness came and Pic nowhere in sight, they "went to straw," having no other choice in this inn-less village. When the porter "strolled jaunt[ily] in" the next morning he received a warm welcome from five inveterate smokers anxious for the special tobacco treats he was to bring with him. Going immediately through their personal belongings, "we seized upon our toothbrushes; but, upon looking for our cigars, we found starvation staring us in the face." Confronted with the prospect of nights around the campfire without their fine havanas, they questioned Pic closely. "Hullo! Monsieur Pic, where are the cigars?" "Messieurs, je suis désolé," said Pic. Brigands on the road, he claimed, had knocked him senseless, ransacked the baggage and stolen the cigars. Furthermore, he said, "I never smoke, *never.*" Although others had seen him smoking Pic insisted he had never spoken truer words. Whymper wryly noted that maybe this last claim was true, "for [Pic] was reported to be the greatest liar in the Dauphiné!"[8]

The party left La Bérade around 1:00 p.m. headed for their main Dauphiné goal, the Pointe des Ecrins. The party's porter was now Rodier, a local "chasseur guide," staggering under a heavy load of blankets. They scrambled first up the westernmost slopes of the Glacier de Bonnepierre, and then over "torrents" passable only because at that height they were still subdivided into smaller streams. In late afternoon, coming to a level spot near the glacier's head, they set up camp for the night. After each man selected his own nook the party settled around a good fire where they "sliced up and brewed" canned Fortnum and Mason soup for dinner.[9] Probably extending his knowledge of cooking to its limit, Whymper noted that because they increased by threefold the soup-to-water ratio recommended in the directions, the soup was excellent. To him, drinking soup around the campfire was as much an art as preparing it. "[A]lways let your friends drink first; not only because it is more polite, but because...one drink of the bottom is worth two of the top as all the goodness settles."[10]

Minus Rodier, the party moved off in the predawn darkness of the next morning. Approaching the Ecrins from the north they arrived at a point on the plateau of the Glacier de l'Encula from which they could clearly see the mountain's upper reaches. It was a daunting sight:

> Imagine a triangular plane, 700 or 800 feet high, set at an angle exceeding 50 degrees. Let it be smooth and glassy, let the uppermost edges be cut into spikes and teeth, and let them be bent, some one way, some another. Let the glassy face be covered with minute fragments of rock, scarcely attached [and] varnished with ice. [I]magine this, and you will have a...faint idea of the face of the Ecrins on which we stood.[11]

From this vantage point they saw that an "enormous bergschrund" completely surrounded the final peak, running east and west about 800 feet below the summit. This crevasse appeared passable only at a higher point on the glacial plateau to their left. Scrambling upward and bearing left they reached the bergschrund at the place chosen to cross it and made it safely to the bottom of the ridge on the eastern edge of the steep northern face. Wanting to avoid the slick surface of the face itself they mounted the ridge but were able to climb only a few feet upward. The rocks were covered with ice and the ridge itself was razor thin, a combination that threatened to send them hurtling down its far side. Turning, they retreated back to the upper edge of the bergschrund where they again surveyed the scene. Their only feasible option now appeared to be a westward traverse along the near edge of the crevasse searching the north face for a route to take them toward the summit.

Croz now began to cut footholds and handholds as they moved carefully along the ice-covered slope above the schrund which dropped sharply off to their right. It was monumentally slow and difficult work; members of the group were roped together at twenty-foot intervals and could not move from their positions except as each new step was cut. Their hands and feet were turning numb from the cold; progress was hardly discernible. Sensing they were getting nowhere someone suggested they should return to the eastern ridge. Croz, in the lead, flared with indignation. Turning he moved toward them with a haste on the slick ice that made Whymper shudder. Glaring fiercely, he said: "By all means, let us go there, the sooner the better."[12] Quickly assured that no slight was intended Croz went back to work as the group's leader, relieved at intervals by Almer as they continued westward.

After nearly three hours they were more directly beneath the summit, but almost as far below it as when they had moved out from the icy rocks of the lower eastern ridge. With the situation still grim they decided they must now either aim for the Ecrins's summit or sound a retreat. Turning back toward a higher point on the eastern ridge, they ascended the steep slope slowly and laboriously, each man carefully keeping the rope taut between himself and the climbers immediately above and below. At 12:30, six and a half hours from the time they had left the col, they finally regained the rocky eastern ridge at a point near the mountain's crest. Exhausted by the hard work and tension of the long morning's climb, they rested to catch their breaths.

With the summit now only a few hundred feet away Almer became impatient, untied himself and advanced toward it. Crossing a snow-bed between some rocks he placed his left foot on a patch of snow and without testing it momentarily for solidity before bringing his right foot forward. As he did so, the patch under his left foot gave way without warning. Completely without support, Almer's flailing body lurched downward, off the precipitous left side of the ridge. He was lost, thought Whymper, but with only an instant to spare the agile guide managed to fall on the right side of the narrow ridge and stop himself. Had Almer initially stepped on the patch of snow with his right foot, thought Whymper, "he would...have fallen several hundred feet without touching anything," finally crashing onto a glacier some 3,000 feet below.[13]

No doubt sobered by his failure to move cautiously, Almer rejoined the group and again took the lead. Though the distance was short they climbed another hour before reaching the Ecrins's 13,462 foot summit. Almer deferentially stepped aside for the rest of the party to pass. The three amateurs called for Croz to come forward for the honor of being the first to set foot on the peak because he had done the most work. When he declined his employers went to the top together, clustering around a pinnacle too small for even one person to mount.

Bone-weary, shivering and balanced on an uncertain perch, they did not shout or raise their arms in victory. But they were quietly ecstatic. With almost superhuman effort they had become the first to conquer the Dauphiné's highest mountain! It was a moment to remember the rest of their days.

As was his custom, Whymper "bagged" a small piece off the summit's highest rock but the climbers did not linger long to celebrate their victory. The day was too far gone for that, and at 2:45 they prepared for the descent. Remembering the horrific conditions of the ascent, they all agreed not to descend by the same route. They wished particularly to avoid the "last rocks" which were icy and unstable. So they turned to the western arête, trusting they could find a route down to the bergschrund and then a way across it.

Apprehension showed in their tense faces. On the ascent the sure-footed Almer had narrowly escaped death. Had he not been momentarily climbing alone he probably would have dragged some of them with him.

Croz, the party's Paul Bunyan, had worked hard enough on the ascent to exhaust even the strongest mortal. They had spent over nine hours in a trial-and-error struggle to the summit. The morning cold had chilled them to the bone; the darkening afternoon promised even lower temperatures. The unfamiliar western arête, chosen for the descent, could become as difficult as their upward path. Aware of the dangers they now faced, Whymper thought that if anyone had called him foolish for venturing upon the Ecrins he would have humbly agreed. And if that "monitor" of his conduct had asked him to swear he would never climb another mountain if somehow guaranteed a safe return from this one, he would have done so. "The game [had not been] worth the risk." But the game was in play and Almer led off, matter-of-factly saying that "the good God has brought us up, and he will take us down in safety."[14]

Whymper's thoughts in that soul-searching moment were revealing. It was the only recorded moment in his remarkably active life to bring forth repentance for bad judgment, a plea for salvation, and a confession of humility. Though the fear he experienced on the Ecrins was undoubtedly genuine, he did not say whether God was also in his thoughts. Indeed, after noting Almer's remark about the Almighty's continuing help, Whymper wrote that it "showed pretty well what he was thinking about," clearly referring to the guide, not himself.[15] An imaginary human "monitor" was his only reference to someone who might be looking over his shoulder.

Whymper's absence of spiritual expression in these circumstances seems somewhat strange for a young man who regularly attended Maze Pond Chapel and believed in God's providence. Some inner restraint may have kept him from publicly disclosing his faith, saving expressions of it for his participation in Sunday morning church services. Perhaps the trauma of the Matterhorn descent made him more a fatalist than a believer. In any case, as his party moved off the Ecrins's summit, Whymper surely felt that although God's design would prevail, every ounce of his own skill, judgment, and remaining strength would be needed to come safely through a difficult descent.

The western ridge presented as many difficulties as the eastern. The rocks were loose, often crumbling when grasped, and the arête so thin the climbers would not know from which side the dislodged pieces would fall. The precipice on one side was almost perpendicular and the slope on the other 50 degrees or more. After descending slowly for some time they came to a "deep notch" lying horizontally across their path that stopped them abruptly. Creeping forward on his hands and knees on the snow to the edge of the ravine, Almer looked at its expanse and the surface of the rock on its other side. Returning, he reported that there was no way around the cleft; they would have to jump across, to what appeared to be an unstable "block" on the other side. As their current leader and the lightest and most agile member of the party he would show them the way. Carrying an extra length of rope Almer leaped across the ravine and landed on the rock which swayed with his weight. Hugging it with both arms, he secured himself there and the rock settled. Releasing their anxiously held breaths during Almer's jump, the others then followed suit, their efforts made easier by the guide's example.

After a while the ridge narrowed even further and became impassable. So they again took to the face of the mountain, now on their right side, descending slowly until they arrived at the top of the bergschrund near its western end, some two hours after leaving the summit. At that point, because the mountain's slope dropped so steeply, they could not see whether the crevasse was passable from their position. The day was ebbing and they were concerned about the possible need to spend the night on the mountain. They had no choice, however, but to restart the slow process of cutting steps down the face to get a better view of the schrund. Now, after all they had been through, good fortune plainly lent a hand. Almer, still in the lead, inched downward until the crevasse became more visible. He then called to the party to brace themselves and hold his weight on the rope as he placed one foot firmly in a step, "made his body rigid," and leaned out toward the crevasse to see if it could be crossed from where they were. Deciding it was passable, he told Whymper, who was next in line, to come close to the edge and untie himself. Whymper did so and the others also moved closer to give Almer more free rope. At that, the Oberlander gave a "loud yodel" and jumped across the schrund into soft snow on the other side. The group, as it turned out, "had hit the crevasse at its easiest point."[16]

Though the climbers now breathed easier, their ordeal continued. The ascent and descent of the final peak above the bergschrund, only 700 feet high, had taken eight and a half hours of physical strain and virtually unrelieved tension. It was now almost 5:00 p.m. and they had been climbing nearly thirteen hours. Forty minutes later in fading sunlight they reached the col where the morning had started, gathered up their baggage and continued downward. Two ice-falls and the traverse of a wide glacier were yet to be put behind them before darkness fell. Descending to the plateau of the Glacier Blanc on the Ecrins' northern side, they traversed it and then crossed over the moraine of the Glacier Noir at 8:45 p.m., just as the daylight faded. Then began a "disagreeable" walk southeast along the Torrent de St. Pierre in the dark, wading through numerous side streams, stumbling over rocks and barely discernible holes. When a huge rock, fallen from the flanks of the Pelvoux, suddenly loomed in their path, an exhausted Moore decided it would make a delightful bivouac. Whymper thought this square monolith would provide little or no shelter but Walker and Almer "with their usual good nature" agreed with their companion and remained there with him.[17]

*Descending the Pointe des Ecrins ("Almer's Leap")*

Under a threatening sky Whymper and Croz decided to keep going in the hope of getting a real roof over their heads. Before moving out they gave their companions what remained of the party's provisions, a dozen cubes of bacon fat and half a candle which their companions gratefully accepted. The two climbers found the way virtually impassable in the darkness. Near the stream they were following Croz suddenly disappeared into the underbrush. Trying to find him Whymper first tumbled into a bush and then fell backward over some rocks, wedging himself between them and rapidly getting soaked with the stream's frigid spray. That was enough for both of them. They found a semblance of shelter under an overhanging rock and built a fire with juniper wood to dry their clothes. With no food and no cigars but plenty of pipe tobacco they smoked and talked at length, swapping tales of past mountain adventure. "How well I remember that night at the rock," said Whymper, "and the jolly way in which Croz came out."[18] The excitement of the day dying at last, they made beds of rhododendron branches and slept soundly.

\* \* \* \*

Although the exhausting but exhilarating first ascent of the Ecrins would not be readily matched, their summer brought several more successes. Soon after the Ecrins ascent Jean Reynaud, Whymper's French surveyor friend of earlier years, joined the party. Two days later the six men became the first to reach the 11,300 foot crest of a pass they named the Col de la Pilatte after the glacier hugging its northern side. On the col as they paused to look about, the Alp's fickle weather changed abruptly: a mist closed in suddenly and blocked their view. Only Croz had been able to glimpse the downward path ahead so they decided to move out while his memory was fresh. The far side of the pass was a fearsomely smooth ice slope which Moore calculated to be 54 degrees. For three quarters of an hour they went slowly downward with Croz cutting steps and regularly cautioning, "Slip not, dear sirs; place well your feet; stir not until you are certain."[19] Then, quite suddenly, Croz's voice became silent." 'What is the matter, Croz?' 'Bergschrund, gentlemen.' 'Can we get over?' 'I don't know; I think we must jump.' The clouds rolled away right and left as he spoke. The effect was dramatic! It was a *coup de théâtre* preceding the

*A night with Croz*

'great sensation leap' which was about to be executed by the entire company."[20]

The crevasse was 7 or 8 feet wide at that point, its other bank a narrow ridge some 15 to 16 feet below them that fell away abruptly on its far side. As the party's leader Croz was the first to jump; Walker followed him and then Whymper stepped up for his turn. "I felt supremely ridiculous. The world seemed to revolve at a frightful pace, and my stomach to fly away. The next moment I found myself sprawling in the snow, and then, of course, vowed that it was nothing...."[21] Though admitting only to feeling ridiculous he had made two large concessions, at least for him: heart pounding, he had suffered a momentary loss of nerve and then, once safe, had tried to conceal it.

Next came Reynaud whose leap appeared to have been encouraged by a friendly boot from Moore that sent him flying, accompanied by a great mixture of provisions and equipment and with arms and legs awry. The Frenchman made a hard landing.

We saw a toe – it seemed to belong to Moore. We saw Reynaud, a flying body, coming down as if taking a header into water, with arms and legs all abroad, his leg of mutton [sailing] in the air, his bâton escaped from his grasp....And then we heard a thud as if a bundle of carpets had been pitched out of a window. When set upon his feet he was a sorry spectacle – his head a great snowball, brandy trickling out of one side of the knapsack, chartreuse out of the other....We bemoaned its loss but...roared with laughter.[22]

Reynaud was less experienced than his companions and had obviously been hesitant about jumping to the other side of the crevasse. "Oh, what a diable of a place!" he had moaned. "Upon my word, it is not possible!"[23] But by the time his turn came it was fairly clear that the jump presented no real danger and once he landed safely the Frenchman was fair game. His awkwardness and disarray gave the others a chance to let off steam at Reynaud's expense, particularly since they genuinely liked him and his "cordial and modest manner." Whymper was protective of his friend, saying that Reynaud was not "a whit more reluctant to pass the place than [the] others,...[just] infinitely more demonstrative – in a word, he was French."[24]

Regrouped on the far side of the crevasse – with Reynaud's diminished liqueur supply in an aromatic knapsack – the party continued downward on the Glacier de Pilatte and reached its snout about 1:00 p.m. From there they descended easily to the valley floor and on into La Bérade. This first passage of the Col de Pilatte ended what Whymper ironically called the group's "little campaign" in the Dauphiné. In only eight days his party had made first ascents of two peaks (the Aiguilles de la Saussaz and the Pointe des Ecrins), and first passages of three high cols (the Col des Aiguilles d'Arves, the Brèche de la Meije and the Col de la Pilatte). He attributed their overall success to good weather and the spirit of his compatriots and guides. Though he did not single out Almer for special praise, he clearly appreciated the crucial role of that "steady man" in the success of the campaign, particularly in his leadership of the party on their hellish descent of the Pointe des Ecrins's western ridge.

Whymper reserved his highest accolade for Croz alone:

I [must] pay...tribute to the ability with which Croz led us, through a dense mist, down the remainder of the Glacier de la

*Reynaud – A Flying Body*

Pilatte. As an exhibition of strength and skill, it has seldom been surpassed in the Alps or elsewhere. On this unknown and very steep glacier he was perfectly at home, even in the mists. Never able to see 50 feet ahead, he went on with the utmost certainty...without having to retrace a single step....[He] displayed from first to last consummate knowledge of the materials with which he was dealing. Now he cut steps down one side of a serac; went with a dash to the other side and hauled us up after him; then cut away along a ridge until a point was gained from which we could jump on to another ridge; then, doubling back, found a snow-bridge, over which he crawled on hands and knees, towed us across by the legs, ridiculing our apprehensions, mimicking our awkwardness, declining all help, bidding us only to follow him.[25]

Between the lines of this tribute ran feelings deeper than Whymper's acknowledged respect for Croz's skill and courage. Following their party's severe trial on the Ecrins he had been pleased at the way he and Croz had conversed freely as the two of them sat around their campfire, smoking and telling "wonderful stories" of past Alpine adventures. In a light moment some days later he had tickled the nose of his sleeping guide with a piece of straw and gleefully watched as Croz awoke squirming and wiggling from an afternoon nap. The shared dangers and relaxed moments of the Dauphiné campaign had created a strong bond between the two men, as close to true friendship as was possible for this reserved young Londoner and his older French guide from the village of Le Tour.

Walker now left them to join his father and sister in further climbs as the rest of the party pushed on to Chamonix where they arrived on July 2nd, crossing three cols en route. Moore and Almer then departed for climbs elsewhere. In town Whymper unexpectedly met up with A. M. W. Adams Reilly, a fellow Alpine Club member, and during the next few days the two of them and their guides scaled three virgin summits: Mont Dolent, the Aiguille de Trélatête and the Aiguille Argentière. These three ascents together with crossings of two high cols ended Whymper's tour of the Mont Blanc Range. Whatever else the summer of 1864 might bring, he had already conducted one of the most accomplished climbing seasons of the Golden Age.

*Portrait of Michel-Auguste Croz*

On July 16th Whymper and Croz left the Chamonix area and went into Switzerland where they rejoined Moore and Almer in the mountain village of Zinal. The only known route between Zinal and Zermatt, Whymper's next and final destination of the summer, was a rather circuitous path over the Triftjoch and the Col Durand. Moore was anxious to find a shorter and quicker route between the two Swiss towns. This suited Whymper, particularly because it offered the possibility of claiming another first passage.

The next day the four-man party crossed the Zinal glacier and headed toward the Arpitetta Alp where, they had been told, a chalet was available for overnight guests. They found it well enough but for Whymper it was the chalet from hell. Cut out of the hillside it had a roof of rough native stone but neither door nor window, and around it were "quagmires" of animal excrement and dirt. It had one room of about fifteen by twenty feet with a sloped roof that was five feet from the floor at one end and seven feet at the other. On the high side was the sleeping area – a raised, six foot square platform littered with dirty straw and dirtier sheepskins. Adjacent was a small space for sitting and eating. The rest of the hovel was a cheese factory, occupied at the time by a lone cheese-maker smoking a pipe as he worked. The man sat on a one-legged cowherd's stool, blowing smoke into a cheese vat he turned by hand. At regular intervals he would take several puffs of his pipe and then blow into the cheese more vigorously than ever. Whymper thought he might well be learning how Swiss cheese got its unique flavor. Wood smoke from the fireplace at the low end of the room mingled with the churner's pipe smoke as both tried unsuccessfully to escape up the room's one narrow chimney.

Several herd-boys trudged into the room for shelter, forced inside by rain now falling in sheets. The chill rain storm also brought the family cows down from the mountain who sought warmth by gathering on the chalet's roof. Pigs and sheep also sought respite from the rain, and all fought for places next to the chimney, nudging the roof stones about as they did so. Leaks stemming from this activity sent Whymper to new sleeping spots twice during the night. He had scraped a clean place on the floor, preferring his plaid on the hard earth to the filthy sheepskins. At one point water from the roof dripped onto the plaid and seeped under his flannels to his skin. Sleep would not come so he went outside for a breath of air but the rain quickly forced him back inside. Then he tried smoking but the leaks made that difficult. The wind howled outside, accompanied by sharp peals of thunder. So he dozed through the night with little rest to prepare him for the challenging day ahead.

The next morning dawned dull, humid and cloudy, an inopportune time to attempt a new and difficult pass. But the thought of spending another 24 hours at the grim chalet eliminated any doubts the four climbers may have had about leaving. They set out at 5:40 a. m. heading southeast from the Arpitetta Alp intending a first crossing of the Moming Pass followed by an easy descent into Zermatt. They got into a jam rather soon, however, just after crossing the lower plateau of the Moming Glacier and coming to the slope leading up to the Moming Pass. Almer recommended that they head for some rocks on their left but Croz urged a course to the right, up a rugged part of the rising glacial face. With the Frenchman's idea accepted, he took the lead. After a while the glacial route grew impossibly difficult – above them were ice-covered boulders and a wall of broken ice that became almost vertical as it rose higher.

They could see now that the rocks recommended by Almer were the preferable route. The problem, however, was that Almer's rocks were even farther to their left, directly accessible from where they stood only by a traverse of the slope that had become too dangerous to ascend directly. Retracing their steps to avoid a crossing would have meant substantial delay and a second night in the Arpitetta Alp's foul chalet. None wanted that, so they began to move horizontally to the left across the icy wall, Croz still in the lead and cutting steps.

Above them near the summit of the pass loomed great seracs looking as if, at any instant, they might fall and sweep away everything in their path. The party's traverse was "a flank movement in the face of an enemy" that could mount a surprise attack without notice.[26] The peril was obvious to all. "It was foolhardiness...an error of judgment," Whymper later confessed.[27] Moore acknowledged that "the whole time we were crossing this slope my heart was in my mouth." Croz told Whymper afterwards that this was the most dangerous traverse he had ever made.[28]

On the way to the rocks Almer emitted an unbroken string of subdued oaths, "indignant," thought Whymper, and full of "self-reproach at being a party to the proceeding." "Quick; be quick," Almer kept saying.[29] Croz needed no urging and went furiously to work.

He was fully as alive to the risk as any of the others....Manfully did he exert himself to escape from the impending destruction. His head, bent down to his work, never turned to the right or to the left. One, two, three, went his axe, and then he stepped on the spot where he had been cutting. How painfully insecure would we have considered those steps at any other time! But now, we thought only of the rocks in front, and of the hideous seracs lurching over above us, apparently in the act of falling.

At length they reached the relative safety of the rocks and drew their first easy breaths in what seemed a very long time. As they rested and drank melted snow fortified with a bit of flask wine the largest of the high seracs suddenly leaned over about 30 degrees and then broke sharply away from its base. Shattering into a thousand pieces it crashed down the slope,

*Moming Pass ("Flogging Down the Icy Foam")*

scoring the surface beneath and driving an expanding snow mass ahead of it like a giant bulldozer. The route they had taken was now a broad sheet of glassy ice with every trace of their path obliterated.

With the dangerous traverse behind them they slogged upward on the route Almer had first recommended. Their long struggle ended thirty minutes later as they reached the near side of the Moming Pass summit. A dense mist clung to the top of the ridge, through which the party could barely discern a high billow of wind-blown snow, frozen like a lofty ocean wave cresting away from them over the far side of the Pass. This overhanging mass of frozen snow, far larger than the one encountered by Wills at the Wetterhorn's summit, blocked their view of the descent and brought Croz again to the fore. Standing behind the wave and using his powerful shoulders, he "flogged down the [icy] foam," cutting through the cornice to the surface of the pass. Without hesitation, he then jumped down to the packed snow on the far side of the summit and bade the others to follow. "Could [Croz] have performed the[se] feats on the boards of a theatre, he would have brought down the house with thunders of applause."[30]

The far side of the Moming Pass was a steep slope as daunting as the treacherous glacial face and looming seracs they had encountered on the way up. Their descent from the high col was another nerve-racking experience which Moore summarized in his journal:

We had to pass along a crest of ice, a mere knife-edge...[O]n our left [was] a broad crevasse, whose bottom was lost in a blue haze, and on our right...a slope falling at an angle of 70 degrees or more. Croz, as he went along the edge, chipped small notches in the ice, in which we put our feet, with the toes well turned out, doing all we knew to preserve our balance....[At] one huge chasm [that] could neither be leaped nor turned...Croz showed himself equal to the emergency. Held up by the rest of the party, he cut a series of holes for [our] hands and feet...and down along this slippery staircase we crept, with our faces to the wall, to the point where we could drop across the chasm....[A]fter a desperate... struggle and as bad a piece of ice-work as it is possible to imagine, we emerged on to the upper plateau of the Hohlicht Glacier."[30]

The party easily scrambled down this last part of the glacier to the Triftjoch and on into Zermatt, arriving at the Monte Rosa Hotel at 7:20 p.m. It had been another long day, bringing with it the first passage of a most difficult col. So difficult, indeed, that the Moming Pass was rarely if ever used again as a route from Zinal to Zermatt.

The next morning, July 19th, Whymper went to the Zermatt post office to collect his mail. To his utter dismay a letter from his father called for his immediate return to London to help with an urgent business matter. Edward was the only son to have joined his father in the family engraving business and though only twenty-four he was Josiah's right arm. Disappointed but dutiful he packed his bags and awaited the arrival of Adams Reilly who was scheduled to join him that day. His companion appeared on schedule and Whymper suggested he try the Matterhorn alone, offering to make Croz available as his guide, but Adams Reilly demurred. Whymper then settled with Croz and walked down the valley to Visp. From there he took the next available diligence to Montreux and continued on to London by rail. This was an abrupt end to his summer and his high hope for a Matterhorn conquest, but he had amassed a season's record of first Alpine ascents that would never be equaled.

* * * *

Before his unexpected summons to England Whymper had planned to try the Matterhorn's east face taking with him a strong team capable of handling any obstacle the mountain might offer. He had written to Adams Reilly on January 18th, 1864: "I think I must have another go at the Matterhorn. I have...a most original idea which I should like to try. Something different from any...I have had before."[32] In his mind was an "attack upon the eastern face" alongside the mountain's notheastern ridge, beginning at the Hörnli.[33] This letter had been the first indication of Whymper's readiness to abandon the Matterhorn's Italian side and the indomitable Carrel along with it. Now that the call of business had ended the summer season of 1864 he would need to wait a year before putting his new strategy into action.

Whymper's deep disappointment at having to leave the Alps without

*Clubroom at Zermatt (1864)*

attempting the Matterhorn gave way to resignation as he worked in London on an agenda for the 1865 climbing season. His last campaign had been an unequaled success overall, and he was now merely "unsatisfied" at the thwarting of his novel plan for the Matterhorn. This low-key reaction was due in part to the great mountain's enduring intimidation of climbers and guides alike. Tyndall, Stephen, Adams-Reilly and other Alpine stalwarts seemed in no great hurry to attempt the unassailable summit. No one – not even Carrel – had tried to climb the Matterhorn in the summer of 1864. The following year, however, would be different. Unbeknown to Whymper a pair of Alpine Club members were quietly considering a Matterhorn attempt. A government-sponsored group of Italian climbers, with Carrel as their designated leader, were also planning an all-out attack on the mountain in July of 1865. The Italian climbers' contest with Whymper's party would go down to the wire in the most fateful and exciting real-time race in the history of mountaineering.

# CHAPTER 11

## *"The Most Brilliant Campaign"*

The letter recalling Whymper to London in 1864 could not have come at a worse time. The accumulated knowledge of four previous seasons had gone into his plan for that year's attempt on the Matterhorn. New rope and a specially constructed ladder would assist him at the most troublesome cliffs and crevasses. Difficult ascents in the Dauphiné and Mont Blanc ranges would prime him for the summer's final assault. Adams Reilly, a friend and seasoned climber, would provide support and companionship. Michel Croz, a skillful Chamoniard with a rising reputation would be his chief guide. All had gone well until he opened his father's letter in Zermatt. The message was brief and straightforward: Come home right away, I need your help. To Whymper it was a time bomb shattering his plans and bringing his extensive preparations to naught.

In London during the early months of 1864 he had thought long and hard about why no one had reached the Matterhorn summit. Was it possible to identify and overcome specific features that made this mountain so difficult? Was there a window of time when the weather might be more cooperative? What route would most likely lead to the top? By the summer of that year those thoughts had coalesced. Whymper's dawning moment came as he continued to sift photographs and reflect on his own experience. Like Poe's purloined letter, the two keys to success on the Matterhorn – though disguised within the foreboding profile of the mountain's northeastern ramparts – were in plain view.

The first of these was the slant of the rock strata on both sides of the mountain. Layers of rock on the rough Italian slope – segments of the earth's crust put in place long ago as continents clashed – dipped slightly to the southwest, toward the climber, with fractured rocks overhanging the upward path in many places. Due to this downward slant, rock fragments and other debris created by frost and erosion did not accumulate on this mountainside to provide better footing. Rather, the broken material fell down the southern slope, often to be swept away by winds of almost hurricane force. Further complicating a climber's task, the surface of the Italian side was composed largely of metamorphic schist – irregular plates of various minerals compacted by heat and pressure at the time of their creation. This material gave little traction to the nails in a mountaineer's boot – less even than the granite rocks Whymper found in France on the Brèche de la Meije and later on the Aiguille Verte. Without the many fissures in these schist rocks the Matterhorn's Italian-side climbers would not have reached the heights they did.

With all this in mind Whymper reasoned that if the downward dip of the schist layers on the southern side persisted throughout the mountain, the rocks on its northeastern side would point slightly upward, thereby assisting climbers instead of hindering them. If this were true the Matterhorn's east side would provide better footing than the southern side.

Whymper's second insight during those winter to spring months in London consolidated his thinking. On his visual surveys of the Matterhorn he had noticed that snow accumulated relatively high on the mountain's eastern slope where it remained through the warmest weather of July and August. He reasoned that snow could not permanently adhere in such quantities on a surface inclined more than 45 degrees. While an icy slope of that angle could mean a difficult climb, he concluded that the eastern face and northeastern ridge were not as dangerously steep as they appeared. This new awareness, combined with the belief that the rocks on those slopes angled upward, flashed through his brain in a sudden "Eureka!" moment: the route to the Matterhorn's summit lay in Switzerland and not, as he and others had long supposed, in Italy!

That was why he had decided to employ the reliable Croz in the summers of 1864 and 1865 despite the French guide's minimal exposure to the Matterhorn's slopes. After all, only two parties were known to have tried the mountain from Switzerland, and Carrel – the patriotic bersagliere determined to scale it from the Italian side – had never done so and almost certainly never would. The Parker brothers in 1860 had climbed without guides to 11,000 feet on the northeastern ridge, and T. S. Kennedy had reached approximately the same point in the winter of 1862. But those climbers had been discouraged by the difficulties met at that height, and by the even more ominous appearance of the sheer cliffs above. Kennedy went so far as to say that "long unweathered sheets of rocks...below the pyramid...[presented] most insuperable difficulties to the climber."[1] Despite these warnings Whymper decided to put his theory into practice by attacking the Matterhorn's summit from the mountain's eastern side near the Hörnli ridge.

Whymper's determination to scale the Matterhorn had become an obsession, but his overall objective went beyond a single mountain. As he immodestly confessed, his "rather ambitious" plans for "the journey of 1865...included all the great peaks which had not then been ascended."[2] His list of candidates for first attempts that summer included the "Grand Cornier [13,022 feet], Grands Jorasses [13,797], Aiguille Verte [13,541], Ruinette [12,727], and the Matterhorn [14,782]."[3] Also on his list was the Dent Blanche (14,318), though he had heard that someone might already have climbed it. On location that summer he carefully charted prospective routes on each of the mountains selected, and with only a "few variations" suggested by his guides these routes were "strictly followed out."[4]

Before his abrupt departure from Zermatt in 1864, Whymper had engaged Croz to be his chief guide for the1865 season. Back in London he had written to another favorite, Christian Almer, seeking his services, and to Franz Biener whom he wanted as a subordinate third guide. Almer and Biener were available and agreed to remain with Whymper for as long as he might need them. Then came a shocking development. In April of 1865 Croz, on receiving a letter from Whymper suggesting the date and place they would meet that summer, replied that he was available only until June 27th, after which he was obligated to another employer. Whymper protested, saying that Croz had agreed last year to serve him during the coming summer season. But Croz would not budge; he felt he had committed himself in good faith to the other climber after not receiving written confirmation from Whymper during the intervening months. That left Whymper no choice but to accept Croz's decision and be thankful that his favorite guide would be available at least for the first part of the season.

Partly because of his limited access to Croz's services Whymper went to the Alps earlier in 1865 than was his custom. On June 12th of that year he met up with Almer in the Lauterbrunnen Valley and they went on to meet guides Croz and Biener in the Valais region of Switzerland. Two days later the foursome was at the Grand Cornier, the first target on Whymper's list. Spotting an upward route to the north that looked promising they stopped momentarily to rope up for the ascent. Here the temperamental Croz, thinking it was too early to do so, decided to show his disdain for what he considered unnecessary caution. "As usual, now that he had got to the front, [Croz] stamped off by himself the moment we decided to tie up, getting a start on us of nearly a quarter of a mile."[5]

At first blush Croz's action might seem unforgivable; why would the lead guide show such blatant disregard for the party's collective judgment? At some level he was behaving like a petulant child who dislikes the rules and quits the game. But Whymper could not get too upset with the man he so respected, who shared his own strong will and self-confidence. He also recognized that Croz never violated his prime duty of protecting those in his care. On the Grand Cornier Croz would separate himself only temporarily, knowing full well that his "*monsieur*" would be safe in the hands of Almer and Biener until all were together again.

The party soon caught up with Croz who then joined them on the rope. Together they ascended slowly but steadily on snow and rocks to within 300 feet of the summit. From there they followed a narrow ridge that led to a great snow cornice blocking their route – a re-occurring barrier near many Alpine summits. Like frozen bars at the entrance to a wintry jail, huge icicles hung from the under side of the cornice's arch to halt the party's advance. Led by Croz they hacked through the icy blockade, went forward under the cornice, and found themselves suddenly on the mountain's summit. It was 12:30, more than nine hours after their early morning departure from Zinal. On this first ascent they had largely avoided rough spots and exploited Whymper's new preference for climbing on snow. It was another notch in the belt of Croz's aggressive young charge.

On the Cornier summit the party "had time to chat." At some point their discussion turned to the subject of "strength" and soon became personal. As Whymper wrote to a friend many years later: "Croz said he could hold me up with one hand, and I challenged him. He took me up by the back of the neck and held me up in the air. Unclothed I weighed 149 pounds, and with the clothing and the things in my pocket must have weighed about 160 pounds."[6] Duly impressed, he rarely spoke of Croz thereafter without mentioning the guide's enormous strength.

The party spent that night at Bricola. On their way to Zermatt the next morning their southward route took them toward the Col d'Herens, just west of the Dent Blanche. A possible first ascent of the Dent irresistibly attracted the acquisitive Whymper. It was a prime target of opportunity and he would never have a better cadre of guides to help him seize it. Although the mountain's summit was rumored already to have been scaled, the party agreed that since there was some doubt about the facts it was worth a try. Another appeal was its reputation as one of the difficult Alpine peaks. "Even Leslie Stephen himself, fleetest of foot of the whole Alpine brotherhood, once upon a time" attempted it and failed.[7] It was a challenge they dared not let slip by.

Their current route to Zermatt was elevated – between 9 and 10 thousand feet – which gave them something of a leg up. As the Dent Blanche climb developed, however, they needed every minute of the extra time available. Bearing left, Whymper and his three guides zigzagged up the glacier at the foot of the mountain's southwest face. At about 11,000 feet a giant bergschrund slashed diagonally across their path, blocking further ascent along their chosen route. Unable to cross it, the party angled upward along the schrund's near edge until they were about 12,000 feet high, some 2300 feet below the summit. There they finally found a snow bridge and on their hands and knees crawled to the other side.

Once over the crevasse the route ahead became a series of small gullies and intermittent rocks. Almer was now leading, followed by Biener, Whymper and Croz, in that order. The work required constant communication among them:

"Are you fast, Almer?" "Yes." "Go ahead, Biener." Biener, made secure, cried, "Come on, sir," and Monsieur endeavoured. "No, no," said Almer, "not there, – here," pointing with his bâton to the right place to clutch. Then it was Croz's turn, and we all drew in the rope as the great man followed. "Forward" once more – and so on.[8]

As they edged slowly upward on the Dent Blanche, the Matterhorn's northern face was clearly visible across the basin of the Z'mutt Glacier. Whymper's "old enemy" looked hopelessly inaccessible. "Do you think," his guides asked, "that you or anyone else will ever get up *that* mountain?" "Yes," Whymper replied, "but not on that side."[9]

Farther into the climb a stiff wind arose bringing with it a bitter chill. Despite the wind at their level, the summit was shrouded in mist. Whymper's fingers began to lose all feeling. Coming to a mound blocking their way they stopped to share the wine bottle and again crept slowly forward. Suddenly and unexpectedly their goal appeared. The clouds lifted and not twenty yards farther on Whymper saw a cairn, a clear sign that someone had reached the summit before them. Without ceremony or an attempt to exchange words – which the conditions would have rendered useless in any event – Whymper tugged on the rope to signal both success and the need to head downward immediately. All had seen the cairn and all turned in their tracks. It was not a first ascent after all but one they would remember with pride – only if they survived the freezing weather and ice-covered rocks of the descent. Whymper described what happened next:

The descent of the [Dent Blanche] was hideous work. The men...impersonat[ed] Winter, with their hair all frosted and their beards matted with ice. My hands were numbed – dead. I begged the others to stop. "We cannot afford to stop; we must continue to move," was their reply. They were right; to stop was to be entirely frozen. So we went down; gripping rocks varnished with ice which pulled the skin from [our] fingers. Gloves were useless; they became iced too, and the bâtons slid through them as slippery as eels. The iron of the axes stuck to the fingers – it felt red-hot; but it was useless to shrink, the rocks and the axes had to be firmly grasped – no faltering would do here.[10]

The party descended cautiously in these miserable conditions for four hours without stopping. They re-crossed the bergschrund at 8:15 p.m. as the light slowly faded from the western sky. Back on the lower side of the glacier they halted to take stock of their condition. Their hands were numb; most of the skin from their fingertips was gone. They knew it had been touch-and-go whether they would leave the face of the Dent Blanche alive. They stumbled down the glacier in a darkening mist, collected their gear and retraced their steps on glacial moraine in the starlight of a black moonless night. They were back in Bricola at 11:45, eighteen and a half hours after the morning's departure. Too tired to care about the night's accommodations they stopped at the first chalet they came to, made arrangements, and fell into an exhausted sleep.

After a late start the following day the party set out for Zermatt but lost their way in a fog and had to return to Bricola. At 7:00 the next morning they made their third start for Zermatt in as many days. The weather was fine and they were able to see their tracks of the previous day. Ironically their footprints ended almost at their objective, the summit of the Col d'Herens. In another ten yards their forward path would have turned downhill toward Zermatt. Whymper thought that if he had just looked at his compass when the fog had first descended they would have known the right direction and completed the ascent easily. That was spilt milk, however, which he was not inclined to mourn.

Some four and a half hours later he was in the Monte Rosa Hotel made cheerful by the warm reception he always received from master innkeeper Seiler. He was glad to see other climbers here as well, T. S. Kennedy among them. This Alpine Club member had plans that might well have changed Whymper's timetable had he been aware of them, but for now Kennedy kept his intentions to himself, presumably without raising Whymper's suspicions. Perhaps he was able to do so because the competition among a relatively small number of climbers to outdo each other in first ascents created an Alpine protocol that frowned on pressing a fellow climber too hard about his immediate plans.

Earlier that day, coming down the Z'Mutt Glacier from the north on their way toward Zermatt, the party had looked closely at the profile of the Matterhorn's northeastern ridge which from their high vantage point gave a rough idea of the slope of the mountain's east face. The guides, to their surprise, could easily see that this slope was not as sheer as they thought. But their deep-rooted belief in the Matterhorn's inaccessibility from the east side kept them wary of committing to Whymper's plan for an attempt on that face. Acknowledging their concern Whymper suggested that they go to the Théodulhorn, a minor peak about three miles southeast of the Matterhorn, to examine a somewhat different route he had in mind. This plan, he felt, would be more to their liking.

At the Théodulhorn the next day, with his proposed climbing area fully within their view, Whymper described his alternate plan. Their ascent would begin on the "immense gully" at the eastern edge of the Matterhorn's southern side. This wide couloir led up from the Glacier du Mont Cervin to a point on the southeastern, or Furggen, ridge. There they would go eastward across the ridge and find themselves at the foot of the great snow-slope lying high on the mountain's eastern face. Traversing that slope diagonally upward to their right, they would arrive at the northeastern ridge, very near the Matterhorn's summit. They would continue from there on the snow and broken rocks of the north face just to the right of the northeastern ridge until they reached the top of the great mountain itself. "Croz caught the idea immediately," said Whymper, "and thought the plan feasible."

With that settled the party went down the Italian side of the Théodule Pass to Breuil. Although the "immense gully" and the remainder of Whymper's alternate route lay in Switzerland, Breuil was closer to the starting point than Zermatt. Besides, Monsieur Favre was a good cook and would willingly prepare all the rations needed for the three days Whymper thought the climb would require. Only one last detail remained and it was quickly settled. Whymper hired his favorite porter, the hunchback Luc Meynet, who was "delighted to resume his old vocation of tent-bearer." Whymper did not say so but it is a safe bet that he was also pleased.

At 5:45 the next morning, June 21st, Whymper left Breuil with his three guides and Meynet as their porter. This new approach would be his eighth attempt on the Matterhorn. It took three hours to come abreast of the large, slightly crooked gully leading up the mountain from the Glacier du Mont Cervin. The couloir's moderate slope looked even more promising close up. The only hints of potential danger were some questionable depressions and holes in the snow at its base. To protect themselves against rock slides, the party climbed in the partial shelter of cliffs on the right side of the gully abutting the mountain's southeastern ridge. About ten o'clock, after an hour of alternately cutting steps in the snow and scrambling on rocks, they took a break to eat and rest.

While the men unpacked the food Whymper wandered farther upward by himself to a slight promontory in order to get a better look at their planned route. Scanning the heights he saw some small stones falling and then a much larger one followed by several others all rushing downward at a fair pace. As yet unconcerned and not wanting to sound a false alarm he kept silent. Then came a crash and a sudden roar leaving no doubt that a fearsome rockslide was underway. About 800 feet above them great masses of stones and boulders – some making leaps of a hundred feet or more – were hurtling downward, crashing into each other and ricocheting off the sides of the winding gully, the sound of their collisions reverberating like rifle shots above the overall din.

Looking down Whymper saw his troops frantically scrambling for shelter. The mutton Almer had been slicing was on its side along with an overturned wine-bag gushing red liquid onto the snow. The men cowered behind rocks; Whymper squeezed into a cleft above them. The rock avalanche flew past in less time than it took to tell, leaving the party shaken but uninjured. Though it had been a momentary life-threatening situation, Whymper could not help thinking later how ludicrous the men had looked in their wild scramble for safety. "Such a panic I have never witnessed, before or since, upon a mountainside."[11] In hindsight he should have warned them, but the mountains rarely gave climbers more than a split second, once danger appeared, to think about means of escape. Sounding an alarm probably would have made no difference. Risks of the sort they had just experienced were as unavoidable as they were common, and mountaineers accepted them as such. Once on the mountain they had no other choice.

Now the party faced a tough decision. The gully that had seemed to offer easy access to the Matterhorn's eastern face had proved unsafe. High

*Cannonade on the Mattehorn*

cliffs, clearly inaccessible, bordered both sides. In Whymper's view, the only possible upward route was on rocks along the base of the cliffs on the right, but all the guides disagreed. They saw that these rocks, though good for perhaps a hundred feet or so, would quickly become impassable. Unable to dissuade them Whymper set out alone, followed by Meynet and then Croz at some distance keeping watch. After a half-hour on the rocks Croz called to Whymper to come down but he refused. This was the Matterhorn and as long as he could move an inch upward he would do so, guides or no guides. He was "getting into a fume" because the men "had no heart in the matter" and kept climbing. Laboriously he was able to get "a good bit higher" but finally could go no farther and reluctantly admitted defeat. "Croz crowed," and Whymper's effort ended.[12]

Down from the rocks Whymper rejoined the party for a council of war. All now agreed that their best option was his original plan – at which they had scoffed – to attempt the east face beside the Hörnli ridge. The most direct way to the Hörnli was over a col near their morning's path from Breuil. They reached that pass without difficulty but were then blocked by an unexpected obstacle. Unbeknown to them the Furggen Glacier had recently shrunk and pulled away from the top of the pass, leaving a precipitous cliff that blocked farther progress.

The party held another discussion. Whymper wanted to go south to the Théodule Pass and then on to Zermatt and the Hörnli ridge. But the guides' strong ambivalence about the Matterhorn resurfaced. Twice that day the mountain had frustrated their efforts; they felt jinxed by whatever forces kept its peak inviolate. Almer asked, "Why don't you try to go up a mountain that *can* be ascended?" Biener echoed this view: "It is impossible," he said. Croz, as forcefully independent in his views as he was stalwart in Whymper's service, was equally opposed – indeed "bumptious" thought his employer. He said that another Matterhorn effort would take three days and probably fail. He reminded Whymper of the latter's desire to make ascents in the Mont Blanc range and that he, Croz, due to his prior engagement, would be unavailable if they spent the last days of his employment on the Matterhorn.[13]

The experienced guide's words made Whymper hesitate; he wanted Croz's strong arms for the difficult climbs in the Mont Blanc area, some of which, he no doubt reminded himself, could add more first ascents to his record. As if to help him decide, the wind came up and it began to snow. Bad weather, they all knew, could indefinitely delay further attempts on the Matterhorn summit. That tipped the balance in Whymper's mind and he ordered a return to Breuil. From there they would head for the Mont Blanc chain via Châtillon and then up the Aosta valley to Courmayeur. After months of careful planning, his eighth attempt on the Matterhorn like those before them ended in disappointing failure.

* * * *

The climb of June 21st, 1865 was Whymper's last outing with the diminutive Luc Meynet. As in their earlier times together the Englishman again showed his respect for the loyal porter. A certain episode did not appear in any of the editions of *Scrambles* published during Whymper's lifetime; it was first reported in *The Matterhorn* by Guido Rey, who learned of it from Meynet himself.[14] While the party sat on the Furggengrat, the Matterhorn's southeastern ridge, debating their next move, Croz had been smoking his ever-present pipe. Meynet "waited patiently" for him to finish and then asked if he might borrow it since he had left his own pipe at home. "You might as well have left your head there, too, *drôle de bossu*, you rascally hunchback. Do you imagine I am going to lend my pipe to a half-man like you?" Taken aback, Meynet said nothing. Overhearing this exchange Whymper gave Meynet two cigars. "Here," he said, "you smoke, too." The peasant immediately lit up and proudly strutted before Croz, puffing hard and blowing smoke, as best he could, in the Chamoniard's face. Later on the descent Croz jerked at the rope tying the climbers together, hoping without success to make Meynet slip. Farther down, as Croz himself began sinking at the edge of a crevasse, Meynet held the rope fast to prevent the intemperate guide from going deeper. The moral of the story was then highlighted by Whymper, who turned to Croz and said, *"Sachez, Croz, qu'on a souvent besoin d'un plus petit que soi."* ("You see, Croz, one often needs a little something more than oneself.")[15]

* * * *

Mont Blanc, the highest mountain in western Europe, straddles the

French-Italian border just northwest of Italy's Val Ferret. In the western end of that small valley nestling at the foot of Mont Blanc is the Italian town of Courmayeur, as close to its giant neighbor as Zermatt to the Matterhorn. Like the Val Tournanche, the Val Ferret is a lush green during the summer and French is the first language of its people. In 1865 Monsieur Bertolini was the town's principal innkeeper, a man known for his hospitality and comfortable quarters. It was to Bertolini's inn that Whymper and his crew went in the early evening of June 22 following their disappointment on the Matterhorn.

They left the inn at 4:00 o'clock the next morning bound for the 13,797 foot summit of the Grandes Jorasses. Under Croz's "dextrous" guidance they passed safely over some smooth rocks that formed their route's only potential hazard and at 1:00 p.m. reached the Jorasses' western summit. The mountain had two peaks, close together, the eastern summit being about 100 feet higher. Neither had been climbed before. Uncharacteristically ignoring the record books, Whymper chose the lesser peak because it offered a better view of the Aiguille Verte, the next mountain on his ambitious agenda.

The ascent had been a walk in the park but not so the descent. On the way back to the valley the snow-crust beneath them suddenly gave way and down they all went, flat on their backs. Instinctively they flipped over and tried frantically to plunge their pointed axes into the icy slope.

> It was useless....[The axes] slid over the underlying ice fruitlessly. "Halt!" thundered Croz as he dashed his weapon in again with superhuman energy. No halt could be made, and we slid down slowly, but with accelerating motion, driving up waves of snow in front....Luckily, [when] the slope eased off at one place, the leading men cleverly jumped aside out of the moving snow. [W]e others followed, and the young avalanche we had started, continuing to pour down, fell into a yawning crevasse, showing us where our graves would have been if we had remained in its company five seconds longer. The whole affair did not occupy half a minute.[16]

It was the sole incident of a long day and they returned to the comfort of Bertolini's inn late that afternoon thankful there had been no other.

The time left to Croz before reporting to his new employer in Chamonix was growing short. One challenge remained for which Whymper wanted the full support of his blue-ribbon team: an attempt to find a new route from Courmayeur to Chamonix. The ususal somewhat meandering route between these towns went over the Col du Géant. Whymper's plan was to try for a more direct and faster route over an unnamed and uncrossed pass near the Mont Dolent. Not knowing what obstacles might await them Whymper decided to allow extra time by starting out shortly after midnight.

They departed Courmayeur at that hour on June 26th. By 8:15 a. m. they were at the head of the Glacier du Mont Dolent and at the foot of the steep couloir leading to the pass they hoped to cross. There were no stones falling at the moment but a great trough in the middle of the gully was proof that the slope would be active later in the day. In the lead was Almer who would bear the highest risk if rock-slides began earlier than usual. Always a true professional he went easily, musing audibly to himself and chuckling occasionally at some pleasant thought or recollection. Climbing steadily for two hours they reached the top of the virgin pass without incident.

The new col seemed an ideal crossing point, lying between the two great peaks of Mont Dolent on their right and the Aiguille de Triolet to the west on their left. Croz was now called forward to cut a trench through the snow that lay piled at the top of the pass. The rest of the party waited expectantly, standing just below the crest. "Can we get down?" Whymper asked excitedly as Croz completed his task. The guide looked down the far slope and then back toward Whymper, triumph in his eyes but caution in his voice: "We shall get down somehow," he said in measured tones.[17]

If conditions on the other side of the pass had matched the compacted snow of the ascent they would have been in Chamonix by late afternoon. But Whymper was skeptical. Still below the ridge on the near side he could hear Croz's axe on the far side cutting steps in what sounded like thick ice. The step-cutting indeed took twice as long as Whymper thought it might; Croz labored for two hours before he was able to anchor himself to a rock, some 200 feet down the far side. During that time Almer and Biener had paid out all of the party's strong manila rope as they held the descending guide. Croz now detached himself, allowing his two colleagues to haul the rope back up the slope. Biener tied himself onto it and descended in Croz's steps with Almer holding the rope above. Whymper could now move over the crest and join Almer on the col's narrow summit, able to see for the first time the awesome slope on the other side.

It was, as he imagined, a solid sheet of thick ice – about a thousand feet from top to bottom and set at what looked like a 50 degree angle, falling unmarked and unbroken to a ledge about 300 feet above the Glacier d'Argentière below. The view was breathtaking but Whymper's thoughts were only on making a careful descent. Almer held the rope as Whymper went step by step down the icy slope. Then came Almer alone, the most vulnerable of all for no one was left to hold the rope for him. Whymper again admired his composure; Almer descended as if on a summer evening stroll. Together again they repeated this procedure for another 200 feet and were then able to leave the ice and descend on rocks at the right side of the gully. Continuing down the rocks an additional 100 yards they arrived at the top of the high cliff about 300 feet above the Glacier d'Argentière. There they stopped to consider their next move.

Two narrowly separated crevasses lay at the base of the cliff; both would have to be crossed to reach the glacier. The guides had been able to see only one snow-bridge across the first schrund, at a point near its center. Because the sheer cliff on which they stood was too steep for a direct descent, they could reach the head of that bridge only by going out on the steep snow slope to the left of the cliff and then moving diagonally downward. Almer and Biener set out with Almer in the lead and cutting steps as Croz and Whymper paid the rope out to them. After descending over 100 feet, they arrived at a point above the bridge leading across the first crevasee. Whymper and Croz then started moving downward, Whymper going first while tied to Biener, well below, "with 150 feet of rope too heavy and unwieldy to be gathered up into a coil." On the steep slope he had to support the weight of this length of rope, barely able to do so because it was soaking wet. As Whymper tersely noted, it was "an exceedingly trying time."[18]

The natural bridge across the crevasse was then about 30 feet below them. The slope leading to it was so steep they could descend only by facing inward, with the first man kicking toeholds in the snow as another held the rope from above. These became handholds and toeholds for the others as each went carefully down, one at a time. Fortunately the snow was in perfect condition for this maneuver: soft, compact and stable. After crawling in single file across the snow bridge they doubled back toward the east and crossed the lower schrund without difficulty. On the other side, however, they had to cut steps for another half hour. Then the ice gave way to snow and they could finally put their axes to rest. It was now 5:30 p.m.; they had spent seven arduous hours on the downward side of this new pass, now known as the Col Dolent. From there they crossed easily over the Argentière Glacier past the Chalets of Lognan and on to Les Tines and the high road to Chamonix. They reached the hotel there at 10:00 p.m., the first passage of the new col completed twenty-two hours after leaving Courmayeur. The hotelier gave them champagne and "other drinks reserved for the faithful," but an exhausted Whymper fell asleep in his armchair leaving most of the offering untouched. On awakening at 6:00 a.m. he took promptly to his bed and went back to sleep.[19]

With customary understatement Whymper acknowledged that their new pass was "unlikely" to compete with the traditional route over the Col du Géant. Indeed, no one made the passage of the Col Dolent again until thirteen years later when two Englishmen, W. E. Davidson and J. W. Hartley, crossed it with their guides in the opposite direction. They knew it would be much easier to climb up the col's northern ice-wall than down it.

The descent from the Col Dolent by Whymper's party was a classic example of how early mountaineers overcame unexpected problems with a combination of skill, ingenuity and physical strength. It showed the value of guides at a time when there were so few experienced amateurs amid such extensive unexplored territory. Guides cut steps, held rope, recommended routes, and found places of safe passage. A good guide needed steady hands, steel nerves, a laborer's strength and bottomless stamina. As on the Col Dolent, a party often benefited from having more than one guide to share the heavy work. There Whymper's party had faced a 50 degree ice slope and a crevasse with only one snow bridge – difficult to access and hidden from all but the most practiced eye. It is easy to imagine a different outcome had there been no guides – or less competent ones – on that formidable passage.

The descent of the Col Dolent also highlighted how skill and luck often go hand-in-hand with an experienced mountaineer. Had the snow been less than perfect on the nearly vertical 30 foot drop to the bridge across the first crevasse – or not located precisely where it was needed – Whymper's party might well have met with disaster. Having those conditions was sheer good fortune but luck alone would not have been enough. It took the skill of all the men to find it and turn it to their advantage. Fortune may favor the brave but it is a mere handmaiden to courage and experience.

Mountaineers instinctively call upon a kind of sixth sense for help in a seemingly impossible situation. On a sheer slope with no apparent way to move up, down, or sideways, a climber senses rather than feels a tiny crevice, crack, or rough spot sufficient to allow movement. This sense, once established, functions naturally as experience accumulates. Novice climbers acquire it gradually, usually at the hand of a knowing guide who sternly commands his employer in moments of crisis simply to "Do Something!" Sometimes, however, skill, good fortune, and six senses are not enough. This was particularly true in the Golden Age as the best guides and amateurs of the day often met unexpected, fast-occurring dangers; the mountains simply reached out and took their toll. In those circumstances destiny gave the climber no opportunity to test his skills or inner fortitude. Very soon Whymper would learn that lesson the hard way.

Michel Croz now left the party and Christian Almer became Whymper's chief guide. Almer lacked some of the qualities Whymper admired so much in Croz: an aggressive confidence, a macho sociability, and almost superhuman strength. But Almer had all the necessary skills: "[T]here is not a truer heart or a surer foot to be found amongst the Alps." Almer also had one attribute that Croz lacked and Whymper prized: the habit of doing his work and keeping his mouth shut. "Almer is a quiet man at all times...and this is one of his great merits. A garrulous man is always a nuisance and upon a mountainside may be a danger, for actual climbing requires a man's whole attention. Added to this, talkative men are hindrances; they are usually thirsty, and a thirsty man is a drag."[21] Whether in the Alps or in London Whymper had no tolerance for those who talked much and said little.

On June 28th Whymper and his two guides, with a porter added, left Chamonix and headed south over the Mer de Glace toward the Aiguille Verte, next on Whymper's list. Late in the afternoon they bivouacked at 7,800 feet on the side of a low mountain known as the "Couvercle," the cap. At 3:15 the next morning they set out for the aiguille's summit. Leaving their tent and food with the porter they headed eastward over the Glacier de Talèfre toward the southern side of the Verte. At 5:30 a.m. they crossed a snow-bridge over a schrund protecting the final peak and from there could see the summit and the entire intervening route. Looking upward the taciturn Almer exclaimed in a rare emotional outburst: "Oh, Aiguille Verte, you are dead, you are dead!"[22] Sunshine and good fortune were theirs that morning: granite rocks on the side of a gully enabled them to avoid the center's slick ice as they climbed higher. Solid footholds took them to a ridge leading to the summit and at 10:15, after a seven hour climb, the party stood in triumph atop the "green needle," the summer's third ascent of a virgin mountain peak.

The Verte's summit was "a snowy dome, large enough for a quadrille" with an exceptional view of the nearby Mont Blanc Massif.[23] Though he celebrated only with a goodly portion of bread and cheese, Whymper was jubilant. Just past his 25th birthday he had now joined Tyndall, Stephen, Wills, T. S. Kennedy, Hinchcliff, and a handful of others in the highest echelon of the British climbers, the elite mountaineers of the Golden Age. Only the Matterhorn remained, and that was to be his next target.

Reveries of dancing on the Aiguille Verte's snowy summit faded as the world rather abruptly intruded. Just south of their position was a small mountain of less than 10,000 feet known as the Jardin. Prettily wooded and easily accessible over smooth glaciers, it was frequented by tourists. As Whymper's party stood on the newly won peak "trying to forget the world...some vile wretch came to the Jardin and made hideous sounds by blowing through a horn."[24] As he and the guides were "denouncing" this noisy intrusion into their unspoiled mountain world, clouds moved in and hid the sun. So the party forgot the distraction and went off in "hot haste" just as snow began to fall heavily.

The descent was uneventful but took longer than they had anticipated due to slippery conditions from the new-fallen snow. They crossed the last schrund and hurried over the glacier back to their camp on the Couvercle, anticipating their tent's shelter and a solid meal prepared by the waiting porter. They found the porter with the tent rolled and about to depart for Chamonix to report that his employer's party had been lost or killed. They roared at him to unfasten the tent straps and get out the food. Alas! When the porter unfolded the tent it produced nothing to eat. "Get out the food," they screamed impatiently.[25] But he could not; he had consumed it all – mutton, bread, cheese, wine, eggs, and sausages. Outraged the hungry party raced toward Chamonix, going at their hardest and leaving the hapless porter struggling in their wake. Whymper was gleeful: "He streamed with perspiration; the mutton and cheese oozed out in big drops....[H]e larded the glacier [and] we had our revenge."[26] After stopping at the Montenvers for an overdue meal they returned to the hotel at Chamonix where they were welcomed by champagne and a traditional cannon salute to their achievement. Their hotelier was almost as pleased as they; every first ascent was sure to bring additional business to his establishment.

The local guides, members of the ancient Association des Guides de Chamonix, did not share the innkeeper's joy. To lead him on the Aiguille Verte Whymper had not employed a guide from Chamonix or the Mont Blanc area, only Almer and Biener, two Oberlanders. In so doing he had not broken any local rules, only taken advantage of an exception. Climbers on the Mont Blanc range were permitted to use foreign guides who had led their employers over a pass en route to Chamonix. The local guides were angry simply because Whymper had not given at least one of them the chance to join his party during its attempt at a first ascent.

The Chamoniards customarily bullied foreign guides and now accused Almer and Biener of lying. What proof did they have of scaling this soaring rock-needle? Where was the flag upon its summit? Further riled by this incendiary rhetoric, a group of angry locals stormed the office of their chief guide in protest. Whymper stayed out of the fray but T. S. Kennedy, recently arrived at Chamonix from Zermatt, came forward and faced off with the crowd's ringleader, hotly disputing his accusations. Shortly three gendarmes appeared, urging the disputants to retire to a cabaret for a glass of absinthe and a more reasoned debate. With the crowd's respect for the "cocked hats" outweighing their anger, they moved on to a local tavern but the argument did not end there. Befogged with drink and oblivious to the supreme irony of their reasoning, the guides made a proposal to Whymper: "Take three of us with you, and we bet you 2,000 to 1,000 francs you won't make the ascent!"[27] He declined their offer but told Kennedy – who was headed for the Verte in a day or so – that if he would accept the wager, Whymper would take a 100 franc share for himself. Kennedy did climb the Verte a week later with two Chamonix guides and one from Zermatt but did not make the bet which, in the end, came to nothing.

From the summit of the Aiguille Verte to the drunken confrontation at the Chamonix tavern, this had been a classic Alpine episode. First, Whymper had scaled a virgin peak only to have its wondrous silence invaded by the discordant bleat of a tourist's horn. Though out of earshot, this callous trumpeter had received a tongue-lashing not only for interrupting Whymper's mountain top reverie but also for showing the typical tourist insensitivity that climbers disdained. Later, feeling grievously cheated by their hungry and dull-witted porter, Whymper's party had unmercifully force-marched the man's overstuffed body. Of course the hapless peasant deserved punishment, but did his employers need to witness his suffering with such apparent relish? Yes, Whymper would say, our behavior was appropriate; his discomfort merely matched our hunger, a fair trade in the circumstances. Also fitting was the gala welcome given them by the hotelier, offered with an entrepreneurial spirit Whymper admired and a geniality he appreciated in those who rendered service. Then came the rather threatening insults from the hostile Chamonix guides, angered by the challenge to their organized monopoly. Though Whymper had stayed aloof, their belligerence surely represented what he detested in unruly mobs back in England: not their anger, necessarily, but their resort to violence against the established order. All in all, the essence of the interplay of personalities and viewpoints in these Alpine settings seemed much the same as in London.

During the previous summer of 1864, as Whymper and Adams Reilly "prowled about" the Mont Blanc area, they had considered the possibility that a new and faster route from Chamonix to Courmayeur might lie over a gap in the ridge between two aiguilles situated almost due east of Chamonix, about one mile southwest of the treacherous Col Dolent. Now, after the latest skirmish in Chamonix concerning the legitimacy of his Aiguille Verte ascent, an attempt on another untrodden pass with only Swiss guides had become something more than the search for a useful route. It was also a way to show the pompous Chamoniards they were not needed, rubbing their noses in the snow of their own backyard.

Whymper's party left the Montenvers at 4:00 a. m. on July 3rd. On this surprisingly easy alternate route they reached the top of the new pass at 9:35. The descent to the Glacier de Triolet was equally trouble-free and by 1:30 p.m. they were on the springy turf of a high meadow, a sign that their work was over and the passage a success. They crossed the Doire River by bridge and were in Courmayeur by five o'clock, confirming that Whymper had indeed found the fastest route from Chamonix to Courmayeur. The new pass came to be known as the Col de Talèfre because it looked down on the glacier of that name. For some reason – probably because it intimidated travellers less skilled that Whymper – the new col never supplanted the Col du Géant as the favored route between these two towns. But with its crossing, Whymper's aggressive program of ascents for the summer of 1865 had gone according to plan. Leslie Stephen, in his review of *Scrambles*, said that Whymper's campaign of 1865 "up to its most disastrous end, was by far the most brilliant ever carried out in the Alps."[28] Only the Matterhorn remained and the aggressive young mountaineer was ready for what he hoped would be the grand finale of the season and perhaps of his climbing career.

Still with Almer and Biener he headed for the Val Tournanche. Whymper intended to attack the great mountain's Swiss side via its east face and the northeastern Hörnli ridge. Along the way there, he and his guides "bagged" the Ruinette, the easiest in his career of first ascents, but they still had doubts about Whymper's main objective. "Anything but Matterhorn, dear sir!" Almer had said during the summer, "Anything but Matterhorn."[29] The guides' caution, Whymper felt, came not from fear but from a conviction that a Matterhorn ascent was impossible and any effort to climb it a waste of time. But their reluctance was real, so he sent them on to Breuil by a short cut while he went to Valtournanche to see if Carrel was available to become his guide.

Whymper knew that the bersagliere was the one man whose desire to climb the Matterhorn was as strong as his own. He felt that if he could outline to Carrel his plan to climb the mountain's Swiss side, the ambitious guide would see the logic of it and forsake, however reluctantly, his determination to scale the mountain's Italian side. Arriving at Valtournanche on Thursday, July 6th, he learned that Carrel was leading a party on the Matterhorn that very day. Noting the low clouds in the valley and on the mountain, Whymper felt reasonably certain that the weather would defeat them. He was right. Walking up to Breuil the next day he met Carrel and his party coming down the path and learned that the previous day's fog and rain had forced them to retreat scarcely before they reached the Glacier du Lion.

Whymper had by now decided that if he could persuade Carrel to guide him he would not need Almer or Biener. Taking advantage of their chance meeting he proposed to Jean-Antoine that the two of them, with Caesar Carrel and another man, take the Théodule Pass to Zermatt by moonlight on the night of the 9th and on the 10th pitch their tent as high as possible on the east face. The next day, if all went well, they would work their way to the northeast ridge and thence to the summit. Carrel urged that they attempt the Italian side instead. Whymper countered with a suggestion that they first follow his plan with the understanding that if it failed they would come back for a try "on the old route." Carrel agreed and they parted company.

Whymper continued on to Breuil to meet with Almer and Biener. These two had served him well and faithfully. The three of them, he calculated, had climbed over 100,000 feet during the eighteen days they had been together. So it was with real sadness that he told them they would no longer be needed. One can only speculate why he did not continue their employment. Perhaps he felt that they – Almer in particular – would take unkindly to being placed under the Italian guide on a mountainside within, though barely, Switzerland's borders. More likely, based on his confidence in Carrel and knowing he would include his cousin Caesar as a second guide, Whymper saw no need for other guides or the further expense they would represent.

That night at the Breuil inn Whymper's hopes for success were as high as they had ever been. He had been frustrated initially by Croz's unavailability and the reluctance of even the best of the Oberland guides to accompany him on the Matterhorn. Croz was physically the strongest of all the guides and there was no one more courageous. But with Croz gone, Carrel was Whymper's next choice, even on the Swiss side of the mountain. He was the only person besides Whymper himself, guide or amateur, who had consistently challenged the Matterhorn and never given up. He was a natural-born mountaineer, the "finest rock climber" Whymper had ever seen.[30] He was a man "of dauntless courage,...with iron nerves, and muscles and sinews of no ordinary kind."[31] Thus Whymper was well satisfied with the arrangements he had put together under the pressure of unavoidable circumstance. Little did he dream, as he slept at the Breuil inn that night, that his plans for an east-face ascent with Carrel would crumble like a rotten rock, leaving him scrambling desperately for a foothold from which to continue his campaign.

# CHAPTER 12

## *Triumph and Tragedy*

A steady rain obscured the mountains as Whymper awoke in Breuil on Saturday, July 8th. No matter; his day would be filled with final preparations for a three-day climb on the Matterhorn starting in the wee hours of the morning of the 10th. He wanted to make sure that everything his party needed – food, equipment, tent, extra rope, blankets, firewood and porters – would be available and waiting for them. The Carrels would be his guides and, he hoped, Luc Meynet one of his porters. The only problem might be the weather; until it cleared no one would be starting for the Matterhorn.

Late that afternoon word reached Whymper that the Rev. A. G. Girdlestone, a mountain-climbing Anglican priest with whom Whymper had spent some time in Chamonix a few days earlier, had fallen ill in the town of Valtournanche. The news took him back to the summer of 1862 when he had languished alone in Breuil recovering from his nearly fatal fall on the Matterhorn. He had vowed then that if he were in the valley when a fellow countryman lay ill or injured he would do what he could to give aid.

The next morning, Sunday the 9th, his Matterhorn plans still on hold under sodden skies, Whymper set out for Valtournanche to offer help to Girdlestone. On the way he met Carrel coming up the valley with several other men, one of whom appeared to be a "foreigner." With them was a pack mule heavily loaded with provisions. Carrel explained that they were helping the foreigner transport his baggage to Breuil. He also told Whymper that he and cousin Caesar had been engaged by a "family of distinction" from the Aosta valley, so the two Carrels could remain at Whymper's call only through Tuesday, the 11th. Whymper was incredulous. Why, he demanded, had Carrel not told him this when he had been engaged only forty-eight hours earlier? Because, said Carrel, his employment by the Italian family had been agreed upon for some time but he had received notice of the actual starting date only upon returning home after their meeting on Friday afternoon.

Whymper was upset but there was nothing he could do about it. Carrel's tone was polite but firm and Whymper knew he was powerless to change the guide's mind. He would learn later that Carrel had something else up his sleeve but at the time he suspected nothing. Carrel, for his part, knew that he was scheduling his consecutive commitments very tightly. He had been expecting his next employer's appearance any moment and was aware that Whymper was planning at least three days on the mountain. But the climbing season was short and Carrel always looked to maximize his earnings. And since Whymper was a constant threat to his Matterhorn ambition, guiding the Englishman to the top was far better than having Whymper succeed without him.

Whymper continued on to Valtournanche to visit his sick colleague. Girdlestone said he felt better but then fainted from the effort of their

*The village of Valtournanche*

conversation. He was obviously in need of treatment of some kind so Whymper tramped down to Châtillon in search of medicine. Though it was a Sunday, he roused an apothecary of sorts and returned to the patient with a recommended potion. By the time his ministrations ended Valtournanche was in darkness and the weather had worsened. It was windy when he stepped outside, with rain falling in buckets.

A figure passed me under the church-porch. "Qui vive?" "Jean-Antoine." "I thought you were at Breuil." "No, sir, when the storms came on I knew we should not start tonight and so came down to sleep here." "Ha, Carrel, this is a great bore....I have sent away my guides relying on you; and now you are going to leave me to travel with a party of ladies. This work is not fit for you" (he smiled, I suppose at the implied compliment); "can't you send someone else instead?" "No monsieur, I am sorry, but my word is pledged...." By this time we had arrived at the inn door. "Well, it is no fault of yours. Come presently with Caesar, and have some wine." They came, and we sat up till midnight, recounting our old adventures, in the inn of Valtournanche.[1]

Whymper's impulsive gesture of friendship despite his frustration and disappointment with Carrel's conduct was revealing. He had often remarked that having the older guide's leadership was the key to a successful Matterhorn ascent. At the time he rightly felt that the bersagliere's abrupt disclosure of his unavailability beyond two days of service was unfair at best and deceitful at worst. And yet, at this tense moment, feelings of friendship and respect for Carrel overcame Whymper's burning ambition and youthful impatience. His invitation to Jean-Antoine and his cousin Caesar to join him for a nightcap also reflected a mature awareness that when circumstances cannot be changed, attitude is everything.

Due to the late hour and the continuing bad weather Whymper spent that night at the Valtournanche inn. The following day, Monday, he went up to Breuil under saturated clouds and intermittent showers. The two Carrels were there and the three of them exchanged greetings but then parted company, all understanding that the little time remaining in Jean-Antoine's working schedule meant that Whymper's dream of ascending the Matterhorn with the *bersagliere* had ended. The inn was almost deserted; Girdlestone had gathered enough strength to come up from Valtournanche but was the only arrival that day. The lingering drizzle had discouraged the people who usually came to Breuil from Zermatt on Mondays in the summer, and Whymper went to bed early that night restless from the weather-induced inactivity.

The next morning a loud knock on his door brought him abruptly awake. It was Girdlestone asking if he had heard the news. "What news?" "A large party of guides went off this morning to try the Matterhorn, and they had a mule with them...."[2] Whymper was instantly alert. He grabbed his telescope and rushed to the window at the front of the inn. In the gradually thinning mist he could see the party already on the mountain's lower slopes. Favre the innkeeper stood beside him. Whymper spoke excitedly: "What's going on? Who's in that party? Who's leading it?" "Jean-Antoine," said Favre, "and Caesar is with him." Knowing that the one day remaining in his agreement with Whymper was meaningless, Carrel had set out with the Italian group on the first clear day giving no prior notice.

Now sick at heart, the hapless young climber learned the details from the innkeeper. The Italian party's ascent had been carefully planned. Carrel and the others whom Whymper had met on Friday the 7th, the day of his first arrival at Breuil, had not been on a failed climb as Carrel had implied. Rather, it had been a reconnaissance mission for the group now on the mountain. The mule Whymper had noticed on his way to help Girdlestone on Sunday was carrying their provisions. Carrel was not in the service of a "party of ladies" but of the family of an important Italian Minister, one Signor Sella. The two Carrels were working for a member of the Italian government! It was a grand scheme to conquer the Matterhorn for the glory of the young Italian nation and its new King Emmanuel II. No wonder they had been so secretive and no wonder that Favre, his "good friend" after five previous summers at the inn, had played along with his compatriots to keep Whymper in the dark! They had "bamboozled and hum-bugged" him and he was "mortified."[3]

\* \* \* \*

The Italian conspiracy – perfectly legitimate, of course – was more extensive than Whymper knew. The Italian Alpine Club had been founded in 1863. Its members, disappointed not to have been the first to climb the high peak of Monte Viso, fixed their sights on the Matterhorn. Two of the Club's founding members – Quintino Sella, a Minister in the new Italian government, and Felice Giordano, a mining engineer – were the leaders and principal funders of this effort. On his way to Zermatt from an ascent of Mont Blanc in 1864, Giordano had met Carrel by chance on the Théodule Pass. After "spend[ing] a whole evening with Jean-Antoine and the [Canon] Carrel," Giordano came to the conclusion that the *bersgaliere* was the man to lead the Italians to the Matterhorn summit.[4]

The Italians' plans took shape during the next year: they would launch an attempt from Breuil in July of 1865 in two steps – a scouting expedition by Carrel followed by an all-out assault if he found conditions on the mountain favorable. Friday July 7th turned out to be the day of Carrel's inspection. That afternoon he had unexpectedly met Whymper on the path and agreed to go with him on the Matterhorn's east side. At that time he knew Giordano was planning to be in Valtournanche soon, with equipment and supplies for Carrel's own attempt on the mountain, but he did not know exactly when. That same day Giordano was in Turin writing of his plans to Minister Sella in a somewhat conspiratorial tone:

I am starting off heavily armed for the destination you wot of. I sent off the day before yesterday the first tent, 300 metres of rope, and some iron hoops and rings, besides various kind of provisions for ourselves, a spirit-lamp for heating water, tea, etc....These things together weigh about 100 kilos. I have also sent Carrel 200 fcs [so] that he may meet these articles in Châtillon and transport them to Valtournanche and Breuil at once....

I am taking with me a second tent, three barometers, and the Yearbook of Longitudes..... You need only trouble about your own personal requirements, viz., your headgear, a few rugs, etc., and some good cigars; if possible, also a little good wine and a few shekels, because I have only been able to bring about 3,000 francs with me.

Let us, then, set out to attack this Devil's mountain, and let us see that we succeed, if only Whymper has not been beforehand with us.[5]

Giordano met Carrel in Valtournanche that Saturday and departed for Breuil the next day with Carrel's group and the heavily loaded pack mule. He was the foreigner Whymper had noticed as the group passed him on his way to see Girdlestone. And it was Giordano's presence that had forced Carrel to shorten his time with Whymper.

Giordano again wrote to Sella on Tuesday, July 11th, the day Carrel's party set off for the Matterhorn. On that day he and Whymper were both guests at the Breuil inn:

I reached Valtournanche on Saturday at midday. There I found Carrel, who had just returned from a reconnoitring expedition on the Matterhorn....Whymper had arrived two or three days before; as usual, he wished to make the ascent, and had engaged Carrel, who, not having yet had my letters, had agreed, but for a few days only. Fortunately, the weather turned bad. Whymper was unable to make his fresh attempt, and Carrel left him and came with me, with five other picked men who are the best guides in the valley.

I have taken up my quarters at Breuil for the time being. The weather, the god whom we all fear and on whom all will depend, has been...very changeable....Carrel told me not to come up...until he should send me word; naturally, he wishes personally to make sure of the last bits....[He must also] ascertain whether we can bivouac at a point higher than Whymper's highest....[P]lease send me a few lines in reply, with some advice, because I am head over ears in difficulty here, what with the weather, the expense and Whymper.

I have tried to keep everything secret, but that fellow, whose life seems to depend on the Matterhorn, is here, suspiciously prying into everything. I have taken all the competent men away from him, and yet he is so enamored of this mountain that he may go up with others and make a scene. He is here, in this hotel, and I try to avoid speaking to him.[6]

Whymper knew none of the details of the Italians' plan as he gazed through the telescope from the Breuil inn. He correctly concluded, however, that Carrel's large party, heavily provisioned, would move slowly. Indeed, as Giordano's letters make clear, the Italians were more encumbered than Whymper thought, not by material excess alone but also by the way they approached the challenge. Although Giordano and Sella were experienced climbers, they relied entirely on Carrel and his group of guides, almost literally, to pave the way. While Carrel was on the mountain, Giordano waited at his lower base feeling lonely and helpless, fretting about Whymper and hoping to receive guidance and support from the Minister. Sella, meanwhile, would remain at his desk in Turin until advised by Giordano that Carrel was ready to escort them both to the top. This was not the way to mount a successful campaign against the aggressive Englishman. They knew him by reputation: he was a guerilla fighter who could shoot straight and move fast. Yet they failed to adapt to his style, sending their troops into battle in classic formation while they sat safely behind the lines until their field commander pronounced the way open. For their flawed tactics they would pay a heavy price.

On that Tuesday morning, however, Whymper despaired of overcoming Carrel's substantial head start. As he looked through the telescope he felt more alone than Giordano.

\* \* \* \*

The devious Italians had stolen a march on him, no doubt about it. Innkeeper Favre had been a party to his countrymen's game from the start and was overjoyed to see Carrel's party finally on their way. He was already counting the increased revenue an Italian-side ascent of the

Matterhorn would bring. But Whymper was not constituted to remain idle for long. After the shock of seeing Carrel's group on the mountain he returned to his room and lit his pipe, his furious puffing soon filling the small chamber with smoke. Tobacco soothed him and helped him think. The Italian party's mule-load of provisions meant that they would move slowly, taking time to prepare meals as they went. The weather had not improved greatly; the rain had stopped but fog and mist still covered the Matterhorn. All things considered this large group might be on the mountain for a week.

As he smoked, a new plan formed in Whymper's mind: he would go to Zermatt, find some guides and attempt the Matterhorn's eastern side. If that failed he could probably get back to Breuil while Carrel was still climbing. The mountain was not "padlocked," so he might even be able to ascend the Italian side alone, overtake the slower moving group and reach the summit before them![7] A wildly over-optimistic scenario but at least it was a plan and it propelled him into action.

Problems arose immediately. He needed help to carry his baggage to Zermatt and though he spent most of the morning making inquiries, not a porter was to be found. They were on the mountain with Carrel, or ill, or somewhere else. Favre was of no help and even the faithful Meynet was too busy making cheese to join him. Around noon that day people at last began to arrive in Breuil, mostly tourists from Zermatt. Among them was a young Englishman accompanied by a Swiss guide, both unknown to Whymper. After introducing himself Whymper told the newcomer of his need for help and asked if he would release his guide for that purpose. He could not do that, the young man said, but added that he was returning to Zermatt the next day and that his guide could assist with Whymper's baggage at that time.

After the young Englishman got settled at the inn they talked further. Whymper told him of his plans for the Matterhorn and in the course of the conversation learned that the new arrival was an English nobleman, Lord Francis Douglas, aged eighteen, whose older brother was the Marquis of Queensberry. Whymper had heard of Douglas from his successful first ascent of the Ober Gabelhorn. Word travelled fast among Alpine climbers; Douglas had reached the Gabelhorn summit only four days before his arrival in Breuil.[8] He also told Whymper that he had been led on the Gabelhorn by Peter Taugwalder, an older guide from Zermatt. Though only forty-five, Taugwalder was known as "Old Peter" to distinguish him from his son, "Young Peter," who was Douglas's guide at the moment. The elder Taugwalder was also in Douglas's employ and in Zermatt awaiting further orders. It was indeed a small world. Old Peter was fresh in Whymper's memory for having the gall – or, Whymper suspected, the empty bravado – to set his fee at 200 francs when Whymper sought a Matterhorn guide in 1861.

Douglas now passed on to Whymper an interesting remark the older guide had made while the two were on the Gabelhorn. Taugwalder said that he had been beyond the Hörnli Pic on the Matterhorn's northeastern ridge a few weeks earlier and felt that the mountain might be scaled by that route. This was generally consistent with Whymper's decision, though it would put them initially on the ridge instead of the eastern face. Knowing Almer and Biener had already left Zermatt he felt that the senior Taugwalder might be his best bet. As he and Douglas talked, the young English Lord became excited at the prospect of attempting the Matterhorn himself and asked if he could join his new acquaintance. For his part Whymper was favorably impressed by Douglas's zeal and his proven success on the Gabelhorn. Before their conversation ended it was agreed: they would go post-haste early the next morning to Zermatt and begin their attempt the following day. Douglas's employment of both Taugwaulders dovetailed nicely into their plan.

They left Breuil early on Wednesday July12th. Favre had belatedly made one of his employees available as a porter. Now that Whymper had joined forces with Douglas and Young Peter, the innkeeper "could no longer hinder our departure"[9] The four men crossed the Col Théodule and made their way to the little chapel at the Schwarzsee, a dark pond located below the Hörnli at about 8500 feet. There they deposited baggage and equipment to be retrieved on the climbers' ascent. Included among these items were almost 600 feet of rope: 200 feet of Manila hemp, 150 feet of a stouter Italian hemp, and over 200 feet of a thinner rope "formerly used" by Whymper which he now called a "stout sash-line."[10] Whymper, Douglas and Young Peter then walked down to Zermatt and found the elder Taugwalder who confirmed his availability as their guide. He suggested that they hire a porter of his choosing and all agreed.

Later in the day, as Whymper and Douglas approached the Monte Rosa Hotel, who should be sitting on the wall out front but Whymper's old favorite Michel Croz. Surprised but happy to see him Whymper assumed Croz was with the employer he had met up with in Chamonix. *Mais non*, said Croz, the Englishman had taken sick and returned home. The Rev. Charles Hudson, a mountaineering Anglican clergyman in Chamonix at the time, had immediately engaged the just-released Croz. Now, said the French guide, they were in Zermatt for the same reason as Whymper: Hudson was set to make an attempt on the Matterhorn!

This was startling news. Whymper had fled from Carrel and Breuil only to find a new adversary in Zermatt. Suddenly climbers were circling the mountain like hunters around a trapped tiger. With another Englishman seeking the same prize, and with the Italians pushing upward on the southern side, Whymper's competition had doubled overnight.

That evening Whymper and Douglas ate dinner at the Monte Rosa. As they finished Charles Hudson and a companion walked into the dining room. In response to questions from "some idlers in the room" Hudson said that the two of them had been surveying the Matterhorn

*Chapel at Schwarzsee*

and were planning an attempt on the mountain the next morning. Hearing this, Whymper and Lord Douglas went into the hotel's common room just off the reception area to assess the situation. They decided it was better to ask Hudson to join them than to have two groups headed for the Matterhorn summit at the same time. Whymper then sought out Hudson to get his reaction.

Hudson agreed that joining forces made sense. Having noticed the young age of Hudson's friend, Whymper wondered aloud if the youth was qualified for a Matterhorn attempt. Hudson identified the young man as Douglas Hadow and assured Whymper that the youngster "had done Mont Blanc in less time than most men." He also mentioned other climbs by Hadow in places unfamiliar to Whymper. In his judgment, the Anglican vicar concluded, his young friend was "a sufficiently good man to go with us."[11]

Hudson was well-respected in the mountaineering brotherhood. He was almost twelve years older than Whymper and had been climbing for several more years than the young scrambler. The priest's confidence in Hadow was enough for Whymper. Hudson further suggested that the three guides already hired would be sufficient and Whymper agreed. With that the die was cast: their new party would consist of four

*Portrait of Charles Hudson*

climbers – Whymper, Hudson, Douglas and Hadow – with Croz and the two Taugwalders as their guides. Old Peter's youngest son, acting as a porter, would go only as far as the first night's bivouac.

Charles Hudson, the Vicar of Wakefield, was a natural-born athlete. In his youth he had been known as a prodigious walker capable of doing fifty miles a day. He was now thirty-five and extremely fit. Like a number of clerics Hudson had taken seriously to mountaineering. He was well known for several climbs, including his ascent of Mont Blanc in 1855 without guides five years before Whymper saw his first mountain. Whymper summed up his assessment of Hudson in *Scrambles*:

> Hudson...was considered by the mountaineering fraternity to be the best amateur of his time....His long practice made him surefooted...not greatly inferior to a born mountaineer ....[He was] a well-made man of middle height and age, neither stout nor thin, with a pleasant face – though grave, and with quiet unassuming manners. Although he had done some of the greatest mountaineering feats...he was the last man to speak of his own doings.[12]

With T. S. Kennedy, Hadow, and fellow Anglican clergyman Joseph McCormick, the Vicar had climbed in the Mont Blanc chain ten days earlier, just after Whymper left the area. The four of them intended to go from there to Zermatt and attempt the Matterhorn together. Of those four only Kennedy, who made no disclosure of their immediate plans, had arrived in Chamonix while Whymper was still there. No doubt hoping their group would be first on the virgin summit, Kennedy knew better than to give Whymper any additional incentive. But neither Kennedy nor the Reverend McCormick made it to Zermatt with Hudson. A business matter had called Kennedy back to London and wet weather had delayed McCormick. Hudson had gone ahead without them, intending to reconnoiter the Matterhorn until McCormick arrived. Hudson's decision to advance the date of his attempt to the morning after Whymper's arrival, accompanied only by Douglas Hadow, meant either that he was not sure when McCormick would arrive or, more likely, that he felt forced to start without him as Whymper was threatening to move out the next day.

Whymper's newest climbing companion, Lord Francis Douglas, like Hudson, was a good athlete. He was also a serious young man who had done well in his studies. The second son of a titled father he was planning a career in the British army. Though only eighteen years old he had spent several seasons in the Alps and shown great agility and climbing skill. In Whymper's opinion the young nobleman was "nimble as a deer" and fast "becoming an expert mountaineer."[13] Douglas's recent ascent of the Ober Gabelhorn had particularly impressed Whymper who had surveyed the peak a few weeks earlier and decided not to attempt it, at that time, because of its difficulty.

At nineteen Douglas Hadow, the fourth member of the new party, "had the looks and manners of a greater age."[14] Hadow had impressed Hudson with a fast round trip on Mont Blanc, but had shown uncertainty on other climbs by seeking extra assistance from guides and fellow climbers. No one was quite sure why Hadow and Hudson were climbing together, though it was probably through family connections. Nor was it clear why Hudson overestimated, or perhaps overstated to Whymper, his young companion's mountaineering ability.

That night the Matterhorn loomed above the town under a starry sky, silently awaiting the first serious attempt on its summit from the eastern side. For all his experience, Whymper had difficulty falling asleep as he thought of Carrel's two-day head start in their race for the mountain's virgin peak. He could not help but reflect on the rush of recent events: the Italians' perfidy, Lord Douglas's fortuitous appearance, and the fate that had reunited him with Croz. Were these omens for good or for ill?

So Croz and I became comrades once more. As I threw myself on my bed and tried to go to sleep, I wondered at the strange series of chances which had first separated us and then brought us together again. I thought of the mistake through which he had accepted [another] engagement;...of his recommendation to transfer our energies to the chain of Mont Blanc; of the retirement of Almer and Biener; of the desertion of Carrel; of the arrival of Lord Francis Douglas; and lastly of our accidental meeting at Zermatt. As I pondered these things I could not help asking "What next?"[15]

"If any one of the links of this fatal chain of circumstances had been omitted," he later wrote, "what a different story I should have to tell!" Though he did not know it as he lay there, the weakest link would be the inclusion of the one climber who should never have been part of the chain.

\* \* \* \*

They left the Monte Rosa hotel at 5:30 the next morning, Thursday July 13th, under the brilliant blue of cloudless skies. In the augmented party were Whymper, Hudson, Douglas, Hadow, Croz, Old Peter and both of his sons, the youngest of which would act as a porter for the first day only. They tramped up to the Schwarzsee chapel at a leisurely pace, retrieved the items left there, and climbed another 2,000 feet to a point just below the Hörnli on the mountain's northeastern ridge. Whymper carried the party's wine-bags, an ever-present addition to even the most difficult Alpine climbs. To make the wine last longer he was secretly adding water to the bags as party members sampled their contents. At each halt the men found the bags full – "a good omen...little short of miraculous."[17] This prank, and Whymper's obvious delight in it, was a reminder of the youthful spirit hidden within the mature body of an accomplished mountaineer. Seriousness in word, bearing, and deed was his hallmark. But occasionally, in excited anticipation of a major mountain summit, the facade cracked.

They were now on the short arête connecting the Hörnli to the Matterhorn's northeastern ridge at the base of the huge three-sided pyramid forming the mountain's upper reaches. Angling left on narrow ledges the party reached the Matterhorn's eastern side, a triangular snow slope whose rocky base and side ridges are each the better part of a mile long. The mountain's pointed summit, though hidden by the steep rise of the face from where they stood, towered more than 4,000 feet above them. It was now 11:30 a.m. All were amazed at the unexpectedly modest slope of the mountain's eastern side; there were places where a climber could actually "run about."[18] Around noon, at about 12,000 feet, they selected an area to erect Whymper's tent and make camp for the night. Thus far Hudson and Whymper had alternated at the front of their team, occasionally cutting steps themselves when necessary. From the beginning the lead twosome had consulted on decisions involving the climb, in effect acting as the party's joint leaders. They now sent Croz and young Peter forward to inspect the route planned for the next day. The two were gone a considerable time, almost three hours. On their return they were visibly excited. We encountered "not a difficulty, not a single difficulty. We could have gone to the summit and returned today easily!"[19] This good news, combined with their uneventful ascent to that point, cheered the party immensely.

> We passed the remaining hours of daylight – some basking in the sunshine, some sketching or collecting. When the sun went down, giving as it departed a glorious promise for the morrow, we returned to the tent to arrange for the night. Hudson made tea, I coffee, and we then retired, each one to his blanket bag; the Taugwalders, Lord Francis Douglas, and [I] occupying the tent, the others remaining by preference outside.

> Long after dusk the cliffs above echoed with our laughter and with the songs of the guides, for we were happy that night in camp, and feared no evil.[20]

They were up before dawn on Friday, July 14th, eager to get moving. Following the route taken by Croz the preceding afternoon they soon rounded the narrow promontory that had blocked their upward view from the campsite. From there they could see the final 3,000 feet of the eastern face in full, rising like part of an enormous ziggurat formed by natural forces to serve a primitive land of giants. Continuing upward they chose a route composed of snow and occasional rocky ground near the Matterhorn's northeastern ridge. The exposed parts of these rocks slanted downward into the mountain, offering the better footing Whymper had predicted.

As the party moved slowly upward he and Hudson again took turns in the lead. Twice they bore further right toward the northeast ridge hoping for better footholds, but to no avail. The ridge's rocks formed a steeper slope – and many were rotten – so the party returned to the eastern face each time. All the while they worried silently about the progress the Italians might be making on the other side of the mountain. Occasionally this concern would become visible: thinking they may have heard a call from somewhere, or even a shout of triumph from the mountaintop, they would stop and listen, but it was only the wind and they would again doggedly haul themselves upward. As they moved on, the thoughts would not stop. Would the Matterhorn prize be snatched from them and their labors be in vain? Would they reach the summit only to be greeted by their victors, or find the footprints of Carrel and the others long since departed?

By ten o'clock they were at 14,000 feet where the eastern face rose sharply, becoming increasingly steeper, then perpendicular, and finally, near the summit, overhanging the vertical. Forced to the right they climbed carefully upward on the ridge, snow filling the spaces among the rocks. Their immediate goal was to find a spot from which to cross over to the north face. Before long they found it and changed the order of the

*Matterhorn from the North East*

ascent. Croz took the lead, Whymper went next followed by Hudson, and then Hadow and Old Peter. Behind them came Douglas and Young Peter, in that order, all seven now roped together. They could see that this would be the most difficult part of the ascent. Looking at it Croz said, "Now for something altogether different."[21]

The rise here was not great – averaging only 40 degrees or so – but the rocks were covered with a thin film of ice and the spaces between them filled with snow, leaving only slippery fragments for minimal support. At first the climbers went almost horizontally to their right, then directly but slowly upward for about 60 feet, then back to the ridge. Caution was their watchword. Whymper would occasionally get a pull on the rope or a hand from Croz, and he would at times extend a hand to Hudson behind him. Hudson invariably declined the offer, saying it was not necessary. Hadow was having difficulty throughout this portion of the climb, requiring continual assistance from Hudson or Old Peter in placing his feet. This slowed their progress and increased the pressure and tension they all felt. They must avoid a fall and yet move fast enough to beat the Italians to the summit.

Their goal was now getting closer. Not long after returning to the ridge they noticed that the snow was smoothing the terrain and the rocks becoming fewer. A few minutes later came a realization that made their hearts leap, the moment they had awaited with a mixture of suppressed emotions: "Nothing but 200 feet of easy snow remained to be surmounted! The Matterhorn was ours!"[22] Whymper quickly untied the rope between him and Hudson. He and Croz, "dashing away, ran a neck-and-neck race which ended in a dead heat" atop the Matterhorn's summit.[23] The others were not far behind. "Hurrah!" The cheers went up; not a footstep could be seen in the snow. They knew, however, that the mountain had two summits: the Swiss peak at the northern end of the narrow ridge on which they stood, and the Italian peak 350 feet to the south. Whymper hastened there as fast as he could and was again elated: the snow on it was also fresh and untrodden. They had beaten the Italians; the world was theirs!

But where were their opponents? Whymper looked over the edge, "half doubting, half expectant," and there they were, about 1,200 feet below the southern summit. "Up went my arms and my hat. Croz! Croz!

Come here!" Croz came over, probably just as excited but less voluble. "Ah! The *coquins*" (the rascals), he said, "They are low down."[24] They yelled at the Italians until they were hoarse. Still not sure someone had heard them, they threw rocks down the slope but got no reaction. Determined to make their presence known they kicked or pried away portions of the ridge and pushed them over the edge; soon a torrent of rocks was hurtling down the mountain. There was no doubt now; the men on the southern slope looked up and saw them. The Italians, shocked and completely deflated by the sudden appearance of the English party on the summit, turned and headed down the mountain back to Breuil.

What a thrilling moment! The party of Whymper and Hudson had scaled the impossible mountain and ended forever the myths and superstitions that surrounded it. They had conquered where others had failed; recognition and honor would now be theirs. The victors' view from the narrow summit was spectacular, enhanced by the excitement of their triumph and the glowing awareness that they were the first to see it.

[On] the southern end of the ridge [we] buil[t] a cairn and then paid homage to the view. The day was one of those superlatively clear ones that usually precede bad weather. The atmosphere was perfectly still and free from all clouds....Mountains fifty – nay a hundred – miles off looked sharp and clear. All their details – ridge and crag, snow and glacier – stood out with faultless definition. Pleasant thoughts of happy days in bygone years came unbidden as we recognized the old familiar forms. All were revealed – not one of the principal peaks of the Alps was hidden. First came the [Pennine Alps]....Behind them were the [giants of] the...Bernese Oberland. Towards the south, beyond the plain of Piedmont, were the Viso – one hundred miles away – and the Maritimes, one hundred thirty miles distant. Then came my first love, the Pelvoux – the Ecrins and the Meije – and lastly, in the west, glowing in full sunlight, the monarch of all, Mont Blanc. Ten thousand feet beneath us were the green fields of Zermatt, dotted with chalets from which blue smoke rose lazily. Eight thousand feet below, on the other side, were the pastures of

Breuil. There were forests black and gloomy, and meadows bright and lively; bounding waterfalls and tranquil lakes; fertile lands and savage wastes; sunny plains and frigid plateaus. There were the most rugged forms and the most graceful outlines – bold, perpendicular cliffs, and gentle, undulating slopes; rocky mountains and snowy mountains, somber and solemn or glittering and white, with walls – domes – turrets – pinnacles – pyramids – cones – and spires! There was every combination...the world can give, and every contrast...the heart could desire.[25]

Amid the whirling emotions of the moment Whymper thought of Carrel, and how distraught the proud *bersagliere* must have felt when the Englishmen suddenly appeared high above him. He regretted that Carrel could not stand with him in his moment of triumph:

He was the man, of all those who attempted the ascent of the Matterhorn, who most deserved to be the first upon its summit. He was the first to doubt its inaccessibility, and he was the only man who persisted in believing that its ascent would be accomplished. It was the aim of his life to make the ascent from the side of Italy, for the honour of his native valley. For a time he had the game in his hands: he played it as he thought best; but he made a false move, and he lost it.[26]

Earlier that morning, as the party left camp, Croz had taken a pole out of the tent and carried it with him. Confident of victory he wanted it for a flagpole when they reached the summit. Whymper cautioned that this would be tempting fate but was ignored. Croz now took and planted the tent pole firmly in the snow. " 'There is the flag-staff,' we said, 'but where is the flag?' "Here it is," replied Croz as he pulled off his shirt and attached it to the pole, donning another from his rucksack to replace it.[27] The well-worn garment hung limply from lack of wind to support it but Whymper learned later that onlookers everywhere – in Zermatt, on the Gornergrat, and throughout the Val Tournanche – had seen it clearly. In Breuil they thought it was the flag of Carrel's party and they celebrated. " 'Victory is ours!' they shouted. 'Bravo Carrel; Viva

Italy!' " But a few hours later their representatives returned "sad, disheartened, and gloomy." Unable to face the truth of Carrel's defeat the villagers had another explanation. "The old traditions *are* true; there are spirits on top of the Matterhorn!"[28]

In time the climbers reluctantly acknowledged the need to end the most thrilling mountaintop celebration of their lives. It was almost mid-afternoon, well into the time when avalanches became more numerous. "We remained on the summit for one hour – 'one crowded hour of glorious life'…and then …began to prepare for the descent."[29] Fortunately they could not imagine the horror that awaited them in the first hour of their downward journey.

\* \* \* \*

The climbers had taken almost nine hours to reach the summit from their previous night's bivouac. Now at 2:30 p.m. by Whymper's watch it was time to begin the descent. Hudson and Whymper agreed on the order. Croz, the strongest and surest of foot, would take the lead. Behind him would come Hadow, the least experienced member of the party. They knew from his performance on the ascent that he would require help on the way down and that Croz was best qualified to give it. Hudson followed so as to be next on the rope above his climbing companion. Douglas came after Hudson, with Old Peter, the strongest of the remaining climbers, positioned above Douglas as the fivesome's anchor. This group began to move downward as Whymper sketched the summit. When he closed his sketchbook and moved toward them, someone remembered that they had not written their names on a scrap of paper to be put in a bottle and left at the top. This was a customary ritual on first ascents as an empty wine bottle was almost always handy. So Whymper made out the list, placed it in a bottle, and put the bottle inside the newly built cairn. He and young Peter then tied up and hastened after the group of five ahead. They caught up with them just as Croz was starting down the ice-covered rocks of the north face, the most difficult part of the mountain.

In talking with Hudson before leaving the summit, Whymper had suggested that they tie a guide-rope around a rock at the beginning of each segment of the difficult area, for an extra handhold as they went down. They carried a considerable length of sashline for this purpose, enough so that each guide-rope could be cut and left behind when no longer needed. Hudson "approved the idea" but the matter was left open.[30] The group was proceeding with great care when Whymper and Young Peter joined them, tied together in that order but not attached to the others. The first group had not fixed a guide-rope on either side of their downward path but Whymper said nothing more about it. A little after 3:00 p.m. Douglas asked Whymper to tie up to Old Peter so that in the event of a slip the elder Taugwalder would have backup support. Whymper did as requested, using one of the strong Manila or Italian hemp ropes, and the party continued downward with seven climbers now roped together.

With this the stage was set; all the players were on their marks. A short time later, around 3:45 p.m., "a sharp-eyed lad ran into the Monte Rosa hotel and said to Seiler that he had seen an avalanche fall from the summit of the Matterhorn onto the Matterhorn Glacier."[31] The lad was Friedrich Taugwalder, old Peter's fifteen year old son who was following the progress of his father and oldest brother with a small telescope. Seiler scolded him for telling idle stories, saying there was not enough snow on the northern side for an avalanche. Unhappily, what the youngster saw was real although it was not snow that was crashing down the sheer cliff of the Matterhorn's north face. Whymper gave his first hand account in the pages of *Scrambles*:

Michel Croz had laid aside his axe, and in order to give Mr. Hadow greater security, was absolutely taking hold of his legs and putting his feet, one by one, into their proper positions. So far as I know, no one was actually descending. I cannot speak with certainty because the two leading men were partially hidden from my sight by an intervening mass of rock, but it is my belief, from the movement of their shoulders, that Croz...was in the act of turning round, to go down a step or two himself. At this moment Mr. Hadow slipped, fell against him, and knocked him over. I heard one startled exclamation from Croz, then saw him and Mr Hadow flying downwards. [I]n another moment Hudson was dragged from his steps and Lord Douglas immediately after him. All this was the work of a moment. Immediately we heard Croz's exclamation, old Peter and I planted ourselves as firmly as the rocks would permit; the rope was taut between us, and the jerk came on us both as on one man. We held; but the rope broke midway between Taugwalder and Lord Francis Douglas. For a few seconds we saw our unfortunate companions sliding downward on their backs and spreading out their hands, endeavouring to save themselves. They passed from our sight uninjured, disappeared one by one, and fell from precipice to precipice on[to] the Matterhorn Glacier below, a distance of nearly 4,000 feet in height. From the moment the rope broke it was impossible to help them. So perished our comrades![32]

*Croz! Croz! Come Here!*

Whymper and the two Taugwalders were frozen in shock at what they had just seen. At first their minds could not fully register what had happened. The image of their fallen comrades' terror was almost more than they could bear – four climbers exquisitely alive one instant and fatally stricken the next. Michel Croz, Douglas Hadow, The Reverend Charles Hudson, Lord Francis Douglas, gone forever in one flashing moment. And then to the stunned survivors came another fearful thought like a second jolt of electricity: but for the broken rope they, too, would have hurtled down the mountain, their breath forever stilled, their bodies torn and broken beyond recognition.

The three remaining climbers trembled but kept their footing, suppressing the panic that squeezes the chest and turns muscles to jelly. After several heartbeats Young Peter momentarily lost his wits. Howling like a wolf over its slain mate he cried in helpless anguish: "We are lost! We are lost!" Old Peter thought first of Croz as he plaintively exclaimed: "Chamonix! Oh, what will Chamonix say?"[33] How could the Chamoniards ever accept that Croz, their strongest son of the mountains, had fallen to his death?

Whymper reacted with shocked silence. His first words were to implore Young Peter to move downward; the rope between them was taut and none of the three could move downward until the uppermost climber did so. But the young Taugwalder stood firm, transfixed by the trauma of the moment. Knowing his son's paralysis endangered them all, old Peter echoed "We are lost!" – and for a moment, it seemed he might be right.[34] But the older guide's instincts quickly returned and he tied his rope around a nearby rock as an anchor for the group. On seeing that, his son recovered his senses and began to move slowly downward. The three soon stood together. Whymper asked to see the end of the broken rope for he wondered, as all of them must have, why it had severed. To his surprise he saw that it was "sashline," the thinnest and weakest of the party's three types of ropes. He was dismayed; it appeared to have broken "in mid-air, and...not...to have sustained previous injury."[35] Old Peter's reason for choosing this rope to tie himself to Douglas would be intensely examined later; for now, however, Whymper simply took what remained of the rope and put it in his pocket.

The accident's emotional impact finally subsided enough for the

*"The Fall" by Gustav Dore*

three to continue downward, again roped together. It was an agonizing descent. The two guides remained "utterly unnerved," causing Whymper to fear for his life. "For almost two hours afterwards I thought almost every moment...would be my last."[36] They managed, however, to take the precaution which the party should have observed from the beginning: at difficult stretches they tied sashline to rocks for additional support. On reaching an easier slope they cut the guide rope and left it in place.

Even with this help the Taugwalders remained shaken. They were still on the north face where even the less dangerous places were trying to men in their emotional state. Old Peter, in the lead, turned several times toward Whymper and with "ashy" face groaned "*I cannot.*"[37] But each time he forced himself to continue, and about 6:00 p.m. the three men were able to move from the north face to the northeast ridge at the spot where they had left it during the ascent. Though they were still high above the Hörnli, the ridge's patches of snow offered more secure footing and a feeling of relief that the most treacherous part of the descent was behind them. Here they paused to search for some sign of their fallen comrades – a piece of clothing or blood on the snow or anything else – but they found nothing. They leaned over the ridge and called out for the lost climbers but only the faint echoes of their own shouts returned. Dejectedly they gathered up the few items which the party had cached there earlier as they had pared down to the essential needs of the higher slopes.

Before they could move downward a strange sight, like an apparition, appeared high in the eastern sky. Lit by the rays of the sinking sun it was a pale, colorless formation of two huge crosses topped by a giant arch spread over them like a canopy. These elements hung in the sky motionless, like a fantastically shaped fog-bow. The ethereal image had come at such an emotionally charged time that Whymper hardly trusted his own eyes. But the Taugwalders were seeing the same thing and had been the first to notice it. As they stood watching, the ghostly image began to dissolve. Though it had formed gradually it disappeared quickly and the three stragglers did not linger or think long about this strange sight.

With better footing now under them – their minds having focused first on the effort to find a sign of their companions and then on the spectral fog-bow – the Taugwalders regained their composure and with it their mundane concerns. After talking together in a patois Whymper did not fully understand, they turned to him and said that they were poor men, afraid that with the death of Lord Douglas, their original employer, they would not get paid. Whymper brusquely assured them that he would compensate them both in full. After more discussion between the two guides Young Peter said that they were not asking for payment. Instead, they wanted Whymper to write in his journal and in the guest book of the Monte Rosa Hotel that they had received no money. "What nonsense! I don't understand you. What do you mean?" "Well," said the young Taugwalder, presuming their failure to be paid would gain them sympathy, "next year there will be many travellers at Zermatt, and we shall get more *voyageurs*."[38] The combination of their language and attitude infuriated Whymper. Too angry to reply, he unroped and took off down the mountain as rapidly as he could manage. The guides had no choice but to keep up with him, asking "more than once" if he was trying to kill them.

Their descent continued in virtual silence. Whymper was still irate over the Taugwalders' behavior. He saw them both as money-grubbing peasants totally insensitive to the loss of their companions, with Young Peter acting as a coward to make matters worse. His own anguish was now tinged with anger at the cruelty of the fate that had changed a joyous celebration into a grievous loss. Night fell but they kept going in the moonlight for more than an hour and a half. About 9:30, finding themselves on a reasonably level slab, they agreed to stop for the night.

For Whymper sleep became a forlorn hope. He could not clear his mind of turbulent thoughts or the incessant images of the accident even as his body sought badly needed rest. His thinking was confused and he was further disturbed by a fear, perhaps irrational, that the Taugwalders' willingness to capitalize commercially on the demise of their employers could also place him in danger. Were he not to return, they would be the sole survivors of this unprecedented catastrophe. And might not his death increase the notoriety of the event, further enhancing the curiosity value of the father-and-son guide team? He was also physically uncomfortable. It was cold and they had chosen a hard slab scarcely large enough to accommodate three people. They passed six truly wretched hours on this narrow perch in almost unbearably close company. At the first light of dawn they again moved on. Once past the Hörnli they practically ran down to Zermatt.

Thus ended the first ascent of the Matterhorn, with triumph turned to disaster. The past two days had held all the elements of a Greek tragedy – worthy protagonists, empathetic figures caught up in terrifying circumstances, a tale of hubristic men punished by the Gods for aspiring to heights fit only for the gods themselves. Their adventure would capture the public's imagination as no other mountaineering story ever before. It would be an oft told tale, the subject of numerous books and countless articles, letters, and much critical analysis. It would achieve legendary status, remembered and told in climbing circles as long as mountains were there to conquer. For Whymper, however, it was only the end of the beginning. Opening before him now was an emotional abyss as threatening as any Alpine bergschrund. He would survive that threat and move on with his life, widely praised for his behavior in the harsh spotlight of the accident's aftermath. But the Matterhorn experience would haunt him to the day of his death.

# CHAPTER 13

## Search and Recovery

On the Saturday morning of July 15th Alexandre Seiler was in the reception area of the Monte Rosa Hotel. The preceding afternoon he and most Zermatters had seen Croz's shirt, the party's "flag," hoisted triumphantly on the Matterhorn's summit. They were already talking about the benefits this ascent would bring their way. As the owner of one of the most popular climbers' rendezvous in the Alps, Seiler was prepared to give the intrepid mountaineers a heroes' welcome. As mid-morning approached he began to wonder why they had not yet returned but told himself it was too soon to be overly concerned. He went about his customary duties, ready to be the first to greet Whymper, Hudson and their gallant band.

At ten o'clock that morning Whymper walked into the hotel. As Seiler strode forward his smile changed to a worried frown at the sight of the haggard figure before him. From his guest's appearance and the distant look in Whymper's eyes Seiler knew immediately that something was wrong. He followed the bedraggled young climber, who had not yet spoken, to his room. "What's the matter?" he asked. "Where are the others?" Whymper replied simply, "the Taugwalders and I have returned." At that, Seiler burst into tears, realizing at once the terrible meaning of those words.[1] The innkeeper was a pragmatic man of action as well as a sympathetic friend. He pulled himself together and went out among the townspeople to break the news, offering his hotel as a meeting place for the search party he knew would soon be formed.

In the faint hope that one or more of his comrades might have survived, Whymper sought out Joseph Weschlen, President of the Zermatt Commune, and urged that men be sent to look for the missing climbers.

Weschlen agreed and immediately went about forming a group of guides for that purpose. By noon, twenty men were assembled and ready. They left shortly thereafter with Weschlen in the lead but without Whymper who badly needed time to recover from his thirty-hour ordeal. He realized that the Weschlen group had probably left too late in the day to reach the scene of the accident before dark. Also aware that he would be the focal point of the investigation that would surely follow, Whymper wanted the company and support of a compatriot when he went back on the Matterhorn.

The Reverend Joseph McCormick, the companion Hudson had decided not to wait for, arrived in Zermatt on Friday morning, the day after the Whymper-Hudson team's departure. He was among the tourists and villagers who had followed the climbers' progress that day and had seen their "flag" on the Matterhorn summit. The next morning as he prepared for a day's outing on the Gornergrat McCormick was not concerned by the party's failure to return. A note to him from Hudson, written at 5:00 a.m. the morning of the latter's departure, had said that the group might spend a second night on the mountain.

Soon after his return to the Monte Rosa Whymper sent a messenger to the Gornergrat to track down McCormick with a note advising him of Hudson's apparently fatal accident and asking that he return as soon as possible to join Whymper in a search party. Early that afternoon McCormick read the note with shock and dismay; he and Hudson were close friends as well as climbing companions. He hurried back to Zermatt ready to join Whymper in the search.[2]

Meanwhile, the Weschlen party had headed southwest toward the accident locale via the Stockli, a large rocky prominence in a field of lower glaciers at the foot of the mountain. From there they considered the route to the far corner of the upper plateau of the Matterhorn Glacier where the fallen bodies were thought to lie. They saw that it would take them over treacherous glacial crevasses and seracs, and that they could not possibly reach the site before dark. So they went back toward Z'mutt, just west of Zermatt. From the heights above the little village, using telescopes, they saw what appeared to be three bodies lying motionless on the Matterhorn Glacier where it joined the base of the mountain.[3] Unable to do anything further at that point they returned to

Zermatt. At 8:00 p.m. that evening Weschlen made his sad report to Whymper, Seiler, and others gathered at the Monte Rosa hotel.

With McCormick now at his side Whymper decided to begin his own search later that Saturday night. Two more English climbers – J. S. Phillpotts and The Reverend James Robertson – had offered to join him. Zermatt guides, some of whom had been in the Weschlen group, initially said they, too, were ready to go with Whymper. Later, however, they withdrew, explaining in abashed tones that the local priests – unwilling to bend the requirement that all able bodies attend Sunday mass – had threatened excommunication from the Church for anyone choosing to be on the mountain that day instead of receiving the bread and wine of Holy Communion. Johann Peter Perren, Zermatt's leading guide at the time, was particularly troubled by the priestly warning. He had led Hudson just days earlier on Mont Blanc and the Aiguille Verte and then accompanied Croz, Hudson, and Hadow on their journey from Chamonix to Zermatt.[4] With tears in his eyes Perren told Whymper that nothing short of this edict – with its accompanying threat of eternal damnation – would have kept him from joining the search.[5]

Five guides from other villages, not encumbered by such intransigent priests, agreed to join the group. Three were from Switzerland: Franz Andermatten of Saas, and Joseph-Marie Lochmatter and Alexander Lochmatter, both of St. Niklaus. Two who had been climbing in the Zermatt area were from Chamonix: Frédéric Payot and Jean Tairraz.[6] The Englishmen and their guides, nine men in all, departed the Monte Rosa Hotel shortly after midnight Sunday morning. Leaving at this hour would permit an early morning passage through the field of seracs guarding the Matterhorn Glacier, pinnacles that could become dangerously unstable as the sun rose higher.

In the preceding two days Whymper had only dozed fitfully. Lack of sleep and the lingering effects of many tension-filled hours had left him drained and weary. But now that his search team was finally in motion his energy began to return. The party first made an easy ascent to the Hörnli under the night sky. From there they went down the right side of the northeastern ridge toward the mountain and in the first light of day reached the Z'mutt Glacier. This put them below and just north of the Matterhorn Glacier, which adjoins the Matterhorn itself. After crossing the lower glacier they began the ascent through the field of seracs where the two glaciers met. Around those icy spires they crept, the guides hurrying them along under the overhangs. Many of the seracs crested like ocean waves in a roiling sea and despite the early hour some of them did fall near the climbers' path. It was difficult going but the only route to the almost inaccessible corner of the glacier that was their goal.

After two hours of climbing in this hostile environment Whymper's party reached the snow-covered plateau of the Matterhorn Glacier at 8:30 a.m. Across the white expanse before them was the glacier's junction with the base of the mountain where their comrades had fallen. Pausing for a panoramic look before moving closer their deepest fears were confirmed. "As we saw one weather-beaten man after another raise the telescope, turn deadly pale and pass it on without a word to the next, we knew that all hope was gone."[7] They approached the corner of death slowly. Glancing up at the almost four thousand foot sheer precipice of the Matterhorn's north side they shuddered at the thought of what awaited them.

Arriving on the scene the party stood momentarily silent, gradually absorbing the ghastly picture of the comrades who had moved so recently among them. The mangled bodies of three stricken climbers lay roughly in a line between the search party and the mountain, each partially sunken in the snow about twenty meters apart. All had been stripped naked and bled dry, their flesh nearly as white as the snow around them. Bones jutted through skin, faces were hardly recognizable on torsos cut and torn. None was identifiable at first sight. The English members of the party were the first to advance to the closest body. Whymper recognized it as Croz's by the beard now pressed into the remains of his neck. Nearby were Croz's trousers, in them a coin purse with six pieces of gold and a string of rosary beads pulverized by the constant pounding of the long fall. Croz's crucifix, which he had worn on a chain around his neck, was embedded in his bearded jaw, the only remaining part of his face.[8] Robertson cut it out with his penknife.[9] Behind Croz was Hadow, identified by hair fragments and nearby pieces of clothing. Hudson's torn body was nearest the mountain. In the shredded clothing lying closest to him was his coin purse, a letter to his wife, and his prayer book. Robertson took a lock of Hudson's hair which he later sent to Hudson's widow.[10]

The three bodies had fallen to the glacier in the order in which the climbers had been descending: Croz forward, followed by Hadow and then Hudson nearest the mountain. Douglas's body was missing. Whymper's telescopic survey of the mountainside revealed nothing. A search by the entire party of the adjacent glacial area turned up only some bits of clothing that might have been Douglas's, plus his boots. Whymper recognized the latter by their small size and by the horizontal cuts Douglas had made along their outside front edges near the soles to make them fit better. The boots of the other climbers were also found. These articles of clothing torn off during the fall were a testament to the awesome angle of the mountainside that had allowed such relatively lightweight objects to escape its grasp. Whymper came away with Croz's hat which had been a gift to him from Whymper, along with a glove belonging to Hadow and the letter from Hudson to his widow. [10] In shock, and in a remote frozen wasteland of indescribable horror, the party decided to bury their comrades' remains at the site. McCormick described the mountainside burial service:

A consultation was held as to what had better be done with the bodies....All agreed that... the best thing we could do would be to bury them in the snow....With our axes we made a grave, cut large pieces of ice, collected the snow, and covered them over.

Out of...Hudson's prayer book...I read psalm 90, so singularly appropriate to time and place....Imagine us...with our bronze-faced guides, leaning on our...alpenstocks around that...newly formed grave in the center of a snow field perhaps never before trodden by man – in the very sight...of the Almighty – and try and catch the sound of Moses's words:

"Lord, you have been our dwelling place throughout all generations. Before the mountains were born or you brought forth the earth and the world, from everlasting to everlasting you are God. You turn men back to dust, saying 'Return to dust, O sons of men.' For a thousand years in your sight are like a day that has just gone by, or a watch in the night...."

Return[ing] to Zermatt, we could not help thinking that a grave in the imperishable snow – lonely, grand, beautiful – was suitable for brave mountaineers.[11]

Fortunately, as if showing respect for the dead, the north face's usual array of falling stones did not interrupt the short burial service. These rock barrages normally peaked in the early afternoon hours as the heat of the day loosened mountainside snow and debris. There were, however, periodic showers during this particular morning. Soon after the party's arrival at the scene, said McCormick, "a shout from one of the guides, and a crack above us the instant after, startled us. We ran down the slope as [rapidly] as we could...and escaped the stones" that fell from the mountain. "We were thus warned that our work...must be quickly accomplished."[12]

Gabriel Loppé, a reporter in Chamonix, wrote a letter published July 23rd, 1865 in a local newspaper, the *Chamonix L'Abeille.* His letter was most likely based on conversations with Frédéric Payot and Jean Tairraz, the two Chamonix guides in Whymper's search party. After describing in grisly detail the picture of death at the Matterhorn's base he added, "In the middle of this appalling scene, Whymper swore bitterly that he would never set foot on a mountain again." This letter also stated that the shower of stones described by McCormick recurred several times during the morning. In those moments, Loppé reported, "Mr. Whymper alone was unperturbed and ignored all entreaties to take cover."[13]

In *A Sad Holiday* McCormick wrote merely that the deceased could not be identified except by the contents of their pockets, and that he grieved over the "shattered tabernacle" of his friend Hudson. For a long time after, Whymper remained unwilling to describe the sight in grisly detail. His initial public reports and personal correspondence excluded such images out of respect for the feelings of the dead climbers' families. His Victorian reluctance to offend readers' sensibilities continued in *Scrambles,* which remained silent on the death scene through all of its editions. Only once did he break the self-imposed restraint – in a French language article in the *Journal de Zermatt.* Published on August 25th, 1895 in Whymper's 56th year, it seems never to have appeared in an English translation. When Whymper's silence finally broke, it burst from him in a torrent of emotion long suppressed. His description of the nightmarish scene summarised above contained the most gruesome language on record.

The discovery of the bodies and the burial of the remains ended the physical part of Whymper's highly stressful ordeal. The search party returned to Zermatt at 2:00 o'clock that Sunday afternoon, almost sixty hours after the fated climbers had broken camp for the final assault on the Matterhorn's summit. The fear, horror and exhaustion of those two and a half days had changed Whymper indelibly. Since childhood he had been circumspect, serious and self-important. As a young man in his early twenties, he was aggressively confident and coldly determined in the pursuit of his goals. These qualities remained after the accident but as part of a more emotionally mature personality. Though still outspoken he showed more concern for others. Also more inwardly directed, he became more temperate though no less judgmental. In the immediate aftermath of the mountain disaster he kept his head. Besieged with questions he responded forthrightly with patience and honesty. No longer the merely critical onlooker of his youth, he had been violently thrust into a wider world, caught in a spotlight of notoriety and buffeted by a whirlwind of controversy.

In later years the emotional impact of the accident faded but never left Whymper completely. He developed a permanent aura of melancholy, often hidden beneath a sardonic wit and a direct, unceremonious manner. Left undiminished, however, was his innate vitality – something more than pure ambition – which kept him involved in adventurous new projects aimed at satisfying his and society's curiosity about the world in which they lived.

Whymper's first step into this new journey would be the challenge of explaining to Swiss authorities, and then to the families of the fallen climbers and to the public, what happened on the Matterhorn descent and why things went so sadly astray.

# CHAPTER 14

## *Troublesome Questions*

The northern half of the Matterhorn lies in the Swiss canton of Valais. The cantonal government, based in Sion, acted quickly to investigate the circumstances of the July 14th fatalities. Early in the week of July 17th it ordered the bodies of the deceased climbers disinterred from the Matterhorn Glacier and returned to Zermatt for a more fitting burial. It also named Joseph Anton Clemenz, a member of the Valais legislature, as Examining Magistrate to preside at a formal inquiry into the causes of the accident. The hearing, it said, would take place later that week.

Clemenz lived in the neighboring town of Visp but was connected to Zermatt by his ownership of the Mont Cervin Hotel, the Monte Rosa's chief competitor. He advised Whymper and other witnesses to be ready to testify at the hearing; he also provided each of them with a list of questions to be answered in writing and submitted prior to their appearances. The Magistrate offered to consider any additional questions Whymper might want asked, either of himself or of any other witness. Clemenz and all hearing participants other than Whymper spoke German. Fortunately a professor of languages from Rugby School was in Zermatt and agreed to translate Clemenz's questions and Whymper's answers, using as a bridge those men's working knowledge of French. The elder Taugwalder, also called as a witness, was helped in the preparation of his answers by his cousin, Alois Julen, a Zermatt lawyer and part-time guide.[1]

Whymper testified on Friday afternoon July 21st; Taugwalder took the witness stand the next morning. Clemenz simply read out his written questions without change. In response each witness also read his prepared answers with no elaboration. During Whymper's testimony the Magistrate asked only two follow-up questions, both of which were inconsequential. When Old Peter's turn came, even though several of the guide's answers were non-responsive or evasive, Clemenz sought no elaboration.[2] He accepted Taugwalder's statement that Young Peter had not been able to see how the accident happened, and he did not call the son to the stand. The other witnesses were the guides Franz Andenmatten and Alexander Lochmatter, both of whom had been in one or both of the search parties. On Sunday, realizing the deficiency of some of Taugwalder's answers of the day before, Clemenz recalled him for re-examination. His questions and Old Peter's answers were again written out in advance. The guide's further responses were largely self-serving, adding little if anything to his prior testimony. His second appearance brought the hearing to a close.

Clemenz and the Recorder, César Clemenz, perhaps a cousin, comprised the Committee of Enquiry. At the hearing Whymper recounted the story of the accident almost exactly as he later described it in *Scrambles*. Upon completion of the hearing the Committee published its understanding of how the accident happened, directly tracking Whymper's testimony. Along with its factual findings the Committee concluded that:

1.  Guilt attaches to no one on the above facts;

2.  Mr. Hadow was the cause of the accident; no one can be accused of a fault or a crime; and there is to be no sequel to the foregoing inquiry, [only this] decision of no grounds for prosecution...[3]

As surprising as it may seem in the light of today's open judicial proceedings and the press's overwhelming coverage of them, no further information about the Matterhorn hearing was made public. The names of the witnesses, their verbatim testimony, the inventories of the deceased climbers' possessions, other documents relating to the inquiry – all went unpublished. There were no contemporaneous published interviews of any of the principals because there was essentially no local press. The record of the proceedings was not made public until 1920, by which time all the participants had died. In *Scrambles*, Whymper expressed the hope that Old Peter had been able to clear himself of any blame in connection with the accident. He had framed suggested questions for Taugwalder intended to do just that. Somewhat sadly he wrote, "The questions, I was told, were put and answered; but the answers, although promised, have never reached me....I should rejoice to learn that his answers...were satisfactory."[4]

Clemenz's halfhearted performance at the hearing reflected the community's view of how the sensitive issues in this case should be handled: the sooner they were wrapped up and buried the better. All of Zermatt – including Clemenz the hotelier – wanted to protect the village's tourist-friendly environment. Crucial to that goal was preserving the good reputation of Zermatt's mountain guides who played a key role in the town's growing "travellers" trade. A finding of criminal negligence or even simple carelessness on the part of either of the Taugwalders would have serious consequences for the town's commercial enterprises.

Greater diligence on Clemenz's part probably would not have changed the outcome of the hearing. But as later events would show, his failure to press Old Peter on why the guide chose the sashline to link himself to Douglas left a void that would attract wild speculation. Those rumors would prove more harmful than anything the senior Taugwalder might have said in his own defense. Clemenz's decision to keep the hearing's record from public scrutiny – a misguided attempt to limit the accident's economic impact – had the opposite effect. Discussion and criticism would not be stifled, and the area's residents and businesses would suffer the consequences for many months to come.

All of the major newspapers in Britain and continental Europe, and one or two in civil war-weary America, carried the story of the Matterhorn conquest and its dramatic outcome. Thousands heard and read Whymper's description of these events in lectures, articles and the several editions of *Scrambles*. Thousands more read scores of other accounts, including a number of books in various languages. Whymper's version of the facts remained essentially unchanged throughout the years. Though examined in microscopic detail from all conceivable angles and points of view, it was never successfully challenged. Unfortunately, however, in much of what was written over the years, speculation and spotty analysis prevailed. Some of the facts about the climb – for example, the resting place of Francis Douglas's bones – may never be known. Some of the climbers' thoughts and motivations, though understood more clearly today, may never escape the shadows. But plausible answers to some of the questions began to surface at the time of the Matterhorn centenary in 1965. More recently the overall picture has become even clearer.

The most intriguing of the unanswered questions has been why Old Peter used the sashline instead of one of the stronger ropes to tie himself to Lord Douglas. The party carried two types of ropes on the mountain. The elder Taugwalder testified at the hearing that he had tied himself to Douglas with a "special rope." He also told of his suggestion to Croz that "before reaching the dangerous place one ought for greater safety to stretch a rope."[5] These statements showed his awareness of the plaited sashline's intended use as a guide rope. But he also believed that the "special rope" was strong enough to protect Douglas from danger. "If I had found the rope too weak, I would have recognized it as such before the ascent of the Matterhorn and would have rejected it."[6] Taugwalder saw no inconsistency in these statements and Clemenz did not bother to question him further.

Whymper himself was partly responsible for the continuing confusion over this issue. In *Scrambles* he called Taugwalder's choice of the plaited sashline "suspicious" because the thinner rope was "old and weak" and there was an "abundance of new and much stronger rope to spare."[7] He also noted that if Old Peter "thought that an accident was likely to happen, it was in his interest to have the weaker rope where it was placed."[8] That was a big "if," however, and also gratuitous on Whymper's part. Indeed Whymper claimed never to have had such suspicions himself. If so, he should simply have said that Taugwalder's rope choice was "questionable" and called for an explanation.

As an experienced guide Old Peter knew that the first part of the descent would be difficult and said as much to Croz. He would hardly have been so rash or cruel as to endanger his client's life, or stupid enough to risk his own reputation with a subterfuge that would leave evidence in the form of a broken rope remnant for all to see. In the same vein, Lord Douglas accepted his guide's choice of the thinner rope without objection. When he asked Whymper to tie onto Taugwalder during the descent he did not ask that a portion of one of the thicker ropes – probably carried by Whymper or Young Peter and thus readily available – be used to replace his own link with the elder guide. The difference in the two kinds of ropes was obvious; indeed, the link between Douglas and Hudson, one end of which was already tied around Douglas's waist, was of the strong twisted hemp.[9]

In *The First Descent of the Matterhorn*, Alan Lyall's encyclopedic research sheds new light on the mystery. He begins with the known facts about Douglas's successful ascent of the Ober Gabelhorn on July 7th, one week to the day before the Matterhorn accident. On that occasion Old Peter Taugwalder was Douglas's lead guide, accompanied by a second guide named Viannin. At mid-morning the three of them – roped together with Douglas in the middle – sat and lunched on what they believed to be the Gabelhorn's snow-covered summit. Viannin, still tied to Douglas, moved a few feet away to retrieve something that lay nearby. Without warning the snow beneath Douglas and Old Peter suddenly gave way. As Douglas and his lead guide hurtled downward the second guide, seeing what had happened, managed quickly to brace himself before the shock of Douglas's and Taugwalder's combined weight came upon him. He managed to stop the two climbers' fall, straining the rope beyond what anyone might have thought possible. But the rope held, and the climbers were able to crawl to safety, their breath coming in gasps and their hearts racing. Miracle of miracles, the rope was a plaited sash-line!

It turned out that Douglas and Taugwalder had been perched on top of a snow-cornice curled above the Ober Gabelhorn's actual summit, a place both Taugwalder and Viannin should have spotted as unsafe. The news of Douglas's first ascent – and of the climbers' nearly fatal fall – had spread quickly throughout the area. No one seemed to have inquired, however, about the ropes used on that climb. Although Whymper furnished the ropes for the Matterhorn ascent, a guide customarily supplied them for his party's use, as Taugwaulder had done on the Ober Gabelhorn.

In *First Descent* Lyall cites the Ober Gabelhorn episode to help explain old Peter's selection of the "special rope" on the Matterhorn and

Douglas's acquiescence in its use. The report of the Alpine Club's Special Committee on Ropes, Axes and Alpenstocks had been published in the September 1864 issue of the Club's *Alpine Journal,* ten months before the Matterhorn accident. It found that only the relatively new ropes of twisted hemp or flax were safe for tying climbers together and also light enough to be conveniently carried. Plaited ropes, on the other hand – like those taken on the Matterhorn for use as fixed ropes – were found to be unsafe as links between climbers. Before the 1864 report, however, mountaineers had confidently used these thinner ropes for that purpose.

Lord Douglas, a new member of the Alpine Club keenly interested in mountaineering, was by all accounts an alert and intelligent young man. Thus he may well have read the Alpine Club's report on ropes before the beginning of the 1865 climbing season. Old Peter, on the other hand, certainly had not read it. And if he had heard about it, it is likely he would have been skeptical of its findings, particularly if he had been told that the Committee had used dead-weights of iron in their tests instead of more resilient human bodies. Presumably, therefore, the ropes Taugwalder supplied for Douglas's Ober Gabelhorn climb were the thinner, plaited ropes that Whymper called sashline. If Douglas had questioned his guide about the absence of ropes recommended by the Alpine Club, Taugwalder would have reassured him of the plaited rope's reliability, and the young man would likely have deferred to the experienced guide's judgment.

Their harrowing experience on the Ober Gabelhorn was still fresh in Taugwalder's and Douglas's minds when they climbed the Matterhorn. Left in Douglas's room at the Monte Rosa hotel was a draft of an article by him intended for the *Alpine Journal.* In it he expressed wonder that the Ober Gabelhorn rope had not broken:

> ...[A]ll of a sudden I felt myself go. The whole top [of the mountain] fell with a crash thousands of feet below, and I with it as far as the rope allowed (some 12 feet). Here, like a flash of lightning, Taugwalder came right by me some 12 feet more, but the other guide...held us both. The weight on the rope must have been about 23 stone, and it is wonderful that [as we were] falling straight down...it did not break too.[10]

That episode had strengthened Douglas's confidence in the ropes supplied by Taugwalder. It must also have confirmed Old Peter's belief in their effectiveness. Lyall thus concludes "that both Taugwalder and Douglas may have had good reason to suppose (albeit wrongly) that the plaited rope [supplied by Whymper] was as strong as the others; an instance of how good fortune can deceive."[11] If correct, that would explain Old Peter's choice of the thinner "special" rope and Douglas's ready acceptance of it. Indeed this scenario has the ring of truth; how else, it seems, could this confusing set of facts make sense?

Given its logic, why did someone not suggest this scenario far earlier? Part of the answer lies in Old Peter's instinct to hold his tongue. At the hearing he was content to say only that the sashline, in his opinion, was not "too weak" for use as a tie-rope between climbers. Knowing his limitations in any battle of words he said nothing about his successful use of plaited ropes over the years, or of the confidence the Ober Gabelhorn experience had given him in their reliability. Lyall suggests an additional reason for Taugwalder's reticence: that he heeded the counsel of his lawyer-cousin Alois Julen to confirm his faith in the "special rope" and stop there.

The fact that the rope broke led to another slanderous attack on the elder Taugwalder, of far greater significance to his reputation than the mystery of why he chose the sashline. Soon after the accident a rumor spread that he had cut the rope to save himself as the others fell. This was a highly speculative charge but devastating in its wide acceptance. Broken ropes were not a common occurrence and it was hard to believe four skilled climbers died accidentally in one long fall. At the time of the hearing neither Clemenz nor Whymper seemed aware that Old Peter was under such suspicion. Whymper kept Taugwalder's end of the broken sashline in his possession for several years before eventually giving it to the Alpine Museum at Zermatt. He wrote in *Scrambles* that the plaited rope "had broken in mid-air and…did not appear to have sustained previous injury," his way of saying it gave no sign of having been cut.[12] He also called the allegation against Old Peter "infamous," saying that "he *could* not [have cut the rope] at the moment of the slip," and that "the end of the rope in my possession shows that he *did* not do so beforehand."[13]

The rumor that Taugwalder cut the rope to save himself gained particular credence in the Chamonix area, home to Croz's brother Jean and his fellow guides. They mourned the loss of their compatriot, refusing to believe that one so strong and able could have fallen to his death without foul play. Old Peter defended himself as best he could. He testified at the hearing that the strain on the rope, before it broke, had bruised him around the waist.[14] He continued to plead his case in the Zermatt streets, plaintively saying to all who would listen: "They say I *cut* the rope. Look at my fingers!" He would then open his hands to show deep burn marks made by the rope as he desperately struggled to hold it.[15]

This charge against the elder Taugwalder is almost certainly without substance. Instinct and experience would have caused him to grab the rope, brace himself, and hold firm. Whatever might have flashed through his mind, there was hardly time for him to extract and open his knife before being struck by the massive weight of the four falling bodies. Fumbling with his knife would have risked his being unanchored at the crucial moment, and the rope burns on his hands should have dispelled any lingering doubt.

But nothing prevailed to staunch the malignant gossip. The senior Taugwalder remained on the hook of public opinion, particularly in Zermatt where the guides blamed him for exaggerating the Matterhorn's difficulty and their resulting loss of business. In the years following the accident his life sank into a downward spiral. In 1867 he suffered the greatest loss a parent can know, the death of his son Joseph by drowning in the Schwarzsee, the "Black Lake" on the Matterhorn above Zermatt. Thereafter, despondent and in virtual isolation among suspicious and distrustful fellow-guides, Taugwalder accepted only limited guiding assignments and never attempted the Matterhorn again or regained his rank as a leading local guide.[16] In 1874 he fled from his problems by emigrating to the United States leaving behind his wife and three remaining children. After living in America for four years Old Peter returned to Zermatt in 1878. He died there ten years later a sad and bitter man.[17]

The years were kinder to Young Peter who was not as deeply affected by the tragedy as his father. He climbed the Matterhorn again in 1872, opening the way for Zermatt guides gradually to regain their pre-eminence on that mountain. In time he expanded his guiding activities to include other parts of the western Alps. He never forgave Whymper's description of him in *Scrambles* as freezing in fear immediately after the accident and then quickly reverting to insensitive chatter while begging Whymper to say that he and his father had not been paid. Finally putting his thoughts in a rough "Narrative" – written in 1917 but not published until 1957 in the *Alpine Journal* – its allegedly new disclosures about the Matterhorn climb were patently incorrect and self-serving.[18]

\* \* \* \*

Over the years a few qualified critics have pointed to certain decisions by Whymper and Hudson as possibly contributing to the fatal accident. One of these was their choice of the order in which the climbers descended. At the hearing Old Peter explained the rationale of putting Croz in the lead to assist Hadow, and Hudson immediately behind his young protégé. On the descent, he said, "Croz led the party, then came Hadow, then Hudson, who regarded himself as a guide; they were followed by Lord Douglas, myself, Whymper and my son. So if you, the Examining Magistrate, accept that Hudson was acting as a guide, you will see that each tourist was between two guides."[19]

The only notable criticism of the climbers' order on the descent came more than fifty years after the event from J. P. Farrar, president of the Alpine Club 1917-19. Farrar would have put Hudson first with Hadow next followed by Croz.[20] His argument was weakened, however, by two questionable assumptions: first, that Hudson was the best amateur climber of the day – which later analysis would seriously undermine – and second, that Hadow was qualified for inclusion in the Matterhorn party, a judgment in which no one else concurred. In any event the order of climbers on the descent never generated widespread debate. The only other issue of concern was whether all seven of the climbers should have been roped together. T. S. Kennedy criticized this decision after the fact but his own prior conduct seriously undercut his argument. Just a week before the Matterhorn accident Kennedy had been one of a party of six climbers tied together on a descent of the Aiguille Verte. As on the

Matterhorn, that party (which also included Hudson) chose Croz to lead them down.[21]

In the immediate aftermath of the accident Whymper did not comment directly on the number of climbers that had been roped together. In a letter to *The Times* written two weeks after his return to London he acknowledged that "if the rope had not broken... [he and the two Taugwalders] could not possibly have held the four men, falling as they did, all at the same time, and with a severe jerk."[22] In that same letter he stated that because the rope between him and the elder Taugwalder was taut at the time of the accident, the shock of the falling climbers' weight had come upon them "as one man." Thus, he said, his tying onto Old Peter at Douglas's request "undoubtedly saved Taugwalder's life."[23]

Whymper did not raise or discuss this question in *Scrambles*. Not until his 1894 article in *The Graphic* magazine did he speak explicitly of it in print. "When climbers are tied together, it is presupposed that everyone will maintain his distance, that in difficult places only one will move at a time, and that the rest will be on the lookout to render assistance. The loss of life in the Matterhorn catastrophe of 1865 did not arise from being tied together, but...was primarily due to the inexperience of one of the party."[24] This practice was outdated or fast becoming so by the time Whymper wrote of it, and his analysis received little or no public comment.

The reason nothing more was made of the Matterhorn party's decision to tie all of its climbers together was that it was not unusual at the time. In those early days mountaineers had faith in the safety of numbers. By the end of the century, however, Alpinists had become concerned with the domino effect of a fall by one of several climbers linked together. They knew that in practice multiple climbers roped together could rarely achieve the coordination or precise individual performances that Whymper cited as necessary. The next generation began to climb with increasing frequency in pairs or threesomes. On the Matterhorn today two persons on a rope is the norm both for climbers who use guides and those who do not.

In his *Graphic* article Whymper candidly admitted that other human errors had led to the Matterhorn ascent's tragic outcome. He maintained that his and Hudson's most serious mistake was including someone of Hadow's inexperience. The other, in his view, was their failure to attach guide ropes at the most difficult parts of the descent. A fixed rope might have enabled Hadow to stop his fall before crashing into Croz.

Whymper also acknowledged that the party's divided leadership between himself and Hudson was a contributing cause of the accident. This was an indirect way of faulting Hudson, which he did again a year later in an interview with a reporter from the *Journal de Zermatt*. "It was incredibly imprudent of Hudson to allow [Hadow] to come with us."[25] In *Scrambles*, after expressly warning that a taut rope between climbers was "of first importance," Whymper made his most direct criticism of Hudson's performance. The Vicar, he said, had not kept the rope taut between himself and Hadow, and that Hadow and Croz fell "ten or twelve feet" before Hudson felt the pull.[26]

Whymper respected Hudson on a personal level. The Anglican priest was a "quiet, unassuming man" who would be "the last...to speak of his own doings" though he was "considered by the [climbing] fraternity to be the best amateur of his time,...a born mountaineer."[27] Later in his life Whymper told a friend that Hudson was "a man many years his senior [with] vastly more experience in mountaineering than he..., [and] that in arranging the [Matterhorn] party he relied mainly on Hudson's judgment..."[28] Though these comments were a bit defensive, they probably reflected Whymper's feelings accurately at the time of the accident. In July of 1865 Hudson was 36, Whymper 25. As a member of the Anglican clergy Hudson held a higher rank in the day's class-conscious society. He had been climbing in the Alps since 1855, five years before Whymper saw his first mountain. In that year he had made the first guideless ascent of Mont Blanc and the first guided ascent of the Monte Rosa. T. S. Kennedy wrote that Hudson "was almost as great as a guide."[29] But later research showed that Hudson's actual achievements did not justify his high reputation. He had climbed "almost wholly on snow mountains" considerably less challenging as a general rule than their rocky neighbors.[30] "Until the Verte in 1865, Hudson had not...a single reputable rock climb" to his credit.[31] The Vicar's actual climbing record is but a footnote to the first ascent of the Matterhorn, but it does help to explain why so respected a climber could have shown such questionable judgment.

Lyall offers an additional perspective on Hudson's decision to take Hadow with him on the Matterhorn. The Vicar had planned to attempt the Matterhorn with his friend and fellow clergyman, McCormick. McCormick was delayed – for how long Hudson did not know – but neither of them was on a tight schedule. Hudson had brought with him a ladder specifically designed for assistance on what he thought might be exceedingly difficult cliffs, along with a wire rope for additional protection on extreme slopes.

This extra equipment suggests to Lyall that both Hudson and McCormick anticipated spending one or two days feeling their way upward, using the special gear if and when necessary. Hadow's participation in the reconnaissance would not present a problem; if the going got tough, Hadow could return to Zermatt and the Hudson-McCormick team could proceed without him. If that was the plan it changed with the arrival of Whymper who was pushing hard to beat Carrel and his group of Italians to the summit. With Whymper ready to start out on the morning of the 14th Hudson realized that to await McCormick's arrival would risk his chance at a first Matterhorn ascent. On joining Whymper he left his ladder and wire rope at the Monte Rosa. The option to cut Hadow from the pack might still have been in Hudson's mind on the 14th, but the excitement of the first day's unexpectedly easy ascent may have banished any lingering reservations about Hadow's ability to continue. Thus the fatal flaw in the party's makeup would remain in place, raising the potential for disaster in this instance to more than likely.

\* \* \* \*

Summits above 4000 meters (13,120 feet) are generally considered major Alpine peaks. Of those the Matterhorn is probably climbed more often today than any other. Although climbers with cell-phones have around-the-clock access to dedicated helicopter rescue crews based in Zermatt, the mountain still takes a surprising number of lives. Fatalities among the Whymper-Hudson party were the first recorded lives lost on the Matterhorn. During the 145 years since then – through 15th August 2010 – 431 climbers have died on the mountain, 58 of them in the 21st century. An interesting subset of these numbers is that no guides – and only one amateur accompanied by a guide – have died on the mountain. The others were climbing guideless – some who were suddenly caught in bad weather and many who fell after losing their way on the descent, arriving at a ledge or other footing from which they could not retreat and then making a desperate and fatal false move. The Association of Zermatt Guides now requires their members to take only one client at a time, and always on a rope between them.

This continuing death toll on the Matterhorn since the end of Golden Age – despite the many advances in climbing equipment, weather forecasting and communications technology – is a forceful reminder of the skill and courage of the mountaineers who first conquered the Alps all on their own.

# CHAPTER 15

## *Into the Vortex*

Barely one week elapsed between the Matterhorn deaths and Whymper's testimony before Magistrate Clemenz, but each of those seven days was filled with unrelieved tension. Awaking Tuesday morning from his first full-night's sleep in four days he could think only of the dramatic turn his life had taken and the public scrutiny he would now confront. As he entered the Monte Rosa dining room all eyes turned toward him, confirming his apprehension. The talk there and throughout Zermatt was of the tragedy on the Matterhorn and its young English survivor. Around him swirled a developing vortex of reports, rumors, and charges that would follow him from Switzerland to England, intensifying as the news spread from the mountaineering community to the public at large. As he wrote to his friend James Robertson in impeccable Victorian prose, "The manner in which I was persecuted by impertinent people on the way home passes all belief."[1]

The next day – like the first aftershock of a violent earthquake – came the news that another Englishman had fallen to his death, this time from the Riffelhorn, a small peak between Zermatt and the Matterhorn. Knyvet Wilson had recently come to town with Robertson and Phillpotts, his fellow masters at Rugby School. The three of them had taken rooms at the Riffelhaus Hotel. Early Tuesday evening they had left the hotel – Wilson with a book in hand, intending to enjoy the sunset and read for a while as night came on. His companions soon headed back to the hotel but Wilson stayed behind to enjoy the mountains' stillness as the shadows lengthened. Returning later in darkness he lost his way. When he failed to appear at the hotel, searchers spent several hours looking for him but found nothing. Adams Reilly, in Zermatt that July, wrote to his friend J.

D. Forbes that they discovered Wilson's body early the next morning "dashed to pieces at the bottom of the peak."[2] This additional loss of life, following so closely on the Matterhorn fatalities, thickened the sense of gloom that permeated the town. "I hate the sight of these bloodstained mountains," said Adams Reilly, "there appears to be [an evil] curse on this place."[3]

\* \* \* \*

Subsequent events confirmed Adams Reilly as a prophet. On Monday of the following week, July 24th, Lord Queensberry, the older brother of the missing Francis Douglas, came to Zermatt in the hope of learning more about his sibling's death and last moments. Arriving on the same day was Henry Hadow, young Hadow's uncle. The following Wednesday they were both in a group that walked up to the Riffelhaus for dinner. On the way back the two of them became separated from the others and had not returned to their hotel after everyone else had been accounted for. Hours later a search party found them stumbling about, confused but thankful that a hidden precipice had not claimed their lives as well.

After breakfast the next day the same group hiked to a spot with a commanding view of the Matterhorn. There they pointed out to Lord Queensberry and Mr. Hadow the sheer cliff where the accident had happened and the corner of the glacier where the three bodies had fallen. Adams Reilly, who was with the group, wrote again to Forbes: "[On] our return we were met by news that a party going up [the] Monte Rosa had been overwhelmed by an Avalanche, and one life, that of a porter, lost. The 6th death in 14 days."[4]

That evening, as if something in the air were causing temporary derangement, another fatality was narrowly averted. Adams Reilly described what happened:

> Next morning we [learned] that Lord Queensberry had started alone at one o'clock the night before with the intention of actually searching the sides of the Matterhorn for traces of his brother! You may imagine our consternation....[We] started at once with a party of guides and I followed them to the top of the

Hörnli. They found [Queensberry] at the end of the Hörnli arrete, happily safe, but the risks he had run were frightful. He had...found his way to the Hörnli in the dark...and had he gone much further would certainly have been killed. He was quite exhausted, and had almost to be carried down the last part of the way to Zermatt.[5]

In Zermatt that year, July was the cruelest month.

* * * *

After receiving Whymper's report on the discovery and burial of the fallen bodies on the Matterhorn Glacier, the cantonal authorities had ordered Joseph Welschen, the Zermatt Commune's president, to recover the climbers' remains and bring them into town for church services and reburial in the town's cemetery. Welschen's twenty-one man party left Zermatt on Wednesday and returned the following day, their mission accomplished. Croz's funeral service began in Zermatt's Catholic church at 8:30 on Friday morning, July 21st. Anglican burial rites for Hudson, Hadow, and the unfortunate Mr. Wilson were held at 10:30 that same day at Zermatt's picturesque cemetery, a lovely site carved out of the hillside slightly below and across the path from the Catholic church overlooking the rushing waters of the Mattbach.

The coffins of the three Englishmen were placed in a common grave in the town cemetery. In 1870, soon after construction of the English Church in Zermatt, their bodies were moved to the church grounds. Whymper, who had been closer to Croz than to any of the fallen climbers, wrote an epitaph in French some months later for the tombstone that marks the guide's gravesite to this day. In crudely chiseled letters it reads "In memory of Michel Auguste Croz of le Tour, valley of Chamounix, an expression of regret for the loss of a brave and devoted man. Beloved by his comrades and esteemed by *voyageurs*, he died not far from here, a man of great heart and a faithful guide."[6]

With the completion of his testimony before the Committee of Enquiry later that Friday afternoon Whymper ended his duties in Zermatt. He left town the following morning and arrived at Interlaken two days later, having spent nights in Visp and Kandersteg along the way. From Interlaken on July 25th Whymper wrote to McCormick, who had cut short his time as the Anglican Church's summer chaplain in Zermatt and returned to London. These two had not known each other well until fate brought them together in the search for the fallen climbers. Their post-accident endeavors created a bond between them and though never close friends they stayed in touch. During McCormick's long life he would be Chaplain to Queen Victoria, Edward VII and George V, and would officiate at Whymper's marriage many years later. In his letter Whymper asked his new friend for the address of the Zermatt official from whom he might seek reimbursement of the expenses he had incurred as he awaited the formal inquiry into the accident. "I am not pleased at having been detained there so long, merely, as it seems to me, to suit M. Clemenz' pleasure."[7]

This was the one instance in which the enormous pressures of the Matterhorn aftermath got the better of Whymper's judgment and controlled temperament. During the four days following the recovery of the bodies, he had kept very busy: composing written answers to Clemenz's questions, preparing questions to elicit information from Old Peter, attending funeral services for his fallen companions, and testifying in person at the hearing. Clemenz could hardly have acted more expeditiously; his proceeding began on the day the bodies were buried. Whymper's frustration probably started at the hearing when he was asked simply to reiterate his written answers and where he could see, first hand, Clemenz's detached manner. No doubt he thought his personal attendance added nothing of substance and hence was a waste of time. His anxiety while at Interlaken stemmed mainly from the thought of the turmoil awaiting him in London.

Leaving Interlaken on July 26th, Whymper headed homeward by lake steamer, diligence, and train via Bern, Neuchâtel, and Paris, and finally by channel steamer to Brighton. He had made up his mind to say nothing more in public about the circumstances or causes of the Matterhorn deaths. Several days earlier McCormick, after talking at length with Whymper about the accident and the events leading up to it, had written a letter to *The Times* describing the episode, signing it semi-officially as the "Chaplain at Zermatt." Whymper hoped and may even have believed that this letter would suffice in England as an acceptable description of the matter for the public. He had also described the accident in a letter to the Secretary of the Swiss Alpine Club, asking that it be forwarded to the foreign press in the hope that it would quiet further speculation abroad. Neither of the two letters, however, had the desired effect.

By the time of Whymper's arrival in late July the London establishment was abuzz with the extraordinary story of the Matterhorn ascent and the awful toll paid by its conquerors. Word of the accident had come earlier by telegraph, and *The Times* had briefly reported it prior to Whymper's return. Thus far the only first-hand account of the disaster was McCormick's letter to the *The Times* which he had abbreviated in order to spare the Hadow and Hudson families additional pain. It made no mention of Hadow's slip or his inexperience, and did not comment on why he had been brought along. It said nothing of the allegedly slackened rope between Hudson and Hadow, or how that had contributed to the outcome.[9] With these omissions McCormick's letter did not begin to satisfy the interest of the mountaineering community or to quell the public's curiosity.

Contributing to the turbulence of the London atmosphere was the leading article in the July 27th issue of *The Times*. In the nature of a lengthy front page editorial, this "leader" reflected the willingness of many mid-Victorian readers to plough through in-depth analysis with their morning coffee. A small sample of its language conveys the flavor of the paper's view.

There are occasions on which a journal must brave certain unpopularity and ridicule, even in quarters where it may most wish to stand well. We desire the sympathies of the young, the courageous, and the enterprising....But we have our Matterhorn to ascend as well as they – not without a cause. Why is the best blood of England to waste itself in scaling hitherto inaccessible peaks, in staining the eternal snow, and reaching the unfathomable abyss never to return?...

As the successful ascent [of the Matterhorn] is utterly

incomprehensible, of course we do not wonder at the disastrous descent....What is the use of scaling precipitous rocks and being for half an hour at the top of the terrestrial globe? The wisdom of the ages points to the...great advantage of combining discretion with valor and the immense improvement which valor itself gains by the connection....

Our argument shows the value we have set on lives that have been lost. [The fallen climbers were engaged in] a fashionable rivalry, as was...natural to their time of life and to a forward age. They will not have died in vain if this writing is taken as it is meant.

The patronizing tone of this article exemplified the vaulted position of the press – and of *The Times* in particular – before the age of mass media. To the modern observer it reflected the press barons' smug self-image as the pre-eminent arbiters of British society. Their opinion piece artfully characterized the establishment's ideas on the nature of true sport and the folly of purposeless exposure to danger.

*The Times's* editors knew, however, they could go only so far in bucking a developing trend. This awareness was clearly shown in their seemingly unwitting homage to the pioneering spirit of the climbers of the Golden Age. Included in the statement was the following concession: "...[O]ur young men will go to Switzerland...they will feel a very natural and irresistible desire to do...what nobody has done...[I]t must be so." This left an opening for those foolish enough to disregard their advice, and the piece concluded with trite exhortations for the use of greater care in the execution of the activities warned against. Dare it be said that like many modern-day editorials, the leading article in *The Times* ended not with a bang but a Whymper.

Whatever its other merits, the front page editorial stimulated an outpouring of letters-to-the-editor, many by poorly informed and outrageously opinionated quasi-mountaineers who should have known better. William Mathews Jr., one of the Alpine Club's founders, aptly summed up the situation in a letter to Whymper: "The bosh being written to *The Times* by a lot of silly people is perfectly sickening, but I don't think it much matters. All sensible persons understand that the accident was caused by...suffering a man to go with the party who was totally unfit for such an expedition, and...the responsibility of having him taken rests mainly with Charles Hudson. As Hudson is one of the victims and has left a widow behind him, one doesn't greatly like to put this in print."[10]

But it did matter – to Whymper, to the members of the Alpine Club, and to the general public. *The Times* was the journal of record for London if not all of Britain. Its influence was comparable to the combined power of a half-dozen of today's Fleet Street dailies or the current *New York Times, Wall Street Journal* and *Washington Post* rolled into one. Its editor urged Whymper to give the paper his personal account of the accident in order to set the record straight and to provide "the full explanation which is so anxiously expected." [11] Whymper resisted, knowing that a detailed description would intensify the public's focus on him and reopen wounds among the families of the deceased that were just beginning to heal. So he declined, advising the editor that he had requested a full inquiry by the Alpine Club which would eventually be made public.

But Whymper was also beginning to see the merits of the editor's argument. Among those encouraging him to publish his own version of the accident was Alfred Wills, the barrister known for his mountaineering exploits and now President of the Alpine Club. Wills was having difficulty assembling the Club's governing Committee for an investigation, and pressure was mounting for Whymper to provide additional information. "It is a great deal better," Wills wrote, "to have the whole truth known and then let people make what they will of it."[12] Whymper had already shown himself open to this course by qualifying his refusal to send the *The Times* his own summary of the Matterhorn descent: "Should you consider it undesirable to [await completion of the Alpine Club's inquiry], I will at once forward a plain statement of the facts."[13] The anxious editor immediately seized upon this opening, renewing his plea for Whymper's statement. Three days later the newspaper published what would become the definitive account of the shocking accident. In the many microscopically detailed analyses of the accident during Whymper's lifetime and beyond, no one successfully challenged the honesty or completeness of this statement.

Whymper's letter to *The Times* was an expanded version of his later-written summary in *Scrambles*. Straightforward and well-organized, it was more than three thousand words in length. It dismantled board-by-board the framework of misinformation and flawed speculation that had been building. It bespoke the author's broad mountaineering experience and the authenticity of his observations. His words rang particularly true to the Alpine Club members who had climbed with him, shared stories of ascents, and heard his views in lectures and informal gatherings. They sensed his reluctance to cast blame and praised what they felt was his simple honesty in describing what happened. They fully accepted, as did the readers of *The Times*, Whymper's statements about his own actions, self-serving though some of them were. One sentence from the letter is quoted more than any other. Like a freeze-frame from a digital video recording, its terse phrasing captures the drama of the moment occurring a half-second before Hadow's slip: "Croz...was absolutely taking hold of his legs and putting his feet, one by one, into their proper positions."[14]

Wills congratulated Whymper immediately after reading his letter. "You have discharged a painful duty – your narrative bears all the intrinsic marks of as much accuracy as possible under circumstances of such extremely painful excitement."[15] The flow of the public's letters to Whymper now became a torrent. Many of these, and his responses to them, were discarded or lost, but enough are preserved in various archives to show a pattern. A few were critical, many were complimentary, and some – from members of the deceased climbers' families – sought solace by way of more information about their loved ones' last days or moments. Whymper took pains to answer all of them promptly and fully, regardless of their source or point of view. His earlier diaries and journals – reflecting the intensity of his youthful views and the robust style of his Alpine climbing – gave little hint of the tact and empathy he would display in his post-accident correspondence. The trauma of that nightmarish descent reached deep within him, releasing a concern for others he had rarely shown.

P. D. Hadow, young Hadow's father, was unhappy at hearing that Whymper had prepared a drawing of the accident from which a print would be made and published in France along with photographs of the fallen climbers.

I can hardly say how much pain and distress such a proceeding would cause to ourselves and to Mrs Hudson, who has written to us on the subject. I have no wish to interfere with parties who wish to publish drawings of the scene of this sad accident, but they might surely spare the feelings of...relatives who have...suffered so much, and abstain from bringing forward again to notoriety the victims of this fatal occurrence.[16]

Thanks to the efficiency of the London post office Whymper was able to receive and reply to this letter the same day Hadow's father wrote it:

For several weeks past Messrs. Groupil have exhibited in Paris two large drawings by Gustave Doré, one of the accident, one of the summit of the mountain....I have been informed by a friend [that they] are grossly inaccurate....

On Saturday one of their employees called here...and I found that they were determined to publish the drawing[s] whether they [were] correct or not. I imagined that I was neither offending against good taste or good feeling in promising to give a sketch of the spot; supposing indeed that you would prefer a correct to an incorrect representation of it....

I greatly regret that anything I have done should have caused you the slightest pain or annoyance and I shall immediately withdraw my promise to help Messrs. Groupil, and... with your permission, forward them a copy of your letter. I am sorry to say that I believe it will [not] prevent them [from] publishing the drawings....[17]

Whymper's solicitous reply to Hadow's father had the desired effect. Mr. Hadow wrote again to Whymper three days later: "I beg to thank you for your prompt reply to my letter. I have forwarded it to Mrs. Hudson to whom I am sure it will be as satisfactory as to me."[18]

Each day brought new letters to Whymper's home. Hudson's widow wrote a gracious note to him shortly after the publication of his article in *The Times*:

I am at a loss to find words to express all the gratitude I feel towards one who wd. have saved the life of my dear husband if he could....When I think of how you started off again, after all the horror & fatigue of the previous days, to look for those whom you knew no human help could avail, I can only say God bless you for it! [19]

Mrs. Hudson signed her letter familiarly "Emily A. Hudson." There is no record of their ever having met.

Douglas's brother, Lord Queensberrry, and his mother, Lady Caroline, also wrote to Whymper. Queensberrry, following his return to London from Zermatt, sought the comfort of a first-hand report of his brother's time with Whymper. At his request the two met and talked. Later in mid-August Whymper reported by telegram to Queensberrry, then in Scotland, news of a rumor from Switzerland that the location of Douglas's body might have been discovered, volunteering to assist in any follow-up the family might wish. "Thank you very much for offering yourself," Queensbury answered, "but I hardly know yet what might be done if his poor body was found."[20]

Lady Queensberrry also wrote to Whymper, requesting a photograph of the Matterhorn and mentioning an article she had seen about her fallen son. He replied:

I have endeavored, but without success, to procure for you the best photograph of the Matterhorn that is published. I am afraid it is not to be had in London, and I have sent to Paris for it.

I am sure that all who met your son feel very deeply the loss you have sustained, and no one more so than myself for he frequently spoke of going home to join you in a way that showed even a stranger how much he loved you. It was terrible to have him taken away and be powerless to help him. I shall ever feel his loss as that of a friend, although I had seen so little of him, for in those days he showed himself as kind and gentle as he was brave and skilful....[21]

Whymper eventually sent Lady Queensberry the Matterhorn photograph he had promised her, marked to show where the accident happened. In her note of thanks she expressed comfort in learning "how very possible it was for my precious one to have remained somewhere above in the rocks, wh. I had always believed to be the case most firmly." Better, she must have thought, to have a place to picture as her son's final resting place than no idea where his body might be. She, too, signed her note familiarly, "Caroline Queensbury."[22]

In due course Whymper replied to other correspondents. In a letter to Richard Glover, an Anglican cleric, he uncharacteristically spoke of the burden the Matterhorn accident had placed on his shoulders and the bitter lesson it had taught him.

> What a series of accidents life is altogether....People talk of the vanity of human wishes and we have all felt at some time or another that they are vanity, but never have I felt it as much as I do at the present. For five years I have dreamt of the Matterhorn; I have spent much time and labor upon it – and I have done it. And now the very name of it is hateful to me. I am tempted to curse the hour I first saw it. Congratulations on its achievement are bitterness and ashes, and [what] I hoped would yield pleasure produces [only] the severest pain. [I]t is a sermon I can never forget...[23]

Ripples from the Matterhorn accident diminished slowly. To help calm the water Wills wrote to *The Times* praising Whymper's "clear and manly narrative." He also assured the newspaper's readers that the Alpine Club "had...not given its sanction and encouragement to rash and ill-considered enterprises." Indeed, wrote Wills, by enabling its members "to compare their different experiences and to profit by one another's successes, difficulties and failures," the Club has "saved many a life and prevented many an accident."[24]

In its early years the Alpine Club had no program of regular charitable giving. When an individual case of need arose Club members made contributions on their own. Following the Matterhorn disaster word spread that at his death Michel Croz had been the sole support of his wife and was contributing heavily to the maintenance of his two sisters. Upon learning of this a group led by Whymper, Wills and Robertson began raising funds to help the Croz family. Under Alpine Club auspices leaflets were printed and distributed describing the family's needs and the Club's desire to honor Michel Croz's memory. On November 21st *The Times* published a letter describing the campaign which ultimately netted over 278 pounds sterling.

In this immediate post-Matterhorn period Whymper was frank in his criticism of the Taugwalders' behavior while the three survivors staggered down the mountain after the accident. In *The Times* he described them as "paralyzed by terror, cr[ying] like infants, and trembl[ing] in such a manner as to threaten us with the fate of the others...[F]or two hours after the accident [they were] utterly unnerved...and incapable of giving assistance."[25] And, he continued, when the three men reached less demanding terrain a heartless Young Peter "was able to laugh, smoke, and eat as if nothing had happened."[26] In a letter to Woolmore Wigram he expressed his "extreme dissatisfaction with both the Taugwalders, but particularly with the younger man. They not only showed a most unmanly fear for their own lives, but directly we got to the easy part of the descent showed a heartlessness that was perfectly revolting."[27]

On his return to London one of Whymper's meetings was with the immediate past Secretary of the Alpine Club, J. J. Cowell, and the latter's father John W. Cowell. Recognizing Whymper's reluctance to put on the public record the details of the Taugwalders' performance, they urged him to make a contemporaneous record of the guides' behavior in the event that his memory was challenged at a later time. Alfred Wills, from whom Whymper sought a second opinion, concurred with the Cowells' recommendation. Whymper followed their advice and put his recollections in a memorandum dated August 17th. In that document – in addition to the facts he would use later in *Scrambles* to describe the Taugwalders' behavior – he included an even more shocking revelation: "...when the Taugwalders suggested that we should continue by moonlight, and again that I should lay down and endeavor to sleep when we stopped, I objected, feeling that men who could view the loss of their fellow creatures with such commercial feelings as these, might not, possibly, be ill pleased if I also slipped."[28]

Perhaps because they were more offended and less forgiving than Whymper, the Cowells felt that he had not reflected the depth of his feelings on this subject. They thus undertook to write their own memorandum. In it they gratuitously magnified Whymper's fears. The Taugwalders, they said:

> ...had urged him to lie down in a manner so importunate and [menacing] as to induce him to place...his back to a rock, and with... axe in... hand to order them to keep at a greater distance... [H]e passed the night standing in that manner... prepared to defend himself.[29]

These memoranda take on heightened relevance only because F. S. Smythe, Whymper's 1940 biographer, used it as a proverbial smoking gun. The first to gain access to the documents, he mistakenly attributed authorship of the Cowell memorandum to Whymper himself. This resulted in Smythe's erroneous claim that "Whymper wrote an extraordinary letter to the Secretary of the Alpine Club in which he accused the Taugwalders of wanting to murder him."[30] Whymper's more moderately worded memo simply expressed one fear among his many agonized thoughts. It made no accusations. He had written it at the prodding of Wills and the Cowells, and expected it to be filed away and used only in the event of a later dispute. As Lyall points out, Smythe's mistake led other writers to expand upon it. One author referred to "Whymper's monstrous accusation" against the Taugwalders, characterizing it as "the fantastic invention of a youthful brain."[31] Another said grandly that "Mr. Smythe has done a disservice to Whymper's memory...but a real service to truth and justice."[32]

Distortions and embellishments in describing a person's character often stimulate more human interest than fact. Stories of misdeeds tend to have greater staying power and find greater credence than recitals of service and sacrifice. Misinformation can hibernate through generations of benign neglect and emerge intact when resurrected. Witness the indication of possible treachery by Whymper, along with Hudson and the elder Taugwalder, in a modern account of the story. Old Peter, says this author, may have "deliberately sanctioned" the use of a weaker rope between him and Douglas to avoid being dragged after the others in the event of a fall. This is followed by the suggestion of knowing complicity by Hudson and Whymper in Taugwalder's action. "Surely Hudson, one of Europe's most experienced climbers, would have noticed what was going on " when Taugwalder made that choice. And Whymper, in writing to Woolmore Wigram that "the rumour [concerning Taugwalder's deliberate choice of a weaker rope] is absolutely without foundation," may also have been "trying to save his own neck."[33] Compounding the harm of this speculation is the fact that in his letter to Wigram, Whymper was actually referring not to Old Peter's choice of a weak rope but to the rumor that the guide had cut the rope to save himself.[34]

Whymper's character provides a particularly tempting target for critics of the Victorian era. Some who allowed Whymper's judgmental nature to form the entire measure of his personality were "overfond of the clichés and half truths with which a certain school likes to belabor the Victorian age and those who lived in it."[35] But in the bright spotlight of the several weeks following the Matterhorn accident Whymper showed a genuine solicitude for those whose lives it had so tragically affected. And he had risen to the challenge of that overwhelmingly stressful experience as few might have predicted.

# CHAPTER 16

## *Glaciers And Sledge Dogs*

As the autumn of 1865 turned to winter, the public's interest in the Matterhorn disaster had waned, and by November Whymper was again working full-time at his father's engraving company. With Christmas approaching he was looking forward to the Alpine Club's annual member-guest dinner. For the last three years this convivial event had been a high point on his limited social calendar. He had enjoyed rubbing elbows with these accomplished men among whom his star had risen rapidly. This year, however, he chose not to attend. "...[I]t would have afforded me great pleasure to have invited you as my guest," he wrote to McCormick, "but I do not intend to go, as I should certainly be called upon to speak, and I do not see how I could make an after-dinner speech there after what has occurred. You will I am sure take the will for the deed."[1]

This must have been a difficult decision. At the Club's annual gathering he would be among supportive colleagues who understood his emotional burden and appreciated the way he had carried it. They would commend him for his forthright account of the accident in the *The Times*, and for smoothing the shock waves of revulsion triggered by news of the "disastrous descent." His remarks could stay within facts already on the public record. Waves of empathy would wash over him as he told of his colleagues' last moments and paid heartfelt tribute to them. Club members' faces would beam with admiration for his unyielding determination to climb the Matterhorn and for his success in finally doing so.

But he would be forced to relive the terrible accident before a hushed audience. He would be the center of attention, pressed to answer questions throughout the evening. And Whymper meant what he had already said to some: mention of the Matterhorn had become "hateful" to him, its conquest "bitterness and ashes."[2] Sadness at the death of his colleagues and vexation at fate's cruelty had replaced the thrill of the Matterhorn ascent and the deeper satisfactions of an unparalleled climbing career.

Peer group opinion also influenced his decision. In times of mourning and shared tragedy, disrespectful or indecorous public behavior was rigorously censured. From Zermatt in August of 1865, Sandbach Parker wrote to his friend, J. D. Forbes, "I think no one will attempt the Matterhorn at present – as it would be a violation of good taste and look like bravado."[3] In Whymper's view, refocusing attention on the Matterhorn disaster even in a low-key after-dinner speech would approach the limits of that strict standard. Also gnawing at him was the perception – not shared by his colleagues – that perhaps he should have more forcefully questioned Hadow's credentials and been more insistent in urging the use of guard ropes on the descent. Though time would gradually diminish these self-incriminating doubts and the melancholy they induced, the accident's emotional impact dominated his feelings in the late autumn of 1865.

J. D. Forbes – "Principal" Forbes, as he was known for his early academic success – was a Scotsman born a generation before Whymper. He was a respected scientist whose special interest was "glaciology," the study of the formation, composition and movements of mountain glaciers. The two men first met in September 1865 in Birmingham at a meeting of the members of the British Association, a national organization formed in 1831 to compete with the more elitist and conservative Royal Society in the discussion and promotion of science. In his conversation with Forbes, Whymper felt free to speak candidly about the Matterhorn disaster. As Forbes described it:

I had the melancholy pleasure of hearing from Mr. Whymper's own lips the details of that awful accident. For a long time it quite haunted me. Mr. Whymper's letter to *The Times*, so perfect in taste and tone as well as in narration, raised him immensely in my estimation, and the impression was confirmed by his bearing and behavior at Birmingham, which was everything that could be wished, though he was subject to the temptation of being violently lionized.[4]

The contacts between these two men continued to the point where Forbes learned something of Whymper's scientific inclinations and of his disinterest, for the foreseeable future, in further Alpine climbing. Based on their conversations Forbes suggested in the spring of 1866 that Whymper might find aspects of glaciology to his liking. In particular, he said, by studying the possible effects of weather and pressure in the formation of ice-layers beneath glacial snows Whymper could make a valuable contribution to the body of scientific knowledge in that field.

Forbes's suggestion struck a responsive chord in the dejected Matterhorn survivor. Within his dark memories of the accident was a resilient nostalgia for his six glorious Alpine summers. He knew the mountains' glaciers like the backs of his hands, and scientific curiosity had been a part of his makeup since his days at Clarendon School. In leisure hours, away from the workaday engraving business, nothing pleased him more than planning foreign travel. Though he was now working full time at the office, a modest glaciology study would require only three weeks or so, and he had become adept at obtaining his father's blessing for such extra-curricular enterprises.

So he committed himself to the project. In typical fashion he made detailed plans, beginning with a study of how to access and measure glacial ice strata. He studied his charts for the location that would best serve this purpose and chose the equipment and personnel for the physical labor his expedition would require. Although he contemplated no serious climbing, Whymper knew the value of having with him an experienced Alpine guide as helpmate in bad weather and unexpected danger, and, in this instance, someone who could act as a straw boss of the project's workforce. To fill this role he arranged for Franz Biener, one of his guides from the preceding year's campaign, to join him.

In late July of 1866 Whymper left London for Zermatt. He had chosen for his outdoor laboratory a familiar locale – the relatively smooth, rock-free Stock Glacier that descended from the Col de Valpelline, a pass about three miles west of the Matterhorn. He knew the area; with Carrel and Meynet he had crossed the Col on the way to Prarayé in 1863. On arrival in Zermatt he met up with Biener and together with three laborers they left town on August 2nd and headed west. That afternoon, short of their objective, they made camp at 9,000 feet on the rocks of the Stockje, a small peak at the head of the Z'mutt Glacier and the point from which the first Welschen search and rescue party had hoped to move toward the fallen climbers' bodies. It began to snow heavily and a gusty wind blew all night. "Great avalanches" of snow cascaded onto the Tiefenmatten Glacier from the surrounding slopes and some smaller accumulations fell from the Stokje itself.

It was hardly coincidental that from his chosen work site on the Col de Valpelline the Matterhorn would be in full view. Though it had become the "hateful" mountain, Whymper seemed irresistibly drawn toward it. Now, in the shadow of the mountain's northern face with his former guide, whirling images of the recent past must have filled his mind. Perhaps he felt that proximity to the fatal scene would have a cathartic effect, and some scientific inquiry in this familiar setting would restore a sense of usefulness that the Matterhorn accident had temporarily diminished.

The next day Whymper, Biener and the three workers set out for the Col at the head of the Stock Glacier. On what should have been an easy ascent they struggled in several inches of new snow against a bitterly cold wind. Leaning forward they plodded upward and reached the Col's 11,650 foot summit in mid-morning. After catching his breath Whymper staked out an area atop the Col 24 feet long and 5 feet wide.[5] These markings established the boundaries of the trench his party would dig in the glacial surface, deep enough to reveal the ice strata to be studied. Biener and the three laborers worked in pairs, one chipping away compacted snow with a pick, the other bringing it to the surface with tosses of a shovel and later, as the depth increased, in baskets carried upward along an inclined ledge hewn in one of the ditch's longer sides. As the trench went deeper it became a deeply frozen chamber. On the glacier above, a cold fog blocked virtually all heat the August sun might otherwise have provided. The men's labor kept their blood going while masses of icicles formed on their beards. Whymper, who merely supervised, became chilled to the bone. After five hours the trench was

*Valley of Zermatt (from Smythe's Edward Whymper)*

nine feet deep and Whymper decided he had had enough for the day. He and Biener scrambled down the frigid slope to their tent on the Stockje and the laborers followed soon after.

During that first day on the Col "...the mists were so dense we dared not use veils or spectacles."[6] The mists did not block the sun's harmful rays, however, and Whymper, who had been in the most exposed position, suffered snow-blindness and a severely sunburned face. In the tent that evening his vision became blurred and he began to see double. The next morning his "eyelids refused to open and the light was painful even when they were closed."[7] The rest of the party returned to the work site leaving him with his eyes bound by a handkerchief, unable to eat and even worse unable to smoke. He was cold and uncomfortable the entire day.

Two days of rest enabled him to return to the Col. Upon viewing the trench he was disappointed to see how little had been accomplished in his absence. Partly because three feet of snow had drifted into the ditch during the first night, the men had been able to dig only four feet deeper, less than half the progress made on the first day. Perversely the wind had strengthened again, its chilling effect dropping the apparent temperature dramatically. Whymper decided that while the men could work in the protection of the trench he would soon freeze to death on the wind-blown surface. He and Biener departed, urging the men to continue their work and promising them their task would end once the solid ice of the glacier was reached. Instead of returning to their bivouac they went westward across the Col and spent the night in the chalets of Prarayé.

After another off-duty day in nearby Bionnaz on other business, Whymper and his guide returned to the work site on the Col the following morning. The workers, having struck an unusually thick layer of glacial ice, had laid down their shovels and sat smoking their pipes. Their employer was furious; relentless cold weather along with the lingering effects of his snow-blindness and sunburn had stretched his nerves taut. Now the men seemed to be slackening their work at every opportunity. "My wrath was somewhat appeased [however], when I went down into the pit. They had struck a layer of ice of much greater thickness than any...previously met with. It extended all around the floor of the pit to a depth of 6 1/4 inches."[8] Seizing a pickaxe himself, he chipped through the thick layer and got the men going again.

After a while his weakened eyes again grew painful. He and Biener left for Zermatt, hiking the entire way through a terrific thunderstorm and very heavy rain. That night Whymper stayed with his favorite Alpine hosts, Alexandre Seiler and his wife. In the Monte Rosa dining room Seiler cut up his dinner and Mrs. Seiler put sulphate of zinc on his face to soothe his sunburn. Then came the inevitable and in Whymper's case, large, nightcap. "After a bottle of champagne," he said, "I slept reasonably well."[9]

The summer's unusually severe weather continued to complicate Whymper's mission as he and Biener headed back the next morning to their trench atop the Valpelline pass. Rain began again and stayed with them as far as their campsite on the Stockje. It then turned to snow, driven hard into their faces. On their tenth and final day on the site they dug through another ice layer to a final depth of twenty-two feet. Late that afternoon Whymper made his last measurements as winds "howled over our heads in a true hurricane." With that, the five-man party, all tied together, "floundered down to Zermatt," arriving there at 9:00 p.m.[10]

Whymper's inspection of the trench's walls showed that layers of pure ice were more numerous near the surface, with successive layers becoming thicker as their depth increased. He estimated that these layers composed at least ten percent of the glacier's mass, more, he thought, than anyone had previously supposed. Also under the heading of new information was the discovery that the stratification of alternate layers of snow and ice within glaciers was caused by pressure-produced agglomeration and not, as many surmised, the infiltration of surface water. This undertaking and the summary of his findings and conclusions were recognized as an advancement of scientific knowledge, all the more impressive for someone with no formal scientific training. Years later, in 1894, sixteen Fellows of the Royal Society included this work among the accomplishments cited in their proposal, never acted upon, that Whymper be elected to their ranks.[11]

While Whymper suffered the rigors of icy winds and snow-blindness in the Alps his father was courting Emily Hepburn, a much younger woman of Scottish descent Josiah had met at Maze Pond Chapel. He had been a guest in the Hepburns' home and served as a Deacon at the chapel with Emily's father. The attraction between them grew, and now some seven years after Josiah's becoming a widower they made plans to marry. He was a vigorous fifty-three; she was an amiable but plucky thirty-four year old, undaunted at the prospect of step-mothering Josiah's eleven offspring. Edward, his father's second child, was only eight years her junior. Emily and Josiah were married in December 1866 and she soon earned her new brood's affection. In the eyes of Annette, the youngest of the Whymper children, the new Mrs Whymper was a "gifted artist and a cultured person."[12] Edward grew quite fond of her, appreciating the support and loving care she gave to her husband and the rest of the family.

Throughout his stepmother's life Whymper addressed her as "Mrs Whymper," despite the closeness of their ages and the cordiality between them. He wrote to her regularly while abroad, for the last time as she lay stricken by an illness from which she eventually died: "I could not have wished a sweeter mother than you have proved yourself!"[13] Today's readers of this letter can only lament the stiffness of their relationship and the loss to Whymper of the counsel and support his stepmother might have offered had he and she been more receptive, which of course they were not. Restrained by Victorian tendencies to avoid probing another's feelings too deeply, neither likely made any serious effort to breach their common emotional defenses.

* * * *

Upon his return from the Alps in the fall of 1866 Whymper again went to work full-time with his father. His engraving apprenticeship had begun some twelve years earlier. Josiah had driven him hard, at least in the early days, and Edward had worked diligently to help the company stay afloat and then to prosper. He had first gone to the Alps not on a lark but as a commissioned agent for a successful book publisher, and had returned with sketches showing more natural talent than perhaps anyone had expected. Those drawings, and the growing success of his mountaineering career, gained him recognition in the society of men whose acquaintances, his father recognized, might one day translate into business profit. He had also worked with Josiah in the company's day-to-day business during the long months between Alpine summers.

Over these years of working together father and son had developed a comfortable relationship. Josiah had come to London a poor young man from Ipswich and with hard work had become a self-made success. To his credit, rather than force Edward or any of his other children to stay within his shadow, the elder Whymper allowed them considerable latitude to follow their own interests. Rather than begrudging them the things he could never have, he generously took pride in his children's expanded interests and achievements. In this atmosphere a tacit understanding developed between Josiah and Edward that travel, exploration and scientific inquiry were acceptable pursuits in their own right and could enhance the Whymper family's standing within the circles of society to which they aspired. This unspoken compact allowed the young engraver to seek outlets for his restless energy, both physical and intellectual, confident he would have his father's support.

Since the days of his teenage diary a yearning for arctic exploration had been a part of Whymper's makeup. The unexpected opportunity to explore the Alps had pushed such hopes aside and under different circumstances might have buried them forever. But as abruptly as William Longman's offer had opened the door to Whymper's Alpine career, the Matterhorn experience had ended it.

Back in London and re-energized by his first natural science venture in the Alps, his scientific curiosity and questing spirit were stronger than ever. In the spring of 1867 he decided to turn his youthful dream of Arctic exploration into reality. As he conceived it, the project would not be on the grand scale or extended timetable of a government-sponsored expedition; he would be on his own – and on his own pocketbook – as a private citizen. But in the tradition of his youthful heroes it would take him to untrodden territory on a useful mission. This time it would be the remote and as yet mostly unexplored interior of Greenland. He would be the first to test its vast inland plateau for travel by dog sledge, believing that new data on this subject would be of value to his nation's continuing program of Arctic exploration.

Greenland is an enormous snowy wasteland of approximately 850,000 square miles, some nine times the size of the British Isles. Almost 90% of the island lies north of the Arctic Circle. A snow-covered icecap, left over from the ice age, blankets virtually all of Greenland's surface. This glacial surface slopes inward from a narrow, broken chain of mountains that encircles the island near its shorelines and contains several peaks above seven thousand feet. Greenland has no woodlands or forests, and no arable land. Today most of its 60,000 residents live in small villages and settlements on the southern portion of the island's western perimeter along the Davis Strait on both sides of the Arctic Circle. These waters offer better harbors and more abundant sea-life than the Atlantic Ocean on the east. When Whymper planned his expedition, Greenland was a Danish settlement and home to some 10,000 people, most of whom were East-Inuit natives who spoke the Inupiaq language. The island was accessible by sailing vessels or steamships coming primarily from Denmark. In 1867 this isolated land lay truly at the edge of the known world's permanently habitable places.

For the twenty-seven year old mountaineer – perhaps before and certainly after his first visit – Greenland held a somewhat romantic attraction: for its remoteness and for the difficulty of its living conditions and the unique character of its people.

> ...[Greenland is] a glacial...land that...compels its inhabitants to live near the sea and upon what they can obtain from it – a treeless country...where the scanty vegetation, pressed down by almost perpetual snow, creeps along the soil upon which it can hardly subsist. A land where none are rich and...all are equal; where there is neither organ-man or wife-beater, and where children are allowed to do just as they like; and, more remarkable, a land without debt or taxes...[14]

With a sense of expectation like the one preceding his first trip to the Alps, Whymper left England by steamer in early March of 1867 for Copenhagen where he would complete arrangements for his expedition. On the way he passed through Belgium and northern Germany. As usual, his first visits to foreign lands left him unimpressed. "Belgium is detestable," he wrote to a friend, "the parts of Prussia worse, and Schleswig worst of all." But Hamburg, the City-State on the banks of the Elbe where the river meets the North Sea, had its good points. "Hamburgers seem to be doing well: I have seen more smiling people

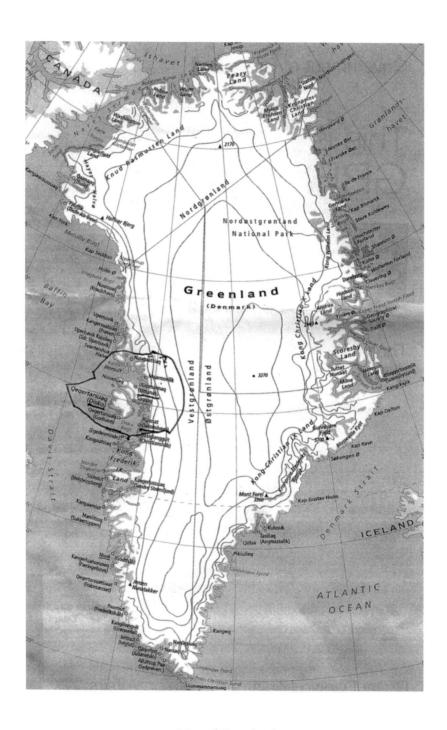

*Map of Greenland*

here than I have during the last five years."[15] He wrote that letter as he lay mired in the city awaiting the delayed arrival of his trunk with most of his clothes and all of his maps and papers. "[T]he Prussians...may have kept my portmanteau to clothe the army. It needs it. The only thing I have forgotten is the thing an Englishman is supposed to stick to last of all – my tooth-brush."[16]

Arriving in Copenhagen in late March he languished for almost two months while unexpected delays kept his preparations incomplete. The principal villain was bureaucratic red tape although some suppliers were also guilty of inefficiency and foot-dragging. Discussions with government officials and tradesmen were irksome and often inconclusive. He finally left Copenhagen in late May on a Danish sailing ship and after a tedious voyage arrived on June 15th at Jakobshavn, a settlement on Greenland's west coast some 200 miles above the Arctic Circle. There he set about two tasks not yet completed: selection of the people who would accompany him inland, and a survey of the shoreline to find the best place from which to launch his party across the mountains and onto the interior's snow-covered icecap.

Greenland was Whymper's first exposure to a culture outside of western Europe. The guile and mendacity of some Alpine natives had hardly prepared him for the similar frustrations he would suffer at the hands of Greenland's Inuits who lived virtually as their ancestors had for centuries. Since he could not change the Greenlanders' ways he made the best of what they offered. Once back in England, with the perspective of time, he would turn the story of his tribulations into a typical Whymperian narrative:

> ...[I]t is distressing, after you have paid...a crew...in advance...to have a man come just before you start and say that he has no boots, or no socks, or no shirt. You remind him that he has [been paid] in advance, but you find that he has nothing [left, having]... settled it all on his wife who has immediately eaten it up. You...pay a little more in advance and [ask him] to go...supply his wants. "The store is closed...tonight." "Go tomorrow then." "Tomorrow is Sunday; the store is not open on Sunday." "Well, on Monday then."

Monday comes [and] there is a gentle breeze which just ruffles the sea.. All your natives shake their heads, for in Greenland it is…the fashion to go to sea [only] in a dead calm. Tuesday comes, the wind has fallen, and…one of your crew [says he is] sick. Again you suggest that you have paid [him] five dollars in advance. The man acknowledges it, and says that he would be most happy to repay you, but points [out] that he has nothing. You can only grin and bear, for it would be no use to appeal to the trader [who supplied the workers and] would tell you he has no power to compel the natives to fulfil their engagements.

At last, after a multitude of delays, the sick man is replaced…and all your natives declare themselves ready to start. You point to the baggage and tell them to put it in the boat. "First, we will drink a little coffee," say they, and all your natives vanish again.[17]

Further delayed by an outbreak of influenza among the Jacobshavn populace, Whymper finally left town with a newly constituted party of five men cobbled together from the best native helpers he could find. Included in the group was an English "collector" who would preserve and catalogue the plants, birds, insects and a few mammals that would return to London as museum specimens, most in fossilized form. Whymper had ultimately obtained three sledges along with drivers and twenty dogs. Men, dogs, sledges and all the party's paraphernalia were loaded onto two rowboats manned by additional Inuits. They were bound for a spot at the inland end of a fiord above Jacobshavn which Whymper had chosen on an earlier exploratory mission as the place to start across the mountains onto the inland glacier. After the party disembarked, one boat took the rowers back to Jacobshavn and one was pulled ashore for possible later use.

Nothing went smoothly. The sledge dogs' behavior was a problem from the start. They seemed to have been poorly chosen, a mistake compounded by their handlers' inability to control them. The inexperienced Whymper thought such canine behavior was the norm. "The dogs, as is their nature, did all they knew to vex us. [They] gnawed incessantly through the[ir] lines…bit us, and fought each other on every possible occasion. If they could have been seized with a unanimous desire to escape in one direction we should have been left without a single brute; but fortunately each one wanted to go a different route...so they neutralized each other's efforts."[18]

Whymper had surveyed this area a month earlier, soon after his mid-June arrival. At that time snow had covered the glacial ice, forming a packed surface on which they could easily walk. He had been able to move on foot at a pace of 3 to 4 miles per hour; natives had said that his party could make 35 to 40 miles per day by sledge over the firm snow. Now, in late July, the snow had melted to expose a thick sheet of ice below. As he gazed at the glistening panorama stretching to the horizon in all directions his heart sank. He saw "thousands and tens of thousands" of icy crevasses that would have to be crossed.[19] "To properly constructed sledges drawn by men, [these crevasses] would not have posed insuperable obstacles. But to sledges such as ours, heavily laden and drawn by those perverse...Eskimo dogs, they presented the most formidable obstacles....[Looking at them] I knew that we could not succeed."[20]

From that point on Whymper's excursion was a disaster. His words painted an indelible picture:

The sledges looked picturesque as they came over the ice-pinnacles, rearing up like ships running before a gale of wind. The dogs, for a moment still as statues, in the next instant would rush away down the opposite slope with ungovernable speed and clear the crevasse at its foot with a bound...[jamming] the sledge...fast between the walls of the chasm. Then the dogs, feeling themselves checked, would tug away to the right and to the left, and, finding their efforts vain...invariably commence to fight among themselves. By the time the sledge was righted, the lines..had become...inextricably tangled and knotted.[21]

At this point Whymper himself was behaving like a trapped animal. He now realized that he had been foolhardy to attempt Greenland's icecap so late in the season. He was no doubt cursing the ineptitude of the Danish authorities and the incredible inertia of the Inuit men, but also blaming himself for not anticipating the extended time the project would require, both for preparation and execution. The straw that finally broke the expedition's back was the collapse of the sledges: a runner on one of them snapped in two; on another, a runner split down its entire length. The third sledge, severely battered, looked as if it might require decommissioning at any moment. Three men sent forward as scouts returned and reported that conditions ahead would only get worse. At that point Whymper knew they could not reach the interior as planned, and so, as he had often been forced to do on the Matterhorn, he ordered a retreat.

Though Whymper's expedition failed in its mission to explore Greenland's interior, he had discovered that it was possible, before summer's sun melted the icecap's snow, to "travel over the glacier-clad lands of the north with sledges."[22] Next time, he vowed, he would find the money to hire men instead of dogs to pull the sledges and would start earlier in the season. The expedition did achieve its secondary goal of collecting rare plant and animal fossils for the British Museum. These were described, and some pictured, in an account published in the British Association Reports of 1869. Whymper thus survived with his pride intact.

In October of 1867 the young explorer was homeward bound. On the "Brig Hoalfisken off the Orkney Islands" northeast of Scotland he wrote a letter to his father "on the chance of coming across a fishing smack," which he thought would be the fastest way to get the letter posted.[23] He asked his father, surprisingly, whether business required his immediate return to London and gave no reason for wishing to extend the almost seven months he had already been abroad. Pushing Josiah further, he also asked if he could live temporarily with the elder Whymper and his new wife at their residence in Haslemere, Surrey – having in mind a plan to use the family home as a base while writing a memoir of his Alpine scrambles.

His letter then became chatty in the style that would permeate his later writings: a folksy description of a commonplace event in an exotic setting, far removed from his readers' own life experiences. "The last pig was killed today. I heard his dying squeals as I was trying to wash myself in a wine glass full of water....I have a young Esquimaux with me – a dog, I mean – who has already devoured the mittens belonging to the first mate and the boatswain and who may be devoured himself yet, being the only fresh meat we have left on board."[24]

At that writing Whymper's sailing vessel had been driven for a week by storms so severe they prevented the use of sails. Apparently the young explorer was unperturbed, either by the boat's lack of headway or its being tossed about in a rough sea. Despite the weather and his recent frustrations in Greenland he was in good spirits, still brash enough to be thinking of future solo expeditions on a shoestring budget. Despite his long absence from the office he was also comfortable writing to his father in that light vein. The sea breezes and salt air of the North Atlantic were a tonic to his body and his spirit.

* * * *

Whymper returned to Greenland five years later in 1872. On this trip he spent most of his time kayaking in the northern part of the Davis Strait where it meets the icy waters of Baffin Bay. There he circumnavigated and mapped Disco Island, for which the current charts were unreliable. Writing little about his exploration of these waters and more for the interests of London lecture audiences, he focused on the customs, lifestyles, and beliefs of native Inuits. He described their seal meat diet, sealskin clothing, and the contribution of sharks to their economy: a single shark liver could yield up to 27 gallons of oil. He talked of the Inuits' good humor, their respect for private property despite their own penury, and how he was able to trust himself among them, "solitary and unarmed without fear of treachery or violence."[25] In Greenland, "murders [were] unknown and quarrels rare....[T]hey had not a single policeman , soldier, or magistrate in the land."[26]

In these writings Whymper sounded more like a 20th century social scientist than a 19th century explorer. At the time, sociology was not yet a formal discipline but people were enormously curious about the alien ways of exotic societies. Lectures by explorers were the most popular means of satisfying their hunger and Whymper gave them the right combination of popular science, adventure and homespun stories of ordinary people in distant lands. He also told them of how the relatively primitive Inuit society dealt with life's challenges in ways extraordinarily

249

different from their own. With the help of his original drawings, and later his own photographs, audiences gave him their rapt attention.

\* \* \* \*

Whymper's two Greenland excursions, five years apart, were his only visits to this remote land. In the time between them he wrote just one article about his arctic travels in the *Alpine Journal*. He spent virtually all of those years writing and making the drawings for *Scrambles*, the book that would bring him a second dose of fame and more fortune than he ever expected.

# CHAPTER 17

## *Birth of A Classic*

On his return from Greenland in the fall of 1867 Whymper moved into his father's home in Haslemere. Josiah, his wife Emily and eighteen year-old Annette, the youngest of the Whymper children, were then living in the house that had once sheltered the entire brood. Josiah realized that his son's reclusive nature and night-owl habits would keep him occupied and largely out of the way. Edward would also be busy writing *Scrambles* and there was plenty of room for him in the spacious house. But it was a generous father who would allow a grown son to join him and his new wife under the same roof.

The arrangement was a great help to Whymper. He would have room and board at no cost, with servants to free him from the time-consuming chores of living alone. Vindicating Josiah's judgment, Whymper stayed with the family at Haslemere for four years and grew closer to his father and his stepmother in the bargain.

His daily routine began typically with a late breakfast around 10:00 or 10:30 a.m., which, according to Annette, had to "be miraculously on the table as he sat down" – a sisterly way of saying that although her brother needed little attention he was demanding about the few things he wanted.[1] He would spend the rest of the morning and early afternoon on correspondence, research and the like. Around 2:00 p.m. he would have his only substantial meal of the day and an occasional word with Annette or his stepmother. Then he would "sally forth on some long tramp," returning home in time for late tea and toast.[2] Thereafter he would sometimes "unbend to some small family interests" which might include a game of bagatelle with Josiah, a diversion that rested his father's eyes after a day of fine block engraving.[3] If something

*Whymper in 1871 (from Smythe's* Edward Whymper)

intervened to prevent his afternoon walk, he would take it in the early evening.

These solitary excursions, which he used for exercise and reflection, became a lifelong habit. Then, at 10:00 p.m., "when the methodical, early household retired to bed," Whymper would lay out his writing and research papers at one end of the breakfast room table.[4] At the table's other end a plain supper would have been spread for him. He would work on *Scrambles* until 3:00 a.m. or later, and "woe to the relative or maid who endeavored to arouse him" earlier than his usual mid-morning hour.[5] Whymper kept to this routine for a year and a half. In the summer of 1869 he returned to the Alps for a few days in late July and early August. This was to be a holiday, a walking tour with no scientific project or mountain ascent in mind. He chose the Dauphiné region of the French Alps for his visit, a remote area that held pleasant memories of his first climbing season in 1861, and of his 1864 campaign with Moore, Walker, Croz, and Almer. As the rugged Dauphiné was still largely unsettled he took with him his old Matterhorn companion Jean-Antoine Carrel, both for companionship and added safety. The execrable food, voracious insects and filthy accommodations of the area now seemed forgotten.

The young Englishman and the grizzled Italian bersagliere – who had reached the Matterhorn's summit from the Italian side soon after his companion's first ascent – were travelling tourists now. They followed much the same route as Whymper had taken in his earlier visits, but this time were content merely to enjoy the region's striking vistas as they talked about the younger man's earlier climbs there. Again passing the massive cliffs of the Meije, which was not scaled until several years later, Whymper decided they no longer looked impossible but was content to leave them for someone else. This brief tour of the Dauphiné ended with his third inspection of the Mont Cenis railroad tunnel through the mountains northeast of Briançon, an engineering marvel he never tired of visiting.

Whymper returned to London in early August. After delivering the first instalment of the *Scrambles* manuscript to his publisher John Murray he returned to Europe and went alone to Turin and then on to Zermatt. There he visited with Alexandre Seiler and others but steered clear of guides and mountain summits. His contentment to walk the Alps as a tourist – and to note with little interest the apparent accessibility of the Meije's grim hulk – showed the drastic change in his outlook since the Matterhorn accident. For now, at least, a respite from the daily grind of an author's life was all he sought.

Back home at Haslemere by month's end Whymper continued working on *Scrambles* – writing, editing and revising his words, over and again, until each sentence and paragraph struck the right note. He also supervised every detail of the work of turning his manuscript into a book. He oversaw the replication of his drawings on the woodblocks used to make the engravings for the book's illustrations. *Scrambles* would contain more than one hundred of his drawings placed strategically throughout the text. Nine employees of the family business copied his drawings onto woodblocks; Whymper and his father did all the engraving.[6] He spent almost as much time selecting the drawings, making the engravings, and supervising the work of the printers as he did on writing the words. To print the book he chose R & R Clark, Ltd. of Edinburgh and spent many days on the company's printing floor with the typesetters and press operators. He was "terribly exacting" in his demands for "the very finest printing results."[7] According to Robert Clark, the company's owner, Whymper "dragged out of his machine-minders the very best that was in them."[8]

In this same period John Tyndall was writing a book of his own Alpine experiences. The memory of their dispute concerning Tyndall's final Matterhorn retreat kept them politely distant, but the feisty natural scientist recognized the young artist's talents and purchased several of Whymper's drawings to illustrate his own text. When published in 1871, Tyndall's *Hours of Exercise in the Alps* contained seven full-page illustrations, six of which bore Whymper's signature.

*Scrambles* was published that same year by John Murray and put on sale at the price of one guinea. Reflecting the care and attention given to its production, the book's handsomely bound text was a fine example of both the printer's and the engraver's art. The design and reproduction of the wood engravings, perfectly complementing the text, were "far in advance of any previously published illustrations of Alpine scenery."[9] The book quickly became a bestseller.

Whymper's memoir generated more literary and social commentary than any previous book on the subject of mountaineering. Preeminent among its reviewers was Leslie Stephen, one of the more flamboyant and outspoken members of the Golden Age's mountaineering fraternity. He had crossed Whymper's path on two or three occasions in the Alps but they had never climbed in the same party. He was the first editor of the *Dictionary of National Biography* and later authored *The Playground Of Europe*, a lighthearted story of his Alpine climbs and travels. Stephen wrote additional articles on Alpinism in *Cornhill*, *Fraser's* and *Macmillan's* magazines, and was one of the early Presidents of the Alpine Club. He is remembered today primarily for extending his family's legacy in the persons of two daughters: the author Virginia Woolf and the artist Vanessa Bell, both of whom were members of the Bloomsbury Group and among the best known women in the literary and artistic circles of the early 20th century.

Considered by some to be the foremost literary critic of his generation, Stephen put his talents on display in a review of *Scrambles* in the *Alpine Journal*:

> The author's place in the records of English mountaineering is so conspicuous that it is a kind of duty to everyone who takes an interest in the subject to read his narrative.... [Some] amateurs are probably quite equal to Mr Whymper in skill, endurance and speed; but he deserves the special credit of having carried to the highest point that spirit which...distinguished all the mountaineers of the [current] epoch from their predecessors. And for that reason I....give him my vote...as occupying the same position in the mountaineering world as Robespierre in the French Revolution....[B]ut for one melancholy circumstance he would have been the most triumphant of us all....

> Mr Whymper's book...is the congenial record of the most determined, the most systematic, and, on the whole, the best planned series of assaults...made upon the high Alps during the period of which he speaks....[His] book contains the most genuine utterance of the spirit in which the victory has been won, as well

as the authentic record of some of the most stirring incidents in the final contest between man and the mountains ....All who have shared...in that spirit will be carried back to those pleasant memories:... solitary rambles, convivial meetings, fine weather enjoyed to the utmost, and bad weather endured by Stoicism and tobacco....[W]e rejoice that he is so able a historian.[10]

Stephen was equally impressed with the engraved illustrations. "Mr Whymper's woodcuts seem to bring the genuine Alps before us in all their marvelous beauty and variety of architecture. Not a line is thrown away, or put in at random; and we could almost lay down the correct line of assault of [any] one of the peaks represented without need of looking at the originals."[11] *The Times* was even more graphic in its praise: "The illustrations [are] remarkable for fidelity to truth and nature. You can almost hear the tinkle of the bells on the Alps and by the chalet; you breathe the fresh fragrance of the pine trees; and fancy listens for the sharp ring of the axe as it makes splinters fly from the ice-walls."[12]

Other print media were dubious. The conservative *Evening Standard* feared that Whymper's book might "foster [a] depraved taste... for doughty deeds in Alpine climbing....[It] had very much the same effect [on us] as sensation headers and tremendous falls have upon the frequenters of...theaters. The shocks are not unpleasant, but they are morally deteriorating, ministering to an unhealthy craving for excitement."[13] *Blackwood's* magazine was similarly critical: Whymper's story portrayed "a great effort of human skill and patience... carried on at the continual risk of life – a risk undertaken with a light heart for no particular reason. This is the weak point of the story. The want of a motive is the only thing which prevents the book, and the adventures it embodies, from taking a very high place in literature."[14] To these critics, Whymper's story of mountain climbing's "continual risk of life," with its occasional violent deaths, shocked and titillated but did not enlighten or uplift.

This stiff-necked attitude represented the view of the mid-Victorian establishment. Its members saw the popular appeal of *Scrambles* as a threat to their entrenched belief that adventuresome conduct should be productive in a utilitarian or patriotic sense. If neither of these, it could be justified only if it provided artistic or spiritual uplift. Their view, however, was already outdated and would soon give way to Leslie Stephen's high-spirited attitude toward mountaineering. By the late 1880s Britain would hail Alfred Mummery as the first modern Alpinist and the father of rock climbing. In the early 20th century England would lionize George Mallory, and Queen Elizabeth II would confer knighthood on Edmund Hillary, the peaceful beekeeper from New Zealand, for his first ascent of Mount Everest and subsequent charitable works.

By appealing to a host of readers beyond the climbing fraternity, *Scrambles* was a catalyst for the rapid erosion of the view that mountaineering was not a true sport. "It did more to break down popular prejudice than any other mountaineering book...ever published."[15] It went through six editions in Britain, three in the United States, and multiple editions in French and German to meet a substantial foreign demand. Whymper was as surprised as anyone by its runaway success. "The book is likely to be a success – an alarming success. So far as I can see, I shall succeed in losing only 500 pounds by publishing it."[16]

His book continued to be read and to stimulate comment well into the 20th century.

Geoffrey Young, a prominent English mountaineer and author, wrote a more modern appraisal of *Scrambles* in a 1923 issue of *Cornhill* magazine:

[T]here are very few works upon a single and rather esoteric subject which young and old alike can continue to read with such unflagging enjoyment. His secret is his veracity, the feeling that he gives us that it is all just happening to ourselves. We feel the conflict, the obstinacy of the man; but we feel also the reality of the forces against him....

Whymper is not self-conscious; he is not capable of regarding himself as an abstraction; he gives us only the concrete incidents of his struggle with mountain forces. We have the lifelike presentation of a flinty mountain and a steely Whymper in continuous concussion, the whole illuminated by [a] firework of sparks....He bullocks into the confusion...his honesty has evoked, [to an] extent made plain to us by the noise of the things falling about him in his charge....Through the attitudes of [other mountaineering] protagonists....he crashed with a rude personal vehemence that remains hopelessly individual.[17]

During the years 1867 to 1871 Whymper had been able to live and write his book in comfort. He had also managed a seven-month expedition to Greenland and one summer holiday in the Alps. In pursuing this lifestyle he was in the mainstream of middle-class Victorian attitudes toward the proper mixture of work and recreation – perhaps near the farther edge of the latter. The working classes spent long and debilitating hours in fields, factories and offices, but among Whymper's peers workaholics were virtually unknown. Their pace of life reflected a special appreciation of the benefits of travel and exploration.

In these last four years he had poured all of his energy and artistic skills into *Scrambles*. During this period he had been only sporadically on his father's payroll and had self-funded his brief trips abroad. The result was a serious depletion of his personal "exchequer," raising the question of how he managed even modest expeditions abroad in those years of minimal earnings. Whymper had always lived simply, however, spending little on entertainment and other luxuries. Josiah had schooled his children in frugality from birth, and his second son learned that lesson well. Throughout his life he watched every outgoing penny, wherever he might be. Part of that training also led him to set aside savings which he could draw upon when needed.

For five or six years following the publication of *Scrambles* Whymper immersed himself in the engraving business. He stuck with it as his most reliable source of income; it was what he did best. He spent most of his work days on the administrative rather than the artistic side of the company, where he showed a good head for finance and management. He found time, however, to write for the *Alpine Journal* on his Greenland experiences and to repackage his Greenland journal articles for some of the many periodicals which for Victorians filled the same demand as reality television does today. Supplementing his income further, he began speaking to some of the many London groups anxious to learn more about foreign lands from the first-hand accounts of adventurers who had been there. From these lectures he began to acquire the skills of a compelling public speaker. Whymper also kept an active interest in the many new products and technologies being produced one after another in the bustling innovation of the mid- and latter Victorian periods. In the next decade he would put his speaking skills to even more profitable use, and make sound investments in start-up enterprises based on new technology.

One of his few summer holidays during this period was a visit to the Alps in 1874. From Zermatt, with guides Carrel, Bich and Lochmatter, he scaled the Matterhorn a second time, the 76th climber to reach the summit since his original ascent. That climb undoubtedly stimulated a flood of memories but Whymper was content to confine such recollections to the pages of *Scrambles*, at least for the time being. His journal commented only on the physical changes he observed on the Matterhorn, all of which met with his disapproval. While ascending the east face he noticed that "little piles of stones [had been] placed here and there on jutting rocks" to mark the ascent route. Those trail guides made it "almost impossible to lose the way, even in bad weather, so soon the biggest duffers in Christendom will be able to go up."[18] As usual, his blunt observation was dead-on; currently, in July and August, forty or more climbers test the Matterhorn's upper slopes each day, weather permitting.

Though he never wrote or spoke of the feelings stirred by this second ascent of the Matterhorn, surely part of Whymper's decision to return to the "hateful mountain" was a desire to confront the memories that still haunted him. Like a general drawn to revisit the site of a great victory won only with the sacrifice of many lives, he would feel again the exhilaration and anguish of his first ascent. This re-enactment of that fateful July 14th served its cathartic purpose; he would never again set foot on its slopes. His second climb to the Matterhorn's summit would be his last.

Whymper's social life in the decade of the seventies revolved around dinners and other activities at the Alpine Club and occasional invitations to gatherings with a literary or scientific flavor. Outings with family members and dinners at their homes filled out his limited social calendar. There is no record of his attempting to find a wife during this period of his life, which would come later. In his thirties and perforce lonely, he most likely satisfied his sexual needs among the swarm of prostitutes in London's many brothels and taverns. His nephew Robert Whymper described his uncle's approach to sex as "distinctly caveman" but gave no details of how he formed that opinion.[19]

Toward the end of the 1870s Whymper began to devote substantial time to the study of the physical effects of high mountain altitude on the human body. His decision to focus on this subject was fueled in part by mountaineers' growing interest in the world's tallest mountains, the Himalayas. He imagined these far eastern giants as his future laboratory for observing the reactions of his own body at levels well above the highest Alpine summits. To him this was a fascinating subject – an irresistible combination of scientific enquiry, travel and physical challenge. At the time, however, a new British foreign policy strictly limited civilian travel through parts of India, effectively blocking non-military entry to the Himalayas. This forced him to consider another mountain chain for his experiments, the high Andes of South America. Disappointed but reconciled to this turn of events – and ever determined to pursue a goal once chosen – he began to make plans for what would become the second great adventure of his life.

# CHAPTER 18

## *The Royal Road To Quito*

To one degree or another, altitude sickness strikes all who venture onto higher altitudes in the open air. Though the percentage of oxygen in the air remains constant, less of this essential gas is available as altitude increases and atmospheric pressure drops. Oxygen levels decrease steadily to a point at which the rarefied air is unable to sustain human life. For some people symptoms of distress begin as low as 5000 feet above sea level and can include severe nose bleeds, headaches and nausea. Often accompanying these symptoms are feelings of apathy or anxiety. At whatever heights they begin, the effects of altitude sickness can be alleviated only by pausing to let the body acclimatize to reduced oxygen levels or by returning gradually to a lower level. Adaptation to reduced oxygen levels brings more rapid breathing, an increased rate of blood flow, and a greater mass of red blood cells. These changes allow muscles to work with less amounts of oxygen. At heights up to 10 or 15 thousand feet, most people can adjust within a few days, but for those attempting the higher Himalayan or Andean summits, acclimatization usually takes considerably longer.

By the mid-1870s altitude sickness was well known but little understood. Diminished air pressure was thought to be the culprit but scientists had yet to determine exactly how it produced the illness's symptoms. The latest laboratory experiments in reduced pressure chambers in France showed only that "oxygen *may* exercise a beneficial influence" on affected persons.[1] But why did some people react differently than others at the same heights? Were the effects temporary or permanent? And why were "aeronauts" – who had flown in hot air balloons since the late eighteenth century – able to soar rapidly to enormous heights with apparent immunity? Students of the subject wondered if something in a particular mountainside's environment – "noxious exhalations from vegetation," perhaps – might be a factor.[2] Whymper thought seriously about these questions and how he might collect new data to shed light on them.

In 1874 he had decided that the Himalayas would provide "the best field for research" on this subject.[3] After months of planning, however, he learned that the British Foreign Office had recently created a kind of "scientific frontier" for India. The nature and purpose of this "frontier" remain unclear but its effect was to discourage, at least temporarily, English citizens from seeking access to the Himalayas through India – the only route to the high mountains thought feasible at the time. Thus on the advice of "experienced Anglo-Indians" he turned his attention and hopes to the high Andes of South America. He first considered peaks in Chile, Bolivia, and Peru but was again deterred by political unrest in each of those countries. Chile had long been at odds with its neighbors Peru and Bolivia, primarily over adjacent territory containing valuable mineral resources. It had gone to war with the Peruvian-Bolivian Confederation in the late 1830s, after which Peru and Bolivia became separate states. In the mid-1870s relations between Chile and its two neighbors were again becoming hostile and in 1878 would descend into open warfare between Chile and Peru.

Time was passing as Whymper persisted with his plans. In the late 1870s he focused on Ecuador as the only accessible country with mountains high enough for his experiments. The peak in his sights was Chimborazo, the nation's highest at an altitude then thought to be above 21,000 feet. On its slopes he could personally test the effects of elevated heights. If he could get to the top of this mountain he would become the first person of record to reach a summit of 20,000 feet or more. No doubt Whymper knew this but did not speak of it as a goal. Perhaps this was because he was aware that earlier climbers had gained greater heights on other mountains though stopping short of their summits. Chief among these were the brothers Adolph and Robert Schlagintweit from Prussia. In 1854, under a joint commission from the British East India Trading Company and the government of Prussia, these two natural scientists mounted an expedition to India and the mountains of Asia.

Over the course of three years they covered thousands of miles and reached an altitude of 22,259 feet on Mount Kamet in northern India. Some twenty years later, in 1874, British Army records showed that two of its officers had reached similar heights, one in the Garwhal region of the Himalayas, the other in the Kuen-lun range to the north. No specific locations or dates were mentioned, however, and these latter climbs were never claimed or recognized officially or unofficially as summit ascents.

Whymper had learned from his first Greenland foray that the price of inadequate preparation was a series of frustrating, potentially catastrophic delays. This time he spent the better part of the year of 1879 making detailed preparations for his Ecuadorean expedition. The route to this distant undeveloped country in northwestern South America lay over the Atlantic Ocean, through the Caribbean Sea, across the Panama isthmus by land, and south through a corner of the Pacific Ocean to the seaport city of Guayaquil. Ecuador's borders encompassed territory on both sides of the equator, the earth's zero parallel for which the inhabitants named their country. The width of the coastal plain between the Pacific Ocean and the Andes averages about one hundred miles. In its sea level rain forests temperatures regularly rise to 85 degrees Fahrenheit while on the highest Andean summits it can drop to 15 degrees or less, well below the freezing point.

In Whymper's day, travel to the country's interior was by mule, donkey, and on foot. There were telegraph lines connecting a few cities but no communication facilities of any sort in the countryside. Accommodations for travelers outside the population centers were usually primitive, offering no real amenities. Necessities for his campaign included canned food, medicine and basic first-aid supplies, blankets, tents, summer and winter clothing, various implements and tools, and chemicals and containers to preserve local samples of flora and fauna. Whymper needed a wealth of additional equipment and supplies for his prospective roles as mountain climber, field scientist and rain-forest trekker. Logistics had to be carefully thought out and delivery schedules closely coordinated with his projected arrival date.

From his Alpine days Whymper knew that the success of his mission would depend in large part on the help of trustworthy guides. In Ecuador his companions would need special talents to complement their technical climbing skills. Months of sustained close contact in a strange land called for men of even disposition, assistants who would take direction well but be self-sufficient and able to think clearly when the need arose. As might be expected, Jean-Antoine Carrel headed Whymper's list of the men who met these requirements. Carrel accepted his old friend's offer and Jean-Antoine's younger cousin, Louis Carrel, also agreed to join the party. Whymper decided to hire a third companion upon his party's arrival in Ecuador.

As part of his planning Whymper realized the need to advise Ecuadorean authorities of his intentions, and to have a local resident on the ground ready to assist him with customs and other logistics. He also wanted someone in the British consul's office in Guayaquil to know of his plans, a fellow countryman who could provide help in case of accident or serious illness. For this he turned to Charles E. Mathews, the Alpine Club President in late 1878, asking Matthews for assistance in making Ecuadorean contacts and introductions. Mathews put him in touch with Ecuador's Consul-General in London, who made the Ecuadorean President's office aware of Whymper's coming and later advised him that government representatives in Guayaquil and Quito were prepared to offer their English visitor every courtesy. The British Foreign Office alerted its staff members in the cities Whymper planned to visit, advising them to be available to their forthcoming English visitor. Mathews contacted his representative in parliament who agreed to "send out in advance, and to place in secure hands," much of Whymper's heavy luggage.[4]

Charles Mathews, Whymper's helpful colleague, was a fellow mountaineer and a man of charm, wealth and influence. The two of them had developed a mutual respect as Alpine Club activists, and their dealings in this matter would strengthen their relationship. They would stay in touch and become regular correspondents in later years. Another friend and mountaineer, Douglas Freshfield – the editor of the *Alpine Journal* at the time – put Whymper together with Frieherr von Thielmann who had "recently ridden through Colombia and Ecuador...and made the ascent of Cotopaxi," an active volcano almost as high as Chimborazo.[5] Others of "the fraternity of mountain-travellers" helped in small ways to prepare Whymper for his journey. He was especially pleased to get "a cheering bon voyage" message from J. D. Boussingault (1802-87), a noted French chemist who had attempted Chimborazo in 1831 but had been forced by fatigue to turn back well below the summit.[6]

On November 3rd, 1879, with his preparations finally complete and the two Carrels at his side, Whymper set sail from Southampton on the steamer *Don*. Three weeks later they arrived in Colon, Panama, then a province of its neighbor Columbia. There they found that heavy rains had recently washed away a stretch of the Panama Railway, forcing a nine-day delay in their westward journey. After finally crossing the isthmus on December 4th they boarded the *Peyta* on Panama's west coast and on December 9th reached the Ecuadorean port city of Guayaquil.

The messages sent out earlier from London on his behalf paid an immediate dividend. "Our ship had scarcely anchored before a Customs House officer sought me out to deliver an ornate speech which commenced, according to the Ecuadorean manner, with declarations that he himself, his property, and other things besides, were mine,...and that he had been ordered to pass my baggage without examination, and free of duty."[7] This effusive welcome to the Republic of the Equator would set the tone for the greetings Whymper would receive throughout his tour of the country. Overblown posturing, he would learn, was a way of life for local officials – more form than substance, often entertaining but rarely helpful.

Guayaquil, with a population close to 28,000, was Ecuador's largest port and second largest city, after Quito, the country's inland capital 167 miles or 269 kilometers as the crow flies to the north. Guayaquil sits on the western bank of the Guayas River which runs southward past the city. This river is a massive confluence of waters formed by two other rivers, each a sizeable stream: the Daule flowing in from the north and the Babahoyo coming down from the northeast. Some thirty miles farther downstream the Guayas widens to flow around both sides of a large island and finally forms a huge estuary as it meets the waters of the Gulf of Guayaquil. The Gulf's indented shoreline runs east from the Pacific Ocean, and then curves southward. The Guayas River drains into the Gulf virtually all of the surface flow from the western side of the Andes that form the spine of Ecuador's northwest region. For fifty miles or so, from the Gulf to Guayaquil, the waters of the big river are navigable by oceangoing ships.

At Whymper's arrival in 1879 this seaport city was bursting at the seams as a result of the war between Peru and Chile. Refugees flooded its streets; tons of cargo, unable to move smoothly through the port's limited facilities, clogged its docks and storage areas. Lodgings were scarce even for those with money. By day the city smoldered in the hot equatorial sun and by night steamed in the heavy atmosphere of the fast-approaching rainy season. Whymper was relieved that he had only two matters to deal with in this oppressive setting. The first was to acquire an interpreter and general assistant. Through word of mouth he found and hired Mr. Perring, an Englishman who had once worked as a courier between Guayaquil and Quito. Whymper's second task was to check on arrangements he had made for pack mules to transport his party's provisions and equipment. They were to be available in Bodegas de Babahoyo, a small town about 45 miles up-river from Guayaquil where the party would begin its overland trek toward Chimborazo's high peak. On the morning of December 13th word came that the mules and their drivers were assembled. Anxious to be underway, Whymper and the two Carrels along with their new team member Perring left by steamer that afternoon.

The width of the Guayas River at Guayaquil was about a mile and a quarter shore to shore. The party's steamer, the *Quito*, moved steadily upstream, overcrowded like the city with passengers and freight. As often on South American river steamers at the time, this one carried an exotic mixture of people and goods including some imported pipe-organs.

The war in Peru caused an exodus of Italian organs from Lima, and thirty refugee instruments landed at Guayaquil just before our arrival. Four of these were on board the *Quito*, concentrated on the fore-part of the upper deck, [with the wind] playing a different tune [on] each. The Ecuadoreans enjoyed the babel, but the alligators in the river seemed more sensitive. They came up and stared with open mouths, [then] plunged down again immediately, out of hearing.

The Guayas and it tributaries are full of alligators. On a [later] trip up the river...I saw a large sandbank completely covered by a horde of them, lying peaceably alongside each other. The natives do not seem...troubled by their proximity, though it is admitted they do occasionally chew incautious children.[8]

At midnight, after an eight-hour upstream cruise, the party's steamer docked at Bodegas, home to about two thousand people. In the town and throughout the region, many houses were built on stilts to protect against flooding. In each rainy season the swollen waters of the Babahoyo River overflowed its banks, turning much of the area into a vast lake. The approach of the current year's wet season thus gave Whymper an increased incentive to get moving and he was relieved the next morning to find the mules and their handlers there as promised. By 1:20 that afternoon, December 14th, all were assembled, loaded, and ready to leave. Carrel led the procession for a while on muleback, followed by Whymper, similarly mounted. Then came the pack-mules and their "arriero" handlers, with Louis Carrel and Perring bringing up the rear.

*On the way to Bodegas*

Whymper and Carrel each carried one of the party's two mercury barometers strapped to his back. These were vital pieces of equipment without which critical height measurements could not be made.

The wisdom of not trusting these instruments to a mule's back was soon confirmed. "Just one hour after the start, when we were jogging quietly along, the leading mule suddenly became possessed by ten thousand devils, and rushed hither and thither, throwing its heels in the air. Succeeding in loosening its load – which turned round under its belly – it then commenced a series of violent fore and aft movements with its hoofs, try[ing] to pulverize my photographic camera and the other things it carried."[9] Temperamental mules continued to be the bane of the expedition as necessary but extremely troublesome components. Whymper thought he might have loaded them too lightly; other parties' mules, he observed, often carried twice the 160 pounds averaged by his. These beasts were never as unmanageable as the sledge dogs of Greenland, but they gave him fits.

It took the party about three hours to reach the "straggling village" of La Mona. There they spent a short night in hammocks on the open front porch of a bamboo hut built on posts. "Sleep was enlivened by super-abundant animal life. Bats flapped our faces and thousands of insects swarmed down upon our candles, while scuttling things of all sorts ranged the floor and invaded our boots."[10] Contrary to his often disparaging remarks about Alpine accommodations, Whymper had no complaints about the lodging he found in La Mona or, with one exception, elsewhere in Ecuador. He was now a more mature traveler and had doubtless been warned to expect only rudimentary night-time facilities.

The party's route from the port of Guayaquil to Bodegas was by river. From there it would take them overland to Guaranda and then to Chimborazo. Because this path continued beyond Chimborazo's southern flank all the way to Quito, it had been known for centuries as "The Royal Road." Though the natives clung to this name, the southern portion of the road had become a rutted jungle pathway hardly navigable by man or beast of burden. "In the matter of mud...it [did] not [take] precedence over all other roads in this country; though it certainly was, in some parts, what Ecuadoreans call 'savory.' The mud is composed of

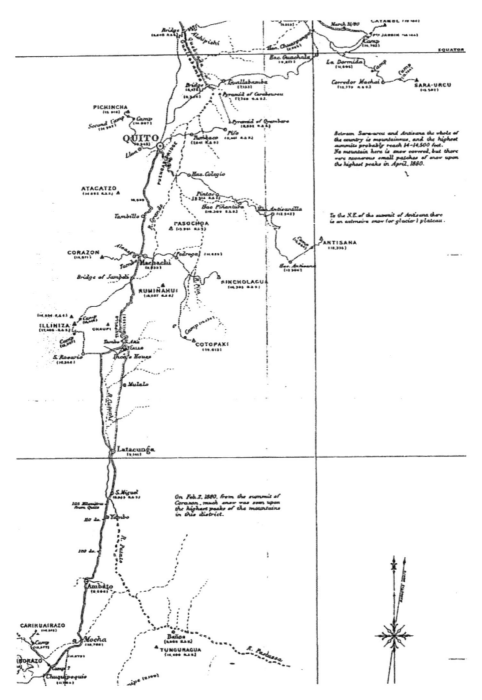

Route map of Ecuador

decaying animal and vegetable matter, churned up with earth, and the product is a greasy and captivating slime."[11]

On the rough road out of La Mona the next morning there was a motley array of traffic over the route in both directions due mainly to the war going on not too far to the east. Metal bedsteads, huge bales of quinine bark, corrugated iron sheets, cases of champagne – all came in sight at one time or another. These caravans held a variety of animals – mules, asses, horses and horned cattle – creating a concert of "snortings, braying, [and] smashing" accompanied by the sharp scoldings and commands of arrieros struggling to keep them under control. Unknown birds flitted about in the thick overhead foliage and in the "hooks and spines" of rain forest vegetation. Sunlight glimmered through holes in the overhead canopy, and alien creatures "thrived on stagnant air in the gloom" of the forest floor. If Whymper had been searching for a place of starkest contrast with the icy solitude and pristine vistas of Alpine slopes he surely found it on the Royal Road to Quito.

The party spent its second night on the road at Muñapamba, in a hut or "tambo" near the road. A throng of assorted beasts surrounded it, probably the domestic animals of other travellers staying at the tambo. The hut offered no food so they ate from their own provisions and retired early. Their beds that evening were planks on which they "passed an uneasy night in the open air." The party was on its way again early the next morning They were now out of the rain forest and into the wooded slopes and moderate climate of the western side of the High Andean Range. The steeply rising road soon became little more than a rut gouged in the forest floor over the course of three centuries of total neglect. Earth fallen from its banks mixed into the muck of mud, decaying plants, and animals that had died there and never removed. That morning they passed two mules "stuck fast and abandoned to their fate." Though their path continued higher, continuing mists limited their view to less than a quarter-mile in all directions.

In the afternoon they entered an area where rain had been falling for eight days, turning the twisting trail into a glassy smooth slope. They pressed forward anxious to gain Tambo Loma, the next shelter marked on Whymper's map. At this point they were joined by a "genial man" on his way to Quito who helped direct them to what he called the "Hotel

On The Hill." On reaching this group of huts their temporary guide steered them across the surrounding "quagmire" to what Whymper generously called the "principal apartment." In reality it was a bare, nine by six foot windowless room with no beds, bedding, food, or a hearth for making a fire. Here they supped again on their own cold rations and slept on their packing cases.

The group left Tambo Loma soon after daybreak the next morning, December 17th. This would be their ninth day in the country but they had yet to see their first mountain peak. Thick mists had been replaced the rain, making the road nearly impassable. The mules sank with each step in mud up to their knees. After struggling upward for several hours at this miserably slow pace, near exhaustion, they gratefully noticed that both the road and the weather were improving. Gradually the mists cleared and at 10,000 feet they could now see, over the tree tops, where they had been and what lay ahead. On the uphill slope about four hundred feet above them was a mountain gap, a low point in a north-south range whose highest peaks Whymper estimated to range from 13,000 to 15,000 feet.

Pushing up and through the pass with renewed energy they reached the other side of the col. There, spread out before them to the east, was a totally different world. Gone were the damp mists and clouds that had covered most of their journey from the Pacific Ocean. The air was clear and dry, its moisture drained by torrential rains on Ecuador's coastal plain and by the rising slopes on the western side of the pre-Andean range they had just topped. From their new vantage point they saw the eastern slope descend into a wide valley, as barren and dry as the Sahara. Going downward, the party's track became a decent road, allowing the mules at last to find solid footing. These new surroundings put everyone in a better frame of mind.

After pausing for lunch, the group continued through two villages on the valley floor and arrived just before dark at the small town of Guaranda. This was the closest settlement to Chimborazo and the site Whymper had chosen as a base for his first survey of the mountain's lofty virgin peak. The party had expected the lodgings at Guaranda's only inn to be more inviting than the bare rooms of the forest tambos of the past three nights. They were disappointed, however, to find the beds "objectionable" and the apartments "filthy" – so unappealing that they all spent yet another night in an open gallery on their packing cases.

Guaranda was about twelve miles in a straight line from Chimborazo's lower slopes. Whymper marveled that he had come so close to the country's highest mountain without having seen it, but such was the fact. The foursome of Whymper, the two Carrels, and their interpreter and aide-de-camp Perring left the inn early the next morning on a one-day scouting mission. They took one arriero with them to point the way but left the mules behind. They went first down a ravine to the west bank of the Chimbo River and then across it on a bridge to the valley's eastern slope. Going steadily up a "regular incline" they were at 11,000 feet by 6:30 a.m. From there, looking back to the east, they saw in sharp relief the high peaks of the mountain range they had crossed the preceding day. None of Whymper's maps showed this chain so he dubbed them the Pacific Range of Ecuador, the name by which they are known today.

Still on the Royal Road to Quito they were now headed to the "Great Arenal," a vast plateau beginning somewhat higher up and extending northeastward to the southernmost edge of Chimborazo and beyond. Their "road" had again become a mountain path, abandoned without maintenance for untold years like its lower section and clearly showing its neglect. The track then disappeared entirely, leaving the party to scramble upward as best they could. The three mountaineers had a fairly easy time of it but Perring, breathing hard, straggled some distance behind. In this manner they surmounted a sandy ridge marking the top of the Chimbo river valley's eastern slope. Before them lay the sandy sweep of the Grand Arenal, "stretching uninterruptedly to the base of Chimborazo."[12] There they had their first sighting of the lower part of the huge mountain, but with clouds surrounding its upper reaches Chimborazo's full grandeur remained tantalizingly hidden.

Nearby was that day's objective, the Tambo of Tortorillas, the only refuge between Guaranda and Chimborazo. At 12,800 feet this one-room hut was "one of the foulest tambos in Ecuador, [its] courtyard a sea of mud." Whymper's party declined even to enter it but were too hungry to refuse the food offered – potato soup, bread and chocolate – which they ate outside. From a grassy knoll near the hut they examined what they could see of Chimborazo and the terrain leading up to it. Coming

*Crossing the Grand Arenal*

off the mountain were buttresses whose moderate slopes ascended to about 15,000 feet. Whymper had been told that mules regularly went to the summits of these buttresses "to fetch ice, which was cut for sale in Guayaquil."[13]

This reconnoiter was useful: it confirmed the mountain's location, revealed the condition of its lower slopes, and showed what would probably be the highest point to which the pack mules could be taken. With those observations noted the party left the area of the Tortorillas and headed back toward Guaranda. Along the way, Whymper became dizzy and feverish, his head throbbing painfully. The staunch mountaineer who had never showed illness during an Alpine climb suddenly needed help staying on his feet. Encumbered by their struggling leader the party moved slowly, regaining the Guaranda inn as darkness descended. Whymper took 30 grains of sulfate of quinine and retired immediately "under a mountain of blankets." On one of the inn's "objectionable" beds – or perhaps again on his packing cases – he managed to sleep well enough to regain his feet the following next day.

That next morning, December 20th, the mist and clouds obscuring all of Chimborazo gave Whymper a welcome day of inactivity and recovery. He and his party used the time to explore Guaranda where they encountered two members of the town's "very thin upper crust." These worthies were the Commissary of Police, known as the Jefo-Politico, and the town Priest. The two officials, anxious to ingratiate themselves with their distinguished English visitor, were particularly friendly. After a few pleasantries, their motive became clear:

'Señor, we understand perfectly that in an affair like yours it is necessary to dissemble, a little. You doubtless do quite right to say that you intend to ascend Chimborazo – a thing that everybody knows is perfectly impossible. We know very well what is your object! You wish to discover the treasures...buried in Chimborazo, and...and we hope you will discover it. But...when you have discovered it...we hope you will not forget us.

'Gentlemen,' I said, 'I shall be delighted to remember you, but in respect to the other matter I...suggest that you shall pay half the expenses of the expedition and take half the treasure we discover.' [At] this they drew long faces and went away. [14]

On the morrow under bright blue skies at last, Chimborazo's upper reaches stood out clearly against the northeastern horizon. This first sighting of the mountain's towering snow-capped crest conveyed a full sense of its awesome size. From a hillside north of town, using telescopes, the party saw near the summit several long glaciers abutted by steep cliffs and gullies of daunting height – all on a scale that dwarfed their Alpine counterparts.

In their fields of vision were two big surprises. The first was that the mountain was double-domed with two snow-covered apexes, not one. Earlier travelers had referred only to its "summit." The discovery of two peaks meant that Whymper would have to measure and perhaps make a scrambling survey of both – as he had done on several occasions in the Alps – in order to decide which was higher. Even more surprising was the revelation that long glaciers streamed in various directions from both domes, covering the upper portion of the mountain's visible side. This was quite shocking, really, because others had reported that the only glacier anywhere near Chimborazo was on another nearby mountain.

Through his telescope Whymper could make out "multitudes of crevasses," including "great schrunds" created by "the dislocation of these icy masses in their passage across unusually irregular ground." At the sight of these deep ravines, some at altitudes he had never attained, he felt more thankful than ever that both the Carrels would be at his side as he explored Chimborazo's untrodden heights.

From their initial sighting the eastern peak appeared to be higher than the western, but theodolite measurements of the angles of both crests created doubt. After a discussion on what approach would most likely lead them to this summit, Whymper and the Carrels decided that the mountain's southwestern ridge appeared to be the most direct feasible route. Jean-Antoine and Louis wanted to leave immediately; for them, Guaranda's minimal leisure time pleasures had worn extremely thin. But Whymper was not ready; he wanted to survey their approach route more carefully before committing men and mules to Chimborazo's unknown slopes. So he sent his two guides out the next afternoon, instructing them to survey the terrain and to find a suitable camping site on the ridge at about 16,000 feet, the highest elevation he thought the mules could reach. Meanwhile he would remain in Guaranda double-checking the serviceability of the mercury barometers so important to the success of his mission.

In his guides' absence Whymper took photographs with the expedition's camera. On their first day in the town he and the others had encountered "a pretty Spanish girl, with lustrous eyes, who captivated the Carrels – by peeling their potatoes." [15] Now Whymper went looking for subjects to record on film, including the girl with the shining eyes. To these wanderers so far from home the Spanish girl was an orchid blooming in the desert, her beauty enhanced by the exotic setting in which they found her.

Whymper was not impressed, however, with the "Authorities" he had met earlier and who now asked him to take their picture. Unwilling to commit a photographic plate solely to them he dispatched Perring to find others who would add local color to the image. The zealous Perring, eager to do his master's bidding, cornered "an old Indian woman – the first person he saw – and drove her into the inn's courtyard." As Whymper put it, "she came in crying and screeching, clasping her hands, and appealing to the Almighty to save her from my cruelty. 'Señor Patron! Spare my life! What have I done to be treated thus?' " [16] He later found out that the office of the Chief of Police was in that same courtyard, causing the elderly woman to think that Perring was one of the Chief's hired ruffians.

The Carrels returned on the morning of December 23rd, their second day out, exhausted but with their mission completed. They had ascended the slow rise of the Arenal to the foot of Chimborazo's southwestern arête, then mounted the ridge and chosen a camping spot on it. Jean-Antoine said that the campsite was at about 16,000 feet as requested. Carrel also confessed that he and Louis had become fatigued while climbing up the ridge's sandy slope. He had therefore chosen a second and lower campsite on the Arenal near the base of the mountain at about 14,000 feet for the party's first night in the open.

With enough information to go forward Whymper proposed to the arrieros that the mule train leave the next day, December 24th. The natives, however, had no intention of spending Christmas day away from their homes so the departure was set for December 26th. At 9:45 that morning the entourage was ready – fourteen mules (four for riding and ten for baggage), three arrieros, and two "Indians" to act as porters and to carry poles for planting on the mountain at various locations to use as reference points on the map Whymper was sketching as his party moved along. At their departure "The priest blessed me and mine, and all we had. The Chief of Police, dressed in his best, came to see us off; while the populace of Guaranda sat on a wall and regarded us with stolidity." [17]

The native pole-handlers proved troublesome from the outset. They obstinately lagged behind, frequently dropping their poles or allowing them to be jarred loose by wayside rocks when the path narrowed. With these disruptions the party took seven hours to reach the broad expanse of the Arenal plain. Drawing abreast of the foothills of Chimborazo's southern flank they abandoned The Royal Road and with Jean-Antoine in the lead angled right to head eastward toward the mountain. By the time they reached the lower campsite chosen by Carrel the sinking sun was casting long shadows on the sand. Under a clear, moonlit sky they bivouacked by a small stream and built a blazing campfire in the chill air. The entire party – "mountaineers, arrieros and Indians" – then sat around the fire and had their evening meal together.

It had been a long day. As Whymper looked around him at the starkly beautiful scene he sighed with relief that they were finally on Chimborazo's slopes, about to begin the ascent. It was "an exceptionally fine night...still and cold...with the temperature falling to...21 degrees Fahrenheit, turning our little brook [into] a mass of solid ice. The remains of the soup in the cooking utensils were frozen up, cruelly hard."[18] But he had no complaint. Conditioned by many frigid nights under starry Alpine skies, Whymper wrapped himself in a blanket bag and was soon fast asleep.

# CHAPTER 19

## *"Time Flew Rapidly"*

Whymper's party awoke at dawn the next morning at their bivouac in the high desert. As Chimborazo's unfamiliar foothills took shape in the sun's first rays the men suddenly realized that someone had raided their campsite. While the exhausted climbers and arrieros had slept soundly, two of their porters had sneaked out of camp taking five mules with them.[1] Fortunately the thieves did not risk the commotion of reloading beasts that had been unburdened for the evening, so the party's provisions remained intact. As Whymper put it, the faithless Indians had simply "deprived [us] of seven backs," a more annoying than harmful loss but one that would deplete the party's portage power and slow their progress. In accord with local custom the native porters, like the arrieros, had been paid in advance for their services.

Whymper labeled the party's present Chimborazo campsite "Camp 1" on the map he was sketching as they went along. At 14,375 feet it was on the edge of the Arenal near the entrance to a small valley that led to a glacier flowing from the mountain's summit. They would now move on to Camp 2, a spot chosen by Carrel on the western slope of the southwestern ridge 2 ½ miles to the northeast and about 2,000 feet higher than their first camp. Whymper planned to take provisions up to Camp 2 sufficient for several days, along with barometers to measure altitudes and climbing equipment to scale Chimborazo's icy cliffs.

At 10:00 o'clock that morning he sent Carrel and Perring up the valley to establish the second camp. They were accompanied by eight fully loaded mules and three arrieros. Whymper and Louis Carrel stayed behind, ostensibly to complete the job of packing up. In truth they remained to block the path of any muleteers who might try to defect, something Whymper thought distinctly possible. As Louis gathered more firewood Whymper "stripped for a real good wash before going to regions where ablutions were unknown."[1] The next thing he knew the one mule left at the lower camp decided to test its masters' patience, which these Ecuadorean crossbreeds delighted in doing at every opportunity. Breaking its bonds:

> the animal rejoiced in freedom, and intoxicated by success went as near to standing upon his head as a mule can go. Its behavior seemed...extremely ungrateful, and I went for the animal. It ran away but...was handicapped [by] a...halter which trailed along the sandy plain whilst I ran unimpeded and gained on it at every stride. When I seized the halter it was I who was captured. The wretched beast dragged me unmercifully over the sandy soil until Louis came to my assistance, and we towed it in triumph back to camp.[2]

*Chimborazo from Guaranda*

Whymper left to his readers' imagination whether the mule had interrupted his bath or had waited until he was again clothed. In any event his wrestling match with the exuberant animal no doubt forced him back to the stream to wash the sand from his newly cleansed body. Carrel and Perring returned at 1:00 p.m., surprising Whymper at how quickly they had been able to unload the mules at Camp 2 and return for a second trip. In their

*Second Camp on Chimborazo*

absence Louis had taken some of their provisions farther up the valley to a spot where earth and rocks formed a safe "depôt" in which to store them for later use. Upon Carrel's return, while the mules rested, the men took a few more items to the cache. That done and Camp 1 now fully dismantled, they reloaded the animals with the remainder of the stores and equipment and headed for Camp 2.

* * * *

In planning his Ecuadorean expedition Whymper realized that he would need food and medicine to supplement such necessities as might be available locally. He spent several months itemizing his requirements, purchasing the items, and selecting their containers. The latter would undergo rough handling throughout their long journey and suffer prolonged exposure to extremes of heat, cold and rainfall. Over time he amassed twenty different foods and medicines, each item packaged either in an individual tin with edges soldered to make it airtight, or in a bottle encased in tin tubing. These items – including beef, mutton, ham, soup, tea, condensed milk, cocoa, sugar, lemonade, dry condiments, powdered laxatives, zinc sulphate, throat lozenges – were arranged into one hundred batches, each composed of all twenty items. Each batch was then put into a flat-oval tin case which Whymper calculated would sustain four men for one day. These larger oval tins, also soldered down, were packed three to a box in sturdy, specially made wooden boxes. In the spaces among them Whymper placed candles in tin tubes, bead necklaces, and other "presents,...jamm[ing everything] tight with cotton wool, tow [flax and hemp strands] and paper."[3] Fully packed these boxes of supplies would together weigh 2,376 pounds, just over one tonne.

Whymper took pride in this imposing array of food and medicine. Though the containers were themselves weighty, they were state-of-the-art packaging. "All the glass bottles were subsequently used for the preservation of natural history specimens. There was no waste...; not a single bottle was broken, and nothing whatever was spoiled or even injured by damp....The boxes were of the best [pine wood], planed smooth...and double-varnished. The lids were screwed down, and the screws worked into metal cups....Many of these [boxes] came back in serviceable condition." [4]Alas, Murphy's Law was at work in Whymper's day even before it had a name. On the slopes of Chimborazo he would wish he had never heard of one particular foodstuff, much less to have included it among his prized list of provisions.

\* \* \* \*

In the early afternoon of December 27th, 1879, the party of seven men and nine mules – with Whymper mounted on one of them – plodded slowly but steadily upward in the sandy soil of Chimborazo's southwestern slope toward Camp 2. For the first thousand feet neither man nor beast showed signs of fatigue. The men dismounted after a while and began climbing, the altitude keeping their pace slower than it would have been in the Alps. Around 3:30 p.m. Whymper, the Carrels and Perring reached the 16,664 foot second camp with only minor fatigue. About two hours later the burdened mules and their arrieros straggled in. Whymper designated one of the muleteers to return to Tortorillas, spend the night there, and return daily to assist in any way he might be needed. The other two, with all the mules unloaded, went happily back to Guaranda, their work done and their wages in their pockets.

Surveying the new campsite Whymper was pleased with Carrel's selection. A wall of hardened lava sheltered their tent on one side; nearby snow-beds provided a source of water; space around the tent would allow exercise when bad weather kept them in camp. But the thought of calisthenics disappeared a few minutes later when the effects of oxygen-depleted air struck the three climbers without warning.

> We were all in high spirits. The weather had been fine and the move...successfully effected....About an hour later I found myself lying on my back, along with both the Carrels...hors de combat and incapable of making the least exertion. We knew that the enemy was upon us, and that we were experiencing our first attack of mountain sickness.[5]

This "first attack" was serious and came on suddenly. "In one hour we were all right and...in the next we were all wrong." Whymper and the

Carrels shared the same symptoms: intense headaches, fever of about 101 degrees Fahrenheit, parched throats and an intense craving for water. They began breathing at an accelerated rate, able to get enough life-giving oxygen only by breathing through their mouths in sporadic "gulps" like fish cast upon a bank. They had trouble swallowing what little water was available and could drink only in small sips between spasmodic, involuntary gasps. Incongruously, Whymper observed that he and Jean-Antoine "wished to smoke" – as if that were a perfectly natural pastime among people barely able to draw breath – and were disappointed that "our pipes almost refused to burn, for they, like ourselves, wanted more oxygen."[6] But tobacco was a great solace to Whymper in moments of stress, no matter what the cause or the circumstances. Food, however, was a different matter; he ate nothing during the forty-eight hours of his affliction.

By evening of the next day Whymper "managed to pluck up spirit enough" to bring out some chlorate of potash brought along specifically for relief of this malady. Dr. Marcet, his London physician, had recommended ten grains of the medicine in a glass of water, taken every two or three hours as needed. Although he was not sure that the potash was the cause, his symptoms diminished with "fewer gaspings" by the end of the following day. Louis Carrel agreed to join Whymper in this medicinal "experiment," but Jean-Antoine would have none of it, regarding all " 'doctor's stuff' as an insult to intelligence."[7]

For all human ills, for every complaint, from dysentery to want of air, there was, in [Carrel's] opinion, but one remedy; and that was wine; most efficacious...if taken hot, more especially if a little spice and sugar were added to it....The wine must be red – "white wine", he used to say dogmatically, "is bad, it cuts the legs..."

[Carrel's] opinions...were often very original and I learned much while in his company; [for instance] that for cure of headache nothing [is] better than keeping the head warm and the feet cold. [H]e practiced what he preached. I can remember no more curious sight than that of this middle-aged man, lying nearly obscured under a pile of ponchos, with his head bound up in a wonderful array of handkerchiefs, vainly attempting to smoke a short pipe while gasping like a choking codfish, his naked feet sticking out from beneath his blankets when the temperature in the tent was much below the freezing point.[8]

Whymper was sensitive enough to laugh good-naturedly at Carrel, not mockingly or with a superior air. Out of respect for his old climbing companion he sensed that the bersagliere's home remedies just might have a degree of merit. Were he twenty-five years later to recount Carrel's idiosyncrasies to a doctor-friend over a glass of wine, he probably would not have been surprised to learn that wrapping the head and baring the feet, by bringing blood from the extremities to the point of pain, was helping the body heal itself. In addition, the placebo effect was always at work.

Perring, the expatriate Englishman, surprised his employer by showing none of the symptoms of mountain sickness. Though a man of "enfeebled constitution" he took care of the hardy mountaineers "in an exemplary manner." He melted snow for water and blew on the campfire to keep it lit in the rarefied air, an essential task which the others were utterly unable to perform. Whymper was puzzled: Perring "was a rather debilitated man... distinctly less robust than ourselves. He could scarcely walk on a flat road without desiring to sit down, or traverse a hundred yards on a mountain side without being obliged to rest."[9] What Whymper would eventually learn was that a person's susceptibility to mountain sickness was unrelated to muscle tone or strength, or to stamina. Among persons accustomed to living at or about sea level, the altitude at which the brain's oxygen deficiency becomes a problem varies in an apparently random fashion.

As might be expected, the mountain-bred Carrels recovered more rapidly than their employer from the effects of the altitude at Camp 2. By the morning of December 29th "they were eager to be off and exploring," so Whymper directed them to seek a new campsite farther up the southwest ridge but below the 17,200 foot snow-line. Alone now but still recovering, Whymper sat up and for the first time surveyed the surrounding landscape.

For the first 500 feet above the party's campsite the southwestern ridge was a "stony waste" of disintegrated lava blocks and patches of sandy soil. Though rising at an angle of about 35 degrees it appeared to be readily accessible. Beyond that stretch the ridge rose less abruptly for some distance until jagged lava boulders blocked the higher view. It was among these crags that the Carrels had disappeared from sight that morning. Whymper's concern mounted as he looked upward from time to time during the day and saw nothing of the two guides, and no clear line of ascent to higher ground.

The Italians reappeared on the ridge above Whymper as daylight faded, but it was after dark when they finally staggered into camp, their energy drained by a full day of scrambling above 17,000 feet. Unable to stand erect, they collapsed on the ground like two sacks of potatoes, falling to sleep without eating, drinking, or making any report of what they had seen. Both of them felt better the next morning but Jean-Antoine was essentially out of commission with terribly inflamed eyes. Squirming like a youngster about to receive a tetanus shot, he reluctantly allowed Whymper to treat his swollen eyes with a solution of zinc sulphate. That done, Carrel told Whymper that he and Louis had forced themselves to an estimated 19,000 feet and come away convinced that Chimborazo's summit was attainable. As Jean-Antoine put it, "the thing is certain."[10]

The bad news was that he and Louis had found no spot suitable for a higher camp. Given their condition, however, and the number of hours they had been gone, Whymper decided not to start for the summit from their location at Camp 2. They would search instead for a smaller, more elevated spot from which to launch an attempt on the final peak. That night the thermometer registered 20½ degrees Fahrenheit. The next morning, December 31st, Whymper and the Carrels climbed up the southwestern arête in search of a niche just large enough for a smaller tent they had with them. Unable to find a protected spot they cleared a small space amid the broken lava near the crest of the ridge, on its eastern side, at a height of 17,285 feet. There they erected the small tent, exposed to the elements, on ground that could be only partially cleared of pebbles and lava fragments. They then returned to Camp 2 where they spent the night. The next day, to say the least, would be problematic. Awaking that morning someone noticed that the sides of a smaller tin containing ox-cheek were bulging outward as if to burst. Whymper recognized what was happening: gas from rotting meat was expanding inside the tin. He ordered the offending tin discarded immediately. Another of the smaller tins showed the same problem so they promptly threw it after the first. Then, after opening one of the larger containers, an overwhelming stench assailed their nostrils. An ox-cheek tin inside the case had burst, ejecting its putrid contents and corroding other tins. Examination of other cases showed the same problem and the faithful guides spent all morning cleaning up the mess. The tins of other foods in the spoiled cases, their contents unaffected, had to be washed several times with soap and water and then rubbed with sand. Even then the rancid odor clung to their seams and a good many of them were also thrown away.

In the end "we were obliged to hurl over the cliffs a mass of provisions which had cost endless trouble to prepare....The worst part of the business, however, was the prejudice...it caused against the...food...[not] defiled by the ox-cheek. Some of my followers flatly refused to touch any of it."[11] Adding to that day's problems was the loss of the rest of their porters. Though already in receipt of their wages they simply decided not to climb further, picked up their belongings and vanished.

The next day, Whymper thought, could only be better. That morning, "cheerfully" bearing the extra duties thrust upon them by the porters' departure, Jean-Antoine and Louis headed to Camp 3 under full loads. About 10:00 a.m. Perring returned from Guaranda with two rifle-carrying guards, a new muleteer, and a boy with a load of wood. Whymper pressed all of them into assisting with the party's move to the small tent-site at higher level. By late afternoon, with the help of these recent additions, the steady foursome of Whymper, the two Carrels, and Perring had transported a three-week supply of provisions from Camp 2 to Camp 3 at just over 17,000 feet.

Now, eight days after leaving Guaranda, the party was at last poised for the main event: Whymper's attempt to measure the effects of extreme altitude on the human body and, incidentally, make the first ascent of a mountain summit in excess of 20,000 feet. During those eight days his party had been occupied less with surveys and exploration than with the logistics of travel in the strange culture of an undeveloped, distant land.

*Third Camp at Chimborazo*

But Whymper stayed focused on his main objective and pursued it with the same determination he had shown in the Alps. Debilitating headaches and fever, food spoilage, rebellious mules, feckless employees – all had been endured with only minimal lingering affects. At Camp 3 his party was within 3200 feet of Chimborazo's summit, ready for the final push.

They struck out at 5:35 a.m. on January 3rd, a relatively late start for experienced climbers. Until then, however, there had not been enough light to guide them through this unfamiliar broken territory. Crossing the southwestern ridge they saw Chimborazo's western dome shining brightly in the morning sunlight. Topping the dome was a huge glacier, the near side of which had sheared off to expose an icy wall several hundred feet high. Just below the severed glacier were about a thousand feet of steep, lava-covered precipices. Another set of lava cliffs, lower down and not so extensive or steep as the upper ones, were at the end of a spur extending southwest from the summit. Atop them was accumulated snow not so thick as the higher glacier.

The southwest ridge on which the party stood led up to the lower lava cliffs. For the first five to six hundred feet the ridge was covered with snow in good condition. Trudging upward the climbers found that the ridge grew steeper as its sides dropped off severely. In some places the hardened lava was covered with ice and in others a mixture of ice, small stones and grit. Overall the surface was coarse enough for them to climb without cutting steps but their treads sometimes loosened the debris, cautioning them to proceed with care. It took two hours of laborious work on the ridge to reach the foot of the lower cliffs. Strewn along fifty feet or so of the stretch Whymper found the "partly fossilized" bones of an animal, probably carried to this lofty spot by a condor or other bird of prey and there "devoured at leisure." He took the bones of this "unhappy ruminant" back to London for examination by Sir Richard Owen, superintendent of natural history at the British Museum, known, among other things, for coining the word *dinosaur*.[12]

Whymper named these lower cliffs the Southern Walls of Chimborazo. A "breach" in this wall, at the point it joined the southwest ridge, rose at a fifty degree angle in front of them. The surface of the breach was a mixture of projecting rocks glazed with ice, the spaces among them frozen solid. "Thus far and no farther a man may go who is not a mountaineer.... The axes went to work, and the cliffs resounded with the strokes of the two powerful cousins. The work was enchanting to [them] after the uncongenial labour in which they had been employed."[13] Then, as in the Alps, an abrupt change in the weather stopped them only part way up the icy cliffs. The temperature had fallen to 22 ½ degrees Fahrenheit and a slowly rising wind had become a furious gale. Convinced that the summit was out of reach under those conditions, they secured their barometers and other equipment in rock crannies and returned to Camp 3 with all possible speed.

In his tent that night Whymper reflected on the day's failed attempt. Calculating that his party had reached an altitude of 18,500 feet he was surprised that the thin air at that height had produced "no...marked effects." At the same time he recalled the party's "perva[sive] lassitude

...and the readiness with which we sat down." Though reluctant to acknowledge that the altitude was a serious challenge, he conceded that he and his companions were still operating at less than their full potential.

Led by Jean-Antoine the party was again on the move at 5:40 the next morning, January 4th. Their way eased by the preceding day's track, they completed the "escalade" of the breach in the lower cliffs by eight o'clock. (Whymper liked the word "escalade" – the French equivalent of "scramble" – which he had learned a decade earlier during the translation of his book for its publication in France). At the top of the cliffs they bore left, zigzagging northward over snow and then onto the westernmost, snow-covered slopes of the Glacier de Thielmann. They passed over its small crevasses, staying clear of the great schrunds nearer the glacier's head. The snow here was stable and frozen hard enough to force the party to cut steps as they ascended.

At this point they were moving slowly. Jean-Antoine's steps had grown progressively shorter until the heel of each forward footprint almost touched the toe of the one behind it. Their breaths were shallower and came in quick succession. But the weather held and they made steady progress. At 10:00 o'clock they were at 19,400 feet and passing the highest outcropping of rocks on the mountain. An hour later they were above the clouds but "fancied" they caught occasional glimpses of the Pacific Ocean 140 miles to the west. At almost 20,000 feet, having circled halfway around Chimborazo's western dome, they saw before them a small plateau between the two summits that were themselves about 600 yards apart. Not knowing which was higher they headed for the western peak, the closer of the two.

Again, as if on cue from a stage director intent on heightening the drama, the wind rose, the skies darkened, and the snow beneath their feet became "exceedingly soft." Carrel sank into this new snow up to his shoulders. After dragging him out and believing themselves trapped in a maze of small crevasses, the party thrashed about, left and right, seeking a firm pathway toward their objective. They finally decided they could proceed only by "flogging down" the snow with their axes and then "crawl[ing] over it on all fours. Even then... one or another would sink down and almost disappear...." Louis Carrel tried to touch bottom with a twelve-foot pole he was carrying but could not. In freezing weather,

*"We were then Twenty Thousand Feet High"*

unaccustomed to this altitude and unable to judge the size of the dangerous soft-snow area, it was difficult to suppress tinges of fear. "Needless to say, time flew rapidly," was the way Whymper put it.[14]

After three hours of this slow crawl they were only half-way to the summit from the point where the snow had softened. Whymper called a halt and in the manner of John Tyndall asked the Carrels whether they wished to proceed or turn back. They talked for a moment in a patois their employer did not fully understand, which seemed a custom among guides burdened with this critical question. Jean-Antoine then replied, "When you tell us to turn, we will go back; until then, we will go on." "Go on," said Whymper, not sure he had made the right choice.[15] An hour-and-a-half later improved terrain vindicated his decision. When the slope to the western summit steepened, the snow firmed and they clambered slowly to the top at 3:45 in the afternoon. There they were dejected to see that the other summit to the east was the higher of the two. Shaking off their gloom they turned eastward. The climax of their arduous ascent came shortly thereafter.

There was no help for it; we had to descend to the plateau, to resume the flogging, wading and floundering, and to make for the highest point....There again, when we got on to the [eastern] dome, the snow was reasonably firm, and we arrived upon the [true] summit of Chimborazo standing upright like men instead of groveling, as we had been doing for the previous five hours like beasts of the field.[16]

The three men had no time for celebration of this hard-earned victory and no thought of doing so. A blustery northeast wind brought slashing snow that stung their faces and made their eyes water. Burdened with barometers and other instruments they were "hungry, wet, numbed and wretched." Fighting the wind they managed to erect a tripod at the summit from which they hung a mercurial barometer, one of the twelve-pound "babies" Jean-Antoine had so carefully protected on their long overland journey and who now held the tripod steady. Louis stood to windward spreading a poncho as a windbreak while Whymper read the barometric pressure. They also checked the pressure with two aneroid barometers, noting that their thermometer registered 21 degrees Fahrenheit. With numbed fingers and freezing faces they returned the instruments to their boxes. As a final gesture they jammed Louis's twelve-foot pole into the apex of the dome, a flag of serge material at its tip. Their summit labor done they headed downward through clouds that had closed in on them as they worked.

At 5:20 p.m. barely an hour-and-a-quarter of daylight remained. Descending the eastern peak and traversing the field of soft snow was easier than coming up; they followed the compacted pathway already made. That took an hour, however, and as the three men pulled themselves onto firmer ground in the dimming light they realized that this was their moment of greatest danger: "We then ran...for our lives, for our arrival at camp that night depended upon passing 'the breach' [in the lava wall] before darkness set in."[17] They arrived at the top of the southern cliffs as the day was dying and cleared the breach just as night fell. In the moonless darkness they literally could not see their feet as they picked their way downward among ice-glazed lava rocks. About an hour later their blood quickened at the sight of a glowing campfire

*Jean-Antoine and the Babies*

twelve hundred feet below them. There, after so many hours alone, a "disconsolate Perring" kept watch. Stumbling blindly down the ridge they reached the bivouac at Camp 3 around 9:15 p.m., "having been out nearly sixteen hours, and on foot the whole time."[18]

The next day Whymper took stock of their successful ascent. The altitude, the deep soft snow near the summit, and the party's unfamiliarity with the terrain – all had combined to stretch a rise of only 3,200 feet into a climb of more than fifteen hours, three of which were in darkness. Reluctantly acknowledging that the thinner air had again slowed their pace, he was puzzled why they had suffered greater discomfort while climbing the 2,100 feet between Camps 1 and 2 a week earlier than during the just completed 3,200 foot ascent between Camp 3 and the domed summit. He seemed not to fully appreciate the ability of their bodies to acclimate to reduced atmospheric pressure during the eight days between those climbs. Nor did he yet understand that for some unknown reason individuals simply react differently. Thus he could only wonder why Louis had been more susceptible to fatigue and shortness of breath on Chimborazo than he and Jean-Antoine who were, respectively, 14 and 26 years older than Louis.

The effects of weather, however, were the same as in the Alps. Louis had failed to wear gaiters and suffered a serious case of frostbitten toes from snow getting inside his boots. The tips of Whymper's fingers had turned white from exposure as he calibrated the summit barometer with bare hands. Both of the guides needed treatment for mild snow-blindness though they had uncovered their goggled eyes only occasionally. Whymper had spared himself that problem by wearing a "knitted head-

*Tripod atop Chimborazo*

piece, and neutral-tint spectacles throughout the day," as well as a linen mask on part of the climb.

Such was the immediate aftermath of the first Chimborazo ascent – 14 ½ years after the Matterhorn conquest and a world away, physically and emotionally, from that event. Here in the equatorial Andes was a more deliberate Whymper, who at 39 probably would not have called himself "middle-aged" though he had used the term in reference to the 37 year-old Charles Hudson when they met in Zermatt. He was now as much an explorer and natural scientist as a mountaineer, more interested in plants and fossilized animal imprints than in peak-bagging, and a serious student of the causes and effects of altitude sickness. But his spirit of adventure still burned brightly. After a few days of rest he would aggressively pursue the next target on his Ecuadorean agenda: the summit of Cotopaxi, at 19,613 feet the world's highest active volcano.

CHAPTER 20

*"Only The Gringos"*

Whymper was the third person of record to attempt Chimborazo's summit. The first was Alexander von Humboldt, a German who in 1802 reported climbing to 19,286 feet on the mountain's southwestern ridge. Dizzy, nauseous and bleeding from the lips and gums, he stopped there and never went higher.[1] The second Chimborazo challenger was Frenchman Joseph Dieudonné Boussingault. In December of 1831, "accompanied by an American (Colonel Hall) and a Negro," Boussingault's party followed Humboldt's route up the mountain's southwestern ridge until they had to pause "every two or three steps to get breath, and even to sit down."[2] Unwilling or unable to go farther, and with their crude barometer showing an altitude of 19,698 feet, Boussingault and his companions broke off their ascent and returned to camp.

When Whymper planned his expedition to Ecuador in 1879, mountaineers believed Chimborazo's summit was at more than 21,000 feet. The high points claimed by Humboldt and Boussingault were well short of that and nothing prior to Whymper's ascent had cast doubt upon their accuracy. With his improved mercury barometer he became the first to measure the mountain's height from the top of its highest dome. His finding of 20,458 feet – refined to 20,561 feet (6267 meters) by today's more sophisticated instruments – showed that earlier estimates of the mountain's height were overstated. Whymper also took barometer readings more than once at the foot of Chimborazo's high "Southern Walls." Standing there he realized that the surrounding landscape matched the description of the place where Boussingault had halted. Combining this with the earlier misinformation about the mountain's height, he concluded that neither of the previous climbers had gone beyond the Southern Walls' base, an altitude he calculated to be 18,528 feet.[3]

These measurements put the earlier climbs in perspective. Until the 1820s when reports from British military units began arriving from the Himalayas, westerners considered the Ecuadorean giant to be the world's highest peak, and in a way they were right. By reason of its location on the earth's equatorial bulge, Chimborazo's apex is nearly 8,900 feet (about 2,700 meters) higher than Mount Everest's when measured from the center of the planet. For the same reason the force of gravity is minimally less on Chimborazo's slopes than on the highest Himalayan summit, and thus its atmospheric pressure lower by a tiny fraction. This difference, however, is too small to affect the height at which climbers on either mountain begin to experience altitude sickness.

\* \* \* \*

On January 5th, the day after Chimborazo's first ascent, cold winds and sleet lashed the party's Camp 3 "eyrie" though they were on the lee (eastern) side of the mountain's southwestern ridge. While Jean-Antoine and Perring gathered firewood near Camp 2, Whymper stayed in the tent "engaged in household affairs," as did Louis, quietly nursing his frostbitten toes. The next morning, refreshed and rested, the three climbers went again to the foot of the Southern Walls where Whymper made some additional barometric measurements and the elder Carrel, with a line around his waist, climbed the rocky breach that had been their path to the top of the Walls. Whymper paid out the line noting the footage as the guide ascended, and by this crude measurement estimated the Walls' height at 455 feet. Bright sunshine highlighted the countryside spread out beneath them.

> The view from this position is one of the most striking upon the mountain. It commands the ridge up which we made our way, and embraces the whole length of the glacier and the vallons below, and in the far distance a little peep of the Arenal road, where by the aid of glasses the passing mule-trains bound from

the capital to the coast could be discerned, and condors sailing to and fro, watching unguarded flocks and herds.[4]

Their day at the foot of the walls ended when the afternoon weather, "following its usual custom," changed suddenly for the worse. As the clouds closed in the party hurriedly cached their instruments among the rocks and none too soon; thunder, lightning, and high winds sent them scampering back to their tent at Camp 3.

January 7th dawned under an overcast sky with reduced wind and no rain. Looking ahead to the book he would be writing, Whymper was regularly mapping the areas described in his daily journal. He planned to stay on the mountain several more days measuring angles and calculating distances to various points on Chimborazo's vast profile. He was anxious to ascend the high mountain again – to the summit, if necessary – to finish that work. Carrel, whom Whymper had dubbed his "Chief of the Staff," took a different view. Jean-Antoine said he wanted to leave Chimborazo now, arguing that the weather was bad and that it would be useless to stay longer. He acknowledged the enormous effort the party had made to construct the camps and stock them for a much longer period, but was adamant that "*he* would not ascend Chimborazo again." Besides, he complained, his body, weakened by dysentery, ached all-over and a longer stay at these heights would further endanger his health. Whymper was surprised by Jean-Antoine's attitude and outspokenness, but having spent so many days in the Alps with the headstrong guide he knew the bersagliere's mind was made up. So he promptly sent Perring back to Guaranda "to bring up the mules for the retreat."

Two days later the mules were fully loaded and the rest of Whymper's party ready to move out. He had directed them to take rooms at an inn near the mountain's base for a period of rest; he would stay another two days at Camp 2 studying Chimborazo's topography and ecology. When the men and mules began their descent, Carrel subtly showed some appreciation for Whymper's willingness to cut short their time on the mountain, along with a shadow of penitence for his own conduct. As "the little procession passed out of sight," Whymper wrote, Jean-Antoine lingered as if, after all, he was reluctant to leave his captain alone on the mountainside. "Turning to wave an adieu, [he]call[ed] out 'Take care of yourself, Monsieur, take care!' "[5] Though not effusive, this farewell was quite out of character for the taciturn guide. Still somewhat puzzled by Carrel's insistence on leaving, Whymper noted with pleasure his companion's parting words and gesture.

The aspiring natural scientist stayed alone at Camp 2 for two more days completing his notes and packing his personal items. Perring returned the afternoon of the 11th, having arranged for rooms at the Tambo of Chuquipoquio located at 11,700 feet near Chimborazo's eastern side. After another day to finish packing they left the second camp, went easily down the mountain and arrived at Chuquipoquio at 10:45 that evening. "The tambo's massive portal was opened somewhat tardily, for all were asleep and the place was in darkness. I went to bed about 1:00 a.m. not in the least knowing what the next move would be."[6]

Early the next morning, the mystery of Carrel's insistence on leaving Chimborazo "was solved."

Louis was found to be a cripple, quite unable to walk...his feet having been severely frost-bitten. They were frightfully swollen, blistered, and discoloured. Jean-Antoine, however, was restored, his dysentery having yielded to frequent internal applications of hot wine and cognac.

[T]hey appeared somewhat shamefaced about these frost-bitten feet...[but] it was not a time for scolding....I saw now why Louis had blundered and floundered about during the descent. The poor man was in a very bad way, and the first thing was to find someone who understood the proper treatment for him as his case was beyond our abilities.[7]

"Shamefaced" indeed but also extremely stoic was Louis Carrel for having suffered in silence for several days what must have been a terribly painful experience

Chuquipoquio's owner, Señor Chiriboga, welcomed Whymper effusively on that first morning. He had come up to the tambo from his home in nearby Riobamba, said the proprietor, " 'to do us honour, to supply our needs, to watch over and care for us.' He fell on my neck and kissed me, and begged that I would write an account of our ascent 'to enrich the Archives of Riobamba.'"8 His family, Señor Chiriboga continued, was one of Ecuador's oldest and had not the country abolished titles he would have been the Marquis of Chimborazo. Whymper accepted the owner's statements at face value but further experience with the good Señor would belie the owners' effusive welcome.

Whymper did learn from the proprietor one useful piece of information: Ambato, a town about nineteen miles to the northeast, was home to "a medical man of good reputation." Perring went immediately to Ambato to find a place for them to stay, with instructions that he return with "means of transporting two...cripples" for Whymper now included himself in that category. In his Andes memoir he confessed to acquiring "a complaint which rendered riding impossible, and obliged me to walk with circumspection." 9 Evidently stricken with hemorrhoids, he, too, needed a doctor's medication.

Though the accommodations were uncomfortable and the food scarce and barely edible, the group's three days at the tambo passed quietly. On one of those days Louis stayed in his room while Whymper strolled gingerly with Carrel along the base of Chimborazo's northeastern quadrant. Perring returned the evening of the 16th "bringing thirteen mules, eight wild-looking Indians, and two persons in uniform...sent by the Governor of Ambato as a 'guard of honour.' " 10 But the party's aide-de-camp had found no wagon or other vehicle for the transportation of the invalids. The improvised plan was for Louis to proceed to Ambato on muleback, and for Whymper to be carried on a litter to be constructed on the spot by the natives. By nine o'clock the next morning Whymper's litter was complete and Louis's feet were "well-bandaged in lint and made up into bundles." After hoisting the younger Carrel into the saddle there remained only the task of paying the bill, a maddeningly frustrating negotiation that became, in addition to the food and rooms, the tambo's final insult.

Tambo employees knew from past experience what to expect when a foreign guest received his bill. As Whymper awaited its delivery the inn's servants locked the gate leading out of the courtyard where the full party now milled about. Astounded at the statement's total, Whymper reviewed the listed items one by one. Portions of each meal – milk, bread, coffee, etc. – were individually priced, with a separate charge for the meals themselves. A number of other billed items had never been supplied, and the final listed total was more than the sum of its parts. Through Perring, Whymper explained all of this to the tambo's major-domo who went off to consult with the proprietor. Meanwhile, the courtyard gate stayed locked.

An hour later word came that Señor Chiriboga would see the unhappy guest in the owner's private quarters. Accompanied by the major-domo and with Perring as interpreter, Whymper found the would-be Marquis "stretched out in a miserable den, in an advanced state of intoxication with a bottle of spirits and a wine glass on a chair by his side." He had been in that room, in bed, during the party's entire stay. Whymper told him that there "might be trouble" if the rest of his troops were kept bottled up in the courtyard, and after some jockeying Chiriboga agreed to their release. With only Whymper and Perring left behind, the tambo servants again locked the departure gate.

> I then wasted a half-hour in discussion with the drunken man, who evaded answers,... sometimes addressing me as "Your Excellency" and sometimes as "Doctor," [saying] that ...it was "quite right, my servant will see to it." "You hear what your master says – you are to do what is right." "My master told me to make out the bill in that way," replied the major-domo. "You hear what your servant says, Señor Chiriboga." "Quite right, Doctor – take a drink; yes, it is all right, my servant will do what is right." [10]

The unscrupulous owner simply outlasted his adversary. Whymper felt he could have taken the keys to the gate by force but feared that word of such aggressive action might spread, causing trouble with other innkeepers. This fear of becoming known as a troublesome guest would later prove needless, but as a practical man of business Whymper decided that "of the two evils...it was best to be swindled." After paying the full amount he and Perring rejoined the rest of the party who had stopped about a mile away, wondering at their leader's delayed appearance.

On the way to Ambato the party's train of mules, porters, and armed guards – with Whymper himself litter-bound at the fore – looked much like a caravan carting an outlaw to prison. But passing natives, "stolid or apathetic, as usual," seemed not to notice. Stopping only once – near Mocha, a town about halfway to their destination – the party reached Ambato at 9:00 p.m., ten hours after leaving Chuquipoquio. There things immediately began to look up. The landlord at the suite of apartments secured for them by Perring charged only four shillings per day. The physician they had heard about, Dr. Abel Barona, provided "skillful attention combined with moderation in charges," another welcome and unexpected benefit of their new surroundings. Under the doctor's care Louis's swelling quickly receded. But with the flesh of the guide's feet coming off in "large gashes" they realized it would be some time before he could walk without pain.

Whymper also received the good doctor's help and was soon able to move about on a limited basis. His first outing was a visit to Ambato's regional governor. The Governor's friendliness encouraged his visitor to mention the blatant overcharging he had suffered at the Tambo of Chuquipoquio. "Everyone [is] robbed at Chuquipoquio," his host acknowledged, and suggested that he bring suit against Señor Chiriboga in Riobamba, the tambo owner's home town. Whymper responded that the proprietor's influence there might lead to an "unfortunate result" in a local court. "It is possible, it is possible," said the Governor, "with an emphasis and look that showed we understood each other." [12] Whymper let the matter drop and was able to say at the end of his stay in Ecuador that his treatment at Chuquipoquio had been an exception to the hospitality he received elsewhere in this unfamiliar country.

Throughout his Ecuadorean travels, whenever Whymper stopped in what might loosely be called a population center, hustlers flocked to the strapping gringo like hungry birds to breadcrumbs in winter. Ambato was typical in this regard with a number of persons "honoring" him with visits. "Besides the usual individuals with visions of gold mines and dreams of buried treasure, there was a General whose sole impediment to opening up a new route to the Amazons was the immediate want of fifty pounds. As this happened to be the exact sum for which I felt a pressing need, we did not do much business together." [13] Importunate locals also accosted Whymper's "Chief of the Staff." One of these, an Italian compatriot of Carrel's by birth, sought financial aid for his business of

*Carried on Litter to Ambato*

producing of dry sherry. "Jean-Antoine's account of the process... made it clear that Plaster of Paris largely entered into it, and that the juice of the grape did not come in at all." [14]

Louis Carrel's lingering frostbite kept them in Ambato for ten days. Whymper's main recreation – for he too was in recovery – was an afternoon stroll as the heat of the day faded, usually with Jean-Antoine at his side. On one of those walks they came across a tame llama. As Carrel went forward to give it a friendly pet, "the gentle creature reared its pretty head and spat in his face."

> Carrel was greatly affronted, and to soothe his ruffled feelings I proposed a walk in the garden of the Minister for Foreign Affairs...Presently we saw a Bishop among the bushes. His Lordship was dressed in orange and black, and had very hairy legs. We did not...know it was a Bishop or we should have been more discreet. Jean-Antoine unceremoniously clapped him on the back, then gave a great yell and the Bishop flew away. I conjecture that Ambato has been unfortunate in its episcopal rulers, for nothing can...be more stinging than the charges of this [colorful] insect. [15]

Often seen in the "Bishop's" company, Whymper later reported, was another "formidable stinger with chrome antennae" and known to the natives as "the Devil."

As the common names of these insects implied, Catholicism was very much a part of the lives of native Ecuadoreans. Surprisingly, however, Whymper rarely commented on their religious practices or beliefs. This omission suggested a significant lessening of his interest in such matters compared to his frequent references in *Scrambles* to priests and their flocks, and to the interest he took in the ethics and religious practices of Greenland's Inuit natives. The *Andes* memoir was the first clear sign that the influence of his Baptist upbringing, formerly a vital element of his personality, was giving way to a more temporal view of life in God's universe. His later writings, including his journals and correspondence, would be similarly barren of references to the spiritual matters in which he had once been so intensely concerned. Those early impressions likely

*"Bishop" of Ambato*

stayed with him in his middle years, carried deeper in his consciousness as the years went by.

After this extended stay the party's mule train left Ambato on the morning of January 24th bound for the town of Machachi. Whymper went slowly on foot but Louis Carrel was once again mounted, his feet still cloth-bound for protection. They stopped to spend the night in Latacunga, a town about halfway to their destination. The "little hotel" of Pompeyo Baquero was immaculately clean, "the best kept house" Whymper found in Ecuador. Outside the hotel the next morning, however, was a reminder of just how far he was from Victorian London. On the doorsteps of every house on the sunny side of the main street leading out of Latacunga were women with babies in their laps. Close by each woman sat a young daughter seeming to stroke her mother affectionately. A second glance showed what was really happening: the family members were eating vermin picked out of each other's hair. The sight revolted Whymper. "Though I shook the dust of this town off my feet, it was impossible to forget the Ladies of Latacunga, for [we encountered]...the same disgusting sight throughout the whole of the interior." [16] These small parasites, as he probably understood, were a source of protein for the undernourished bodies of the participants. But his revulsion at this animal-like behavior overwhelmed any urge to view or discuss it with his usual scientific curiosity, and his Andes narrative made no further mention of the Ladies of Latacunga.

Perring, who knew the road to Machachi from his days as a courier, was now the party's guide. From Latacunga they crossed the bridge over the Cutuchi River and proceeded north on its western side. Beyond the town of Callo, about 12 miles upstream, the road rose in a series of serpentine bends until it reached 11,500 feet. From there it descended gently over undulating hills and then led downward in a number of zigzag turns before entering the Machachi basin. Once out of the hills, the route became the longest stretch of straight road in Ecuador. With darkness now fallen their passage over it seemed interminable. When they reached the tambo where Perring had arranged for them to stay it was boarded up for the night.

> Pleadings for admittance were unheeded [so we knocked with] whip handles and hob-nailed boots. Presently a husband and wife were heard in consultation. "My dear," said the masculine voice, "it's robbers; you had better go to the door." It was opened very reluctantly by a disheveled female, who found it was "only the gringos." [We were then] admitted to the tambo of Antonio Racines who became our host for several weeks. [17]

Señor Racines' tambo would be the party's headquarters for a lengthy stay in Machachi. During their first ten days Louis rested in his room as his sorely damaged feet slowly healed. Whymper's condition improved sooner, allowing him and Carrel to make daily excursions to the surrounding countryside while Louis sat on the tambo's balcony enjoying a sweeping view of the great basin of Machachi. In the early mornings, herdsmen moved along the Quito road, sometimes with a wild bull restrained fore and aft by a horseman's lasso and prodded by lances when he balked. Arrieros and their teams were the most common passers-by. Less frequently, mounted men visiting friends in other villages – or perhaps on courting missions – would display their finest outfits: colorful multi-layered ponchos, chaps or buskins of wild animal skins, and triple-decked Panama hats protected by an outer casing and a final oilskin to guard against rainfall. Their shoes, often toeless, were armed with formidable heel spurs that jangled constantly to warn of their owner's presence. From the buttonholes of their colorful shirts hung carved wooden drinking cups, and at their sides large machetes, more for show than for clearing pathways. Some, in the style of "great cavaliers," rounded out their appearances with whips having wrought-iron handles, and guitars tied to their horses' saddle-bows.

Primarily for diversion, but also to collect high-altitude flora and fauna, Whymper decided to attempt Illiniza and Corazon, two nearby summits of 16,800 and 13,700 feet, respectively. Early on February 1st he and Carrel set out for Corazon's summit, which they reached after a long but uneventful climb. They spent three hours atop the mountain gathering a variety of plants and insects to add to Whymper's steadily expanding collection of indigenous flora and fauna. "I collected five lichens and as many mosses, three Drabas, a Lycopodium, a Werneria and an Arenaria.... From amongst this vegetation, I disinterred an earthworm, a beetle, a bug, and some spiders....When the atmospheric conditions were favorable, something was always obtained...; and at the greatest heights I laid hands upon everything that was seen, either animal or vegetable, anticipating that the zoological side, at least, would yield much to new science." [18]

The samples from Corazon's summit were but a tiny drop in the sea of specimens Whymper gathered during his stay in Ecuador. He filled footnotes and appendices to his *Andes* memoir with the Latin names of hundreds of different species and types he collected: including flowers, ferns, vines and other plants; butterflies, mayflies, dragonflies, bees, wasps, daddy-long-legs, lizards, spiders, crickets, beetles, worms, frogs, scorpions and crayfish. "In the *Supp. App.* there will be found 98 species of insects which were taken at 10,000 feet and upwards. Of these, 15 are known, 71 are new to science, and 12 are not identified." [19]

All would be carried back to Whymper's headquarters where the party's rooms at the inn "became a museum, and sometimes almost a menagerie." Curious Machachi children came early every evening to the tambo to see the gringos with strange customs and foreign countenances. "See! That is the Señor patron. Look!" – pointing to Jean-Antoine – that is Señor Juan. What a fine beard!" Whymper enlisted some of these youngsters as his collection assistants:

> They...angled for reptiles which they would not dare to touch and brought them in alive, dangling from cotton nooses at the end of sticks. "What," my young friends timidly [asked],..."does the Señor Doctor do with all these things?" [On learning] that they were collected [for] the future, the rumour was circulated that we lived on lizards and frogs and [we] were thought more odd than before.[20]

For five days following his Corazon ascent Whymper, Carrel and Perring took life easy, collecting and labeling specimens, waiting for Louis's feet to heal. They went outside in the early mornings but equatorial summer storms usually brought them inside before noon. The clouds and rain lasted only two or three hours at most.

> When the thunder-echoes ceased to roll between Corazon and Rumiñahui, Jean-Antoine and I used to turn out for our walks in the lanes of Machachi. The short equatorial day was nearly over. The hum of the bee and the chirping of the cricket had ceased, and the toilers in the fields had already retired. We met no one, and there were no sounds (except perhaps the distant notes of a reed-pipe played by some Indian lad wending his way homewards) until the frogs began their music. When this...died away, an almost perfect stillness reigned – the air was scarcely disturbed by the noiseless flight of the gigantic moths and the gentle twittering of the little birds making snug for their long night.[21]

This idyllic natural setting was not always peaceful. On Whymper's first solitary evening walk along residential lanes he encountered guard dogs kept by Machachian householders to protect their property. Several of these "mongrel curs" rushed from the darkness and made for him, snarling and snapping as they angrily tore at his clothes. He managed to escape uninjured but when he complained to their owners the next day they assured him that their dogs were not "savage" as he had reported. Rather, they said, these

*The Head of the Expedition*

were fine dogs, of such good reputation that when anyone in that region wanted a dog "he would come to Machachi to *steal* one."[22]

Thereafter Whymper went walking armed with a stout club for protection. He thought about what might happen if he lost his life to these man-eaters. The Machachi men, if taken before a judge, would have deplored the fact that "there [was] nothing left of the Doctor except the buckles of his braces." They would claim it was not the dogs' fault, "the best dogs in the World. The fact is the Señor *would* go on foot, he would not ride on horseback, and the dogs did not understand it...."[23] Their defense would have carried the day, of that Whymper was certain.

During the long rest in Machachi, Louis Carrel's frostbitten feet had improved substantially. Though he was not yet ready for full service he could hobble around without pain. Whymper was relieved to see this and to know he could now begin to put together a full party of men and mules to continue his Ecuardorean program. Believing they could leave Machachi in the next few days, he began to focus again on the plan he had formulated three weeks earlier while at the Tambo of Chuquipoquio. Implementation of this "scheme" would compensate him, he felt, for his having been forced to quit Chimborazo's slopes before his work there was complete. Knowing Jean-Antoine well enough to believe that his prickly guide might be cool to this next project, Whymper considered how he might best present the idea to his Chief of the Staff. It was a bold plan, whose success would require everyone's full commitment. After a day's thought and a good night's rest he was ready to make his case.

CHAPTER 21

## *Inferno At Night*

Located 20 miles southeast of Machachi, Cotopaxi is the world's highest active volcano. Its 19,347 foot summit rises some 9,000 feet above the high desert plain that surrounds it. The mountain's massive snow-covered cone begins at 15,500 feet and slopes upward at an angle of roughly thirty degrees to the jagged edges of its broad summit. Successive eruptions over the ages have blown away Cotopaxi's original crown leaving a deep, oval-shaped crater measuring 2,300 feet north to south and 1,650 feet east to west. When the mountain's cloud cover occasionally dissipates to permit a wide-angle photograph, Cotopaxi's image calls to mind the stark silhouette of its African cousin, the dormant Mount Kilimanjaro.

Only three years before Whymper's Andes expedition Cotopaxi exploded with staggering force. People living in the mountain's shadow had grown accustomed to its periodic blasts of steam, often clouded with fine particles of mineral rock swept up in the rushing column. Over the years spectacular but harmless displays had built up a false sense of security among these residents. When the volcano began belching smoke in mid-June of 1877 it received little attention, even at night when flames and molten rock lit the sky above its vast crater.

Several days later Cotopaxi fired an even louder warning shot. Around noon on June 25th a dark column of hot volcanic ash shot skyward to a height of more than three miles, accompanied by loud rumbles signaling prodigious subterranean turmoil. In Latacunga to the south and in Quito 35 miles to the north, townspeople saw the smoke. That afternoon gritty ash fell on passenger steamers in Ecuador's coastal waters heralding Cotopaxi's increased agitation. When darkness came on and the mountaintop glowed, still the local population remained calm.

At 6:30 the next morning eruptions of ash and steam began again. Then, about 10:00 a.m., the volcanic summit suddenly boiled over. Like a dragon's fiery tongue, incandescent molten lava gushed between the crags of the crater's rim as the mountain itself disappeared in thick black smoke. The hiss of escaping material became an ear-splitting roar as a devil's brew of molten lava, mud, and rock poured down the mountain, leaving only devastation in its wake. This fast-moving flood, following the slope of the land southward, reached the area of Latacunga some 25 miles distant in only 30 minutes.

Reading about the volcano's 1877 eruption Whymper wondered at the power that could raise "hundreds of millions of tons – its heat at thousands of degrees Fahrenheit" – to a level almost four miles above sea level and send it "cascad[ing] downward in furious leaps, ploughing up the mountain like cannon-shot....[It had crossed] the bed of the River Catuchi...and then...turned towards Latacunga, rooted up the road, and swept away arrieros with their teams,...erased houses, farms and factories, and destroyed every bridge in its course." [1] Arriving in this region of Ecuador in 1880 – a geologic microsecond after the volcano's latest blast – he "found the country a wilderness."

\* \* \* \*

Whymper felt sure that success on Cotopaxi would fully compensate him for having to cut short his scientific studies and measurements on the heights of Chimborazo. He was excited at the thought of camping near an active crater's edge and at having the chance to look "by night into the bowels of a first-rate volcano." To carry out this "scheme" he would need Jean-Antoine's full cooperation. It would not be a strenuous ascent but would entail hard physical labor and a possible recurrence of altitude sickness after their long layover in Machachi. He would need the help of both guides in measuring air pressure, temperature and mountain angles, and in other less physical activities, thereby frustrating the Italian bersagliere's desire to spend his time on truly challenging climbs.

Whymper realized that his customary direct approach would be unlikely to stimulate Carrel's interest in the Cotopaxi project. He thus "broached the matter...circuitously" with what must have felt to him like Machiavellian cunning. Saying nothing of his scientific objectives, he spoke only of Cotopaxi's "famous eruptions," pleasurable nights in a warm tent, and the chance to examine an unknown "subterranean world." Initially Carrel merely listened, showing neither interest nor objection, so his leader kept talking. Perhaps, Whymper added, they might also gain knowledge of volcanoes as yet unknown in scientific circles. At length the imperious Chief of the Staff said, "You have raised within me a great desire to look into this animal."[2] That was enough; Whymper knew he had carried the day and that Jean-Antoine spoke also for Louis. Now, he felt sure, both of them would put their hearts as well as their strong bodies into the new project.

The unified party readied themselves for the Cotopaxi ascent not knowing how long they would be on the mountain but preparing for an extended stay. The three climbers divided among themselves the barometers, theodolite and other instruments; Perring would remain behind as the party's quartermaster and rear guard. Axes, ropes, poles, shovels, provisions, cooking equipment, additional heavy clothing, and their tent – all were sorted, inspected and assembled. Whymper decided that they would take a closer look at the volcano from the Machachi hinterlands and, to help solidify Jean-Antoine's commitment to the main objective, begin the project by first attempting an ascent of Illiniza, a nearby virgin peak of 16,800 feet.

On February 7th Whymper and the Carrels, along with several local guides, eight arrieros and nine mules, left Machachi bound for a hacienda farmhouse near Rosario, a hamlet just south of mount Illiniza. Carrying with him a letter of introduction obtained in Machachi, Whymper was received "very courteously" and shown by his host to what appeared to be the hacienda's little used master bedroom suite. Though comfortable by the standards of their place and time, these private chambers held some surprises even for the veteran traveller of flea-ridden Alpine inns and unspeakably filthy Ecuadorean tambos. "My apartment [in Rosario] had the appearance of not having been cleaned or even swept since the building was erected. The whole ceiling was covered with a dense black mass of house-flies clustered over one another to the depth of perhaps half an inch. I could not have imagined that such a spectacle was possible. There were also tens of thousands on the upper part of the walls....Feeling something hard under the pillow I looked underneath and found a prayer-book, a revolver, and a guitar."[3] Whymper did not say whether the gun was loaded or how well he slept under this repulsive canopy.

After leaving the hacienda early the next morning the party spent a day and a half in a toilsome, four-mile climb to reach a ridge leading up Illiniza's southern side. There, during a momentary break in the clouds, Jean-Antoine and Whymper saw the mountain's summit briefly for the first and last time. That glimpse, however, showed them that while they might advance another 200 feet, they could not reach the summit. An ice wall rose vertically between two glaciers that came together on the ridge above them leaving no way around it on either side. Stymied and disappointed the two climbers retreated. On the descent they became "mist-bewildered" in a thick fog, unable to tell one direction from another. After shouting for some time in the hope that Louis would hear them they were rewarded when he appeared through the fog, having "pluckily hobbled" out to meet them. At 4:30, as they went back to the hacienda, Whymper silently conceded that on Illiniza "we were fairly beaten."

For the next four days, as Louis's frostbitten feet continued to heal, they rested and restocked in Machachi. On February 14th the party headed directly for Cotopaxi with mules, arrieros and porters, plus Perring and a couple of sheep. A violent storm that first day delayed their progress and forced them to take shelter at a hacienda in the moorlands near Pedregal, a small hamlet only five miles east of their starting point. They spent the night "by invitation" at a ruined chapel on the hacienda's grounds and the next morning set out toward Cotopaxi, 15 miles to the south. Though the path was not steep they had to pick their way around lava blocks and slog through drifts of powdered lava as they went upward. Whymper had chosen as their path the route used two years earlier by Max Von Thielmann on the fourth successful ascent of the volcano, a route Von Thielmann had described to him when they met before Whymper left London. Around 3:50 that afternoon, at about 15,000 feet on Cotopaxi's western side, they came to a "rude framework of poles." Looking around they discovered – from a record contained in a bottle at the site – that this had been Von Thielmann's campground.[4]

Deciding to set up camp there, Whymper sent the animals and their keepers back to Machachi.

Their first night passed uneventfully at this site though the mountain's bowels rumbled continuously, punctuated by sharp noises like the "slam of doors in a...stone corridor." Snow fell while they slept, covering the camp in a thin white blanket. At dawn the next morning the temperature was 24 degrees Fahrenheit, but the warmth of the volcanic cone rapidly turned the snow into water that sank into the porous soil causing the mountain to steam from top to bottom. Whymper gave the porters an option: they could return home or stay, and those who remained would receive small, silver-tipped wooden crucifixes which Whymper had brought from England, plus their pay. Three of the six natives elected to continue on the mountain with the party. As they could not go higher in their straw hats and open-toed shoes, they were "rigged out" in some of the party's extra clothing.

*Cotapaxi from Rosario Hacienda*

*Cotapaxi Crater from Below*

Whymper's next goal was to establish a higher camp near the Cotopaxi summit. He dispatched the guides and two natives upward with the small tent, along with equipment, instruments and provisions needed for the final push. The party's instructions were to find a spot near the top of the mountain where these materials could be safely placed – a dépôt or cache for necessities enabling the climbers to stay near the summit for several days if need be. Whymper planned the final ascent for two days hence, intending to choose the location for the uppermost tent when they reached higher ground above the dépôt. The work party spent that day, February 16th, establishing the cache in the worst weather they had yet encountered: hail, snow, fog, high wind and intermittent thunder and lightning throughout the day.

That night, with everyone back in camp, the mountain was calm. At 7:00 a.m. the next morning, as the clouds parted briefly, they saw steam issuing from the top of the cone. Although the foul weather continued, Whymper spent the day "exploring the neighborhood," updating his journal and adding to his plant and animal collection. The others made a last trip with supplies to the upper slope and on their return finished assembling the clothing and personal items they would need for an extended stay near the summit.

The next morning, February 18th, in "unusually fine" weather, Jean-Antoine and two porters set out at 5:20 a.m. Whymper and Louis followed at 6:00 and caught up with the others at 17,000 feet. For most of the way, "the ascent...was a walk, [with] no climbing necessary." They did rope up, however, and cut a few steps in the snow here and there. At 11:00 a.m. they arrived at the bottom of a "great slope of ash" on the mountain's western side that led up to the crater at an angle of about 37 degrees. Leaving their rucksacks and porters there, the three climbers "hurried up this unstable slope as fast as we could go," its grainy mass aggregated only by occasional streaks of ice. They reached the rim of the crater exactly at noon. Smoke and steam partially obscured the crater's opposite side and hid the bottom completely. Soon after their arrival the "animal," as Carrel kept calling it, gave a great roar just to let them know it was very much alive. The explorers had agreed in advance that in case of trouble they would drop everything, each man then shifting for himself. At the sound of the roar the expressions of all three showed that such a moment might well have arrived. But before they could react a cool cloud of steam enveloped them. Taking this as the mountain's welcome, they stayed put.

The question now was where to erect their tent. Whymper wanted to stay close to the volcano's rim, but the slope they had just climbed "was naked, exposed" and unstable. He and Jean-Antoine spent the next three hours touring the crater, looking unsuccessfully for a more suitable spot. Returning to the point of their ascent they went down about 250 feet below the rim and there, joined by the two porters, scraped out a level area on the slanted ashy slope. It was difficult work. The fine lava particles would not cohere when trampled or beaten; attempts to rake out a platform only brought down more material from above. Finally, by digging horizontally into the slope and "tenderly pouring many tons" downward they were able to establish a relatively stable base. Completing the erection of the tent they attached tent-ropes to large lava chunks which they had laboriously manhandled from sites hundreds of yards distant and then buried in the surface of their makeshift ashen platform. They took their longest rope upward by one of its ends and secured it at a crag on the crater's rim. This was intended as a guide rope during their stay near the rim, and with that their work was complete. The porters returned to the lower camp leaving Whymper and the Carrels alone on the slope just below the rim.

As they finished a cold supper in their newly erected tent the weather – which had held off all that day – again turned violent. A snow-laden wind lashed the side of the mountain, threatening to demolish their tent before they could occupy it. But after an hour the squall departed as quickly as it had arisen. In the sudden stillness they noticed the unmistakable smell of india-rubber, the source of which Whymper found by flattening his hand on the tent's mackintosh flooring. The edge of the fabric facing into the mountain felt the warmest. At 110 degrees Fahrenheit, it seemed near the melting point while the rubberized fabric's outermost edge registered only 52 degrees. But the tent flooring held up, and its range of temperatures remained unchanged during their summit stay.

"When night fairly set in" the three men left the tent for the "cold and tranquil" outside air. Using the long rope to guide them and to make their steps lighter on the unstable slope they ascended steadily toward the mountain's summit. Nearing the top Whymper squirmed forward on all fours, his face increasingly illuminated by the flames and molten lava in the crater's basin. Not knowing quite what to expect but "prepared for something dramatic," he asked Carrel to grasp his legs as the made the final push and peered into the unknown.

Ben[ding] eagerly forward...[I]...saw a [huge] amphitheater... surrounded by perpendicular and even overhanging precipices mixed with steep slopes – some bearing snow and others apparently encrusted with sulphur. Cavernous recesses belched forth smoke; the sides of cracks and chasms...shown with ruddy light; and so it continued on all sides...with...the fiery fissures becoming more numerous as the[y went deeper]. At the bottom, probably twelve hundred feet below us and towards the center, there was a rudely circular spot about one-tenth the diameter of the crater. [It was] the pipe of the volcano [from its] lower regions, filled with incandescent if not molten lava glowing and burning, with flames travelling to and fro over its surface and scintillations scattering as from a wood-fire – [all] lighted by tongues of flickering flame which issued from the cracks in the surrounding slopes.[5]

Whymper was probably the first person to gaze on that extraordinary night-time scene from such a precarious vantage point, and certainly the first to write about it so vividly. The three men stayed in this position long enough to note that Cotopaxi ejected what appeared to be pure steam at about half-hour intervals, sounding like a steamship blowing its boilers at sea and surrounding the climbers each time with a damp sulphurous cloud. At length they descended to their high camp and as Whymper had promised, slept on a warm tent floor if not a warm tent. That night the outside thermometer registered 13 degrees, the coldest temperature Whymper recorded while in Ecuador. Lacking insulated sleeping bags or any sort of effective protection against the cold they carried "extra ponchos and wraps" for that purpose. More closely resembling a hibernating bear than a pioneering natural scientist,

*Fire Below,*
*from Cotapaxi*

Whymper wore "an extra flannel shirt, a thick woolen sweater, a down dressing-gown and a huge Ulster coat over all. [His] head was protected by a knitted woolen headpiece, crowned by a Dundee whaling-cap, with flaps."[6]

The next morning they were up before dawn. Though they had seen no particles in the prior night's mist, they found their tent "almost black with...ejected...matter." At first light Whymper took photographs and mercurial barometer readings, marked out 600 feet on the mountainside for reference, and measured angles for calculating the mountain's dimensions. At 11:30 he decided it was time to leave the summit but the porters who were scheduled to return about that time to help with the baggage failed to show. In the "abominable weather they preferred to leave the work to us," and somehow the three climbers managed to get themselves and their equipment to the foot of the ashen slope. Whymper and Jean-Antoine raced down to the party's lower camp as Louis, still hampered by his tender feet, followed more slowly. There they spent two more days in bivouac, awaiting the arrival of the mule train to take everything down to Machachi.

Back in their hometown, the party's porters were questioned by the authorities who were convinced the gringos had been searching for gold. "Tell us, what did they do?" Said the men, "The Doctor, dressed like a king [in his Ulster coat and Dundee whaling-cap], went from one place to another, looking about; but after a time Señor Juan and Señor Luis seemed afraid of him for they tied him up with a rope." "Enough of this; tell us, did they find the treasure?" "We think they did. They went down on their knees searching for it, and they wrapped what they took in paper and brought it away." "Was it gold?" We don't know, but it was very heavy."[7] These "treasures" were in fact samples of Cotopaxi's jagged crest and debris from the slope leading to the summit.

* * * *

Whymper was pleased that his ascent of Cotopaxi had gone according to plan. The unprecedented opportunity to spend twenty-six hours on a boiling volcanic summit, including a night-time view from the rim of its fiery crater, was more than enough to justify the effort. Several scientifically-oriented activities enhanced the experience: further observance of the effects of prolonged exposure to rarefied air, measurements of Cotopaxi's features and recordings of its temperatures, a collection of lava samples, and additional plants and animals preserved for London biologists.

The Carrels, however, had a different perspective. In their view, the ascent was "severely scientific" and unduly prolonged. "They pined for more work in harmony with the old traditions; for something with dash and go – the sallying forth in the dead of night with rope and axe to slay a giant; returning at dusk with shouts and rejoicing, bringing its head in a haversack."[8] Recognizing this restlessness in his top assistants and wanting to keep them motivated, he decided to give Jean-Antoine a "sugar plum" by allowing him to select a target peak and allotting a full day to its attempt. The bersagliere happily chose the 16,350 foot Sincholagua, an aiguille-shaped extension of the Cotopaxi massif accessible by one route only.

Their jumping-off place for Sincholagua was the chapel at Pedregal where they had stayed before the ascent of Cotopaxi. At 7:00 a.m. on February 23rd the three stalwarts left there on muleback bound for Carrel's chosen mountain. An easy ride took them to 14,800 feet, where they placed the animals in the care of an arriero. After two hours of climbing on a snow-gully under sunny skies they were at 16,000 feet and headed for the top. Suddenly, out of nowhere, a furious storm of one-half inch hailstones sent them scurrying to nearby cliffs for protection. They left their refuge twice during lulls but each time a renewed shower of icy bullets beat them back. When the hail turned to snow amid thunder claps and lightning flashes they continued the ascent. Near their goal, as their ice-axes "hissed ominously" in the charged air, the slope steepened. By thrashing down the snow as they went they scrambled up the last yards to the summit as the storm raged about them. The top of the mountain was too small to accommodate even one person so Jean Antoine "knocked off its head – a compact dark-colored rock" – which they put in a bag. Staying not a moment longer the three climbers turned tail and went rapidly down the mountain. Arriving in Pedregal around 7:00 p.m. Jean-Antoine, in his laconic manner, was thrilled. He had slain the giant and would carry its head back to his home in Valtournanche as another hearth-side trophy.

* * * *

For the last month the party's headquarters had remained at Señor Racines's tambo in Machachi. The bulk of their clothing and scientific equipment and all their containerized plant and animal specimens had remained there during the party's climbs of Cotopaxi and Sincholagua. Whymper was now ready to move on. Ecuador's capital city of Quito would be his next stop. It took just one day back in Machachi to pack their breakables in leather bags against the rigors of mule-back transportation. That done the party took leave of their host and the Machachi residents they had come to know so well.

> When the time came for departure, quite a little crowd assembled. We had entered the place strangers. [O]ur ways appeared odd to the natives and we could not converse [easily]. But in course of time, a good understanding had arisen. The language of kindness is understood everywhere. They had been useful to us and we had not been unmindful of them. [A]nd now... all our young friends... David and his wife, Gregorio, Lorenzo the poncho-maker, and many others came together to say goodbye. Antonio Racines, arrayed in his best, accompanied us several miles on the road and took leave with many good wishes and profound salutations.[9]

Whymper's party would pass through this town again but only for brief stops en route elsewhere. He would remember Machachi as the locale in which he felt most welcome, and perhaps the only place from which the Englishman and his Italian guides would carry fond memories of ordinary Ecuadorean citizens.

# CHAPTER 22

## Rest, Robbers and Resurrection

During his three months in Ecuador Whymper had successfully blended a scientist's curiosity with an explorer's taste for adventure. On Chimborazo, Corazon, Cotopaxi and Sincholagua, in an unprecedented use of nature's laboratory, he had recorded the effects on the human body of sustained exposure to high altitude. He had been the first to measure accurately the height and dimensions of two of the Andes' most inspiring peaks. He had gathered and preserved hundreds of unknown and little known insects, reptiles, plants and flowers, most at heights above ten thousand feet. Enduring serious bodily ailments, pestilential inns, miles of impossible roads, rebellious animals, untrustworthy employees and atrocious weather, he had cast an observant eye on people, places and customs largely unknown to his contemporaries. And through those distractions and hardships he had kept a detailed journal, the mark of a serious travel author.

Deeply Victorian in his esteem for leisure time well spent, Whymper would remain in this distant country for an additional four months. His pace would be slower due in part to a lengthy battle with the Andean equivalent of Montezuma's Revenge. But he would make five more ascents of virgin peaks ranging from 15,500 to 19,000 feet, add native pottery and other artifacts to his burgeoning collections, and extend his notebook with more accounts of Ecuadorean customs and other exotica.

\* \* \* \*

In late February of 1880 Whymper made his first entry into Quito, Ecuador's ancient Capital City. With an estimated 35,000 residents, this

*Fourth Camp on Chimborazo*

was the country's largest center of population. At 9,300 feet it hugged the lower eastern slopes of Pichincha, an extinct volcano fourteen miles south of the equator. A combination of mountain air and tropical sunshine gave the city a springtime climate year-round. Its older buildings retained something of their early Spanish origins but most of Quito's structures were flat-roofed one-story houses with no fireplaces or rooftop chimneys. Like an amphitheatre with low-backed seats, the city's sloping contour and smooth skyline afforded unimpeded views southeastward toward the green fields and wooded areas of the Tumbaco Plain below.

Douglas Hamilton, the local British Minister, had arranged lodgings for the newly arrived party in a rustic but well-appointed center-city hotel. He had also obtained an invitation for Whymper to visit the Ecudorean president, General Ygnacio de Veintemilla. When the two Englishmen arrived for their appointment the day after Whymper's arrival, the President was meeting with one of his army colonels. Greeting his new visitors effusively, the General waved the Colonel to the far end of the spacious office. Fascinated by the news that his English visitor had recently made the first ascent of Chimborazo, Veintemilla asked to hear all about it. Hamilton began a lively description of the climb in Spanish, embellishing Whymper's words as he caught the spirit of the moment. Noticing the ostracized colonel's black felt hat lying nearby, he seized it as a prop to illustrate Whymper's route up the mountain. In the process he made a deep furrow in the "shining nap"of the Colonel's formal military headpiece. Whymper described what happened next.

> While this tête-a-tête was progressing, [with] the President leaning forward on his elbows intently following Mr. Hamilton's discourse, I...glanc[ed] round...[to find]...the colonel writhing in agony....He was on the point of exploding with suppressed rage at seeing his Sunday headgear used as a blackboard for 'that wretched gringo'....Notic[ing] my glance...the President turn[ed] and [saw] the state of affairs...[as did our Minister,who dropped] the hat....With grim humor (which I fear made the Colonel go over to the Revolutionary party), the President requested Mr Hamilton to continue;...and then by a few light touches, which fortunately [followed] the nap, the ascent was completed.[1]

Several ravines in Pichincha's lowest slopes ran through Quito, acting as natural drainage for the city's daily rain showers and helping to keep it free of "bad smells and...pestilence." The city's only reliable sources of water, however, were the fountains in its public plazas. Whymper described the fountains' output as contaminated with various "abominations." But the infested water was good enough for many wealthier Quito citizens who paid water carriers to deliver it to their homes. One of these carriers, an older man with white hair and a pink face, was a well-known figure. Whymper "offered to take his portrait and told him that he should have a shilling if he stood quite still and only fourpence if he moved. 'Señor,' said the old fellow, 'though several gentlemen have proposed to do the same, you are the first who has suggested any remuneration.' "[2] The water carrier's photograph has vanished but Whymper's sketch of him is preserved in one of the most charming of the many lithographs in his *Andes* account.

For Victorians, Ecuador's customs were as distant as its geographic location. Aware of this Whymper laced his journal with vignettes aimed at satisfying his readers' curiosity. In Quito, he noted, visitors in the homes of others doffed their hats upon entering, only to be invited by their hosts to put them back on. In this way, respect was paid and good sense honored; no householder wanted a guest to catch cold in his unheated parlor. On the streets a different etiquette prevailed. When lightning lit the sky, men removed their headgear with each flash even in

*Old Water Carrier in Quito*

a pouring rain. This placatory gesture to a higher power was made "as punctiliously as the homage...paid to religious processions" passing by.[3]

Procrastination, another inveterate Ecuadorean habit, was prevalent even in the country's capital city. This *mañana* philosophy, Whymper decided, went hand-in-glove with the people's tendency to promise the moon only to find a "well-sounding excuse" when it came time to deliver. He attributed this in part to the monotony of living continuously in days of equal length, and months of unchanging temperature. Jean-Antoine succinctly agreed: " 'It would be good for these people,' he said, 'to have a winter.' " In the end, Whymper took a charitable if somewhat patronizing view of this habit: "[T]he enthusiastic kindness of their hearts frequently causes Ecuadoreans to make promises small and great, which afterwards escape their memory or are beyond their ability to perform."[4]

Such kindness could not be found, however, in their commercial transactions: Ecuadorean businessmen were quick to disregard contracts and eager to make false claims to justify their doing so. A local trader in the city's marketplace spoke from experience: "I never consider a transaction terminated unless I give my customer a whipping." To most, that might have seemed merely an apt metaphor but Whymper appeared to take the man literally. Here in the city, he said, "the marks of the whip answer[ed] in place of a receipt-stamp."[5]

Whatever the distractions of life in a foreign country, Whymper paid close attention to matters of personal finance. He used a letter of credit from a London bank to obtain funds while abroad, which the Bank of Ecuador had reissued to him on his arrival in Guayaquil. Now, when Whymper sought coins from a Quito bank for use in the interior, he received a large amount of reals and medios in a closed bag. After examining the contents he decided that "the arithmetic of the bank differed from that in common use." But he had left the Bank before counting his money and knew there could be no appeal. After several more transactions he closed his account at the local bank with a final withdrawal. On that occasion the bank manager deducted four pounds sterling – a relatively large amount in the circumstances – "for what he was pleased to term his 'advances.' " As the bank had had the use of his money for several months, Whymper took issue with the charge but was assured that this was the local bank's "usual custom." "Your custom is novel and interesting," said Whymper, "and it shall be mentioned in a book I intend to write upon my journey, as it is a thing that ought to be known."

Shortly thereafter the Quito bank manager returned the four-pound fee to Whymper, saying it was not because his customer was writing a book, but because "it would be more regular" to charge the Bank of Ecuador. Whymper doubted that the national bank's office would reimburse its local manager, and on his return to Guyaquil some three months later had his opinion confirmed. "I found that the Bank of Ecuador had snapped its fingers at its brother in the Capital."[6] Whymper had shown once more that he and his money were not easily parted .

\* \* \* \*

Mr. Perring had been the party's interpreter and aide-de-camp since their arrival in Ecuador. Because the English-born ex-courier had performed admirably on Chimborazo and helped with accommodations, arrieros and travel routes, Whymper had put up with his one weakness: an over-fondness for alcohol. Occasionally, under the influence, Perring had slipped off his mule into the dust, once into a fast-moving stream that soaked him head-to-toe. On some days he would be missing for hours and then show up with a lame excuse. In Quito, with time to search for someone to replace the errant aide, Whymper let him go. That someone was Mr. Verity, a mechanic temporarily between jobs, who appeared – wrongly, as later events would show – to have the reliability Perring lacked.

While in the Capital City Whymper formulated loose plans for the remainder of his Ecuadorean expedition. He knew roughly what he wanted to accomplish, but having experienced the vagaries of life in this primitive land for a good while he realized that only with a flexible agenda could he get them done. Ascents of additional Andean peaks were his first priority. In this way he could continue his study of the body's reaction to high altitudes, add to his growing collection of plants and animals, and in the process enhance his stature as the foremost high-mountain climber of his day. These climbs would also boost his Italian guides' morale, keeping them – if not happy – at least in a state short of open rebellion. His two other objectives were to find more artifacts of Ecuador's earlier days and to return to Chimborazo for further measurements of the mountain and its surrounding terrain. Another three months or so seemed a reasonable timetable to complete these tasks.

Setting out from Quito on March 4th his party headed for Antisana, his first climbing target. After two days of travel to a campsite on the mountain's slopes, their first attempt to reach Antisana's summit ended in failure. It also left Whymper with a bad case of snow-blindness for neglecting to wear his goggles at all times during the climb. With two days of rest, however, he and the two Carrels tried again and were successful. After two hours on the summit the three climbers began their descent. Near the bottom they were roped together, with Whymper in the middle between the two Carrels. They discussed untying themselves but decided against it as they were "close to home" and wanted no additional delay. They could not have imagined at the time that this decision, though casually made, probably saved Whymper's life.

[We were] striding along...about fifteen feet apart, Louis in front and Jean-Antoine last, keeping step as we walked. [Suddenly] the surface gave way and I shot down, as [if] through a trap-door, nearly pulling both men over; and in the next second found myself dangling between two varnished walls of glacier which met seventy feet beneath.

The voices of the cousins were nearly inaudible for the hole was no bigger than my body, and they could not venture to approach it. With slow and anxious pulls they hauled away, fearing that the rope would be severed by the glassy edges; but...more of the brittle structure yielded and I went down again. This was repeated [until] Jean-Antoine, seeing that their efforts must be ineffectual as long as they were on opposite sides, leaped the chasm. [Then], with united pulls, the two cousins landed me with a jerk — through the frozen vault and its pendent icicles — onto the surface, poorer by a cap though not otherwise the worse for the immersion.[7]

Twenty minutes later they were safely back in camp, and from there they returned immediately to their temporary quarters in a farmhouse near Antisana's base.

The party returned to Quito two nights later. Groping their way through a maze of darkened streets on a moonless night, only Verity's familiarity with the neighborhood enabled them to find their hotel. The city, said Whymper, was lit "very economically." Local law required all residents to place a lighted candle in front of their homes at dusk, but did not specify a minimum length of time. The homeowners thus set out candle remnants – or as Whymper put it, "the fag-ends of tallow dips" – whose remaining lifetimes were in minutes not hours. Thus every night, soon after sunset, the city again became wrapped in total darkness.

* * * *

*Second Camp at Pichincha*

Whymper's party next made "an excursion to the top of Pichincha," more for curiosity and the collection of local fauna than for mountaineering challenge. Back in Quito, having restocked their provisions and reloaded everything on a fresh train of eight mules with their arrieros, they left the city on March 25th bound for the summit of Cayambe mountain. In addition to Verity and the two Carrels, the group now included three new men from Machachi: David Beltran, a "willing and pleasant-tempered native;" a principal arriero named Cevallos; and despite the recent unpleasantness with the bibulous Perring, an assistant muleteer named Domingo, a "lad of...jovial temperament, much given to strong waters."

After two days and nights on the road they reached Cayambe village. Setting out the next morning with a local guide to lead them to the mountain's base, they made good progress. Jean-Antoine, with a mercury barometer strapped to his back, had moved out in front of the group – partly to avoid the chance that a "floundering animal" might injure his precious cargo but also because he had "an abominable habit" of forging far ahead in a show of independence, even though it irked his employer greatly. Having failed to catch sight of the bersagliere for some time, Whymper went to look for him. He climbed part way up a ridge on one side of their track and soon sighted the missing guide some distance ahead. Whymper kept going but Carrel never reappeared.

Steep cliffs soon separated him from the rest of the party, whom he could no longer see or hear. Hoping to rejoin his companions when the land flattened he continued on, whistling and shouting without success to attract their attention and re-establish contact. Suddenly there appeared before him a stray deerhound – one of the dogs accompanying the local guide – who looked "equally perplexed" and ran about, stopping regularly to listen. As the lost climber and his new companion struggled ahead, Whymper had to help the hound over some difficult spots. Snow began to fall and soon became a blinding storm, obliterating any semblance of a path. On they went for two more hours with no sign of other party members.

Whymper halted to take stock of their situation. The snow had stopped but he and his four-footed friend were at 16,000 feet with no compass, extra clothing, food, shelter or matches. He decided to go downward regardless of where it might take him and by 4:00 p.m. was below the clouds. Halfway across a wide stream he looked back and saw the hound standing on the bank, howling in frustration, afraid to enter the water. Returning and gathering the "big baby" in his arms he waded back into the stream but found he could not mount the fissured bank on the other side. For the next two hours he and the dog continued downstream among the reeds of the far bank, struggling through what became a slimy morass threatening to swallow them both if they made a false step. Finally they were able to ascend the far bank and find a "semblance of shelter...[in] a little thicket" where Whymper decided to spend the night. After settling in he realized that he had chosen a lair made by wild cattle, making him doubly glad to have the hound at his side for warmth and for protection should the den's owners return unannounced.[8]

Cold and hungry the wanderers left the thicket at "earliest dawn." Sensing a faint path through the underbrush of a thickly wooded area the dog stayed low and instinctively kept to the track as Whymper, "driven to make long detours," followed as best he could. He confessed that had not the "sagacious" hound stopped several times and waited for him – or if necessary come back to lead him – he might never have made it. Around 7:30 the woods thinned and they were soon in an open space with help suddenly at hand. On a grassy plot below he saw an Indian couple working outside their hut in the bright morning sunshine. Blue smoke curled upwards bringing with it the smell of warm food.

Nearly famished and relieved to find this outpost of civilization, an eager Whymper confessed that he forgot his manners. " 'Have you locro?' 'Yes, Señor.' 'Give me some locro.' 'That I will, Señor'," and at once his host brought out two pots of potato soup, the smaller one for the dog.[9] After a breakfast tasting as good as any Whymper could remember, the man led them along the bank of the stream until outlying houses of a native village came into view. As the peasant turned to leave with a polite farewell, Whymper stopped him and put in his hand all of the loose money from his own pocket. "I left him in stupefied adoration, uncertain whether he had seen a vision or entertained a gringo."[10] Whymper and his canine companion were back in Cayambe village by 9:00 that morning, from which he dispatched a messenger to the main party announcing his safe return. To them, who had suspected the worst after long hours in a fruitless search, his reappearance unharmed was more like a resurrection.

Over the next two days, continuing their assault on virgin peaks, Whymper's party moved upward to a campsite at 14,762 feet on Cayambe's slopes. This site, at the same height as the Matterhorn summit but the better part of a mile below Cayambe's highest point, was a reminder of the Andean scale to which Whymper's party was now accustomed. Early on the morning of April 4th he and the two Carrels scrambled upward through a maze of snow-covered crevasses, traversed the mountain's Grand Plateau, and on steeper slopes "overcame several large open crevasses and numerous concealed ones" to reach Cayambe's virgin summit at 10:00 o'clock that morning.

Two days later, Whymper's party headed southeast across the equator toward Sara-Urca, their next mountain objective. Thus began the hardest passage of their Ecuadorean journey. They slept that night in a dilapidated thatched-roof shack surrounded by the fallen trunks of rotting trees. There, stricken by a bug that made "his internals go...wrong," Whymper "lay feverish under a pile of ponchos for the next three days."[11] The party spent the next night on swampy ground where "if you stood still, you sank up to the knees in slime." The next day they went through difficult marshland, bloodying their hands on razor-sharp reeds they grasped to pull themselves along to avoid sinking into the bog-like earth. Their difficulties continued for four more days as they struggled through swampland using the tracks of bears, pumas and other wild beasts to support their weight. For two of those days they were marooned in camp by continuing rain, sheltered only with mackintosh ponchos suspended on ropes tied to nearby trees. Thick clouds blocked the sun daily for two weeks; the country, said Whymper, was like a giant sponge. Throughout this time he made no progress in his battle with diarrhea.

The weather broke at last on the morning of April 16th when low clouds replaced five straight days of continuous rainfall. When the mists lifted around 5:00 p.m., Sara-Urca made its first appearance under overcast skies. Whymper immediately took its bearing in case the weather again closed in, and sketched the mountain for his notebook. The next day they began a "forced march" toward their goal. Finally on Sara-Urca's

*At Camp on the Equator*

slopes, they "could not see a hundred yards in any direction" but the mountain's fog-covered glaciers were a welcome relief. As a back-up to their compass Louis Carrel took four-foot reeds from a bundle he was carrying and stuck them in the snow along their track, planting a new reed as the one behind grew dim. Suddenly they saw Sara-Urca's "pointed snow peak" emerging above the clouds about 500 feet above them, guarded only by a sharply edged snow ridge. "With out-turned toes" they went "cautiously along the crisp arête" and at 1:30 in the afternoon stood on the mountain's high summit.

Following this ascent the party spent three miserable and depressing nights on the trail, arriving back at Cayambe village on the 20th. At this point Whymper recalled the 16th century story of Gonzalo Pizarro's fruitless two-year search in the Amazon basin for the wealth of *El Dorado*. The younger half-brother of Spanish conquistador Francisco Pizarro lost thousands of his troops to starvation; those who survived emerged naked, their clothes having rotted in the unrelenting moisture of the equatorial jungle. Now, after only ten woeful days on the trek to Sara-Urca, Whymper knew "why, upon returning to Quito in 1542, Gonzalo Pizarro *kissed the ground* when he again stood on *terra firma*."[12]

\* \* \* \*

During the next three days Whymper and the Carrels reached the summit of Mount Cotocachi. This 16,300 foot summit, along with Antisana, Cayambe and Sara-Urca, marked the fourth virgin peak in his current round. Whymper's health was still poor and his strength sapped. But he felt well enough to pursue a search for artifacts of Ecuador's older Indian civilization. He sent the Carrels back to Quito, and with only Verity and a single arriero began an archeological exploration among the old villages and Indian burial mounds in the northern province of Imbabura.

For the next six days Whymper travelled throughout the province enlisting the help of priests and Jefo-politicos in his search for pottery, carved stone ornaments, implements, utensils, arrowheads and weapons of bronze and stone. He collected a hundred or more of these artifacts, some of which weighed several pounds, and kept his two assistants busy packing the pottery in straw, then in wooden or cloth containers, and finally placing everything in saddle bags contoured for transportation by muleback. He said nothing about the cost of this effort, which he would almost certainly have mentioned had there been any meaningful cash outlays. Either the local population had no sense of proprietorship in these items or he bought them for a song. He pictured scores of them in his *Andes* narrative, along with a good many pages of text describing them in detail. In this, and in the listings and descriptions of flora and fauna he collected almost daily, he was as thorough and methodical as in his earlier observations in the Alps and in Greenland.

* * * *

On his return to Quito on May 3rd, Whymper felt "more dead than alive," being told by someone he looked "fit for the grave."[13] He wrote to a friend that during his absence of more than 5 weeks he had lost "five inches...around the waist."[14] He then spent more than a month in Ecuador's capital city regaining his strength and arranging for the dispatch of his various collections to Guayaquil for trans-shipment to England. Ever practical, he sold off excess equipment and food, taking in over £100 in the three days of his unusual bazaar. He had wisely decided to accept cash only, following the admonition of a sign he had seen in Panama on his outward journey. Composed, he was told, by "a California miner of unusual literary ability," it read:

NO TRUST GIVEN
To Trust Is To Bust
To Bust Is Hell
No Trust-No Bust-No Hell[15]

During his stay in Quito Whymper dismissed Verity, his most recent interpreter, who had proved untrustworthy after all. To fill that position Whymper hired a half-breed Indian/Hispanic from Quito, Francisco Javier Campaña, a man who had provided part-time assistance before Verity left. Campaña was a diminutive and somewhat prideful man who "aspired to look *comme il faut*" with a heavily adorned saddle that weighed almost as much as he did. He wore knee-high boots and multiple ponchos, carried a carved drinking cup and a macheta as status symbols, and allowed the tails of his woolen scarf to float out behind him in the wind. He was nevertheless pleasant and efficient and Whymper felt he had finally hired the right man.

With Campaña now joining roustabout Beltran, arriero Cevallos, and Domingo, the latter's assistant, the seven-man party left Quito on June 7th bound for Whymper's second ascent of Chimborazo. Not far down the road stood a number of people waiting for them to pass. These were Campaña's relatives gathered to bid him farewell, "including his wife who cried and screamed and fell on his neck as if he were going to execution....[A]mong the Indians, a display of grief upon the departure of a husband is quite the correct thing," said Whymper, "but [I] am unaware whether his *return*...produces a corresponding amount of joy."[16] Beltran added his own color to the party by bringing along a borrowed llama. Trotting easily beside them with head held high, the llama earned its keep by carrying 24 pounds of photographic and other equipment. Buoyed by his party's quickened spirit and his own realization that this was the last leg of his Ecuadorean odyssey, Whymper welcomed the return of his good health and bountiful energy.

By June 11th the party was in Machachi. In the nearby village of Penipe they had come upon "a poor half-starved [mongrel dog] with a good-natured countenance." Once fed with chicken bones and other leftovers, he could not be discouraged from following their caravan. Initially called "Penipe," the dog's ears went up when someone tried out the name of "Pedro," so "Pedro de Penipe" officially became the party's newest member on the road to Chimborazo.[17]

* * * *

"To test the snow-going abilities" of new assistants Beltran and Campaña, Whymper decided to take them on a warm-up climb of Carahuairazo, a high peak adjacent to Chimborazo. On June 25th, the seven-man party set up camp between the two mountains, about four miles north of the Tambo of Chuquipoquio, the scene of Whymper's memorably unpleasant lodging. From this camp he would survey part of the "high road," adding data points to his map of the Chimborazo area.

Here a new threat arose, greater than any they might expect on the mountain. The next day, while Domingo kept watch, two men rode in, seized the arriero's macheta, and took all his money. This was only the first sign of new trouble. At dusk a horseman Whymper recognized as an employee of Chuquipoquio – the tambo where the perfidious Señor Chiriboga had cheated Whymper out of 6½ pesos – came up and demanded payment for the use of the ground and for the grass on which the mules were feeding. Told, in effect, to get lost, the man rode off, shouting that he and others would return that night to seize the party's animals. About 9:00 o'clock Campaña and Beltran came in, very upset as they told how two men on the road into camp had used white cloths to frighten their mules and then tried to overpower and rob them. The two had managed to fight off their attackers losing only a few "trifles."

Putting these things together it seemed to Whymper that Señor Chiriboga must have again come up from Riobamba 'to watch over and care for us' " as he had on Whymper's first visit to the infamous landlord's establishment. By fortunate chance the party's camp was on a strip of land that narrowed to a point between a rushing stream on one side and a deep earthquake fissure on the other. In view of the latest threat they placed the animals at the protected point and themselves between the point and the area where the land opened out. Whymper's journal told what happened next:

> Kept watch until midnight, then roused Louis to take a turn for an hour, but before his time was half over he was snoring again. Continued to watch, and at 2:00 a.m. heard whistling and low voices of persons approaching . Said nothing; took my whip and aroused the others; hung out the lanterns to show [the intruders] the way, and shouted defiance. Apparently, the thieves thought they might have a warm reception and went off. Night being very dark, we saw no one. After this, [as] my people [kept] watch, I went to sleep. A windy, rainy night. [18]

The next day a muleteer from Machachi rode in and reported the theft of eleven of his cattle the night before. With that, Whymper decided to abandon the road survey and move beyond the reach of "the robber of Chuquipoquio."

After a delay of two more days the party, including the four-footed Pedro de Penipe, set out by lantern light for Carihuairazo, the 16,500 foot mountain where Campaña and Beltran would be given "a little preliminary exercise" before the planned second ascent of Chimborazo. Their scramble to Carihuairazo's summit was laborious, made more difficult by having to pass Pedro from one climber to another over the jagged mountain's roughest spots. This made for slow going but they all made it to the mountain's icy peak before noon in good spirits, including Pedro de Penipe. Campaña and Beltran were excited by the day's successful ascent and elated to hear that they would be included in the upcoming Chimborazo ascent.

Their euphoria ended, however, when the mountain gods belatedly levied a toll for this latest invasion of their sanctuary. Back at their campsite, when the novices' eyes began to blur and sting, Whymper recognized the first symptoms of snow-blindness and immediately brewed a large batch of sulfate of zinc. Though applied liberally the medication took two nights and a day to do its work. The Ecuadoreans wailed piteously in their small shelter while Pedro de Penipe – similarly afflicted – whimpered and staggered about, "knocking his head unwittingly against the [surrounding] branches.[19] Unable to move about, the men were attended by the party's two arrieros.

Two evenings later, with all snow-blind cases fully recovered, the party was encamped on Chimborazo's northwest side. The next morning, as all pitched in to complete final preparations for the summit ascent, an idea suddenly popped into their heads:

Let us take Pedro. He was already entitled to bow-wows from all dogs who had stood on lesser eminences – let us enable him to take precedence over the entire canine race. "Ha! Pedro; good dog, come here!" Pedro was sociable and came willingly so long as we were round the fire, but moved away when we began to load, and looked doubtful...Calls were in vain and finally he put his tail between his legs and bolted down the hill as fast as he could scamper. "No, my masters. You may go up but I shall go down – no more snow-blindness for me."[20]

Perhaps Pedro went back to Penipe to live out his life, content with having reached on Carihuiarazo a height greater than Tschingel, the greatest of the canine Alpinists. Or perhaps he simply disappeared. Whymper's journal said nothing more on the subject.

The five climbers, now including Campaña and Beltran, set out for Chimborazo's summit at 5:15 on the morning of July 3rd. About a half-hour later as Whymper halted to chafe his hands against a cold wind, Cotopaxi put on a spectacular show. Silhouetted clearly against a bright blue sky 60 miles to the north it was emitting no smoke or steam, the first time Whymper had seen it so calm. Then suddenly, after belching two puffs of steam, the volcano ejected a thin column of "inky blackness" at terrific speed straight up into the air. In one minute the dark pillar had risen to a height of 20,000 feet above the crater's rim, or 40,000 feet above sea level. At that height, a high wind forced it into an abrupt 90 degree bend to the horizontal, where it swept westward only slightly dispersed from the tight column in which it first shot upward. Later, donning his natural scientist's cap to examine samples of the volcano's dust collected at several points, Whymper calculated that Cotopaxi had that day deposited over two million tons of ash on the surrounding countryside.

As the climbers ascended, Cotopaxi's eruption continued for the better part of an hour. Clouds then formed between the volcano and themselves. Viewed from Chimborazo through this grit-laden filter the sun's orb became a coppery green that turned a bright red and then a duller brick-red, finally glowing with the color of shining brass. "No words can convey the faintest idea of the impressive appearance of these strange colors in the sky – seen one moment and gone the next – surpassing in vivid intensity the wildest effects of the most gorgeous sunsets."[21]

Whymper had chosen to begin his second ascent of Chimborazo along its northwest arête, the most distant of the three ridges seen six months earlier from the slopes above Guaranda. Along that ridge the party arrived at the western base of the mountain's Northern Walls.

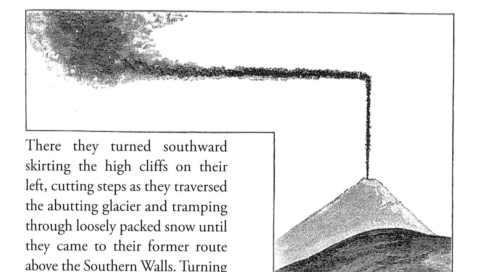

*Eruption of Cotapaxi, 3rd July 1880*

There they turned southward skirting the high cliffs on their left, cutting steps as they traversed the abutting glacier and tramping through loosely packed snow until they came to their former route above the Southern Walls. Turning left they pushed upward to the plateau between Chimborazo's twin domes and in knee-deep snow headed for the eastern peak, the higher of the two. At 1:00 p.m. as they neared the summit "a great clamor and cackling" came from Beltran and Campaña, thrilled to have made it this far. What they had seen, breaking the dome's smooth outline, was the top of the twelve-foot pole Whymper's first party had placed there in January. A few tattered remnants of the pole's red flag, frozen solid, pointed to the southwest, the direction of the prevailing wind that had shredded the cloth material as the flag's remaining fragments stiffened in the cold.

About ten minutes after their arrival, fallout from Cotopaxi's earlier explosion began to settle on Chimorazo's summit, its grey cloud gradually obscuring the surrounding countryside. Over the next hour the black volcanic dust turned the mountain's pristine snows into dirty, soot-colored ripples. It coated the climbers' lips and eyelids, penetrated their nostrils, and drove away any thought of eating or drinking. It finally got so bad that they began breathing through handkerchiefs. At 2:30 p.m. the summit thermometer registered 15 degrees Fahrenheit and the climbers shivered as the winds whipped their numb faces. Though it was obviously time to leave Whymper decided he would first record this exceptional moment in a photograph. The result was a striking representation of the scene: a crusty, white-bearded Jean-Antoine in the center beside the torn flag and on his flanks Beltran and Campaña in their hats, goggles, and layers of ponchos. The sullied snow under their feet and the grey sky above created an atmosphere of deep gloom. Whymper's equipment included a black and white "instantaneous plate" exposed for one minute behind a lens that required regular wiping during the entire procedure. An engraving of this photo graphically depicts the scene in Whymper's *Andes* narrative.

Happy to be headed downward, the party "slipped along quickly" on newly hardened snow – roped together with Louis leading, followed by Beltran, Campaña, Whymper and finally Jean-Antoine as their "sheet anchor. Though Campaña, the 'little interpreter,' tumbled about gloriously, he tugged no more than a good-sized fish at the end of a line and we descended boisterously, cutting the zigzags and finding great advantage from the sticks which had been planted to mark the route...."[22] They were back in camp on Chimborazo's northern side by late afternoon.

\* \* \* \*

With the second ascent of Chimborazo, Whymper's Ecuadorean mission was almost complete. On July 6th, after circling the high mountain's western and southern slopes, the party came to the village of Chuquipoquio on their way to Riobamba. Whymper had no intention of stirring up sour memories by returning to Señor Chiriboga's tambo; he paused by the side of the road only to make some notes. At that moment, however, fate put temptation squarely in his path. Along the road came the "rascal[ly]" major-domo who had locked Whymper inside the gates of the tambo on his last visit and helped the drunken hotelier collect his extortionate fees. Stopping him and establishing that the man remembered the incident, Whymper demanded the return of his fraudulent overcharge. The man refused, telling Whymper he would need to take up the matter with Señor Chiriboga at the latter's home in Riobamba. Whymper replied that the tambo's owner would only refer his major-domo back to Whymper saying "do what is right."

*The Sky was Dark*

Remembering their earlier encounter the assistant conceded that Whymper was probably correct.

> "Now," I said, "as you will not give me the [money], although you [were] told to do what [was] right, I intend to give you something....[With that,] I produc[ed] my horse-whip from behind my back...and forthwith...gave him...a sound whipping. Campaña and Carrel did not interfere,...[nor] did two people of the tambo looking on...[T]he fellow was bigger than myself,...[but] after making the big brute howl and blubber, I told him that I was now going off to Riobamba to give the same to his master.[23]

With this example of frontier justice Whymper again showed that he was a "hard man" on the slopes and off. As good as his word he sought out Chiriboga in the latter's Riobamba home but learned that the dishonest innkeeper had left town, warned, Whymper believed, that retribution was on its way. He felt confirmed in this when he learned in Guayaquil that Chiriboga had returned to his house the day after Whymper's departure.

Whymper was now ready to start for Guayaquil on the last leg of his Ecuadorean journey. In Riobamba, after bidding farewell to all but one of his native companions, Whymper, the two Carrels and Campaña set out on a new route to the coast through Guamote, Chimbo and Yaguachi. Lying about 30 miles to the south of the Royal Road and roughly parallel to it, this was known as the "Railway Route" because its last leg – from Chimbo to Guayaquil, a distance of about 55 miles – was served by a new railroad. They were told before leaving town that the walk to the rail head at Chimbo village would take two days, and that food would be plentiful along the way. Once there, a "capital" hotel would provide overnight lodging. Thus primed, and wishing to travel light, they left Riobamba on July 8th with only one day's supply of provisions. It soon became clear that they had been badly informed: the trip to the rail head took three and a half days and potatoes alone were available for the first few miles with no food of any kind thereafter.

At the point where the Chimbo River turned sharply westward, the new track lay "hidden away in the jungle." The rail line began at the river where the only sign of civilization was an unoccupied contractor's shed on wheels at the track's end. There was no train or station or anyone to provide them with information. No village, much less a hotel, was anywhere in sight. Campaña went down the tracks and found someone who said the train might arrive that day or perhaps mañana. Hungrily, they waited.

The train arrived at noon carrying three people and no freight. On boarding Whymper showed the conductor a flowery letter written by President Veintemilla asking the Railway Authorities to provide the Englishman and his party "every assistance [and] attention." Whymper told the trainman that he and his companions were hungry and wished to purchase whatever food might be available. Duly impressed, the conductor offered two pineapples, declaring that "the pineapples were mine, he himself and all that he had were mine, etc." Refusing Whymper's offer of payment he cut the fruit into five portions, four for them and one for himself. The train then got underway and went smoothly along until just before the station at Chimbo where it jumped the track. This gave Whymper an opportunity to buy provisions with which he prepared a meal and invited the conductor to share it with them. "Now," thought the satisfied traveller, "the pineapple account is balanced."[24]

This conclusion, he would soon discover, was premature. As he prepared to leave the train in Yaguachi and was thanking the conductor for his services, the trainman stepped in front of him. "The fares!" he demanded politely. Whymper was puzzled; he thought the President's letter "might have covered anything from special trains downward," surely including the matter of a ticket. "No," was the reply, "it embraces everything *except* that." "How much?" "Three and a half pesos each." Whymper paid the amount "like a lamb" but as he moved off, the conductor restrained him once more. "There is the baggage." "How much?" Whymper again paid the charge but noticed that the official still had something on his mind. "Is there anything else?" "Yes, Señor. Your Excellency has forgotten to pay for the pineapples!"[25]

On that note Whymper's long sojourn in the Ecuadorean interior finally ended. A steam launch took the four men down-river to Guayaquil. The Carrels planned to leave Whymper in a few days and return by steamer to Panama. As he handed over the rather substantial sum due to the guides in back wages he urged them to guard it carefully. Regrettably, the party's Chief of the Staff forgot he was a proud bersagliere and acted more like a bosun's mate on shore leave after six months at sea. He and Campaña went on a colossal binge, gambling away what they did not spend on liquor or what had not been stolen from their pockets. Unconscious, they were hauled to a police station where they awoke disheveled, disconsolate and penniless. Whymper gave Jean-Antoine another £20 gratis, but Carrel – this time with false pride – gave his employer no thanks. His stubborn silence put a doubly unfortunate edge on their parting as it was the last time the two men would be together.

Whymper spent the next two weeks conducting further research on the hundreds of plants and animals in his treasured collection, and adding to the notes of his seven and a half months abroad. On July 29th, 1880 he boarded a steamer for Panama, the first leg of an uneventful one-month homeward voyage. On the first day out he took a long last look at his final mountain conquest. "In the eastern skies, above the alluvial flats, Chimborazo arose dim and cloud-like in the far-off distance....[A]s we steamed away, I lingered to give it another and yet another farewell glance, gazing upon it as one might upon the features of some good old friend for the last time, knowing full well I should never see them more."[26]

CHAPTER 23

## *"A Raconteur Hardly Surpassed"*

While on his far-flung travels Whymper wrote faithfully to family members and a number of colleagues and acquaintances. In Ecuador this had been difficult. Its rudimentary postal system discouraged regular writing sessions, forcing the English visitor to remain virtually incommunicado while in the nation's remote countryside. The lack of reliable service also required him to write letters from the one or two places offering a reasonable hope of ultimate mail delivery. Chief among these was Quito where a special courier handled the official correspondence to and from the British foreign office. Whymper gained access to the "minister's bag" through Mr. Hamilton, the resident British minister, which made his writing to London a far more appealing option. During each of his three sojourns in Quito he spent long hours "delightful[ly] employ[ed]" in personal correspondence.

Included in his March output was a letter to his stepmother, Emily, a fellow artist and one of his favorite correspondents. Beginning respectfully with "Dear Mrs Whymper" it continued for six chatty pages. With evident pride he told her of his visit with President Veintemilla and of the calls paid on him by some of Quito's social lions: Carlos Aguirre, "head of the most powerful family in the country," and the "diplomatic representatives" of France, Germany and Chile. He also offered the thought that she might one day "make a nice sketching tour here."[1] Less lighthearted in a second letter to Emily in May, he spoke of his lingering illness and of his thoughts of returning home. "To my father say that I shall pitch into business directly I get back, and that I shall hope to ease his work very speedily."[2]

Whymper returned to work at his father's engraving business in the fall of 1880. Josiah was now 67, Edward 40, the lives of both at a juncture. Proud of the business he had founded before his son's birth the senior Whymper sought a means of assuring its continuity and, in the bargain, gaining financial security for himself and his wife. Edward had worked for his father's company since the age of 14 and needed to continue earning a living. He also wanted to pursue his foremost interests: writing, travelling and natural science. After months of discussion the two found a way to satisfy both: Edward agreed to buy the business from Josiah and pay him a lifetime annuity of £350. Considering that the engraving business was struggling against photography's growing competition, this was a generous sum. It was made more so by Josiah living longer than his expected lifetime. But the arrangement worked. Under Whymper's oversight the business continued for many years and Josiah lived in financial security until his death.

In the decade following Whymper's return from Ecuador the engraving business was only a part of his busy life. He wrote papers on altitude sickness; his pamphlet on *How To Use the Aneroid Barometer* brought compliments from scientists and fellow climbers. He consulted with zoologists and geologists to help identify and assemble the specimens in his Ecuadorean collections. *The Times* and other newspapers carried stories of his expedition, as did the *Alpine Journal*. Several magazines also bought and published some of his stories. This notoriety created a demand for paid lectures, to which he happily responded. One of his free lectures, given in 1882 to the Alpine Club and held at the Royal Institution, was attended by the Prince of Wales, later Edward VII, who moved for a vote of thanks when the lecture ended. At the reception following the lecture Prince Edward told Whymper that he understood him to be a great traveller. "Not so great as your Royal Highness," Whymper replied, combining tact and flattery in equal measure.[3]

In these immediate post-Ecuador years Whymper became seriously interested in photography, a relatively new art medium made popular by improvements in an older process. The first photograph, called a heliograph, was developed in 1827 by a Frenchman, Joseph Niépece. After Niépece's death his partner, Louis Daguerre, invented the "daguerreotype," the first practical photographic method. Relatively expensive and potentially harmful in its use of mercury vapor, the daguerreotype gave way to wet-plate photography. Developed in 1851 by Frederick Archer, the wet-plate was part of a cumbersome process involving the use of four different chemicals. After a relatively short lifetime it was replaced by the dry-plate. Though first described by Richard Maddox in 1871, dry-plate photography came into vogue only after 1878 when Charles Bennett, another Englishman, developed a process by which plates using this new method could be mass-produced and sold in the marketplace.

This was a revolutionary advance. Hundreds of amateurs, Whymper among them, rapidly adapted to this technique, relegating the wet-plate process to history. Soon after his return from Ecuador he met and began working closely with Alfred Harman, a British entrepreneur of his own age and founder of the Ilford Company named after the village of Ilford, Harman's birthplace. He was a tireless worker who began by making dry-plates in the basement of his home using a gelatin emulsion of his own formulation. The Ilford Company would in time become England's largest manufacturer of this new type of photographic equipment. Through his collaboration with Harman, Whymper helped to pioneer the development of the dry-plate process.[4]

Whymper's increasing interest in photography evolved naturally. Early on he had begun experimenting with chromolithography as a means of adding variety to his drawings. In 1870 he had submitted one of these colored prints to an "Exhibition of Chromos and Engravings" in South Kensington, which the curator rejected. "I was told," he wrote years later to his friend Henry Montagnier, "that the exhibition was for chromos and not for watercolor drawings. I replied that [the curator's mistaking Whymper's colored lithograph for a watercolor] pleased me more than if they had given [my entry] a medal."[5] His life-long experience as an engraver did not blind him, however, to photography's potential. He foresaw the increased use of photographs for book illustrations and selected several pictures, mostly by other photographers, for the 4th and later editions of *Scrambles*. With an eye for subject matter and picture composition, Whymper became a recognized amateur photographer particularly praised for his Alpine scenes.

Four of his mountain photographs, well-preserved through their hundred-plus years of life, are still on display in the Monte Rosa Hotel.

Two of these are particularly appealing. In the Arvenstube – a first floor room handsomely paneled with arola pine – is a photo of a lone climber with a toehold on an almost vertical mountain face, stretching for the aid of a fixed rope. The viewer can almost feel the texture of the climber's woolen jacket, long trousers and felt hat; the damp, tight strands of the hempen rope; and the rough surface of the rocks on which it hangs. The picture was taken at fairly close range, possibly during Whymper's re-visitation of the Matterhorn slopes in 1892 or on his Alpine tour of 1893. Another photograph hangs in the stairwell leading up to the Arvenstube: a captivating view of several climbers among enormous seracs taken at a distance to offer an Ansel Adams-like panorama. The climbers appear to be moving cautiously in the dull light of a cold, grey afternoon, their small figures dramatically offset by the harsh terrain. As with many of Whymper's drawings and photographs, both of these pictures invite the viewer into the scene.

Perhaps the best known of Whymper's photographs is a picture of Queen Victoria's Jubilee celebration taken from the window of his office on Ludgate Hill in 1888.[6] With the publication of his two guidebooks in the 1890s, Whymper was able to market some of his photographs to the general public. One of several advertisements in the front of each book offered a package of eighteen of his Alpine photographs. Of these, one entitled "Seracs on the Zinal Side of the Gabelhorn" was probably the striking photo now in the Monte Rosa Hotel.

Robert Whymper, the son of Edward's brother William and not a consistently complimentary critic, summed up his uncle's artistic talents and the part they played in his life: "His technique was brilliant. Had he not spent so much time in mountaineering and exploration, he might well have been a great artist."[7]

*Travels Amongst the Great Andes of the Equator*, Whymper's account of his Ecuadorean expedition, was ten years in the making. During this period other responsibilities had kept him busy. The engraving business's bottom line was now his prime responsibility. Fees from lecturing and writing helped support his free-ranging lifestyle. As ever, the summertime Alps provided therapeutic getaways which he spent mostly in Chamonix, Zermatt and Grindelwald. Now among the tourists flocking to these increasingly popular resort towns, he was also about the business of gathering information for future guidebooks already taking shape in his mind.

Another reason for his upcoming book's long gestation period was its length and enormous detail. In his view, *Andes* was his magnum opus, more important than *Scrambles*. It was first published in two volumes in 1892: the first a narrative of mountain travel; the second a volume of ten appendices on subjects including barometer readings, mountain heights, and earlier attempts on Chimborazo. As in *Scrambles*, lithographs made from his drawings filled the book – 20 occupying full pages and 118 smaller drawings decorating the narrative's text. Whymper's hand guided every step of the printing process, again assigned to R & R Clark, Ltd. of Edinburgh who had performed so well with the *Scrambles* manuscript.

Reviews of his *Andes* travelogue surpassed Whymper's expectations. Said *The Times*, "It is rare to find a traveller so many-sided as Mr. Whymper. He is an artist, a keen and cautious scientific observer, an admirable collector, a daring mountaineer...a humorist of the driest brand, [and] a raconteur hardly surpassed...[A]n explorer in the truest sense...[he is] entitle[d] to rank among the few whose 'Travels' never grow stale or obsolete."[8] Confirming this view, a verbatim copy of Whymper's 1892 *Andes* with all of its illustrative lithographs was published in the U. S. in 1987. This edition adds several striking color photographs of Ecuador's mountains and other outdoor scenes by Loren McIntyre, who also wrote an Introduction to the *Andes* reprint.[9]

The *New York Times* gave American readers its opinion of Whymper's Ecuadorean travelogue. "Much of what [Sir Henry] Stanley has done for an unknown region of the earth's lower surface, Mr. Whymper has done for remote and comparatively unknown regions of the earth's most interesting and lofty altitudes."[10] Adding a second U. S. voice to Whymper's accolades was Theodore Roosevelt, the future rough-riding Bull Moose and U. S. President. "Mr. Whymper was not content merely with the conquest of the mighty Chimborazo; he also campaigned against the greatest of its fellow peaks. The story of his travels, of the hardships he endured and the triumphs he achieved, is of interest not only to mountaineers, but...to all lovers of manly adventure."[11] Americans' familiarity with *Andes*, and to a lesser extent with *Scrambles*, led to a successful U. S. lecture tour by Whymper in the late 1890s.

Between his ascent of the Matterhorn in the mid-1860s and his departure for Ecuador in 1879, Whymper had spoken often before the Alpine Club and other English audiences about his mountaineering exploits. His two Greenland expeditions provided material for updating and expanding his stories, and additional pictures with which to illustrate them. Following his return to London in 1880, his travels in Ecuador became the focal point of his increasingly popular presentations. His clear speech, confident air and commanding physical presence consistently impressed his audiences, and with increasing experience at the podium he developed "an unfailing sense of the dramatic."[12]

His success on the lecture circuit led him to hire Gerald Christy of The Lecture Agency to handle his speaking schedule and attempt to increase his bookings through better promotion. During his summers abroad in the early 1890s, Whymper's illustrated talks on the Alps and the Andes began attracting the attention of travellers to Grindelwald, Davos, Chamonix and other Alpine watering holes. In 1896, with demand for his lectures increasing, he turned to the Lunns travel agency for help with his European bookings. That summer he left London on a speaking tour with slides, a magic lantern complete with gas cylinders, a lantern operator and a full speaking schedule. His formula for successful lecturing was the same as for his writing: carefully selected and tightly organized subject matter with scrupulous attention to detail – all presented with a flair and self-deprecating humor that revealed a hint of vulnerability not apparent in his imposing appearance.

\* \* \* \*

Ten years after Whymper's return from Ecuador and two years before the publication of *Andes*, Jean-Antoine Carrel met his death on the lower slopes of the Matterhorn's Italian side. In August of 1890 the 61 year-old Carrel, still active as a mountain guide, was hired by Leone Sinigaglia of Turin for an ascent of the Matterhorn. The three-man party, with Charles Gorret as a second guide, spent their first night at a recently built hut at the foot of the Great Tower. Before dawn "a most violent hurricane of hail and snow" struck the mountain. It raged "all night – and the day and night following – with incredible violence."[13] By the

351

fourth night their situation had become dangerous; provisions were low and the party was using the seats of the hut for firewood. They decided to head downward the next day, weather permitting.

On the morning of August 25th the three climbers left the hut under cloudy skies. As they reached the Col du Lion the "dreadful hurricane" returned. A blizzard of snow made communication difficult; the men had to wipe ice from their eyes with almost every step. Due to a lost glove Gorret's hand was already frostbitten. Daylight turned to darkness with the party still creeping cautiously down the ice-covered rocks. Despite their intimate familiarity with the Matterhorn's south side, Carrel and Gorret became confused about which direction they should take. After a brief rest and a slug of brandy they rediscovered the descent route and labored downward with Carrel still in the lead. He then stumbled two or three times and his pace slackened. Concerned for his comrade, Gorret suggested that he take the lead and that Jean-Antoine move to his usual anchorman position on the rope, with their client Sinigaglia between them. Carrel did so and the threesome, thus rearranged, arrived at the final slope leading to the pastures above Breuil.

The two lead climbers then felt a tug on the rope. They shouted up to Carrel but got no reply. Alarmed, they took a few steps upward and then heard the guide's faint voice, "Come up and fetch me, I have no strength left."

> We went up and found that he was lying with his stomach to the ground, holding on to a rock in a semi-conscious state [and] unable to get up or to move...." I no longer know where I am," [he said]. His hands were getting colder and colder, his speech weaker and more broken, and his body more still. We did all we could for him, putting with great difficulty the rest of the cognac into his mouth....We tried rubbing him with snow, and shaking him and calling to him continually, but he could only answer with moans.
>
> We tried to lift him, but it was impossible – he was getting stiff. We stooped down and asked in his ear if he wished to commend his soul to God. With a last effort, he answered "Yes," and then fell on his back, dead, in the snow.[14]

*Portrait of J.A. Carrell (1890)*

In the Breuil inn, with no sign or word from the climbers since their departure, a relief party had waited all day in frustration as the weather pinned them down at the inn. Sinigaglia and Gorret reached the village in the small hours of the morning of the 26th and joined with villagers at dawn to recover Carrel's body. Jean-Antoine was buried at Valtournanche on August 29th. Two years later an iron cross was erected at the spot on the Matterhorn where he died.

In a later edition of *Scrambles'*, published in 1890, Whymper paid tribute to his companion of twenty years. "Jean-Antoine Carrel...[had] a pure and genuine love of mountains....[He was] a man of originality and resource, courage and determination, who delighted in exploration....I preferred him to all others as a companion and assistant upon my journey amongst the Great Andes of the Equator....It was not in his nature to spare himself and he worked to the very last. The manner of his death strikes a chord in hearts he never knew. He recognized to the fullest extent the duties of his position, and in the closing act of his life set a brilliant example of fidelity and devotion...."[15] This tribute, made several years after their uneasy parting in Guayaquil, left no doubt that the enduring image of the old bersagliere in Whymper's mind was formed in their days together among the high Alps.

The vivid memories of those times remained with Whymper as he visited the Alps almost every summer of his remaining years. During this period his life would slow down but his entrepreneurial spirit would spur new ventures and keep him on the move and productive well into the next century.

CHAPTER 24

## *"Mony A Mickle Mak's A Muckle"*

Whymper went to Zermatt in 1892 to take photographs and there he met up with one of the best-known mountaineers of that day, J. P. Farrar, seventeen years his junior. Together with the guide Franz Biener they went hiking on the slopes surrounding the town. Still competitive in his middle years, Whymper executed what was for him a classic maneuver. "As I wanted to see how fast Farrar could go on a path I gradually increased the pace as we came back but I could not stimulate him and presently both he and Biener were far in the rear. I got back in time for dinner, but Farrar did not turn up at the *table d'hôte* at all!"[1] A day or so later Whymper scrambled on the Riffelhorn with his long-time Alpine Club comrade W. E. Davidson, and Farrar came with them. As dusk approached and the party continued upward, Whymper turned back. In Zermatt he sent Biener with a lantern "to light the others home. They got in at some late hour of the evening and I got back to the *table d'hôte*."[2]

At least in some respects Whymper was behaving here like a typical 52-year old tourist. A hot meal was evidently more satisfying to the former young lion of the Alps than a leisurely climb with a new companion. The Matterhorn conquistador now considered his day a success if he returned in time for the dining room's nightly special. But the competitive fire in Whymper's belly was only dampened, not extinguished. If in relatively easy climbs with younger men he could also show superior stamina, well, so much the better.

Farrar never put clearly on record whatever opinion he had formed of the older climber during those two summer days. In 1920, however, he wrote a revelatory critique of the first Matterhorn ascent in the *Alpine Journal*. In it he praised Charles Hudson as "the one man of all his generation, of mature judgment…upon whom the E[ast] face of the great mountain, however apparently inaccessible, failed to lay a spell….[T]he death of Hudson and Croz held up the tide of mountaineering for fully half a generation of man."[3] Farrar's opinion flew into the face of well-known and widely accepted facts, unconscionably implying that the Matterhorn's east face intimidated Whymper. Even as late as Farrar's 1920 article the British mountaineering community knew perfectly well that Whymper chose to climb the east side of the great mountain before learning of Hudson's plan to do likewise. In a similar vein, Farrar's praise for the man who brought young Hadow into the Matterhorn climbing party and disregarded Whymper's suggested use of a guide rope on the descent, was clearly overblown. Farrar's inflated description of Hudson's mountaineering skills probably derived as much from his distaste for Whymper's combativeness on their two Zermatt climbs as from his respect for the Anglican clergyman.

In the summer of 1893 Whymper went on his first mountain camping trip since Ecuador. It was to be a modest outing aimed primarily at testing an improved version of his original tent design. He made only one ascent, the well-worn but still imposing summit of Mont Blanc. His first stop was Randa in the Valais region of Switzerland. From there he went by way of Zermatt and the Théodule Glacier to the spot above Breuil where Jean-Antoine had died three years earlier. After pausing there to pay his respects to Carrel's memory, he took their familiar trail through Prarayé to Courmayeur, from which he planned to attempt Mont Blanc along the Dôme route. Foiled by bad weather he had to settle for an ascent of the mountain via the customary route from Chamonix. His party reached Mont Blanc's summit on a cold afternoon under clear skies. They spent a frigid night there in the framework of the Jannsen Observatory, then under construction. His journal described the next morning's spectacular sunrise:

A vast sea of cloud [lay] motionless over the Italian valleys…[with] all the peaks [visible through them]….The sun rose with a bound behind the Mischabel; Monte Rosa was in the shadow but other great peaks broke out like watchfires…. Shortly after sun[rise]…the shadow of Mont Blanc was seen projected in the direction of Aix les Bains. It was at first grey in tone and might have been mistaken for another mountain. [I]t deepened, then died and sank away. The air was still and intensely cold.[4]

Whymper climbed Mont Blanc's snow-covered dome again the next year and once more spent the night on the mountaintop. In the 108 years since the mountain's conquest only two other climbers had slept on Mont Blanc's summit: the pioneering Professor Tyndall in 1859 and J. Payot in 1887.[5] In the next morning's bright sunshine, the distant Matterhorn monolith was a tiny triangle on the far southeastern horizon. Among the other giants of the Pennine Alps it was recognizable only to an experienced eye. Thoughts of his two narrow escapes on its slopes must have gone fleetingly through his mind as he gazed at the peak virtually synonymous with his name. He knew that this might be his last distant view of the Matterhorn and other high Alpine peaks in grand array. That would indeed be the case; his 1894 ascent of Mont Blanc essentially ended Whymper's mountain climbing career.

In later years he undertook another mountain project, but for surveying purposes only. In four of the summers between 1901 and 1905 he went to the Canadian Rockies as a consultant to the Canadian Pacific Railway Company. The beautiful peaks and valleys of these northern mountains are similar to the Alps in climate and topography, and the Railway Company was the largest commercial landowner in that region of western Canada. Company officials held Whymper in high regard as one of the Alps' most experienced climbers and the author of two popular guidebooks. He was a logical choice to explore and photograph land along the Company's rights-of-way, and to advise them on their properties' potential for resort development.

Though Whymper's assignment involved a good bit of strenuous hiking, the tracks of the Canadian Pacific railroad turned out to be more of a physical challenge than the Canadian Rockies. In 1903 he and a hired assistant were walking along a track at night when a train rounded a curve behind them running almost silently. He sensed its presence only when a glint of light on the track made him look backward. There, fifty yards behind them, the train was fast approaching. Whymper pushed his companion off the track and then jumped quickly aside and into the darkness alongside the track to save his own life – all in a day's work for an energetic sexagenarian.

Two years later his Canadian journal recorded a train accident in which he was a passenger. "A sudden jar and a crash occurred....I was projected backwards...and struck the back of my head against the carved woodwork of a sleeper and...rendered insensible. The breakfast tables were swept clean before their proper time; and the Chef de la Cuisine got cooked in his own boiling water. Two trains going in opposite directions had been in combat....[A]bout sixty people were cut...or damaged."[6] The railway's final insult was a derailment that came five years later, when Whymper was seventy, in which he was shaken but uninjured.

\* \* \* \*

In the last two decades of the 19th century and the first five years of the 20th, Whymper's brief forays into the Alps and the Canadian Rockies were a sideline to his principal activities. He was managing his engraving company and investing some of his savings in photography-related businesses. His program of lectures was expanding to include European resort areas, and he was working with Henry Kündig of Geneva to supply guides to Alpine inns and hotels. His *Andes* narrative had been published and was selling well. The engraving business was surviving in a declining market. It was then Whymper embarked on his last literary endeavor: authoring guidebooks for tourists in the regions of Chamonix and Zermatt.

He could see that travel guides to the resort areas of the western Alps were inadequate and out of date. Pamphlets published by travel agents were overambitious and misleading. By 1892, in the course of more than thirty summers, he had prowled the streets of scores of Alpine towns and villages, supped and slept in most of the mountain inns of France, Switzerland and Italy, and tramped or climbed pathways and mountainous slopes in all of those areas. Now, during his annual Alpine lecture tours, he began systematically to chronicle his experiences as if through the eyes of a first-time tourist. Four years later he would turn those notes into travel guidebooks for two of the Alps' most popular resorts.

When preparing for a trip abroad Whymper was a fusspot. In his trunk and suitcase were compartments, partitions, and cloth pockets. Invariably, as he packed for a summer month in the Alps, the same items went into their same reserved niches. His journals, pencils, drawing paper, account books, records, instruments, articles of clothing, maps, knives, matches, medicines, personal items – all had their assigned places. This fastidious habit served him well; in foul weather, darkness, or an emergency he could find what he wanted with minimum effort. It saved time, especially when his eyesight and other faculties began to fade. It was also one of the traits that revealed Whymper as a study in complementary contrasts: cautious in planning but bold in execution, entrepreneurial in spirit but tight-fisted with the cash in his pockets.

In the libraries of London from October to May he studied the history, architecture and culture of Chamonix and Zermatt. The months of summer and early autumn found him in the towns themselves. Local libraries provided historical records; village elders offered oral versions of ancient legends. He frequented a variety of hotels, inns, and spas to sample their rooms, food and other amenities. No new construction, ownership change or landmark disappearance escaped his attention. If offerings improved at one establishment and deteriorated at another, he recorded and published both pieces of information. Whymper paid special attention to the prices charged for lodging and meals and woe to the innkeeper who did not give value for the amount paid. Over the years some proprietors would ruefully discover he had told the world of their excesses, no matter how small. "Was charged 1 franc 25 centimes for *café au lait* and a penny-worth of biscuits at Hotel de la _____. Mark them *dear*."[7]

Whymper carefully sorted and organized the great variety of information he had accumulated about each location. By way of introduction to the area being described he added selected stories of his own mountaineering days interspersed with the exploits of other notables, past and present, who had climbed in those regions. He revised his guidebooks annually, keeping their information current for the new readers who bought copies each year.

*Chamonix and the Range of Mont Blanc* was published in 1896; *The Valley of Zermatt and the Matterhorn* in 1898. Both became bestsellers as much for their literary interest as their reliable, up-to-date information. Each of them, wrote Whymper, is a "little book...which some may desire to have at home and others will wish for on the spot. It deals with both past and present. The historical portion is followed by the topographical."[8] After that rather high-blown introduction he moved on to more savory details. The summary of *Chamonix's* chapter one contents could have been mistaken for a six-pence scandal sheet: "...Chamoniards Bought and Sold – Heresy, Sorcery and Capital Punishments – Peronette Charged with Eating Children at the Synagogue – The Priory Changes Hands and the Natives Behave Violently...."[9]

The Zermatt guidebook contained equally graphic introductory titles: "A Legend – The Bishop Outwits Satan – Murder of the Comptesse de Viège and Her Son – War in the Valais – The End of Bishop Tavelli."[10] The text went on, of course, to recount the story of the first Matterhorn ascent and descent, but it was described as: "...Terror of the Taugwalders – An Apparition – An Infamous Proposition – Surprised By Night...." Subsequent deaths on the mountain also got attention: "Another Catastrophe on the East Face – Death of Jean-Antoine Carrel – Death of Miss Bell and Dr. Black."[11] Few would-be tourists could resist these tabloid enticements. Whymper's "little books" happily combined the talents of an author, mountaineer and hard-nosed businessman.

The first pages of the guidebooks were devoted to advertising. Much of that was for Whymper-related products including: "Alpine Photographs: Each Print Bears Mr Whymper's Signature;" "Volcanic Dusts From The Great Andes of the Equator (perfectly pure, sold in bottles...set of eight specimens in a box, post free for 10s)"; "Boots by Norman (maker of the first boots which trod the summits of the Matterhorn and Chimborazo);" "Flexible Waterproof Coverings;" and "Telescopes, Field Glasses and Aneroid Barometers." Others were for "Hand Cameras;" "Schweppe's Soda Water;" and "Swiss Maps and Guides."

The most prominently displayed ads were for Whymper's books, crammed with blurbs of warm praise. From *Blackwood's Magazine* on "*Scrambles Amongst The Alps:* "It is a drama, a tragedy... mov[ing] us to wonder and fear, admiration and pity; it holds us breathless by moments, hanging on the story-teller's lips. The pictures alone are enough to make the fortune of any volume." From *The Independent* on *Travels Amongst the*

*Great Andes:* "Of this book we would say what Jules Verne sought to do in the realm of romance Mr. Whymper achieves in the literature of travel." And from the *Saturday Review*: "A more manly or more modest chronicle of great exploits than this we have not read." Also advertised was Whymper's pamphlet *How To Use The Aneroid Barometer*. "If Mr. Whymper's theory about the aneroid is maintained, a large number of peaks and heights on the earth's surface will have to be calculated all over again." *St. James's Gazette*. As in his approach to mountain climbing, there was nothing bashful or academic in Whymper's literary self-promotion.

Indeed, the mature Whymper pursued the success of his guidebooks with the same determination that drove him to Alpine summits as a youth. He methodically set out to place at least two or three copies in every inn and bookstore in the Chamonix and Zermatt regions, no matter how small or out-of-the-way. He would leave them on a "sale or return" agreement under which proprietors would hold sales receipts until Whymper came back to collect. As this could be anywhere from two to twelve months later, he often had difficulty getting his due. Even some of the better hoteliers and booksellers would learn in advance of his coming and leave their premises before he arrived. But Whymper was a modern "repo" man; his debtors could run but they could not easily hide. He would doggedly look in every room on all floors within a debtor's establishment, banging on doors that were locked. Then, if necessary, he would search next door and around the corner. His persistence paid off; both guidebooks sold well in Europe, earning Whymper an annual five-figure income in French and Swiss francs.[12]

Perhaps the most intriguing advertisement in these guidebooks appeared in their last editions. In toto the ad read:

**IN PREPARATION**

A BOOK FOR BOYS
YOUNG AND OLD
ONE HUNDRED STORIES
(Not To Be Read By Women)
By Edward Whymper
'Mony a mickle mak's a muckle.' Scotch proverb.[13]

Obviously intended to be humorous, the ad seems a stretch even by Victorian standards. The warning to women presumably meant not that they would be embarrassed – after all, young boys were the primary targeted readers and the author retained a fine-tuned sense of propriety. The message was merely that the stories were not a female's cup of tea. The book was never published and no incomplete manuscript surfaced. So the question remains: would Whymper's upcoming anecdotal "mickles" together have made, as advertised, a popular book-length "muckle?"

# CHAPTER 25

## *Aging Lion*

Frank Smythe, Whymper's 1940 biographer, wrote the introduction to a 1949 edition of *Andes.* Whymper, he said, was a "cold and unimpassioned" mountaineer and a "soured and crusty old man."[1] He called Whymper "foolish" for letting the Matterhorn tragedy induce a lingering sadness and for using alcohol to ease his burden.[2] This view put Whymper in a classic double bind: hardhearted for being unmoved by the grandeur of the Alps and softhearted for allowing the Matterhorn tragedy to affect him so deeply. Elements of truth float within Smythe's assessment, but missing are the deeper colors and subtler shades of a full-toned Whymper portrait.

Two photographs provide striking bookends for the story of Whymper's life. The best known picture of Whymper shows a 25-year old mountaineer garbed for a climb, gazing into the distance as if assessing his next mountain target. Though relaxed, his face reflects determination and strength; the lips are full but the mouth is firmly set. Forty-three years later, in November 1908, Whymper is the aging lion of the Alps. He appears in a jacket, tie and watch-chain, holding a pipe in one hand and what appears to be a manuscript in the other. Scrubbed, combed and neatly dressed, he is a successful man of business and letters, wise in the ways of the world and no stranger to emotional conflict. Like an optical illusion his eyes convey acceptance and defiance, the look of a person who takes people and events at face value but stays guarded against life's manifold threats. On his lips, tighter and thinner now, is the knowing half-smile of someone in whom the flame of life burns low but still generates heat. In both portraits, Whymper cuts a fine physical figure.

Anecdotes, family remembrances, and friends' reflections add depth to the 1908 portrait made three years before his death.

\* \* \* \*

On June 24th 1897, an Englishman named James Cooper left his hotel in Zermatt and never returned. Arriving there later that summer Whymper found the townspeople indifferent to the fact that no trace of Mr. Cooper had been found. After making inquiries on his own he wrote a letter to *The Times* decrying the apathy of the mountaineering community and urging that the matter be cleared up. The missing body was discovered that October. Mr. Cooper's relatives were grateful for Whymper's concern and offered to reimburse any expenses he might have incurred. He refused payment but accepted an invitation from the deceased climber's older daughter, Edith, for a visit to the home she and her aunt shared in the English countryside.

*Portrait of Edward Whymper (1908)*

The two women described their time with Whymper in a piece published under the pseudonym "Michael Field."

> He (Whymper) comes fresh and gaping from half a day's Turkish bathing. He fights a tendency to stoutness with the patient force that got him to the top of the Matterhorn. He is a curious triune being – one-third hero, one-third old bachelor, one-third mysterious man of business and lecturer....His head is combative...but with refinement softening the fierceness. [T]he eyes are blue, reticent of glances, but each glance is frank and has the modesty of genuine manliness, though...in his nature....there is a whimsical care for recognition, as an homage to [his] personal force.

> [His] features will not stamp memory;...they give the vague impression one would have [of] a giant smothered in rose leaves. The smile comes rarely but it is royal, the gift of a king when it is bestowed. Like all people of fine strain who live much by themselves, his talk is often on the things he likes to eat and drink, and he has many fads. His sugar must be sifted that he may have only a suspicion of the fattening sweet in his tea.

> He rolls on the couch, bows over Musico [a pet chow] and kisses my little hound. When the hour comes for dressing he asks whether we have a strong desire to see a black coat – "I don't think it's a pretty thing to see, but if you wish, it shall be put on." We pray him to do as he like, and he wears a grey suit for dinner.[3]

Whymper and the two spinsters bantered pleasantly at the evening meal. He suggested that despite their self-professed "infirm[ity]" they could reach Mont Blanc's summit under his guidance one way or another, "dead or living." Asked if their dogs could come along, Whymper said that this "would add considerably to the contract." The next morning his hostesses were surprised that he slept late. "[T]he hero of the Matterhorn is not punctual at breakfast – the coffee...and the eggs grow cold!...All the morning he...stud[ies] our Swiss bills, disentangling them as if they had been sent to him. We take him up to Reigate Hill; our discourse is simple and most friendly. When he goes after lunch we miss the only guest who has given us the feeling of whole-hearted sunshine."[4]

One of the people close to Whymper in his later years was his nephew Robert Whymper, son of his brother William. Robert had known his uncle since the days of his own childhood in the early 1880s when, as part of the training for "his expeditions," Whymper would walk 12 miles to visit William's family at their home in Surrey. He would "get a meal, stay beyond [my] parents' bedtime, and walk back."[5] The two kept in touch and at one point Whymper thought of adopting the young man as his son – probably believing he had the means to offer his nephew an education better than the boy's father could afford. Nothing came of that however. Robert did well in school, became a chemist, and often attended Whymper's lectures. Thus they had much to talk about, including his nephew's opinions on various scientific subjects.

> I used to lunch often with Edward Whymper at the old Anderton's Hotel at the bottom of Fleet Street where scientific matters were usually discussed between us. There, he was well known and respected in spite of the fact that he would usually appear in a sweater that showed his bare, bull-like neck to perfection. [H]e seldom wore anything under the sweater....At all times, E. W.'s appearance was impressive, his fine head and physique often causing people to turn in the streets as they passed by. The only time I attended a public function with [him] – except for his lectures – was the presentation to [Robert F.] Scott of the R[oyal] G[eographic] S[ociety] medal – a memorable occasion that impressed upon me how well E. W. was known and regarded.[6]

Robert genuinely respected his uncle but forthrightly appraised him as "self-centered and oblivious to social convention." One of the ways Whymper showed arrogant indifference to his surroundings was in his smoking habits, which were much the same as when he sat around the campfire of a mountain bivouac. Following his presentation in the lecture hall he would light his pipe and smoke "throughout the subsequent introductions" much to the "horror" of the ladies present. Using finely ground tobacco he puffed away so vigorously that burning fragments regularly overflowed onto "carpets, tablecloths and bedclothes...profusely scar[ring] his chest" when he smoked in bed. Whymper's bluff manner infused his closer relationships as well. His way of showing affection "was rather like that of a big bear [without] sentimentality....He had no friends but thousands of admirers."[7]

Geoffrey Young, a distinguished British mountaineer of Robert Whymper's generation, saw the Matterhorn conqueror as the foremost mountaineer of his day though "inferior to most of his fellow [climbers] in sensibility, imagination and culture." Young praised him, however, as an "honest egoist...in life...and as a writer," and kept a steadfast admiration for Whymper's unchanging persona.[8] In the early 1900s he encountered the famous climber in a Zermatt street preceding a ceremony marking the opening of a new mountain hut.

> For my generation, the familiar squared jowl and the unchanged idiosyncrasies in dress brought...into [a later] century the sense of Zermatt in the '60s. His myth moved with him out of the past, isolating him as a legendary figure even in the company of greater nobilities. We did not expect him to behave quite like present day men, and he never disappointed us. The grim mannerisms and...bluff oracles were always consistently in the Whymper tradition: he was so aggressively himself as to give the close-up magnification of a film...looming a little larger than life.

> I remember him last...in the Zermatt street, with courteous officials pressing him to attend...the opening ceremony of the Schönbühl hut. Impassive and dour, he waited a dramatic moment and then, the harsh growl anglicizing his accent effectively – *Il faut avoir de la bière!* We all smiled and sighed happily – Whymper was still Whymper. [T]he officials beamed and flaunted a whole menu of wines, and Whymper rolled on imperturbably.[9]

Young's encounter with the dour Englishman in the streets of Zermatt showed that Whymper's idiosyncratic ways were as familiar to

367

mountaineers of the Edwardian generation as to their Victorian predecessors.

This was not the case in Canada where mountain men knew him only by his renown as a pioneer of the Alps. Their first exposure to his thorny personality came when he went to the Canadian Rockies in the summer of 1901. Not knowing quite what Canada's mountains would require in the way of climbing, he had brought Swiss guides with him. Canadian packers would provide horses, camping equipment and supplies. They would also lead his party to the mountains; the imported guides would then take over. His trek would begin in the Upper Yoho region near the town of Field.

To that point in time Whymper had worked only with Alpine guides and porters, Inuit dog-sledgers and kayakers, and Ecuadorean arrieros and interpreters. He came to Canada expecting to employ natives of a similar stripe, people he consistently treated peremptorily until they proved themselves worthy of his respect. This attitude was dangerously wide of the mark and almost ended his Canadian venture before it began.

Canadian packers were a different breed altogether: individualistic, educated for the most part beyond the boundaries of their daily duties, and proud, somewhat defensively, of their skills. Whymper's abrupt manner and haughty stare alienated everyone with whom he came into contact. By the time he left the dining room of the Banff hotel after his first breakfast the staff was furious at his imperious manner. Next to receive his cold look was the hotel manager whom he curtly ordered to inform the packing company's representative to report to him that afternoon at 3:00 o'clock sharp. When the outfitter arrived at 2:55 Whymper admonished him for being five minutes *early*. The brusque mountaineer then advised the outfitter that he had brought canned food from England packed in sturdy wooden boxes so that it could not be "pillaged." With this final insult to the packer and his Canadian crew the young man exploded. The rude Englishman could go to hell, said the outraged oufitter, and try to get help from the devil.

Faced with this rebellion by one of his lead packers, the owner of the outfitting company brought Whymper into his office and told him that if he did not stop treating the Canadians who were there to serve him as lackeys he would soon have no one to turn to. Suddenly humbled – no one had abandoned him in the field since one of his early guides turned tail on their way to Breuil forty-one years earlier – Whymper accepted the message. The outfitter brought in a new leader and the expedition got underway. On the trail, however, further troubles between the visitor and his new packer resulted in a second defection that left Whymper again in the lurch. Still hoping to retain his company's unruly client – who, after all, held the promise of considerable business over this and possibly other summers – the outfitter's CEO persuaded a third young man to lead the crew in service to the famous mountaineer who had thus far proved such a disagreeable customer.

Robert Campbell, a seasoned leader though only in his twenties, was the man chosen for this intimidating task. Wisely he got Whymper alone and set some ground rules for their going forward together. He reminded the haughty Englishman that Campbell's men – because they were more familiar with the terrain en route to Whymper's mountain destinations – would be in charge of the party for that leg of the trek, emphasizing that the Swiss guides would take their orders from the Canadians. To minimize further confrontations, he said, Whymper's guides would handle all menial camp duties under the Canadians' supervision. The canned food from England would be removed from their heavy boxes and packed in saddle bags where they belonged. To all of this Whymper agreed. He realized, even through the fog of his misconceptions, that he had no other choice.

Despite the resultant good intentions on both sides, trouble broke out during the party's second day on the trail. Unused to their duties as chief cooks and bottle-washers the Swiss guides were surly and Whymper disgruntled. Campbell heard them talking in a mixture of German and French and described in a later memoir what happened.

We did not know a word of that tongue nor did we need to. From the[ir] tone...we knew they were not having a prayer meeting. Suddenly Whymper's right [fist] flew out, connecting with [the lead guide's] jaw, [who] hit the dust....We yelled at them to stop, and they did. I told Whymper he shouldn't do that.

He glared at me and reminded me that I had insisted he run his own camp, and he would thank me to mind my own affairs....

When you know you have the upper hand you can afford to be cool. 'That is just what I propose to do. I assume you know something of the authority...of a Justice of the Peace in England?' 'Quite,' he retorted, 'What has that got to do with it?' 'Quite a lot. You have committed an assault. I am a J. P.' His face went blank. Used to seeing all the trappings of a court in England [he could hardly] realize that before him stood a young man...[in] a buckskin shirt...with his thumbs shoved under a belt from which hung a gun on one side and from the other a sheath knife – embodying all the majesty of British law.

Whymper was flabbergasted. After a moment's silence he asked, 'Well, what do you propose to do?' I replied that I hoped that I would not have to do anything more than suggest he apologize to his guide for hitting him. Loss of face before one of his servants was a bitter pill. But he might be treated to a more bitter one if he refused. Walking over to his guide, he reached out his hand and made some remark in German. The four Swiss smiled. I gathered that the apology was not only ample but accepted....Turning to Whymper I told him I would bring him his afternoon tea.[10]

Things improved after that tense moment. Whymper approached Campbell after the evening meal and asked if they could find a way to work together. Campbell seized the opportunity, saying to the somewhat abashed client he would be glad to work cooperatively with Whymper if he would accept the Canadians' way of doing things, particularly their manner of dealing with "the help." He explained that many of the young packers were medical students, one of whom was a practicing dentist taking time off, who could cook as well as pull teeth. Amazed to find that the outfitter's employees were "men of that class" Whymper's attitude changed abruptly. With Campbell's crew now providing all of the camping services everyone got along well over the next two weeks the party spent together. When the newly chastened mountaineer found that two of the men shared his interest in botany and geology, they "got along swimmingly."[11] The end of the story was that Campbell outfitted Whymper during several more summers with "never an unpleasant word between him and my boys."[12]

The growth of the relationship between the crusty Victorian and his Canadian outfitters – from contentious aloofness to friendly accommodation – would be repeated by those who came to know Whymper in his later years. Campbell, who spent several weeks at a stretch with his famous client, was able to add a detail that these others never saw or alluded to only in passing. This was Whymper's heavy use of alcohol as he grew older and his exceptional capacity to resist its effects. "On the trail," Campbell wrote, "his daily allowance was a [pint] bottle of House of Commons Scotch and ten pints of ale." In town the quantity was about the same though with a different but always regular pattern.

> With his fish and soup it was a pint of sauterne. His meats were washed down with a pint of Saint Julien. His dessert was always MacLaren's cheese and soda biscuits, and with this he sipped a pint of Mumm's. Often after dinner...he...and his drinking pal, the C.P.R. trainmaster...would each have a pint of champagne. Then he would escort his friend down three flights of steps to the railroad platform and [lead] him...home.... [He would then] return to the hotel as brisk as a teenager going on a date. His room was on the third floor, and there was no elevator. Up those stairs he would go, [with] never a hand laid on the bannister....[O]ften he would finish the day by writing a scientific treatise for the British journals....I have never seen him under the influence of liquor![13]

Whymper obviously used alcohol – greater quantities as he grew older – to endure the strain of the hard physical life he had chosen and the heavy emotional baggage of the Matterhorn accident. Compounding these burdens was the emotional pain of his self-imposed loneliness. He was unwilling to use his dampened Baptist faith as a conduit to his soul, and he was disinclined to bare his feelings with any of his contemporaries.

The Alcoholics Anonymous revolution of recovery without institutional help had not yet begun and he would have scoffed at it had it been available. Josiah's genes kept him going, assisted only by Whymper's energetic and itinerant life style.

In the summer of 1903, two years after his initial summer with Campbell, Whymper was in the United States headed home from his second expedition to the Canadian Rockies. On the night before boarding the ship for England he slept at the Manhattan Hotel in New York City. Signing the register he asked to be called at a certain hour the next morning. He had difficulty sleeping which he blamed on "hotel noises." The wake-up call came 10 minutes early, an unwelcome arousal for the man who liked to sleep late when not in the open air. "I answered it as well as I could, saying sometimes, 'All right,' and at others, 'All right, I'm getting up.' " The front desk clerk, apparently unsure that his mumbling guest was fully awake, kept on calling. Roused and dressing Whymper did not answer the persistent tolls. A bellboy finally came up and "commenced a tirade against me which [in] plain English would be 'What the devil do you mean by not answering us?...Have you ever used a telephone before?' "[14]

Whymper's journal left it at that, but a New York newspaper reporter got wind of the incident either through the hotel clerk or from an interview with Whymper himself. With a public press even more aggressive than today, and the old mountaineer still a celebrity, the story came out differently in print. According to the reporter Whymper angrily yanked his room telephone from the wall by its roots, rushed out the door and threw the instrument down the corridor after the retreating bell boy. This version of the story could have been outright distortion, embellishment, or the simple truth. In any case the newspaper article did not portray Whymper out of character.

Throughout Whymper's life, strangers crossing his path were quick to remind the famous mountain climber that they had brushed shoulders or perhaps shared a drink, a meal, or a story with him at some earlier time. Reminiscences by some of these status-seekers came as late as a quarter century after his death. H. H. Bellhouse, Secretary of the Yorkshire Ramblers Club 1893-99, remembered Whymper as "modest and unassuming...one of the easiest men to entertain I ever met, and in...conversation over a pint of ale...one of the most entertaining....He was a kindly and charming man."[15] One of Whymper's fellow mountaineers wrote a paper in the *Alpine Journal* entitled *Ten Years Without Guides.* Following the article's publication its author received from Whymper a complimentary copy of the latter's Chamonix guidebook, unaccompanied by any reference to the Journal piece. His colleague appreciated the gesture, believing it signified approval of his writing. This illustrated, he said, Whymper's "rather aloof way of doing a kind thing."[16]

* * * *

In his late fifties Whymper met Charlotte Hanbury, the only woman outside of his family for whom he developed a deep affection. He first mentioned her in his journal of September 21st, 1899, where he noted with obvious pleasure their meeting in Chamonix. Though ten years older, she had Whymper's high energy and shared his love of mountaineering. Charlotte had gone to the Alps as a young woman in her twenties, first visiting Chamonix in 1856. She subsequently climbed several Alpine passes and minor peaks, thereby earning Whymper's praise for her lasting stamina: "She walks wonderfully well...[coming] down from the top of the Flégère last Friday without stopping."[17] He was also delighted to learn she had read and admired his books, with *Scrambles* at the top of her list. Charlotte was a free spirit, able to deal with Whymper as an intellectual equal. Given her age and the restrictions of their Victorian upbringing, the intimacy they shared was almost certainly that of warm friends only. But she sensed his loneliness and sympathized with it; he was delighted at last to have a talented and attractive female companion, though older, in his life. His sister Annette and nephew Robert approved of Whymper's new friend though they never met her. Charlotte, who "was said to have been as beautiful as she was good and pious, dominated his thoughts for a considerable time."[18] Then, just over a year after their meeting, fate intervened to cut short their relationship. Had it not done so, and they had been able to share each other's companionship for a few more years, the last chapter of Whymper's life would almost certainly have told a very different story.

He returned to London from the Alps in September of 1900 to find that his dear friend had rather suddenly been diagnosed with a fatal illness. Deeply saddened he visited her often. In early September "she was...bright and cheerful..., but the interview was...most painful." Two weeks later "her face [was] losing its colour and [she was] looking older."[19] On September 28th his diary noted: "Took my final adieu before leaving for America. Her face was getting more aged but her hands were wonderfully strong, under the circumstances, and she was as cheerful as usual."[20] The two friends, tacitly recognizing the likelihood of her death before his return from an American lecture tour, sensed this would be their last time together. But they likely gave no thought to a postponement of the tour. Both would simply soldier on, for this was their habit and the custom of the times in which they lived.

Underway to America Whymper wrote to Charlotte while off the coast of Ireland and again on the high seas before docking at Boston. On October 23rd, ten days after his arrival, he received a cablegram from Cornelius Hanbury announcing his sister's death. Whymper wrote to Annette: "The news came to me as I was starting a lecture. My beloved friend gone! I hardly know how I carried on."[21] Back in London he found that Charlotte had left a roll of French silk to be delivered to his sister Anette with Charlotte's "dying and undying love."[22] Several "literary men" had been friends to Miss Hanbury during her lifetime but she had never married. The tender feelings she brought out in Whymper receded upon her death, resurfacing later only in his concern for children.

Whymper's lecture tour was a financial success but the American audiences were disappointing. They attended in respectable numbers but lacked the knowledgeable appreciation shown by their British counterparts. With the occasional exception of a group of "chattering" women his listeners gave him their attention, but in none was he able to stir emotional involvement. In Boston he "went through the entire performance without getting a laugh or raising the faintest applause....Good, bad and indifferent slides seemed all alike to them." The receptions for him after the programs were equally frustrating. Many of his American hostesses brimmed with affected enthusiasm, a quality Whymper had disdained since the days of his youthful diary. One woman told him "that when she read my account of the first ascent of the Matterhorn she cried and read it out loud to a party of her friends, sen[ding] them [all] into hysterics."[23] One can easily imagine the pained look on his face as he stood there, helpless to escape the well-intentioned but fatuous compliments of his gushing female admirers.

American men seemed equally insincere. "Doctors, Professors, Judges, etc. – not one of them should I remember again if we met....[I]t gave them the greatest pleasure to see me there...the Matterhorn had made a profound impression on them, etc. They came up one after the other using almost exactly the same words."[24] Small talk was also the norm at London social gatherings but Whymper had no time or disposition for it anywhere. By the time his lecture tour ended he had had his fill of American society. In the future he would stop in the United States only for overnight stays on his way to and from western Canada.

Few people outside of Whymper's immediate family got to know him intimately. One of these was Frank Aylett, his trusted aide, secretary and manservant for the last decade of his employer's life. According to Robert Whymper, Aylett "was as close and cautious about...his master...and as honest and faithful to [him]...as any man I have ever met."[25] This long tenure confirmed Whymper's ability to instill loyalty in his servants and to find someone who met his rigid demand for personal privacy. Aylett died leaving no recollections of the colorful character he had come to know so well.

Not so constrained was Coulson Kernahan, Whymper's fellow author and lecturer, who delighted in telling the world about his controversial friend. Kernahan's book, *In Good Company*, offered personal recollections of several literary figures he had known over the years including Oscar Wilde, Charles Swinburne and Whymper. Published only a few years after Whymper's death, the book gives insights into his character that ring as true as Michel Croz's axe cutting steps on the icy descent of the Col Dolent.

During the years he kept Whymper's company – roughly the decade between 1895 and 1905 – Kernahan lived in Westcliff, a ten-minute walk from Whymper's home in Southend. On many days they took the same train to and from their London offices. It was as his fellow commuter, before they became acquainted, that Kernahan first observed the man some called "The Sphinx." "To the good folk of the town he was indeed always something of an enigma. In the street he stalked straightforwardly along, looking only in front of him, set of mouth, stony of eye and severe of brow if anyone spoke to or stared at him." [26] On the train Whymper rarely read a newspaper, often working with papers from his black bag or staring out the window while smoking his ever-present pipe.

When first introduced at a London gathering the two promptly "fell out." Hearing that Kernahan lived in the Southend area Whymper sought his agreement that nowhere else would one meet such "objectionable people" as their fellow commuters to and from the City. Kernahan acknowledged that Southend was not "the home of rank and fashion," but said he found these travellers and other residents quite sociable and had many friends among them. This brought forth a tirade from Whymper.

> "My good sir," he stormed, "I ask you where else in England, where else in God's world if you like, will you come across such a collection...of defaulting solicitors, bagmen, undischarged bankrupts, shady stockbrokers and stock jobbers, potmen, pawnbrokers and publicans as on that particular railway which you and I use?"

> I did not agree with him, and told him so plainly if courteously. [W]hereupon, seeing that I was more amused than annoyed by his storming, he suddenly turned good-tempered, diverted the conversation into other channels, and when we parted was quite friendly.

> His attitude, as I afterwards discovered, was characteristically Whymperian. He could respect a man who stood up to him and was undismayed by his storming; [but]...had no use...for one who was ready...insincerely, to profess himself entirely in agreement. He would at any time rather be bearded than humored, and [my refusal] to be browbeaten was, I now believe, one of the reasons why he and I...became good friends. [27]

Another graphic image of his new friend remained firmly in

Kernahan's memory. One morning he was seated on a commuter train ready for imminent departure. As the conductor blew his whistle and waved the "all clear" flag to his engineer, "a closely-knit, sturdily built man of middle height" walked slowly along the platform beside the train. Frantically waving his arms, the trainman urged Whymper and other late-comers to "hurry up." Amid this commotion Whymper "never lengthen[ed] his step by so much as one inch, never quicken[ed] his pace by as much as...one second, but stroll[ed] as leisurely as if the train were not to start for an hour...looking at each carriage for the face he [was] seeking."[28] Whymper's brazen defiance of conventionality succeeded; the train waited until he found Kernahan, entered the coach, and took a seat next to his new Southend friend.

While ignoring the hostile stares of the conductor and impatient commuters Whymper showed a keen sense of his commanding presence, and of how far beyond the bounds of ordinary behavior he could go without challenge. The incident was also a sign of the times: today's trains and subways would leave the tortoise-like, seemingly befuddled older gentleman standing on the platform in their wake, shaking his fist and cursing the insignificance of the individual in the modern rush-hour maelstrom.

Once seated Whymper varied his morning routine only in his initial greeting to Kernahan, which would be either a nod or a brief "good morning."

Then he puts his bag upon his knee, produces a packet of biscuits, and, looking out the window the entire time, munches them with jaws that move as rhythmically and methodically as...clockwork. His breakfast of dry biscuits finished, he dives into his bag for a flask, solemnly removes the stopper...[and] lifts the flask to his mouth, takes a drink, smacks his lips, replaces the stopper in the flask and then the flask in the bag, snaps the lock and puts the bag at his side. This done, he fishes in his pocket for pipe, tobacco and matches, charges and lights his pipe, takes with evident enjoyment two or three long draws at it, sniffing...with relish and with open nostrils the smoke which rises from the bowl, settles himself comfortably in his corner, and then, and not until then, turns to me with a cheery "Well, how are you this morning?" I reply with equal cheeriness, and probably the whole way up to town we talk – only we two – incessantly.[29]

Whymper enjoyed the company of people he could talk to with no risk of their seeking his friendship as an equal: he would chat with "a barber, a bird-stuffer, a boatman or a net-mender" without the "pompous precision" he affected with others. He seemed genuinely interested in the specialized information they shared with him and would talk to them for hours.[30]

It was not so with people of his own station. Kernahan was the only one in that category ever invited, he believed, to Whymper's Southend residence, a thoroughly "unhomelike place." It was three stories high, with servants' rooms in the basement. The first and second floors were unoccupied working areas. Two or three rooms on the top floor comprised Whymper's living space, "carpetless and barrack-bare" with only a few pieces of necessary furniture and "curtainless" windows. On the walls of the main room were photographs he had taken of mountains and wastelands in the Alps, Greenland and Ecuador, along with more recent scenes in Canada. Whymper pointed to a rolled-up mattress on the floor. " 'That,' he said to his visitor with a queer smile twisting at the corners of his mouth, 'is my bed. The rugs and pillow are inside. At night I unroll the thing and there I am. What could be simpler?' "[31]

Whymper slept less than most and at odd hours. He would usually take to his bed shortly after a 4:00 p.m. dinner, rising later at night for a "nocturnal ramble, which he loved." Sometimes he would not return until dawn. Kernahan often heard him discourse animatedly on the "joys of finding himself afoot and alone when more conventional folk were abed," self-satisfied, one might suppose, at this confirmation of his unique lifestyle and outlook.[32]

After their first meeting, except for a nod when their paths crossed, Kernahan left Whymper strictly alone. He realized later when the two had become friends and visited often that this had been the key to the formation of their relationship. Whymper was churlish to many but courteous and friendly to strangers as long as he made the first overture. "If it came from the other, he was at once on his dignity, withdrawing...instantly into his shell....No curled hedgehog could present a more prickly front than when in a train, in a club, or elsewhere, some representative of the lion-hunting fraternity, or of that class of person who dearly loves to claim acquaintance with a celebrity, made overtures to him.... [When] left to himself [however, he would] often,...like the hedgehog, uncurl of his own accord."[33]

On learning from their early conversations that his new friend had done some climbing in Switzerland, Whymper became more affable and eventually sought Kernahan's companionship on their train rides to London. Finally he wrote to his train-mate: "Come and crack a flask with me on Sunday next, any time you like after 8:30 p.m."[34]

Kernahan arrived punctually and was immediately offered a cigar from his host's selection of 25 year-old Manila favorites. Whymper then talked "incessantly, incisively and brilliantly" until past eleven o'clock when a two-way conversation began. Not until 12:30 as Kernahan's attention waned and his hunger pangs grew stronger did Whymper remark "And now, what do you say to supper?" "When you're quite ready," his guest replied foolishly, which led Whymper to relight his pipe and begin a discussion of the photograph of himself on the mantelpiece. Finally, when asked to comment on his host's appearance in the photo Kernahan saw his chance. "You look so cheerful, so well fed and happy. I can only suppose you had just had your supper...and I'm horribly hungry and in want of mine." Responding with only a "come along," Whymper led the way to a lavish cold supper spread on a table in the next room. "But such a supper! Anchovies, chicken, calves foot jelly, clotted Devonshire cream and other delicacies, with rare old Burgundy and the best of Champagne."[35]

Kernahan acknowledged that he felt warmly toward Whymper, contrasting himself with the many distinguished contemporaries who merely "liked" his company. Whymper was a man of considerable achievement, a member so to speak of the London meritocracy. But "the mold into which he was cast was austere, stern, and at times forbidding. He was a 'marked' man wherever he went; and in all companies a man of masterful personality. He inspired attention and respect in everyone, and something like fear in a few, but...except in the case of children, rarely inspired affection."[36]

Kernahan believed that Whymper was aware of his forbidding look and that others sometimes saw it wrongly as a lack of goodwill. To buttress this view Kernahan related a story that Whymper told on himself. " 'I was walking up Fleet Street one day,' he would begin, pursing his lips [and] almost smacking them over his words," as if relishing their flavor. Looking down, he chanced to see a sixpence lying on the ground but did not pick it up. The law required property found in a public place to be turned over to the authorities and, said Whymper, he did not want to bother with a trip to the nearest police station. Behind him he noticed "a poor ragged devil" without a shirt or shoes to his name. As his good deed for the day he caught the man's eye and then looked down at the coin. Confident that the man had seen the coin and understood the message, Whymper walked silently away. Farther down the street he became aware that the man was following him, no doubt, he thought, to thank him for the gift. But no! When he stopped and half-turned to receive the man's blessing, the latter "hissed, almost spat in my ear: 'You blank, blank, blankey blank, blank! Too blanky proud blank, are you, to pick up a sixpence? [Well], blank you!' "[37]

Whymper's first thought was that he hardly deserved such contempt for an attempted act of charity. Mulling it over, however, he felt there must have been "something unintentionally offensive or...patronizing in the way I looked at the man and then at the sixpence – something which he resented so bitterly that he had to follow me all that way to spit it out."[38]

Like a parable this story was subject to multiple interpretations. Would Whymper truly have felt bound to turn in something of as little value as a stray sixpence or did he use this as an excuse for a small act of charity to someone society might regard as undeserving? Was the vagrant's venomous outburst the result of anger and perhaps embarrassment at having to accept a gift from someone who seemed to scorn him, or simply from a hatred of Whymper's class? For whatever reason, was it justified? In any case, Whymper's concession was a rare expression of self-awareness, a sign that he knew more about himself than he ordinarily showed.

Such self-awareness sometimes surfaced in very different circumstances. On occasion, sensing that his overbearing manner had been uncalled for, he would make a conciliatory gesture. One Sunday morning he and Kernahan walked four miles to the neighboring village of Shoeburyness. Citing the "salt bloaters" he had eaten for breakfast, Whymper suggested that they stop at the local inn for something to slake his thirst. The inn was closed on Sundays except to "bona fide travellers" who by definition were those who had come more than three miles from where they had spent the preceding night. Responding to their knock the innkeeper opened the door slightly and asked if they were bona fide travellers.

"Well," remarked Whymper, "...there was a time early in my career when some doubts were cast upon my qualifications as a mountaineer...but this is the first time I have been challenged as a bona fide traveller. I'll say nothing about the qualification of my friend here, but considering that since the last time I passed this hostelry I have traveled some seven or eight thousand miles, I think I'm entitled to describe myself as a traveller in a very bona fide sense. As a matter of fact, we have come from Southend this morning, which I believe is outside the statutory three miles. Do I look, my good fellow, like a man who'd tell you a lie about a thing like that?"

"I don't know," replied the man, looking Whymper very hard in the face, but I'll tell you what you do look like if you wish. You look like a man who, if he'd made up his mind to have a drink, would have it whether he was a bona fide traveler or not, and wouldn't let no one else stop him from having it...."

"I observe, my man," said Whymper sententiously, as the door was opened to admit us, that you are no indifferent judge of character, but I am curious also to know whether you are disposed to have a drink yourself.[39]

The man's answer, in parliamentary parlance, was in the affirmative. Thus the Sunday morning visitor who began with a bit of heavy posturing ended by treating his host to a drink. As Kernahan had observed, Whymper was comfortable befriending low-born strangers, especially those who refused to be intimidated.

Kernahan injected himself into the aftermath of one of Whymper's more obnoxious displays of rudeness to a man who least deserved it. Grant Allen, a friend of Kernahan's, was known to all as a learned, gentle and generous man. At a London dinner gathering Allen, after being introduced to Whymper and having no idea of the latter's sensitivity on the subject, asked about the historic Matterhorn ascent and was told curtly, in effect, to mind his own business. Kernahan realized without being told that Whymper later regretted his brusqueness with Allen and sought some way of indirectly conveying an apology to the modest gentleman which pride and stubbornness prevented him from doing directly.

Sometime later Kernahan invited Whymper to a dinner at which Edward Clodd, a close friend of the wronged Allen, would also be present. Whymper admired Clodd as a "profound thinker...brilliant writer...and a "true friend." Kernahan saw this as an opportunity for Whymper to make amends to Allen via their mutual friend. " 'You know,' said Whymper in accepting the invitation, 'how generally I hum and ha when anyone asks me to a function or a dinner, and that I'd rather...dine on bread and cheese...in pajamas...here in Southend than be at the trouble of getting into a black coat and journeying up to London to eat a ten-course dinner. But, if Clodd is to be one of your guests, I'm your man.' "[40] Though Kernahan made no report, the dinner presumably allowed Whymper to make amends to the man he had offended.

Clodd wrote to Kernahan years later after reading a draft of the latter's chapter on Whymper. "I read the enclosed last night. Like Cromwell, Whymper would say, 'Paint me, warts and all,' and you have done as he would have wished, producing a faithful and withal sympathetic portrait....You truly assess him as a lonely man, but there was a soft place under a hard shell, and this comes out in the tenderness toward children and all helpless things of which you speak. I am glad to have your witness to his liking for me. His visits to me remain a cherished memory."[41]

Two vignettes in the Kernahan portrait account for Clodd's reference to Whymper's compassion for children. Sponsored by London charitable organizations, young girls came often to Southend for a week by the sea in Holiday Homes for the Poor. On his way home one day Whymper discovered a young girl wandering about, lost and crying helplessly. After comforting and quieting her he learned that she was staying at a Holiday Home and promptly became her guide. Kernahan happened upon the incongruous pair as they walked down the street. "I saw him stalking in front of me arrayed in a black greatcoat and a top hat and black leather leggings. In one hand he carried his bag and by the other he clasped the hand of a tiny girl-child, poorly clad and hatless, whom he stooped to comfort as tenderly as could any woman, and in fact took out his own handkerchief to wipe away her tears."[42]

Through visits with Kernahan Whymper came to know his friend's stepson. The boy was twelve years old and a cadet on H.M.S. *Worcester*. He "was devoted to [Whymper], being especially proud that the greatest of mountaineers was at the trouble of giving him lessons in climbing. Up and down the cliff slopes of Southend Whymper marched the lad, impressing upon him the importance of always going at one steady and uniform rate, [and] teaching him to walk from the hips mechanically and machine wise...." Back on his ship, the young cadet sent his autograph book to Whymper for his signature. "In it, the man whom some people (including himself, Kernahan might have added) thought grim, surly, and morose, wrote: 'I have been dying to see you again. When *are* you coming along? Edward Whymper. Feb 24th, 1905' "[43]

Kernahan was Whymper's closest friend. To him as to no other person Whymper opened the folds of the protective cloak he always wore, allowing rare glimpses of the aloof and reclusive man's inner self. To create Whymper's image, Kernahan relied "not upon bold strokes...but upon the...painting-in of comparatively unimportant but nonetheless cumulative details."[44] From Kernahan's brush Whymper emerged as a man "of absolute self-dependence, self-containment, and self-contentment... [with] no wish [for] the happiness or sorrow...[that others had] the power to contribute....[Although he] believed himself to be a happy man, Edward Whymper was...not only the loneliest but the most pathetic human creature I have ever known."[45] Pitiable, that is, in the sense that Whymper never experienced – on any level – the love for another that generates the deepest satisfactions available to the human spirit. Perhaps he never realized such joy was possible.

Positive feelings for Whymper were the bedrock, however, of Kernahan's friendship. "[Neither] rank and title, great social position, the power of the purse and the power of the Press, nor his own self-interests, could ever move Edward Whymper to seek the favor of those who for their own sake, or for the sake of what they have done, he did not already respect. Secure in the knowledge of his own just and honorable dealings with all men, and seeking only the approval of his own conscience, he was content to go his own way in the world, a strange, strong, lonely, but in many respects a remarkable man – I think in force of character and determination the most remarkable man I have ever known."[46]

\* \* \* \*

Kernahan moved away from the town of Westcliff shortly before Whymper's marriage in 1906 and did not attend the wedding. He had little hope that the upcoming union would succeed. A "born bachelor...he always seemed to me....[I] cannot imagine him as a married man."[47] Kernahan knew his friend only too well.

# CHAPTER 26

## *Last Lap*

The last lap of Whymper's extraordinary life began in the spring of 1906. On April 25th of that year, just two days short of his 66th birthday, he married Edith Lewin, age 21, a young woman he had known since she was a child in grammar school. At that time she had lived in the basement rooms of Whymper's Southend home with her aunt, his housekeeper. According to his sister Annette the aunt was "a most respectable, old-fashioned" lady.[1] Not so the niece. "She was wholly unsuited by character as well as by education for such a marriage. Love of dress and extravagance were [her] outstanding features."[2]

Edith was a christened Anglican and the couple were married in a church of her faith. The Reverend Canon Joseph McCormick – who had joined in Whymper's search for the Matterhorn victims and read the burial service at their temporary grave sites – officiated in the Rite of Holy Matrimony. Edith was attended by three bridesmaids and given away by her father. Edward's nephew Robert was his best man.

The reception celebrating this rather bizarre union perfectly reflected the groom's eccentricity. Though Whymper tried "to keep the matter as quiet as possible," twenty-five guests attended, all at the bride's behest.[3] Other than Robert, the groom invited not a single member of the Whymper family nor any of his friends or associates. The faithful Aylett came as Whymper's servant. McCormick, six years Whymper's senior, sermonized about the beauty of youth administering to old age, a theme Robert predictably found "rather revolt[ing]."[4] Robert was under a general order from his uncle to "search" the guests before they left. He later said – perhaps tongue-in-cheek, perhaps not – that this prevented the loss of silver though not of champagne. Whymper gave Edie twenty presents; she received eleven gifts from his friends. Ninety-five announcements of the marriage went out in the mail.

Whymper referred to his new bride as "Edie," she called him "Ted." For their honeymoon they went to the popular seaside resorts of the Southern Counties. From their base in Bournemouth they took beach walks, rode in "donkey chaises," and visited Whymper's sisters Liz and Nettie who were on holiday in nearby Poole. Whymper most enjoyed their visit to *H.M.S. Ocean*, a ship of the channel fleet docked at Weymouth. Its "upper deck," he wrote with barely tempered scorn, "was encumbered with a multitude of...hanky panky devices [which] one well-directed cannonball" could have put out of action. Other aspects of their honeymoon were less pleasing. He – and Edie if he judged her correctly – were disappointed by a theatre performance of *Uncle Tom's Cabin*. "The first part was not bad but the end was rubbish and drove us out before" the final curtain. On a steamer trip around the Isle of Wight Edie became "unwell" due to lively wind and waves. They also visited the town of Swanage by steamer. Though "not so deadly dull as Poole, Wimborne and Warsham...[it was] not particularly attractive."[5]

Back in London by late May the couple took up residence in Forest Gate. As an inexperienced sailor on the unfamiliar seas of matrimony, Whymper chose popular landmarks to guide Edie's entry into his world. He took her to the National Gallery, Hampton Court Palace, the Tate Gallery, Lambeth Palace, Madame Tussaud's and the Hippodrome Theater. He arranged for her brother and sister to join them for lunch in his office on Ludgate Hill where they watched King Edward's entourage on its way to Saint Paul's Cathedral. All the time, however, he was confiding to his diary that the sightseeing jaunts were a bit boring. "The performance was bad" at the Hippodrome. The National Gallery put on a "poor show," and they were "made to pay handsomely" at the Hampton Court tearoom. "Don't go there again," he firmly reminded himself.

Signs of marital stress developed early. On June 1st Edie went to sleep after lunch and forgot their meeting set for later that afternoon. Whymper arranged for them to have lunch at 1:15 p.m. the next day but Edie arrived at 2:30. Later that summer he took his new bride to Europe, the first and last time they would visit his old haunts together. Before embarking he provided her with a "dress and other allowances." Upon their arrival in Paris, however, she got no opportunity to examine the latest fashions or to spend any of her allotted funds. Whymper had scheduled them to leave immediately for Geneva, probably because Paris no longer held his interest. In the Swiss capital he introduced Edie to H. F. Montagnier, an enterprising 29 year-old expatriate American whose interest in mountaineering and the Alps had led him to Whymper. Like Kernahan, Montagnier refused to be intimidated by the older man's bluff manner, becoming instead his admirer and friend. From Geneva the Whympers went on to Zermatt and then to their final stop in Chamonix. There "Edie did her first ice-cutting on the Mer de Glace."[6]

In Chamonix they took a room at the Hotel Couttet, the town's leading inn. The Couttet brothers and the hotel staff knew Whymper well from the many times he had been its guest over the years. At the time of the newlyweds' visit Adeline Payot was in her third year as the maîtresse d'hôtel. She saw to it that Whymper's favorite sandwich, gruyère cheese with mustard, was prepared to his liking and that the house's best champagne was in plentiful supply. Mrs. Whymper also received the staff's special attention. Mlle. Payot noticed that when Whymper left the hotel on his afternoon rounds to promote sales of his Chamonix guidebook he would lock the door to his room and leave Edie inside without a key. Wanting to comfort her on these occasions a hotel employee would climb a ladder to the balcony of the Whympers' first floor room with refreshments for the abandoned bride.[7] Perhaps an insecure Whymper convinced himself that Edie liked her afternoon naps and wished not to be disturbed. In any event it is little wonder she chose not to accompany her husband on his future business trips to the Alps.

Whymper invariably stayed at the Hotel Couttet when in Chamonix. In his later years he followed a regular pattern on his return to the hotel from a day of business. At dinner time, if sober, he would join the other guests at the table d'hôte. When "ivre" he would eat alone. On the good nights he would invite one or two others to join him in his room for a "séance" with after-dinner spirits and more conversation. Each floor of rooms in the Hotel Couttet had its own maid who was on duty around the clock. Several times on convivial evenings during which several bottles of champagne were consumed Whymper would emerge from his room, throw an empty bottle down the corridor toward the maid and in his commanding voice shout, "Marie! *Apportez-nous une autre bouteille!*" The hotel's staff and guests always knew when the famous mountaineer was among them.[8]

Much of what is known of the next three years of Whymper's life comes from letters and postcards from him to Montagnier at the latter's home in Geneva. More than anything else this correspondence shows the stress imposed by the steady decline of Whymper's marriage. In the spring of 1907, however, he sounded positively chipper. "Mrs Whymper sends you her kind regards. She keeps very well, bright and lively."[9] In April during or just before Montagnier's visit to London he wrote, "Mrs Whymper...hopes you will take lunch with her on Saturday next at 1:30 p.m."[10] In October a rather lighthearted letter to Montagnier had only one dissonant note: "My Missis joins me in wishing you long life and prosperity. She will not accompany me to Geneva this year, as she has not yet finished unpacking her bonnet boxes."[11]

The next February, 1908, he wrote to Montagnier: "Mrs Whymper instructs me to offer you all sorts of tender expressions."[12] On May 14th of that year Ted and Edie became the parents of a daughter whom they named Ethel. In a letter to Montagnier of July 5th Whymper was buoyant. Forsaking his usual notepaper or postcard penned in a close-lined somewhat cramped hand he wrote in a free-flowing style on a large sheet of white paper. "Madame and Miss Whymper are both very well, but they will not accompany me to the Alps this year. Mademoiselle does not Whimper, as she ought to do. Her lungs are good, and she squalls. If this goes on for long, perhaps the Squalls will become Gales....Give my regards to all good people and leave out the rest."[13]

That October while her husband was in Europe Edie wrote to Montagnier in the voice of her daughter: "My Dear Mr Montagnier, Mamma tells me it is you who so kindly sent me this beautiful rattle. It is exceedingly good of you, and I only wish I could thank you personally for such a charming present. How is Daddy? I am so longing to see him again, and feel sure that I shall remember him when he comes back. Mamma wishes me to say that she hopes you will come and see us when you are in London again. I am five months old on the 14th and I grow very fast. With lots of love, I remain, yours truly, Ethel Rosa Whymper."[14]

Edie had made the bed she lay in but the poignancy of her words was touching. Between the lines of her letter was a sense of longing, a wish for more than she could give or receive in her hapless marriage to Whymper. Her joy as a new mother shone clearly but not brightly enough to conceal her loneliness. The warmly expressed thanks made in her young daughter's voice were tinged with sadness – for Edie's plight and from concern for the future of young Ethel herself to whom Whymper would always seem an emotionally distant grandfather. The cautious venting of those feelings provided some relief, including the bittersweet pleasure of making contact with Montagnier, the one person she might dare to include in her fantasies.

Across the Channel Whymper was faring poorly. Having adopted Montagnier as his close friend now that Kernahan had moved from Southend, he opened himself more and more to the young man who had become his favorite correspondent. On November 2nd, 1908, he sent a long, disjointed letter to Montagnier written in a faltering hand. After speaking of more ordinary things he ended with a description of the head injury he had suffered three years earlier in a train accident on the Canadian Pacific Railway. Since then, he said, his sight had "grown worse and worse" to the point that he could not read "anything" and could "only guess at" his own handwriting. "[Where] it will end I cannot tell, but I write seriously in saying that I do not care to live as a log, and frequently think of suicide."[15] This was the lowest point of his life to that time, his black mood brought on by more than poor eyesight. It lingered through Christmas into the following January when he wrote to Montagnier from London. "How are things in Geneva?...Here, we are as usual Damp, Dreary, Dismal."[16]

Whymper struggled through the next year, 1909, as his correspondence with Montagnier continued. He told his friend that the American Alpine Club had recently granted him honorary membership and thanked Montagnier for what he believed had been a helping hand in that decision. He also told Montagnier that he had proposed him for membership in the Royal Geographic Society and in the "Sierra Club" of America.[17] In July he attended a reception for Ernest Shackleton whose ship *The Nimrod* had just returned from Antarctica, and whose crew had reached the magnetic pole. Shackleton himself had come within a hundred miles of the geographical South Pole. It was a "striking occasion" at Albert Hall where the guest of honor "spoke well." But Whymper believed – correctly, as time would show – that Shackleton's book would not "display literary capacity."[18]

Earlier that year Edie wrote to Montagnier that "our daughter is getting along splendidly and trys (sic) very hard to talk and walk." Not until April of the following year, 1910, in the letters that survive, did Whymper again mention his daughter Ethel to his friend in Geneva. "The infant by way of amusing herself set fire to her nursery last Tuesday morning. A third of the room was [aflame] before it was noticed, and she was found standing in the middle of the room, admiring the conflagration. In another minute she would probably have been on fire herself & burnt to death."[19] Given the Whympers' relationship, this last remark, besides being intentionally silent on how the accident happened, probably cloaked substantial anger. It was the first shoe falling ominously to the floor as a sign of Whymper's marital distress.

If Montagnier then listened for the other shoe to fall he did not have long to wait. In late August he received a letter from Whymper leaving no doubt as to his friend's crumbling life. "Mrs Whymper is past redemption, and it is best not to discuss the matter except sotto voce."[20] Among Whymper's surviving letters this isolated sentence seems a bolt from the blue. More likely, however, he had dropped earlier hints in lost letters or when he and Montagnier were face to face. Late that year the Whympers' troubles became public knowledge. On December 9th *The Daily Telegraph* noticed the issuance of a "decree of judicial separation" on uncontested grounds of cruelty.[21] The court's order allowed them to live apart but did not dissolve the marriage or fix Whymper's financial obligations to his wife.

Alone again Whymper was angry, bitter and defensive. On a clipping of *The Daily Telegraph* article enclosed in a letter to Montagnier he suggested that the judge should have noted that he was "only too glad to get rid of her." In his mind the future appeared bleak; he anticipated "constant demands for money and no peace." Feeling the need for Montagnier's friendship more than ever he added a postscript: "I think it is time to drop the *Mr* Whymper."[22]

Ten days later he invited Montagnier to attend the Alpine Club's annual dinner as his guest, adding that "I am the sole surviving founder of that Organization."[23] Though he had joined the Club four years after its 1861 founding Whymper was well remembered as one of the small group whose early exploits helped sustain the association in its fledgling days. Acknowledging the septuagenarian's forty-nine years of active participation and support, most Club members of the early 20th century would probably have been happy to second Whymper's claim of founder-ship status.

In February of 1911 Montagnier suggested to Whymper that he escape London's winter and the pressures of his marital estrangement by visiting the young American and his wife in their new home in San Remo, Italy. Sounding both appreciative and a bit envious Whymper contrasted Montagnier's life with his own. "[B]efore long you will sit under your own vine and fig tree, none daring to make you afraid." Changing then to a minor key he continued with a nearly audible sigh: "I have not a penchant for olives; [if] I do eat them it must be...in Jerusalem...upon Mount Olivet. After that, the Dead Sea comes naturally."[24] He declined Montagnier's invitation on the ground that "the troubles in connection with my wife's desertion are not finished."

The correspondence between London and San Remo continued. Although Whymper never visited Montagnier's villa, the town's romantic aura stayed in his thoughts. That spring he thanked his friend for sending him a book conjuring up scenes of gentle sea breezes and warm Italian sun. "It made me wish to roll in the grass at S. Remo."[25] Montagnier could hardly have pictured Whymper frolicking on his lawn but he probably recalled that image four months later when he learned that his friend was gone, never to return.

* * * *

In the mid-summer of 1911 Whymper's marital problems hit bottom. That July he told his sister Annette how bad things were. "I cannot say when I shall be off, for Mrs E. Whymper is doing her best to annoy me....All who are concerned with the matter know that her sole aim is money. I have already lost £2,000 over her, and if I am forced to leave the country to escape from her, I shall lose as much more. I shall be obliged to sell...the greater part of my cherished belongings and...be almost completely cut off from the family and my friends...."[26]

Though he perhaps exaggerated his potential monetary exposure his psychological sufferings were acutely real. He never gave full expression to his deepest feelings but his heart surely told him that he had made a colossal mistake. At some level he must have blamed himself for ignoring the internal warnings before the marriage and for not foreseeing the inevitable and bitterly painful consequences of such a mismatched union. Now after five years he likely would have exchanged the wife and child he had so strongly desired for the comfortable routine of the single life he had so misguidedly relinquished.

\* \* \* \*

On August 8th, 1911, Whymper left London for his annual round on the Zermatt-Chamonix circuit to promote and update his guidebooks and to collect revenue from their sales. Travel was faster now and he was in Paris by seven o'clock that same evening. In Zermatt two days later he sold six guidebooks to the Wega outlet at "reduced prices" and seven to the guide Anderegg "at two francs each."[27] Like an aging peddler he walked down the valley to Randa and then went by train on the circuit to Stalden, Sierre, Martigny, Montreux and Bern.

Next on Whymper's agenda was a side trip to Grindelwald for a pre-arranged meeting with W. A. B. Coolidge, an American by birth who had lived in Europe since his childhood and was now in his early sixties. Coolidge was ten years younger than Whymper and an avid mountaineer. Through a lifetime of scholarly writing he had become known as the dean of Alpine historians. Thin-skinned, irascible and a loner much like his scheduled visitor, Coolidge was a controversial figure. The two men had first crossed swords when Whymper mistakenly wrote in *Scrambles* that Coolidge had not been the first to ascend the Ailfroide. On finding that he had been in error he apologized to Coolidge and they corresponded politely over the years.

In his heart, however, Coolidge never forgave Whymper and kept his resentment bottled up. More than twenty years later he wrote an obituary for Christian Almer following the famous guide's death in 1898. In it, no longer able to contain himself, Coolidge challenged the accuracy of Whymper's description in *Scrambles* of Almer's daring leap across a chasm on the descent of the Pointe des Ecrins in 1864. Whymper wrote to the Alpine Club asking for a special meeting of the members to review the issue, but after considerable back and forth among the Club's Executive Committee and the two disputants, Whymper's request was denied. But while it was pending Coolidge resigned his Club membership, effectively calming the waters.

For all his brusque manner and outward confidence Whymper was never comfortable with Coolidge's alienation. He respected the latter's scholarship and on occasion had sought his advice on lecturing techniques. The renowned historian was an entrenched member of the establishment, a position for which Whymper, despite his own accomplishments, retained something of a sense of awe. Seeking now to repair the relationship between them he sent word to his contentious colleague that he wished to visit Coolidge at the latter's home in Grindelwald. Unbeknown to Whymper, his friend Montagnier – who was gradually becoming Coolidge's peer as a leading Alpine historian – had probably acted as an intermediary to help bring the two together.

On September 3rd Whymper went from Bern to "Chateau Montana," Coolidge's Grindelwald home. Anxious to bury the hatchet and having heard that his host might be growing senile, Whymper wanted to see Coolidge while the latter was still sensible. Though the two men talked together until late that afternoon neither of them revealed the topics or the outcome of their discussion. On Coolidge's mental state Whymper said only that he "did not detect any signs of insanity," leaving the impression that their meeting, if not wholly cordial, had at least left the two aging antagonists in a strained peace.[28]

In Geneva over the next three days Whymper combined business with pleasure. He worked on guidebook and other matters with his long-time friend and partner, Henry Kündig, and dined on separate evenings with the Kündigs with whom he was staying and with Madame Montagnier, his friend's wife who was visiting Geneva from San Remo. On this latest visit to the lakeside city Whymper displayed, ironically, a bit of creeping senility that led him to choose unlikely situations in which to prove to himself that his faculties were in fact undiminished. In

Geneva a year earlier he had sought the help of a city policeman in finding a street on which one of his guidebook outlets was located. Though the details are not clear, he thought it was in one direction while the policeman insisted it was in another. With an excess of Swiss wine perhaps contributing to the heat of Whymper's reaction, the policeman decided to take the angry Englishman to the station for cooling off. Now back in Geneva a year later, after determining from a street map that he had been right all along, Whymper returned to the police station to prove his point. With him he took two good cigars giving one each to "the gendarme and the man in charge."[29] No doubt he felt better as the policemen, puffing on their cigars, shook their heads at yet another lesson in the vagaries of human nature.

By September 9th Whymper had moved on to Chamonix. The next day he met with booksellers and innkeepers on guidebook matters. Either that afternoon or the next he had a chance encounter with Georges Casella, a French journalist, on the terrace of the Hotel de Paris. In an article published after Whymper's death, Casella wrote that he had been talking to two friends about his stay in a hut on the Aiguille Verte, from which he had just descended. They were discussing the hardiness of pioneer climbers who had bivouacked on rough and rocky slopes without the comforts of a hut. " 'That's true, that's true,' said a voice close to us. Someone was listening to us....The accent disclosed an Englishman. 'Yes,' said the man, 'and since you have climbed the Verte you should understand the problems I had at that time in reaching the virgin summit before the others. Yes, indeed, a lot of problems, even more than with the Matterhorn.' 'Whymper!' I cried.....''[30]

The words Casella ascribed to Whymper seem genuine in their tone and substance. Even more true-to-life was Whymper's next remark: "Besides, I explained all that to *The Times* on the orders of the Alpine Club. But what I can tell you is that the Matterhorn was very easy, and that we only took Hadow – a fool, I can tell you – because the guide...no, I am not going to tell you that...Let's drink!"[31] These were his final words on the subject. In compulsively bringing up a horror he wished to forget and then abruptly turning to drink as a more bearable alternative, he stayed completely in character.

On September 11th Whymper asked Michel Payot, the guide, to join him in a search for the bodies of climbers who had disappeared somewhere on the Glacier des Bossons during an ascent of Mont Blanc in 1870. Applying a generally accepted formula for calculating the pace of glacial movement, Whymper believed that the preserved bodies were about to be disgorged at the foot of the Bossons glacier. Payot agreed, probably just to humor his aging friend, but Whymper took him seriously and gave him "instructions [on] what to do." In his September 12th journal he wrote in huge print, spread out upon the page: "Fire! fire!! fire!!!...A shed belonging to Couttet caught fire...and created some excitement." The same entry ended: "Did not feel at all well towards the end of the day." Whymper wrote his last words the next evening: "September 13th, Wednesday – at Chamonix,"[32] Though somewhat shaky, the handwriting was clearly legible. Portions of some letters were thicker and blacker as if the ailing writer had pressed on the pen to steady his hand.

This final dateline seems intended as the usual preface to his notes of the day's activities. But he was simply not up to continuing with the entry before he retired. The next morning, in a service provided daily to all guests at the Hotel Couttet, a maid came to his room with hot water. Whymper told her he would stay in his room until further notice and wished not to be disturbed. Knowing that a failure to follow the instructions of this particular guest meant a swift and certain tongue-lashing, she advised the staff and they left him alone. Perhaps they knocked on his door that night or the next day, Friday, and perhaps they thought they heard his gruff voice telling them he wanted nothing. On Saturday the 16th, finally alarmed, they entered Whymper's room and found him dead.

Speculation has it that the weary mountain lion, knowing he was dying, retired to his den to let nature take its course. By most accounts, however, the cause of death was "cerebral congestion" or a stroke. While Whymper's stubborn reclusiveness may have kept him from consulting a doctor, the stroke probably disabled him before he could form a conscious wish to die. The Couttets immediately took charge, sending telegrams to London and seeing to the preparation of the body for burial. Word also went out to European Alpine Clubs, associations of guides, and other members of the mountaineering community. Every British and European newspaper of note published the news of Whymper's death, as did the *New York Herald*. In his scrapbook Montagnier collected obituaries from 41 London newspapers and periodicals and 148 others throughout Britain. Some carried follow-up stories in later editions. The scrapbook also held over 170 obituaries and Whymper profiles from publications in France, Italy and Switzerland.

Whymper's funeral was set for Wednesday, September 20th. Early that day members of the Compagnie des Guides de Chamonix went to homes, inns and shops announcing Whymper's death and urging attendance at the burial service scheduled for 2:30 that afternoon at the town cemetery. The funeral procession started from the Hotel Couttet where his body had been kept. Pallbearers were ten Chamonix guides, including Frédéric Payot, one of the five guides to join Whymper's search party following the Matterhorn disaster. They placed the coffin in a horse-drawn hearse, stayed beside it as the cortege moved along, and carried it from the hearse to the grave site at the town cemetery.

Leading the line of mourners were the firemen of Chamonix with their shiny bugles on prominent display. Following them were a sizeable number of wreath-bearers carrying alpine flower arrangements from individuals and organizations. Next in the line were Whymper siblings Charles, William and Elizabeth, representing the six surviving brothers, their sister Annette, and a dozen or more nieces and nephews. After them came delegates from the English, French and Swiss Alpine Clubs, the Mayor and other town officials, the Couttet brothers, the Payot family, and several other old friends from Chamonix. The coffin was covered with two large sprays of flowers sent by Whymper's widow Edith and by the Winter Alpine Club of Manchester.

Behind this group was a dense line of townspeople and transient tourists, some with sadness in their hearts and some attracted only by curiosity about the famous mountain climber they did not know. As all gathered around the open grave, representatives of the three Alpine Clubs paid brief but respectful tribute to their departed comrade. After a simple prayer service conducted by The Reverend Chadwick, Whymper's coffin was lowered into the ground and the mourners slowly went their separate ways.[33]

The family and the deceased himself could hardly have sought a more appropriate setting. Under an overcast sky the encircling crags and snow-capped domes of the Mont Blanc range stood silently guarding the ages-old ritual taking place below them. As symbols of nature's enduring power against the transience and frailty of human life, these majestic peaks lent special significance to the burial of the Golden Age's most vigorous climber. Among the mountains with which he would forever be associated, Edward Whymper was finally at rest.

# SOURCES

The following abbreviations have been used:

| | | |
|---|---|---|
| AC | – | Alpine Club |
| ACA | – | Alpine Club Archives |
| AJ | – | *Alpine Journal* |
| BL | – | British Library |
| NLS | – | National Library of Scotland |
| SPRI | – | Scott Polar Research Institute |

## Preface

1. Edward Whymper, *Scrambles Amongst the Alps*, London: John Murray, 6th edition (1936) p. 334
2. Leslie Stephen, 5 *AJ* 237
3. Claud Schuster, 57 *AJ* 432-33
4. Geoffrey W. Young, *Mountain Prophets*, 54 AJ 97-117, pp. 105-06 (1943)
5. Schuster, *op. cit.*, p. 432
6. *op cit.*, Scrambles, p. 333

## Prologue – Storm on the Mountain

1. Edward Whymper, *Scrambles Amongst the Alps*, London: John Murray, 6th edition (1936), p. 255
2. *Ibid.,* p.124
3. *Ibid.,* p. 125
4. *Ibid.*
5. *Ibid.,* p. 124
6. *Ibid.,* p. 125
7. *Ibid.,* p. 126
8. *Ibid.,* p. 127
9. *Ibid.,* p. 130
10. *Ibid.*

11. *Ibid.*

12. *Ibid.,* 131


Chapter 1 – A Victorian Family

1. ADD MS 63112, folio # 1, BL (hereinafter # only)

2. T. G. Bonney, *Whymper's Obituary*, 26 AJ 54 (1912)

3. F. S. Smythe, *Edward Whymper*, London: Hodder & Stoughton Ltd. (1940), p. 15

4. *Ibid.,* p. 61

5. G. M. Young, *Victorian England: Portrait of an Age*, London: Oxford Univ. Press (1954), p. 84

6. *Ibid.*

7. *Ibid.*

8. Gertrude Himmelfarb, *Victorian Minds*, Chicago: Ivan R. Dee (1968), p. 276

9. *Ibid.,* pp. 276-77

10. W.D. Rubinstein, *Britain's Century*, New York: Oxford University Press (1998), p. 65

11. *Ibid.,* p. 150

12. *Ibid.,* pp. 156, 173

13. *Ibid.,* p. 172

14. *Ibid.,* p. 299

15. *Ibid.,* pp. 288-89

16. Russell M. Goldfarb, *Sexual Repression and Victorian Literature*, Lewisburg: Bucknell Univ. Press (1970), p. 49

17. *Ibid.*

18. *Ibid.,* p. 43

19. *Ibid.,* p. 31

20. *Ibid.,* p. 36

21. *Ibid.,* p. 27

22. T. G. Bonney, *Whymper's Obituary*, 26 AJ 55 (1912)

23. *op cit.,* Smythe, p. 11

24. *Ibid.,* p. 5

25. ADD MS 63112, # 133, BL

26. *Ibid.*

27. *Ibid.,* # 14

28. *op cit.,* Smythe, p. 42

29. *Annette's Note*, ADD MS 63112, # 143, BL

30. *Ibid.,* # 128


Chapter 2 – Ambitious Dreams

1. F. S. Smythe, *Edward Whymper*, London: Hodder & Stoughton (1940), p. 2

2. *Ibid.*
3. ADD MS 822/1/1-9, SPRI
4. *op cit.* Smythe, p. 15 (28 Jan. 1856)
5. *Ibid.,* p. 46 (20 Oct. 57)
6. *Ibid.,* p. 42 (13 Aug. 57)
7. *Ibid.,* p. 63 (19 Jan. 59)
8. *Ibid.,* p. 58 (24 Apr. 58)
9. *Ibid.,* p. 5 (2 Feb. 55)
10. *Ibid.,* p. 6 (3 Mar. 55)
11. *Ibid.*
12. *Ibid.,* p. 8 (17 Jun. 55)
13. *Ibid.,* p. 35 (17 Jan. 57)
14. *Ibid.,* p. 43 (17 Sep. 57)
15. *Ibid.,* p. 46 (27 Oct. 57)
16. *Ibid.,* p. 9 (8 Jul. 55)
17. *Ibid.,* p. 14 (5 Jan. 56)
18. *Ibid.,* p. 40 (19 Jul. 57)
19. *Ibid.,* p. 44 (4 Oct. 57)
20. *Ibid.,* p. 56 (28 Feb. 58)
21. *Ibid.,* p. 64 (20 Feb. 59)
22. *Ibid.,* p. 20 (8 Feb. 59)
23. *Ibid.,* p. 27 (14 Jun. 56)
24. *Ibid.,* p. 13 (30 Dec. 55)
25. *Ibid.,* p. 18 (19 Feb.56)
26. *Ibid.,* p. 35 (1 Mar. 57)
27. *Ibid.,* p. 27 (15 Jun. 56)
28. *Ibid.,* p. 25 (15 May 56)
29. *Ibid.,* p. 27 (10 Jun 56)
30. *Ibid.,* p. 16 (8 Feb. 56)
31. *Ibid.,* p. 38 (6 Jun. 57)
32. *Ibid.,* p. 44 (22 Sep. 57)
33. *Ibid.*
34. *Ibid.,* (22 Sep. 57); (24 Sep. 57)
35. *Ibid.,* p. 59 (3 Jun. 58)
36. *Ibid.,* p. 61 (10 Aug. 58)
37. *Ibid.,* p. 68 (31 Aug. 59)
38. *Ibid.,* p. 65 (11 Apr. 59)
39. *Ibid.,* p. 67 (8 Jun. 59)
40. *Ibid.,* pp. 19-21 (5 Mar. 56)
41. *Ibid.,* p. 47 (7 Nov. 57)
42. *Ibid.,* p. 57 (27 Mar. 58)
43. *Ibid.,* p. 59 (4 Jun. 58)

44. *Ibid.,* p. 53 (30 Dec. 57)
45. *Ibid.,* p. 67 (10 Jun. 59)
46. *Ibid.,* p. 16 (7 Feb. 56)
47  *Ibid.,* p. 30 (16 Oct. 56)
48. *Ibid.,* p. 63 (25 Jan. 59)
49. *Ibid.,* p. 39 (2 Jul. 57)
50. *Ibid.*
51. *Ibid.,* p. 55 (12 Feb. 58)
52. *Ibid.,* p. 29 (2-14 Aug. 56)
53. *Ibid.,* p. 30 (17 Oct. 56)
54. *Ibid.,* p. 6 (22 Feb. 55)
55. *Ibid.,* p. 7 (6 April 55)
56. *Ibid.,* p. 15 (23 Jan. 56)
57. *Ibid.,* p. 16 (12 Feb. 56)
58. *Ibid.,* p. 38 (4 Jun. 57); p. 41 (30 Jul. 57)
59. *Ibid.,* p. 64 (24 Feb. 59)
60. *Ibid.,* p. 38 (4 Jun. 57)
61. *Ibid.,* pp. 54-55 (25-26 Jan. 58)
62. *Ibid.,* p. 56 (18 Feb. 58)
63. *Ibid.,* p. 64 (11 Feb. 59); p. 67 (1 Jun. 59)
64. *Ibid.,* p. 26 (1 Jun. 56)
65. *Ibid.,* pp. 50-51 (15 Dec. 57)
66. *Ibid.,* p. 54 (7 Jan. 58)

Chapter 3 – Beauty, Mystery, and Adventure

1. W. A. B. Coolidge, *Swiss Travel and Guidebooks*, London: Longman Green (1889), p. 76
2. Roger Frison-Roche and Sylvain Jouty, *A History of Mountain Climbing*, New York: Flammarian Press (1996), p.19
3. *Ibid.,* p. 18
4. *Ibid.,* p. 20
5. *Ibid.,* p. 40
6. Leslie Stephen, *The Playground of Europe*, London: Longman, Green (1894), p. 14
7. *Ibid.*
8. *Ibid.,* p. 15
9. *Ibid.,* p. 3
10. *Ibid.,* p. 7
11. Claire Engel, *Mont Blanc, An Anthology*, George Allen & Unwin Ltd. (1965), p. 55
12  *op cit., Playground of Europe*, p. 53
13. *Ibid.,* p. 49
14. *Ibid,* p. 51

Chapter 4 – A Perfect Match

1.  *New York Times*, 2 Feb. 2001
2.  F. S. Smythe, *Edward Whymper*, London: Hodder & Stoughton, 6th ed. (1936), p. 36 (18 Mar. 57)
3.  *Ibid.*, p. 47 (9 Nov. 57)
4.  *op cit.*, *Scrambles*, p. ix
5.  *op cit.*, Smythe, p. 59 ( 4 Jun. 58)
6.  *op cit.*, *Scrambles*, p. 3
7.  *Ibid.*, pp. 3-4
8.  *Ibid.*, p. 15
9.  *Ibid.*, p. 4
10. *op cit.*, Smythe, p. 83
11. *Ibid.*, p. 83 (*Whymper's Journal* of 9 Aug. 60)
12. *Ibid.*, p. 85 (12 Aug. 60)
13. *Ibid.*, p. 83 (9 Aug. 60)
14. *Ibid.*, p. 84 (10 Aug. 60)
15. *Ibid.*, (11 Aug. 60)
16. *op cit.*, *Scrambles*, p. 8
17. *op cit.*, Smythe, p. 85 (*Whymper's Journal* of 13 Aug. 60)
18. *op cit.*, *Scrambles*, p. 9
19. *op cit.*, Smythe, p. 88 (*Whymper's Journal* of 17 Aug. 60)
20. *Ibid.*
21. *op cit.*, *Scrambles*, p. 10
22. *op cit.*, Smythe, p. 89 (*Whymper's Journal* of 19 Aug. 60)
23. *Ibid.*, p. 93 (28 Aug. 60)
24. *Ibid.*, p. 95 (2 Sep. 60)
25. *Ibid.*, p. 96 (4 Sep. 60)
26. *op cit.*, *Scrambles*. p. 14
27. *op cit.*, Smythe, p. 98 (*Whymper's Journal* of 12 Sep. 60)
28. *Ibid.*, pp. 99-100 (13 Sep. 60)
29. *op cit.*, *Scrambles*, p. 15
30. *op cit.*, Smythe, p. 101 (*Whymper's Journal* of 14 Sep. 60)
31. *Ibid.*, pp. 102-03 (16 Aug. 60)

Chapter 5 – The Golden Age Begins

1. Walter Unsworth, *Hold the Heights*, London: Hodder & Stoughton (1993), p. 70
2. Fergus Fleming, *Killing Dragons*, London: Granta Books (2000), p.187
3. Alfred Wills, *Wanderings Among the High Alps*, Oxford: Basil Blackwell (1871), 1937 ed.

4.  *op cit.*, Unsworth, pp. 47-49
5.  *op cit.*, Wills, pp. 215-16
6.  *Ibid.*, p. 206
7.  *Ibid.*, pp. 203-06
8.  *Ibid.*, pp. 206-08
9.  *Ezekiel*, NIV Compact Bible, Grand Rapids: Zondervan Corp. (1984), p. 92
10. *op cit.*, Fleming, pp. 166-67
11. *op cit.*, Wills, p. 217

Chapter 6 – The Wild Dauphiné

1. Edward Whymper, *Scrambles Amongst the Alps*, London: John Murray, 6th edition (1936), p. 21
2. *Ibid.*, p. 15
3. *Ibid.*, p. 22
4. *Ibid.*, p. 26
5. *Ibid.*, p. 28
6. *Ibid.*
7. *Ibid.*, p. 36
8. *Ibid.*, p. 38
9. *Ibid.*, pp. 38-39
10. *Ibid.*, p. 39
11. *Ibid.*
12. *Ibid.*, p. 42
13. *Ibid.*, pp. 42-43
14. *Ibid.*, p. 43
15. *Ibid.*, p. 9
16. *Ibid.*, p. 48
17. *Ibid.*, pp. 48-49
18. *Ibid.*, p. 46
19. *Ibid.*, pp. 101-02
20. *Ibid*, p. 49
21. *Ibid.*
22. *Ibid.*
23. *Ibid.*
24. *Ibid.*
25. *Ibid.*, p. 56
26. *Ibid.*
27. *Ibid.*, pp. 49-50
28. *Ibid.*, p. 56
29. *Ibid.*, p. 57
30. *Ibid.*, pp. 59-61

31. *Ibid.*, p. 61
32. *Ibid.*, p. 63
33. *Ibid.*
34. *Ibid.*, p. 64

Chapter 7 – The Monomaniac and the Bersagliere

1. *op cit.*, *Scrambles*, p. 67
2. *Ibid.*, p. 68n
3. *Ibid.*, p. 68
4. *Ibid.*, p. 72
5. *Ibid.*
6. *Ibid.*
7. *Ibid.*, p. 73
8. *Ibid.*
9. *Ibid.*
10. *Ibid.*
11. Charles Gos, *Alpine Tragedy* (1934), p. 227
12. *Matterhorn Man*, Walter Unsworth, London: Victor Bollanz (1965), p. 35
13. *op cit.*, *Scrambles*, p. 373
14. *Ibid.*
15. *Ibid.*, p. 74
16. *Ibid.*, pp. 74-75
17. *Ibid.*, p. 75
18. *Ibid.*, p. 76
19. *Ibid.*, p. 79
20. *Ibid.*, pp. 79-80
21. *Ibid.*, p. 83
22. *Ibid.*
23. *Ibid.*, p. 84
24. *Ibid.*
25. *Ibid.*, p. 81
26. *Ibid.*, p. 85
27. *Ibid.*, p. 86
28. *Ibid.*
29. *Ibid.*, p. 88
30. *Ibid.*, pp. 87-88
31. *Ibid.*, pp. 89-90
32. *Ibid.*, pp. 57-58
33. *Ibid.*, p. 90
34. *Ibid.*, p. 91
35. *Ibid.*

36. *Ibid.,* p. 92
37. *Ibid.*
38. *Ibid.,* p. 93


Chapter 8 – The Professor and the Matterhorn

1. John Tyndall, *Hours of Exercise in the Alps,* New York: D. Appleton & Co. (1896), p. 30
2. A. S. Eve and C. H. Creasey, *The Life and Work of John Tyndall,* London: Macmillan & Co. (1945), p. 29
3. *Ibid.,* p. 71
4. Douglas W. M. Freshfield, "Professor Tyndall's Attempt on the Matterhorn in 1862," 5 AJ 329-36, 335
5. *op cit., Hours of Exercise,* p. 32
6. *Ibid.,* p. 33
7. *Ibid.,* p. 35
8. *Ibid.,* p. 38
9. *Ibid.,* pp. 41-46
10. *Ibid.,* p. 46
11. *Ibid.,* p. 121
12. *Ibid.*
13. *Ibid.,* p. 48
14. *Ibid.,* p. 63
15. *Ibid.,* p. 114
16. *Ibid.,* p. 122
17. *Ibid.*
18. *op cit., Scrambles,* p. 32
19. *op cit., Hours of Exercise,* p. 63
20. *Ibid.,* p. 114
21. *Ibid.,* p. 157
22. Claud Schuster, *Postscript to Adventure,* London: Eyre & Spottiswoode (1950), p. 161
23. *Ibid.*
24. *op cit., Hours of Exercise,* p. 162
25. *Ibid.*
26. *Ibid.,* p. 163
27. *Ibid.*
28. *Ibid.,* pp 163-64
29. *Ibid.,* p. 164
30. *Ibid.,* p. 165
31. *op cit., Scrambles,* p. 95
32. *op cit., Hours of Exercise,* p. vii

33. *op cit., Scrambles*, p. 101

Chapter 9 – Intermezzo

1. Ronald Clark, *Victorian Mountaineers*, Boston: Charles T. Branford & Co. (1954), p. 79
2. W. D. Rubinstein, *Britain's Century*, New York: Oxford University Press (1998), p. 97
3. *op cit., Victorian Mountaineers*, p. 82
4. *Ibid.*
5. Arnold Lunn, *Switzerland and the English*, London: Eyre & Spottiswoode (1944), pp. 131-32
6. *op cit., Scrambles*, p. 97
7. *Ibid.,* pp. 97-98
8. *Ibid.,* p. 97
9. *Ibid.,* p. 98
10. *Ibid.,* p. 103
11. *Ibid.,* p. 109
12. *Ibid.,* p. 110
13. *Ibid.,* p. 116
14. *Ibid.,* p. 117
15. *Ibid.,* p. 118
16. *Ibid.,* p. 133
17. *Ibid.,* p. 133

Chapter 10 – "Strength and Skill Seldom Surpassed"

1. *op cit., Scrambles*, p. 136
2. *Ibid.*
3. *Ibid.,* p. 137
4. *Ibid.,* p. 141
5. *Ibid.,* p. 144
6. *Ibid.,* p. 149
7. *Ibid.,* p. 151
8. *Ibid.,* p. 157
9. *Ibid.,* p. 158
10. *Ibid.*
11. *Ibid.,* pp. 167-68
12. *Ibid.,* p. 168
13. *Ibid.,* p. 169
14. *Ibid.,* p. 171
15. *Ibid.*

16. *Ibid.,* p. 173
17. *Ibid.,* p. 174
18. *Ibid.,* p. 175
19. *Ibid.,* p. 183
20. *Ibid.,* pp. 183-84
21. *Ibid.,* p. 184
22. *Ibid.,* p. 185
23. *Ibid.*
24. *Ibid.,* pp. 184-85
25. *Ibid.,* p. 25
26. *Ibid.,* p. 213
27. *Ibid.,* p. 215
28. *Ibid.,* p. 213
29. *Ibid.*
30. *Ibid.,* p. 216
31. *Ibid.,* p. 216-17
32. *Ibid.,* p. 219
33. *Ibid.,* p. 250

Chapter 11 – "The Most Brilliant Campaign"

1. Thos. S. Kennedy, 1 AJ 77-82
2. *op cit., Scrambles,* p. 221
3. *Ibid.,* p. 224
4. *Ibid.*
5. *Ibid.,* p. 228, n. 1
6. Whymper's letter to Wm. Edw. Davidson, May 20, 1911, AC Library Archives
7. *op cit., Scrambles,* p. 234
8. *Ibid.,* p. 237
9. *Ibid.,* p. 238
10. *Ibid.,* p. 251
11. *Ibid.,* p. 254
12. *Ibid.,* p. 257
13. *Ibid.,* pp. 255
14. Guido Rey, *The Matterhorn,* Oxford: Basil Blackwell (1946), p. 268
15. *Ibid.*
16. *op cit., Scrambles,* p. 269
17. *Ibid.,* p. 271
18. *Ibid.,* pp. 276-77
19. *Ibid.,* p. 278
20. *Ibid.,* p. 281
21. *Ibid.,* p. 283

22. *Ibid.*
23. *Ibid.*, p. 284
24. *Ibid.*, p. 285
25. *Ibid.*
26. *Ibid.*
27. *Ibid.*, p. 287
28. Leslie Stephen, 5 *AJ* 237
29. *op cit., Scrambles*, p. 299
30. *Ibid.*, p. 58
31. *Ibid.*, p. 121


Chapter 12 – Triumph and Tragedy

1. *op cit. Scrambles*, p. 301
2. *Ibid.*
3. *Ibid.*, pp. 301-02
4. Alan Lyall, *The First Descent of the Matterhorn*, Llandysul: Gomer Press (1997), p. 94
5. Guido Rey, *The Matterhorn*, Oxford: Basil Blackwell (1946), p. 97
6. *Ibid.*, pp. 97-98
7. *op cit., Scrambles*, p. 302
8. *op cit., First Descent*, p. 86
9. *op cit., Scrambles*, p. 304
10. *Ibid.*
11. *Ibid.*, p. 306
12. *Ibid.*, p. 308
13. *Ibid.*
14. *Ibid.*
15. *Ibid.*, p. 306
16. *Ibid.*
17. *Ibid.*, p. 308
18. *Ibid.*, p. 309
19. *Ibid.*, p. 310
20. *Ibid.*
21. *Ibid.*, pp. 311-12
22. *Ibid.*, p. 312
23. *Ibid.*, p. 313
24. *Ibid.*, p. 314
25. *Ibid.*, pp. 317-18
26. *Ibid.*, pp. 314-15
27. *Ibid.*
28. *Ibid.*, p. 316

29. *Ibid.*, pp. 316-17
30. *Ibid.*, p. 320
31. *Ibid.*, pp. 320-21
32. *Ibid.*, pp. 321-22
33. *Ibid.*, pp. 322-23
34. *Ibid.*, p. 323
35. *Ibid.*
36. *Ibid.*
37. *Ibid.*, p. 324
38. *Ibid.*, p. 326

Chapter 13 – Search and Recovery

1. *op cit.*, *Scrambles*, p. 326
2. Joseph McCormick, *A Sad Holiday* (pamphlet) London: James Nisbet & Co. (Sep. 1865)
3. Alan Lyall, *The First Descent of the Matterhorn*, Llandysul: Gomer Press (1997)
4. *Ibid.*, p. 148
5. *Ibid.*, p. 240
6. *Ibid.*, p. 363
7. *op cit.*, *Scrambles*, p. 327
8. *op cit.*, *First Descent*, pp. 470-75 quoting Whymper's interview in French in the *Journal de Zermatt*, 25 Aug. 1895
9. *Ibid.*, p. 241
10. *Ibid.*
11. *op cit.*, *A Sad Holiday*, pp. 16-17
12. *Ibid.*, p. 16
13. *op cit.*, *First Descent*, p. 363

Chapter 14 – Troublesome Questions

1. *op cit.*, *First Descent*, p. 508
2. *Ibid.*, pp. 501-02
3. *Ibid.*, pp. 500-01
4. *op cit.*, *Scrambles*, pp. 328-30
5. *Ibid.*, p. 376
6. *Ibid.*, p. 375
7. *Ibid.*, p. 330
8. *Ibid.*
9. *Ibid.*
10. *op cit.*, *First Descent*, p. 375
11. *Ibid.*, p. 377

12. *op cit.*, *Scrambles*, p. 323
13. *Ibid.*, p. 329
14. *op cit.*, *First Descent*, p. 499
15. *Ibid.*, pp. 468-69
16. *Ibid.*, pp.172, 199
17. *Ibid.*, pp. 172-74, 199
18. *Ibid.*, p. 216
19. *op cit.*, *Scrambles*, p. 377 (App. H)
20. *Ibid.*, pp. 369-70 (App. F)
21. *op cit.*, *First Descent*, p. 128
22. *The Times*, 8 Aug. 1865
23. *Ibid.*
24. *Ibid.*
25. *op cit.*, *First Descent*, pp. 112, 474-75
26. *op cit.*, *Scrambles*, p. 321n.
27. *Ibid.*, p. 308n
28. *op cit.*, *First Descent*, p. 113 (letter from H. F. Montagnier to J. P. Farrar, 1917)
29. *Ibid.*, p. 112
30. D. F. O. Dangar & T. S. Blakeney, 61 *AJ* 132, 118
31. *Ibid.*

Chapter 15 – Into the Vortex

1. *op cit.*, *First Descent*, p. 446 (letter from Edward Whymper to J. Robertson, 27 Aug.1865)
2. *Ibid.*, p.393
3. *Ibid.*
4. *Ibid.*, p. 411
5. *Ibid.*, (letter from A. Adams Riley to Principal J. D. Forbes, 1 Aug. 1865)
6. Author's photograph
7. F. S. Smythe, *Edward Whymper*, London: Hodder & Stoughton, 6th ed. (1936), p. 205
8. ADD MS 63090, # 284, BL
9. *op cit.*, *First Descent*, pp. 394-96
10. *Ibid.*, p.109
11. *Ibid.*, p. 412 (letter from *The Times* editor to Edward Whymper, undated)
12. *Ibid.*, p. 417
13. *Ibid.*, p. 413
14. *The Times*, (8 Aug. 1865)
15. *op cit.*, *First Descent*, p. 432
16. *Ibid.*, pp. 442-43
17. *Ibid.*, pp. 443-44

18. *Ibid.,* p. 444
19. *Ibid.,* p. 436
20. *Ibid.,* p. 438
21. *Ibid.,* pp. 450-51
22. *Ibid.,* p. 451
23. *Ibid.,* p. 439 (letter from Edward Whymper to Rev. Richard Glover, 18 Aug. 1865)
24. *Ibid.,* pp. 437-38
25. *The Times,* (8 August 1865)
26. *Ibid.*
27. *op cit., First Descent,* p. 430
28. *Ibid.,* p. 448
29. *Ibid.,* p. 449
30. F. S. Smythe, *Introduction* to *Travels Amongst the Great Andes* (1949 edition)
31. *op cit., First Descent,* p. 296
32. *Ibid.*
33. *op cit. Killing Dragons,* p. 282
34. *op cit., First Descent,* pp. 426, 430
35. Claud Schuster, Review of *Travels Amongst the Great Andes of the Equator,* 57 AJ 432

Chapter 16 – Glaciers and Sledge Dogs

1. F. S. Smythe, *Edward Whymper,* London: Hodder & Stoughton (1940), p. 216
2. *op cit., First Descent,* p. 439 (letter from E. Whymper to R. Glover, 18 Aug. 1865)
3. *Ibid.,* p. 415
4. *Ibid.,* p. 283 (letter from P. J. D. Forbes to Alfred Wills, 2 Feb.1866)
5. *op cit., Scrambles,* p. 384, App. J
6. *Ibid.,* p. 385
7. *Ibid.*
8. *Ibid.,* p. 386
9. MS 822/2 , SPRI
10. *op cit., Scrambles,* p. 387
11. ADD MS 63112, # 347, BL (signed by 16 supporters)
12. *Ibid.,* # 135 *(Annette's Note)*
13. *Ibid.,* # 136
14. Edward Whymper, 5 *AJ* 1-23
15. *op cit.,* Smythe, p. 219
16. *Ibid.*
17. Edward Whymper, 6 AJ 209-20, 210
18. *op cit.,* Smythe, p. 222
19. *Ibid.*
20. *Ibid.,* p. 223

21. *Ibid.*
22. ADD MS 63112, # 40, BL
23. *Ibid.*
24. *Ibid.*
25. *Edward Whymper,* 6 AJ 216
26. *Edward Whymper,* 5 AJ 1, 21

Chapter 17 – Birth of a Classic

1.  ADD MS 63112, #135 *(Annette's Note),* BL
2.  *Ibid.*
3.  *Ibid.*
4.  *Ibid.*
5.  *Ibid.*
6.  *op cit., Scrambles,* p. xxii
7.  ADD MS 63112, #s 177-80, BL (letter of Wm. Maxwell of Clark, Ltd. to Ethel Blandy, Whymper's daughter, 21 Oct. 1938)
8.  *Ibid.*
9.  *op cit.,* Smythe, p. 228
10. Leslie Stephen, 5 AJ 234-40, 237, 240
11. *Ibid.,* p. 235
12. *The Times*
13. *op cit.,* Smythe, p. 228
14. *Ibid.*
15. *Ibid.,* 234
16. ADD MS 63090, # 285, BL (Whymper letter to J. Robertson, 23 Mar. 1870)
17. *op cit.,* Smythe, p. 230 (quoting Geoffrey W. Young in *Cornhill Magazine,* 1923)
18. *Ibid.,* p. 236
19. ADD MS 63312, # 154 (notes of nephew Robert Whymper)

Chapter 18 – Royal Road to Quito

1. Edward Whymper, *Travels Amongst the Great Andes of the Equator,* New York: Charles Scribner's Sons (1892), p. viii, n1
2. *Ibid.,* p. vi
3. *Ibid.,* p. xi
4. *Ibid.,* p. xiii
5. *Ibid.*
6. *Ibid.*
7. *Ibid.,* p. 1
8. *Ibid.,* p. 4, n1
9. *Ibid.,* p. 6

10. *Ibid.*, p. 7
11. *Ibid.*, p. 8
12. *Ibid.*, p. 21
13. *Ibid.*, p. 22
14. *Ibid.*
15. *Ibid.*, p. 37
16. *Ibid.*, p. 39
17. *Ibid.*, p. 40
18. *Ibid.*, pp. 40-41

Chapter 19 – "Time Flew Rapidly"

1. *op cit.*, *Great Andes*, p. 42
2. *Ibid.*
3. *Ibid.*, p. 46
4. *Ibid.*
5. *Ibid.*, p. 48
6. *Ibid.*, p. 49
7. *Ibid.*, p. 50
8. *Ibid.*, p. 51
9. *Ibid.*
10. *Ibid.*, p. 59
11. *Ibid.*, pp. 61-62
12. *Ibid.*, p. 65
13. *Ibid.*, p. 66
14. *Ibid.*, p. 68
15. *Ibid.*, p. 69
16. *Ibid.*
17. *Ibid.*, p. 70
18. *Ibid.*

Chapter 20 – "Only the Gringos"

1. *op cit.*, *Great Andes*, p. 29
2. *Ibid.*, p. 31
3. *Ibid.*, p. 76
4. *Ibid.*, pp. 77-78
5. *Ibid.*, p. 80
6. *Ibid.*
7. *Ibid.*, pp. 81-82
8. *Ibid.*, p. 82
9. *Ibid.*

10. *Ibid.,* p. 87
11. *Ibid.,* p 89
12. *Ibid.,* pp. 91-92
13. *Ibid.,* p. 91
14. *Ibid.,* p. 93
15. *Ibid.,* p. 96
16. *Ibid.,* p. 98
17. *Ibid.,* p. 99
18. *Ibid.,* p. 114, n2
19. *Ibid.,* p. 103
20. *Ibid.,* p. 116
21. *Ibid.,* p. 118
22. *Ibid.,* p. 119

Chapter 21 – Inferno at Night

1. *op cit.,* *Great Andes,* p. 127
2. *Ibid.,* p. 122
3. *Ibid.,* p. 130
4. *Ibid.,* p. 139
5. *Ibid.,* pp. 151-53
6. *Ibid.,* pp. 148-49, n1
7. *Ibid.,* p. 155
8. *Ibid.,* p. 158
9. *Ibid.,* p. 165

Chapter 22 – Rest, Robbers, and Resurrection

1. *op cit.,* *Great Andes,* pp. 172-173
2. *Ibid.,* p. 168
3. *Ibid.,* p. 170
4. *Ibid.,* pp. 176-77
5. *Ibid.,* p. 177
6. *Ibid.,* p. 182
7. *Ibid.,* pp. 197-98
8. *Ibid.,* p. 226
9. *Ibid.,* p. 227
10. *Ibid.*
11. *Ibid.,* p. 241
12. *Ibid.,* p. 250
13. *Ibid.,* p. 286
14. *New York Times,* 12 July 1880

15. *op cit.*, *Great Andes*, p. 293

16. *Ibid.*, p. 295

17. *Ibid.*, p. 314

18. *Ibid.*, pp. 312-13

19. *Ibid.*, p. 318

20. *Ibid.*, pp. 321-22

21. *Ibid.*, p. 324

22. *Ibid.*, p. 327

23. *Whymper's Journal*, July 1880

24. *op cit.*, *Great Andes*, pp. 389-90

25. *Ibid.*, p. 390

26. *Whymper's Journal*, July 1880


Chapter 23 – "A Raconteur Hardly Equaled"

1. ADD MS 63090, # 289, BL (letter dated March 18, 1880)

2. *Ibid.*, # 296, BL (letter dated May 8, 1880)

3. *op cit*, Smythe, p. 281

4. ADD MS 63112, # 155, BL (notes of Robert Whymper)

5. *Ibid.*, # 94, BL (letter dated November 17, 1909)

6. *Ibid.*, # 155

7. *Ibid.*, # 156

8. *The Times (unknown date)*

9. *Travels Amongst the Great Andes of the Equator*, Salt Lake City: Peregrine Smith Book (1987), photographs and new Introduction by Loren McIntyre

10. *New York Times (unknown date)*

11. *op cit.*, *Great Andes* (1987 ed.), back cover

12. *op cit.* Smythe, p. 289

13. *op cit.*, *Scrambles*, p. 364 (L. Sinigaglia's letter to Italian Alpine Club, 1890)

14. *Ibid.*, p. 366

15. *Ibid.*, pp. 366-67


Chapter 24 – "Mony a Mickle Mak's a Muckle"

1. *op cit.*, Smythe, p. 284

2. *Ibid.*, p. 285

3. *op cit.*, *Scrambles*, p. 366

4. *op cit.*, Smythe, pp. 286-87

5. *The Graphic*, Oct. 1884

6. *op cit.*, Smythe, p. 312

7. *Ibid.*, p. 290

8. *Chamonix and the Range of Mont Blanc*, Introduction (1896)

9.  *Ibid.*, p. 1
10. *The Valley of Zermatt and the Matterhorn*, p. ix (1898)
11. *Ibid.*, p. x
12. *op cit.*, Smythe, p. 293
13. MS 41269, *A Book for Boys*, NLS


Chapter 25 – Aging Lion

1.  Edward Whymper, *Travels Amongst the Great Andes of the Equator*, London: John Lehmann Ltd. (1949), pp. 7, 20
2.  *Ibid.*, p. 13
3.  Misses E. Cooper and K. Bradley, 46 *AJ* 164-65 (1934)
4.  *Ibid.*
5.  ADD MS 63112, #s 151-159, 151 BL (notes by nephew Robert Whymper)
6.  *Ibid.*, # 157
7.  *Ibid.*, #152
8.  Geoffrey W. Young, *Mountain Prophets,* 54 *AJ* 97-117, 103
9.  *Ibid.*, p. 105
10. Robert E. Campbell, *Tales from the Canadian Rockies, Edward Whymper*, Brian Patton, editor, Toronto: McClelland & Stewart, Ltd. (1993), pp. 160-61
11. *Ibid.*, p. 162
12. *Ibid.*
13. *Ibid.*, pp. 162-63
14. *op cit.*, Smythe, p. 309
15. ADD MS 63112, # 171, BL
16. *Ibid.*, # 177
17. *op cit.*, Smythe, p. 297
18. ADD MS 63112, #s 151-59, 159 (Robert); # 148 (Annette), BL
19. *op cit.*, Smythe, p. 298
20. *Ibid.*
21. *Ibid.*
22. ADD MS 63112, # 148, BL
23. *op cit.*, Smythe, p. 298
24. *Ibid.*, p. 299
25. *Ibid.*, p. 305
26. Coulson Kernahan, *In Good Company*, The Bodley Head, London: John Lane (1937), p. 149
27. *Ibid.*, p. 151
28. *Ibid.*, p. 152
29. *Ibid.*, p. 153
30. *Ibid.*, p. 158
31. *Ibid.*, pp. 158-59

32. *Ibid.,* p. 159
33. *Ibid.,* p. 160
34. *Ibid.,* p. 161
35. *Ibid.,* p. 163
36. *Ibid.,* p. 173
37. *Ibid.,* pp. 173-75
38. *Ibid.,* p. 175
39. *Ibid.,* p. 176
40. *Ibid.,* p. 180
41. *Ibid.,* pp.183
42. *Ibid.,* p. 186
43. *Ibid.,* p. 187
44. *Ibid.,* p. 185
45. *Ibid.,* pp. 178-79
46. *Ibid.,* p. 185
47. *Ibid.,* p. 186

Chapter 26 – Last Lap

1. ADD MS 63312, # 148 (Annette), BL
2. *Ibid.*
3. *Ibid.,* #s 151-159, 153 (Robert)
4. *Ibid.*
5. MS 822/23, SPRI
6. *Ibid.*
7. Oral statement, René Simond, President, Les Amis de Vieux Chamonix and son of Adeline Payot Simond, 26 June 2001
8. *Ibid.*
9. AD MS 63112, # 44, *letter to H. F. Montagnier* dated 30 Mar. 1907
10. *Ibid.,* 10 Apr. 07, # 45
11. *Ibid.,* 28 Oct. 07, # 49
12. *Ibid.,* 27 Feb. 08, # 55
13. *Ibid.,* 5 Jul. 08, # 59
14. *Ibid.,* 12 Oct. 08, # 62
15. *Ibid.,* 22 Nov. 08, # 63
16. *Ibid.,* 13 Jan. 09, # 70
17. *Ibid.,* 26 Jan. 09, # 71
18. *Ibid.,* 2 Jul. 09, # 80
19. *Ibid.,* 25 Apr. 10, #103
20. *Ibid.,* 24 Aug. 10 # 102
21. *Ibid.,* 12 Dec. 10, # 104
22. *Ibid.*

23. *Ibid.,* 22 Dec. 10, # 107

24. *Ibid.,* 20 Feb. 11, # 110

25. *Ibid.,* 11 Apr. 11, # 115

26. *Ibid.,* 28 Jul. 11 to Annette, # 27

27. MS 822/26, SPRI

28. *Ibid.*

29. Montagnier Scrapbook, *Daily Chronicle*, 18 Sep. 1911

30. *op cit.*, *First Descent*, p. 277 (from *L'Auto*, 18 Sep. 1911)

31. *Ibid.*, p. 278

32. *op cit.*, Smythe, p. 318

33. G. Casella, *Les Sports d'Hiver et l'Alpenisme* (1911)

# ACKNOWLEDGMENTS

Various people encouraged me to tell the story of Edward Whymper's life, others helped me research and write it, and some did both. I especially want to thank those noted here.

Anthony M. Schulte, my college classmate and former Executive V-P, Alfred A. Knopf, led me by the hand into the turbulent world of book publishing. He introduced me to his colleagues in every sector of the industry, both in Britain and the U.S. He unfailingly supplied new sources of potential assistance and gave me sound advice during every step of my journey to publication. I stayed the course thanks to Tony.

Jane Fletcher Geniesse's beautifully written *Passionate Nomad: the Life of Freya Stark* (Random House, 1999), inspired me to choose biography as my non-fiction genre. Through her introduction, I met with the seventh John Murray of the storied London publishing house bearing his name. There I bathed in the aura of generations of prominent authors including Whymper, who had conducted business in the office library in which we sat. This meeting confirmed my decision to pick the famous mountaineer as my subject.

Alan Lyall, author of *The First Descent of the Matterhorn* (Gomer Press, 1999), provided additional inspiration by spending a day with me at the Pen-y-Gwryd Hotel, North Wales, in the early stages of my research. From then until the completion of my manuscript, he and his book were wellsprings of accurate information on Whymper's most famous climb. Alan's book also offers original and extraordinarily insightful answers to questions surrounding that memorable episode. In short, his contributions to my book were invaluable.

Daughter Sherrye Henry faithfully edited the first draft of my manuscript, helping me to better appreciate elements of the author's craft. She increased my awareness of attitudes and methods likely to bring out whatever authorial talents I might have. She emphasized the importance of "story," whatever the format. She gave me genuine emotional support for the challenge I had undertaken. Sherrye knows of my gratitude, which I happily repeat here.

Thanks also to Jeremy Thompson and his stalwart Matador staff members Terry Compton, Jane Rowland, Sarah Taylor, Jennifer Liptrot and others, all of whom worked diligently and creatively in the production and marketing of *Triumph and Tragedy*. Aimee Fry developed my website, Ian Skillicorn my podcast, and I thank them both.

In the beginning, the Alpine Club's librarian Margaret Ecclestone gave me a warm welcome and extensive research assistance. Robert (Bob) Lawford provided access to his impressive collection of alpine photographs and mountaineering lore. Both are no longer with us, but I remember them most favorably. More recently I received a similar reception and helpful assistance from the Club's current librarian Thadeusz Hudowski, and from its Honorary Archivist Glyn Hughes.

Though I spent less time in the library of the American Alpine Club in Golden, Colorado, its staff also offered me valuable and much appreciated help. Robert Headland, prior to his retirement as Archivist and Curator of the Scott Polar Research Institute, gave me access to Whymper's early writings and Greenland papers.

Thanks also to London literary agent Andrew Lownie for his generous references to editors and his encouragement to persevere. Similarly supportive in guiding me through London's literary maze were publisher Duncan Baird and agent Christopher Sinclair-Stevenson. I appreciate the efforts of this trio on my behalf.

I have attempted to obtain prior permission for the use of copyrighted material in this book. I apologize for any inadvertent omissions, and will be pleased to include missing acknowledgments in any future editions.

# INDEX